ROOSEVELT IN RETROSPECT

BOOKS BY JOHN GUNTHER

Roosevelt in Retrospect

Behind the Curtain

Death Be Not Proud

Inside U.S.A.

Inside Latin America

Inside Asia

Inside Europe

D Day

The Troubled Midnight

The High Cost of Hitler

John Gunther

ROOSEVELT
in
RETROSPECT

A Profile in History

New York

HARPER & BROTHERS, PUBLISHERS

Dedicated to

CORNELIUS HORACE TRAEGER, M.D.

It is perhaps as difficult to write a good life as to live one.

— LYTTON STRACHEY

For, the noblest deeds do not always shew men's virtues and vices, but oftentimes a light occasion, a word, or some sport makes men's natural dispositions and manners appear more plain, than the famous battels won, wherein are slain ten thousand men, or the great armies, or cities won by siege or assault.

— PLUTARCH, *Alexander the Great,* i

Je n'impose rien; je ne propose rien; j'expose.

CONTENTS

FOREWORD

This book is an attempt at analysis as well as a mere narrative; a gathering of sources and an interpretation rather than a reminiscence or revelation, though it contains a great amount of new and fresh material. But it does not pretend to be a full-dress history of the Roosevelt years nor a biography in the orthodox manner; for these we shall have to await the slow sifting of years of scholarship. What I have written, sizable as it may seem, is little more than a preliminary sketch, an estimate, a survey, an appraisal—moreover an appraisal from a personal as well as a political point of view.

Books about Roosevelt are pouring out by the dozen, but it is a fact that no reasonably full biography exists in print today of the only man ever to be elected President of the United States four times. That my own effort to fill this gap should have turned out to be so packed with detail is suggestive indication of the richness of the subject.

I began to think of doing a book about F.D.R. long ago—back in 1944, in fact, when I started work on *Inside U. S. A.* It was obvious even then that Roosevelt was bound to become a figure like Lincoln. Myths and legends had already begun to spring up around him, obscuring the truth. And, whether you liked him or not, you could not get away from the fact that he made a greater imprint on American history than any president since the foundation of the republic.

First I talked to scores of people in all walks of life who had known Roosevelt well—or slightly. The testimony of a servant at Hyde Park was often as illuminating as that of a member of the Cabinet. I tried to think of my assignment as a reporter's job, and I never met anybody who ever knew FDR who did not have something new to contribute. The President was inexhaustible. Then I proceeded to read as widely as possible, dig up old newspaper and magazine files, consult the official records, and knit the results together. I have read all the relevant books—there are a lot—and a bibliography appears at the end of this volume.

But I got much more from people than from books, much more by ear than from eye. My real bibliography is a long list of men and women. Some material was confidential as to source, and I have had to give many anecdotes without naming those who supplied them. But I can assure the reader that every detail has been carefully checked and to the best of my knowledge and belief there is no word in this book that is not true. To all those who helped me, let me say warm thanks, without inflicting on them any specific responsibility for what I wrote.

When I began writing after many months of research I thought in terms of a comparatively brief character sketch, nothing more. Then I found out that to explain the character I had to proceed to a longer account of the main elements of Roosevelt's life as well. I tried to write as objectively as possible, and always from the point of view of hoping to get at the bottom of the mysteries and contradictions of the Roosevelt personality, his root qualities and basic sources of power.

So let us proceed and explore and try to take Mr. Roosevelt apart and then put him together again, and see what kind of picture may be built up of Roosevelt the President, Roosevelt the man, and so, however tentatively and inadequately, pin something of his great substance against the wall of time.

J. G.

New York City, March 15, 1950

Chapter 1

THE HISTORICAL PERSPECTIVE

It takes a long long time to build the past up to the present.
—FRANKLIN DELANO ROOSEVELT

Franklin Delano Roosevelt, thirty-second President of the United States and Chief Executive from 1933 to 1945, the architect of the New Deal and the director of victory in World War II, Franklin Delano Roosevelt who is still both loved and hated as passionately as if he were still alive, was born in Hyde Park, New York, in 1882, and died in Warm Springs, Georgia, in 1945. It was his fate, through what concentration of forces no man can know, to be President during both the greatest depression and the greatest war the world has ever known. He was a cripple—and he licked them both.

Was he a great man? Of course. But what made him so? How did the greatness arise? His career, by almost any criterion, is one of the most extraordinary in modern times. But exactly why? What controlled his character? What did Roosevelt himself contribute to his own proliferating destiny? What transformed him from a not very exceptional young man into a mature colossus? What came from the *Zeitgeist*, what from him?

I once heard it said that Roosevelt's most effective quality was receptivity. But also he transmitted. He was like a kind of universal joint, or rather a switchboard, a transformer. The whole energy of the country, the whole power of one hundred and forty million people, flowed into him and through him; he not only felt this power, but he utilized it, he retransmitted it. Why does a country, if lucky, produce a great man when he is most needed? Because it really believes in something and focuses the entire energy of its national desires into a single human being; the supreme forces of the time converge into a single vessel. Roosevelt could manipulate this power, shooting it out at almost any angle, to provoke response, to irradiate ideas and men, to search out enormous issues. He was like a needle, always quivering,

3

oscillating, responding to new impulses, throbbing at the slightest variation in current—a magnetic instrument measuring ceaselessly the tone and intensity of public impact. But no matter how much the needle quivered and oscillated, it seldom varied far from its own true north.

But this analysis, however suggestive, is too artificial for my taste, because the essence of F.D.R. was not mechanistic, but sublimely (and sometimes ridiculously) human. Of all his multifarious qualities the dominant was probably his extreme humanity. Later we shall try to break this term down; suffice it to say now that, being a man, he believed in men. The term "humanity" covers a wide arc—from amiability to compassion, from fertility in ideas to subtlety in personal relationships, from the happy expression of animal vitality to the deepest cognizance of suffering and primitive despair. The President was inveterately personal, and people were inveterately personal about him. A lady I know, by no means a sentimentalist, said two or three years after his death, "He made me glad I am a woman. I miss him actively, personally, every day." At least a dozen people all over the country told me early in 1945—the remark became almost trite—"I never met him, but I feel as if I had lost my greatest friend."

His radiant, energetic smile—even with the touch of glucose in it, even when it seemed contrived—stirred people with confidence and hope. His lustrous voice, so soothing, so resonant, so alive, said, "My friends . . ."—and the people were. They were not merely his followers, but partners. He led by following, which was one of the most distinctive sources of his power. He lifted people above themselves—he gave them a goal—and hence no one was ever able to take the masses away from him. He gave citizens the sense that they, we, the country, were going forward, that life was still the kind of adventure it had been in pioneer days, that the pace was fast and that substantial rewards were attainable.

Yet, more than any modern president, he split the country—which is one of the more obvious Roosevelt paradoxes. Why was he hated so, defamed and calumniated so? Because he took from the rich and gave to the poor. But that is only one explanation. Why, five years after his death, is he still hated so? Because what he did lives after him. But that too is only part of the story.

Roosevelt stood for the "common man" (though this ambiguous phrase is a cliché earnestly to be avoided) but he was certainly not common himself. In fact he was a storybook Prince Charming, a fairy-tale hero to the millions; he ruled with a wand—even if it was an ivory cigarette holder. Out in the rain, men and women strove—literally—to touch the hem of his cape as he passed, this man who could not walk. The "common" people chose him, a prince, to lead them, and he did things for them, as a good prince should. What was the New Deal except a vast exercise in *noblesse oblige?*[1]

To a supreme degree Roosevelt had five qualifications for states-manship: (a) courage; (b) patience, and an infinitely subtle sense of timing; (c) the capacity to see the very great in the very small, to relate the infinitesimal particular to the all-embracing general; (d) idealism, and a sense of fixed objectives; (e) ability to give resolution to the minds of men. Also he had plenty of bad qualities—dilatoriness, two-sidedness (some critics would say plain dishonesty), pettiness in some personal relationships, a cardinal lack of frankness (for which, how-ever, there was often good reason), inability to say No, love of im-provisation, garrulousness, amateurism, and what has been called "cheerful vindictiveness." Amateurism?—in a peculiar way, yes. But do not forget that he was the most masterfully expert practical poli-tician ever to function in this republic.

Observations on Whether or Not He Was a Great Man

I have said that "of course" he was a great man. He fulfilled a concrete historical function, his career epitomized the cardinal pressures of his era, he was what Emerson might have called a Yea-Sayer, a world-man, and no erosion by history will ever efface some of the things he did. He was admired and loved all over the world, not just in the United States; his appeal was universal.

Yet it is difficult to summarize in a single word what he stood for, as one may say that Socrates stood for Reason or Napoleon for Conquest. In a sense Roosevelt was an instrument, not a creator. He was not a true Original. He was not pure, like Joan of Arc, nor profound, like Dante, nor did he breathe fire, like Shelley. He had plenty of moral grandeur, but he was multiplex and multiform. He was neither a poet, a philosopher, an artist, a mystic, nor even an intellectual. He had few

---

[1] A good many writers on FDR have used this *noblesse oblige* analogy, but it should not be pushed too far. Certainly the early New Dealers themselves never thought of the New Deal in *noblesse oblige* terms, nor, I think, did Roosevelt him-self. They thought in terms of emergency and social justice.

Ideas. In sheer brain power, he was outweighed by several of his contemporaries, and somehow he lacked wholeness of soul, in the way that
St. Augustine, let us say, had wholeness of soul, or, on a different level,
Cromwell or Spinoza. He called himself a Christian and a democrat,
but one does not associate with him the overwhelming, overpowering
creative impulse that comes to a man with a permanent, absolute
devotion to a single principle. Roosevelt was never a man obsessed.
He was not a Goethe, whose whole career may be crystallized by the
use of a single word, Nature, or even a Gladstone (Liberalism), or a
Bismarck (Prussia).

Probably what it all boils down to is the matter of contribution. He
did not create a country, as did Masaryk, nor a continent of the imagination, like Beethoven, nor a new world of science, like Freud. He
may not have been as stupendous a human being as, say, Michelangelo
or Tolstoi, but if you measure a man practically by the work he leaves,
FDR ranks very high. A Roosevelt advocate might say: (1) Almost
singlehanded he saved democracy in the United States; (2) he brought
the United States to world leadership for the first time. Certainly he
belongs in the category of Washington and Lincoln as one of the three
greatest presidents in American history, whether you like all he did or
not. And think how he is missed!

Greatness? What is greatness? Consider on a different level the
peculiarly revealing item that, though he was as much of a cripple
as if both legs had been sawed off at the hip, it was inconceivable that
anyone should ever have thought of him as an invalid.

Conservative or Liberal?

Of this we shall say more later. An easy definition is that a conservative
is someone who wishes to conserve things; a liberal is someone who
wishes to liberate. Of course this definition breaks down at once when
we consider that, in order to conserve, the conservative may have to
liberate; he may be unable to conserve the larger order except by
liberalizing various institutions. Conversely, the liberal will have
nothing left to liberate if he does not conserve the rudimentary essentials. Roosevelt was a liberal about old-age pensions; but he was a
conservative about the Bill of Rights. He was a liberal on issues like
social security, child labor, and a hundred others; but he was an
extreme conservative about democracy. It goes without saying that he
belongs to the line of liberal, progressive presidents: Jackson, Theodore

Roosevelt, Wilson. Yet it should not be forgotten that some reforms of the New Deal helped to strengthen and even preserve the free-enterprise system in this country, and considered from this angle FDR was one of the most conservative presidents in our history.

Roosevelt himself thought in terms of action and results, not abstractly. In fact one of the most extraordinary things about his mental structure was that he almost never had abstract thoughts at all.

Once I asked someone very much on his side who was as well qualified to know as anybody, "Just how does the President *think?*" The answer was, "My dear Mr. Gunther, the President never 'thinks'!"

Roosevelt and Roosevelt

If anybody had ever predicted to Theodore Roosevelt that Franklin Delano Roosevelt, his fifth cousin and nephew-in-law, would be elected President of the United States four times, let alone once, the response would probably have been an indignant snort. Nevertheless T.R. had a considerable regard for FDR when Franklin was a youngster, and FDR had a deep respect and admiration for TR. The first vote for president FDR ever cast was for TR—probably his only vote for someone not a Democrat. Later Woodrow Wilson became FDR's leader, but, the late Josephus Daniels told me once, they were never particularly close; even when FDR became Wilson's Assistant Secretary of the Navy, he was still much more under the influence of his great cousin Theodore. Most Roosevelts have a habit of sticking together, politics aside.

The two Roosevelts had strikingly parallel lives to a point. Both came of prosperous and sturdy Dutch stock, both were born in New York State, both went to Harvard (Theodore, '80; Franklin, '04), both opened their careers in the New York legislature, both were Assistant Secretaries of the Navy,[2] both were Governors of New York, both ultimately reached the Presidency. Their policies were often similar too. TR waved "the big stick" at "malefactors of great wealth" and spoke with pugnacious contempt of the "vested interests," one of many phrases invented by him that have become fixed in the language; FDR—his words were milder—talked of "economic royalists" and

---

[2] Actually five different members of the Roosevelt family have at one time or other filled this post in this century, a remarkable fact that should have interest for the historians. The other three were Theodore Roosevelt, Jr. (under Harding and Coolidge), Henry L. Roosevelt (under FDR), and Theodore Douglas Robinson, a cousin, under Coolidge.

"driving the money changers from the temple." Both were Big Navy men, and pursued an extremely active foreign policy; TR acquired Panama, sent the fleet around the world, and was an international hell-raiser in general. Also TR worked out the Peace of Portsmouth between Russia and Japan; FDR had peace problems at Casablanca, Teheran, Quebec, and Yalta. But the strongest analogies remain domestic; for instance both men were ardent conservationists. TR stood for the "Square" Deal; FDR for the "New" Deal. The very phrase New Deal derives from the concepts of two former Presidents, Woodrow Wilson's "New" Freedom and the Square "Deal" of Theodore.

Similarities in temperament between the two Roosevelts are also marked, but one must withstand a temptation to exaggerate them. The same family background, which we will go into in considerable detail later, produced certain common traits, though not those that might be most easily imagined; both were rich men, with deeply ingrained aristocratic impulses, and both stood for social justice. There is a strong reformer streak in Roosevelts. Another item is that both surmounted onerous physical handicaps, though at different ages; TR's asthma, however, even though it threatened to make him an invalid, can hardly be ranked as a catastrophe with FDR's paralysis. Still, like FDR, TR spent years in conquest of an illness. Another point is the intense interest both men had in natural history and the outdoors, and their somewhat infantile delight in shooting birds and beasts. FDR had a considerable bent for natural science, particularly in childhood, but he never developed it as TR did; even if he had not been paralyzed, it is almost inconceivable that he could have written such a muscular book as *African Game Trails*. FDR's passion for ships and water is widely known; not so well known is that TR once wrote a history of the Naval War of 1812. Still another item: both had a deep and adhesive family sense, and loved children. Still another: both were immensely curious, with agile fresh minds and variegated interests. Still others (we are getting down to minutiae): both loved to read aloud, to do business at meals, to go on picnics, and to pamper dogs.

But there were differences too. TR was like a dragon; FDR was like a faun, at least as a youth. There was much more buncombe and bluster in TR. He was less urbane and graceful, and more bellicose. He was, Henry Stimson records, "the most commanding natural leader" he had ever known; certainly FDR was a great leader too, but not in quite that way.

Of course FDR never had the opportunity to toughen himself in the West on the fist fights and hand-to-hand brawls that TR loved. One cannot quite imagine him saying, as TR did, "I am as strong as a bull moose, and you can use me to the limit!" The accent is gentler—for instance consider FDR's words in the 1944 campaign, "I am an old campaigner, and I enjoy a good fight." He did—but he used his head more than his fists. He did not have the elder Roosevelt's fierce industry: for instance TR wrote more than 100,000 letters during his seven years in the White House, incredible as this feat may seem, and Ike Hoover tells us that he often read "three or four" books a night. But also FDR had qualities that TR didn't have—resilience, a magical serenity, and consummate delicacy of political approach. FDR envied TR his vitality. Once he sighed to an interviewer, "TR needed only six hours' sleep a night, but I have to have eight."

At Campobello, FDR's summer camp in New Brunswick, Canada, one trail was tough in the extreme. It led along the shore and then over precipitous rocks and broken hills; in one place you had to swim a few yards where the path broke off, and the water was icy cold. FDR, before illness struck him, made a point of taking this hike just once every summer. But TR would have done it every day, and before breakfast at that. (Incidentally Eleanor Roosevelt told me once that one of TR's own hikes near Oyster Bay was so rugged and difficult that it terrified her when she was a child.) TR loved obstacles. He loved to overcome something just for the sake of doing so. FDR was one of the greatest fighters who ever lived, but, prudently, he much preferred to go around an obstacle rather than blast it off the road, if he could get to the other side just as expeditiously.

FDR liked to use phrases from TR in his speeches, and enjoyed quoting remarks like "weasel words." Incidentally it was to FDR himself that TR once said, "If I can be right 75% of the time [as President] I shall come up to the fullest measure of my hopes."[3]

Bonds between the two men remained close for a long time if only because of their abstrusely interlocked family relationship. When

---

[3] *The Public Papers and Addresses of Franklin D. Roosevelt,* edited by Samuel I. Rosenman, 13 Vols. (New York, Random House, 1938, Vols. 1928-36; The Macmillan Co., 1941, Vols. 1937-40; Harper & Brothers, 1950, Vols. 1941-45), Vol. II, p. 165. I shall draw frequently on this great repository of Roosevelt documents, hereafter to be called "Rosenman."

Eleanor Roosevelt married Franklin, it was TR, then the President of the United States, who gave the bride away; Eleanor was TR's godchild and favorite niece. All this we shall deal with in a chapter below. One detail is that when the ceremony was over, TR turned to Eleanor with the words, "You've done well to stick by the name of Roosevelt!"

Recently I asked one of FDR's sons, Franklin, Jr., if he had any childhood memories of TR; he replied that when he was growing up in Washington "Uncle Ted" was at Sagamore Hill most of the time, but that when he visited the capital he would usually drop in on the Franklin Roosevelts for tea and that he was always boisterous, jovial, and aggressive. In fact, he would rush up to the room where the small Roosevelts were getting ready for bed, grab young Franklin with one arm and his brother John with the other, and then haul them across the room, roaring, "I'm taking two little pigs to market!" Franklin was scared half to death (he was about five at the time) because he thought, first, that Uncle Ted might well be actually carting them off to a butcher shop, and second, that he might slip and drop them down the stairs.

TR and FDR began to be less friendly after 1917. The old Rough Rider wanted to raise a volunteer division to serve in France; Pershing overruled him, and Wilson had to stand by Pershing. But TR resented it that Franklin, as Assistant Secretary of the Navy, did not support his project—though it was hardly in FDR's proper field to do so. I once asked Alice Longworth, TR's daughter, what had been her father's final judgment on Franklin before he died in 1919. She said, "Father had no opinion about him one way or another at that time."

Roosevelt and Wilson

Likewise, the influence of Woodrow Wilson on Franklin Roosevelt was profound; likewise, these two Presidents shared some striking traits. Each was of the upper gentry; yet each was a people's man. The career of each can be stratified into four clear periods—domestic preoccupations, a foreign crisis, war, and interest in the future peace. Each was a gentleman; each had qualities of grace and gallantry; each had charm and courage. But whereas FDR's charm was natural and spontaneous, Wilson's was more sporadic, though considerable; he had to turn it on. Wilson was much more intellectual than Roosevelt; he really used his beautifully articulated mind. It would have been unimaginable for Wilson to use a dozen collaborators on a single speech, as FDR often did. Nor did Roosevelt have Wilson's ear for cadenced prose. Wilson was more austere than FDR, brittler, and less fluid and receptive. Wilson was a Scots Covenanter; FDR a Dutchman of good will. Both men were idealists, who believed firmly in Right; but FDR was much less doctrinaire. FDR was of course the better politician, sensitive whereas Wilson was stubborn and dogmatic, relaxed whereas Wilson was often hurt and tense. Wilson was never a back-slapper or a hail-fellow-well-met; he seldom called anybody outside his family by a Christian name, whereas, as is notorious, FDR used first names at sight. Wilson feared people; Roosevelt loved them. Wilson, a genuinely shy man, never really *liked* politics, whereas FDR adored every nuance of the art and science of political maneuver.

One analogy, not often thought of these days, is that Wilson, too, was paralyzed after his stroke on October 2, 1919. And it is a pungent forgotten detail that, before the stroke, Roosevelt flirted with the idea of trying to persuade Wilson to run for a third term.

Another analogy, on quite a different level, is that neither ever told anybody *every*thing. (But does any president?) Another is the way each used people. But Wilson gave men orders; FDR cajoled them. FDR sent Harry Hopkins to Europe almost exactly as Wilson sent Colonel House; but whereas House was a kind of supermessenger, Hopkins was a friend, a genuine intimate. Also FDR—so complex, so given to several motives—thought that the trip would be useful for Hopkins's own education and development.

Wilson was, we know, more orderly than FDR. But when he played golf he never kept score—something which would have shocked Roosevelt profoundly. One point of difference, which tells a good deal about their contrasting attitudes toward social affairs, is that whereas FDR belonged to a covey of clubs at Harvard, Wilson set out to abolish clubs at Princeton. Wilson, with his stern aloofness, was a creature devoid of personal emotion—so one might think. But it is unlikely in the extreme that FDR could ever have behaved as Wilson did when he was courting Mrs. Galt, when, for days on end, the business of government all but stopped while the President pressed his torrential, neurotic suit.

Yet the bond between the two men is unmistakable. FDR often quoted Wilson, as he quoted Theodore; one Wilson maxim he used was, "Reactionaries can always present a front because their program is so negative." And one can easily imagine FDR reading with satisfaction Wilson's definition of statesmanship: "The resolute and vigorous advance towards the realization of high, definite, and consistent aims, which issue from the unreserved devotion of a strong intellect to the service of the State." One can imagine, too, how indulgently he might have smiled at such an example of Wilson's frosty humor as his remark on bureaucracy, "I shall create no more boards. I find that most of them are long, wooden, and narrow."

Then, too, FDR might well have been amused—and impressed— by Wilson's instruction to one emissary he sent abroad: "Pay no attention to our ambassador there. If you get along too well with him, we will know that you yourself are doing nothing; but if you get into too much trouble, remember that we will call you home."

World War I took Wilson by surprise, and at the outbreak of hostilities in 1914 he appealed to the American people to be neutral "even in thought"—something FDR would never have done. Indeed FDR did the exact opposite. Wilson thought that the war was caused "by nothing in particular" and for a considerable interval he saw little to choose between the British and German varieties of illegality. FDR, as we all know, took a sharply different line.

The following is an excerpt from an extemporary speech Roosevelt made in 1939 at a dinner for the trustees of the Hyde Park library:

I always remember an episode in 1917. It occurred at the White House. I was Acting Secretary of the Navy and it was the first week in March. It was perfectly obvious . . . that we were going to get into the War within the course of two or three weeks. . . . I went to see the President and I said, "President Wilson, may I request your permission to bring the Fleet back from Guantanamo, to send it to the Navy Yards and have it cleaned and fitted out for war and be ready to take part in the War if we get in?" And the President said, "I am very sorry, Mr. Roosevelt, I cannot allow it." But I pleaded and he gave me no reason and said, "No, I do not wish it brought north." So, belonging to the Navy, I said, "Aye, aye, sir," and started to leave the room. He stopped me at the door and said, "Come back." He said, "I am going to tell you something I cannot tell to the public. I owe you an explanation. I don't want to do anything, I don't want the United States to do anything in a military way, by way of war preparations, that would allow the definitive historians in later days to say that the United States had committed an unfriendly act against the Central Powers." I said, "The definitive historian of the future?" He said, "Yes. Probably he won't write till about the year 1980 and when he writes the history of this World War, he may be 'a German, he may be a Russian, he may be a Bulgarian—we cannot tell—but I do not want to do anything that would lead him to misjudge our American attitude sixty or seventy years from now."[4]

In domestic fields Wilson was a definite precursor of FDR's New Deal, though people are apt to forget this now. Under Wilson came the Federal Reserve banking system, attacks on monopoly in big business, woman's suffrage, federal loans to farmers, the eight-hour day for railway workers, much miscellaneous social legislation, and, above all, the income tax. Also Wilson created an "ethical climate," as it has been aptly defined, which Roosevelt inherited after a long and dreary gap. But the more important analogies are in the realm of foreign policy; both Wilson and FDR helped carry America out of international provincialism. One reason why FDR did prepare for war is that Wilson had not prepared; this is probably Wilson's chief gift to him. Wilson created the League; FDR helped create the United Nations. But FDR learned well from Wilson's supreme mistake: Wilson cared so much for the United States of the World that he forgot the United States of America. This classic blunder FDR never made. Painstakingly, never-endingly, from the beginning of the crisis over isolation in the mid-1930's until his final preparation for the San Francisco Conference in 1945, FDR kept in mind Wilson's defeat by the Senate. "The tragedy of Wilson was always somewhere within the rim of his consciousness," as Sherwood[5] points out. Wilson was, in short, his stop sign, his warning signal, for year after crowded year. He took no steps at all for bringing the United States into world commitments without the most scrupulously calculating eye to Congress, because the red light that was Wilson always shone.

Roosevelt and Churchill

One may easily forecast the weight of dissertation that will come about these two prodigious virtuosos and their equally prodigious inter-relation in future years, as more and more documents become available. Material exists already for a round dozen Ph.D. theses.

A celebrated ambassador once said mischievously to an equally celebrated Washington hostess, "What do you think you would find if you cut Roosevelt open?" The reply was, "What you would find if you

---

[4] Rosenman, Vol. VIII, p. 117.

[5] *Roosevelt and Hopkins*, by Robert E. Sherwood (New York, Harper & Brothers, 1948), the best book on FDR yet written.

cut open a paper doll. Nothing." This is not to be taken seriously of course, but in point of fact Roosevelt sometimes did give the impression of being two-dimensional. Churchill seems fuller-bodied, with greater depth; one thinks of him as all one color, the scarlet of the beefeater guardsman or the purple of the Renaissance; FDR had a multiplicity of shadow tones and reflecting surfaces. Churchill, one feels, is always one man, though astoundingly various within his single flesh; Roosevelt was every sort of man who ever was.

Many obvious points of similarity exist between the two, but Churchill was probably a better gambler, and took chances more; also he was a better bargainer. It is unlikely that FDR would ever have put up such a bluff as, for instance, Churchill did in 1943, when he tried to bludgeon the Turks into entering the war by threatening to "give" the Dardanelles to Russia. Churchill wrote more eloquent and brilliant prose. He had a deeper apperception of historical realities. He trusted his experts more, and avoided government-by-crony. He was more accessible to controversy. It is interesting that Henry Stimson records that he "could cut loose at the Englishman as he never felt free to do with his chief"; he argued with Churchill much more freely than with FDR. A minor point is their relation to the scientists in their entourage. Roosevelt bears more responsibility for the atomic bomb than any single man, but he did not like scientists much and never had them close by. Churchill and his chief scientific consultant, Lord Cherwell, were inseparable.

Oddly enough FDR and Churchill were eighth cousins once removed, if the researches of one genealogist are correct. Both men, it appears, can trace a common descent from a personage known as John Cooke who came to America on the *Mayflower*. John married Sarah Warren; one of their daughters was the great-great-great-great-great-great-grandmother of Sara Delano, FDR's mother, and another was a direct ancestress of Churchill's American-born mother, Jennie Jerome.

Some confusion has existed as to exactly where and when the two men first met. Churchill himself says that, when Roosevelt visited England during World War I, they encountered one another at a dinner at Gray's Inn; Churchill was "struck by his magnificent presence." But, remarkably enough, he appears to have forgotten this episode when the two leaders saw one another for the first time in World War II; it irked Roosevelt that Churchill apparently had no recollection of their previous meeting. What seems to be a mystifying item appears in

Volume II of Roosevelt's letters: "I am just back from lunch with Winston Churchill. He saw the President yesterday and apparently had a pretty satisfactory talk." This was in July, 1917. But the Churchill involved here was the American novelist Winston Churchill, not the British statesman.

As one reminiscence follows another we learn more of the profound complexity and scope of the Roosevelt-Churchill intercourse during World War II. Between them something like 1,700 telegrams, letters, and other communications passed in five and a half years, starting with Roosevelt's sympathetic initiative to the "Naval Person" when Churchill became First Lord of the Admiralty in 1939. This letter is a good example of FDR's touch and tact, and it disproves, incidentally, the charge sometimes made that the exchange by-passed Neville Chamberlain, the Prime Minister:

> It is because you and I occupied similar positions in the world war that I want you to know how glad I am that you are back at the Admiralty. . . . What I want you and the Prime Minister to know is that I shall at all times welcome it, if you will keep me in touch personally with anything you want me to know about. You can always send sealed letters through your pouch or my pouch.
>
> I am glad you did the Marlborough volumes before this thing started—and I much enjoyed reading them.[6]

Churchill's letters to Roosevelt from this date until Pearl Harbor constitute one of the supreme feats of political argument of all time. He "armed" FDR with patient lessons; he laid the framework for the destroyer transfer; he ceaselessly cajoled, explored, exhorted; he wheedled him, encouraged him, and called out sternly "Do it now"; he prompted Roosevelt to the idea for Lend Lease in the celebrated 19-point letter of December, 1940; he kept at him artfully through his ambassador in Washington; he analyzed history for him as he made it, in documents of unprecedented insight, brilliance, variety, and vigor. But one must not think that Roosevelt was a dupe or that he played second fiddle. The Churchill salesmanship was masterly; but FDR did not need to be sold on the major premises.

The President and Prime Minister met ten or twelve times during the course of the war—on the *Augusta* (where the Atlantic Charter was drawn up), four times in Washington, twice in Quebec, and at Casa-

[6] Quoted in Mr. Churchill's *Their Finest Hour* (Boston, Houghton Mifflin Company, 1949).

blanca, Cairo, Teheran, and Yalta. According to Churchill's own calculation they had 120 days of close personal contact in all. Nothing in
contemporary—or other—annals quite matches the dramatic intensity
and importance of this series of monumental conferences; it is quite
safe to say that never before has talk between two men so influenced
the course of world history, both military and political. Roosevelt once
telegraphed to Churchill, "It is fun to be in the same decade with you,"
which would appear to be one of the more massive understatements
of the age.

After the Atlantic Charter meeting, when the two leaders returned
to their respective ships, each immediately asked one of his adjutants,
"What did *he* think of me?" FDR was inclined to be boastful later. He
told a friend, "I had thirteen warships at that meeting, but Winston
had only two or three. One of his broke down, and I had to *lend* him a
destroyer!" Incidentally no formal document embodying the Charter
was ever signed, which fact has caused much puzzlement and controversy. One story is that FDR, picking up the press release that had been
prepared, jotted down his own initials on it and then Mr. Churchill's
too. The British did not take the Charter as seriously as we did, though,
as we know from the latest installment of the Prime Minister's memoirs,
the actual draft closely follows a memorandum Churchill himself had
prepared. Roosevelt's own words about this, as reported at a subsequent
press conference, are, "There isn't any copy of the Atlantic Charter, so
far as I know. I haven't got one. The British haven't got one. The nearest thing you will get is the [message of the] radio operator on the
Augusta and *Prince of Wales*. That's the nearest thing you will come
to it. . . . There was no formal document."

General Eisenhower met Churchill at Casablanca in 1943. Roosevelt
hardly knew Eisenhower then, but the President turned to him when
the Prime Minister left the room: "Isn't he a wonderful old Tory to
have on our side?"

FDR and Churchill bickered and bargained and nettled one another
as the strain of waging coalition war became almost intolerable, and
often this issue of Toryism was at the bottom of their difficulties.
Roosevelt exasperated the Prime Minister almost beyond speech by
pushing for the independence of India, by constantly adducing the
need of colonial peoples for self-development and self-improvement.
FDR stated openly at one press conference late in the war that Winston was "mid-Victorian on all things like that" (i.e., things having to

do with the British Empire), and that "he would never learn." Once—at Teheran—they had a spat over the status of Newfoundland, and Sherwood and Elliott Roosevelt recount some other lively episodes. Think what the Prime Minister must have felt when FDR quite casually urged the British to give up Hong Kong! Churchill had great anxiety at Yalta when Roosevelt "flabbergasted" him by telling him that he was going to meet the kings of Egypt, Saudi Arabia, and Ethiopia in Cairo. "Churchill . . . thought we had some deep-laid plot to undermine the British Empire," Hopkins wrote.[7] Eleanor Roosevelt writes, "He [FDR] never minced words in telling Mr. Churchill that he did not think the British had done enough in any one of the colonial areas in really improving the lot of the native peoples."[8] FDR had an extremely generous and copious imagination about anything to do with improving anybody's future.

Another important point of difference was the Second Front; the British did not want to risk a major operation across the Channel until 1944. Of course this issue involved the Russians, who thought that they were being bled white in the east while the western allies stalled. At one of their conferences, trying to break through Stalin's implacable suspiciousness and reserve, FDR "ganged up" on Churchill (having given him due warning), and proceeded to bait him in the Russian dictator's presence. But the baiting went a little far. I asked someone who was present if this episode actually had taken place as frequently described. "You bet it did, and it wasn't funny, either!"

On smaller counts, personal counts, there were other irritants. For one thing Churchill, as is notorious, liked to take gargantuan naps in the afternoon, "naps" sometimes two or three hours long, and then stay up most of the night, whereas FDR worked straight through the day and wanted to be in bed by midnight. And Churchill was puzzled and irritated by the President's discursiveness. The Prime Minister annoyed Roosevelt by bringing his own Map Room to the White House; FDR, who was good at tit for tat, retaliated by bringing *his* own Map Room to Quebec. Churchill, the record would indicate, was much more generous than Roosevelt in comments of each about the other. Modestly he would describe himself as the President's "first lieutenant." He was the elder; yet he liked to address him as "Mr. President,"

[7] Sherwood, p. 871.

[8] The quotation from Mrs. Roosevelt is from her second volume of autobiography, *This I Remember* (New York, Harper & Brothers, 1949).

though of course FDR called him "Winston" practically from the moment they met.

Churchill began to be worried about Roosevelt's health at Quebec. Shortly thereafter, in the campaign against Dewey, FDR made his famous campaign ride through the streets of New York in icy rain; at once Churchill telegraphed him, appealing to him to take better care of himself. Once the Prime Minister (at Quebec) said that to encounter Roosevelt, with all his buoyant sparkle, his iridescence, was like opening a bottle of champagne. Roosevelt was not so given to such pleasant compliments. It is recorded that, in their last meetings together, Churchill always looked "as if he were going to get hit," and Roosevelt is once supposed to have said, "Yes, I *am* tired! So would you be if you had spent the last five years pushing Winston uphill in a wheelbarrow."

James F. Byrnes writes in *Speaking Frankly* that the President complained at Yalta about Churchill's too frequent and lengthy speeches, "which held up business." Byrnes replied, "Yes, but they were good speeches." Then FDR chuckled and admitted, "Winston doesn't make any other kind." On the other hand Edward R. Stettinius, who was also present at Yalta, reproduces in his book a handwritten chit FDR passed across to him on one occasion when the Prime Minister began to speak, "Now we are in for ½ hour of it," which would seem to be a comment somewhat snide.

Astonishing things occurred at the second Quebec meeting, according to Henry Morgenthau. Roosevelt took Morgenthau with him to Quebec, because the agenda included the British monetary situation— "Churchill keeps saying he [not personally of course] is broke," Morgenthau records. The conferees had a violent argument about the status of Germany after the war, and Churchill attacked Morgenthau ("I never had such a verbal lashing in my life") for his projected scheme of transforming Germany into a pastoral, industryless state. "The President . . . said very little. This was part of his way of managing Churchill. He let the Prime Minister wear himself out attacking me. . . . Then, when the time came, he could move in with his superb and infectious humor and compose the situation." Churchill demanded, "What are we going to have between the white snows of Russia and the white cliffs of Dover?" (i.e., if Germany were destroyed) and Morgenthau asked the President what to do. FDR replied simply,

"Give me thirty minutes with Churchill." He was sure that he could "handle" him.

Roosevelt's death was probably no great surprise to Churchill. "At Yalta," the Prime Minister has said, "I noticed that the President was ailing. His captivating smile, his gay charming manner, had not deserted him, but his face had a transparency, an air of purification, and often there was a far-away look in his eyes." In a way the President's death contributed to Churchill's defeat at the British general election that summer, because the war with Germany had been won even though FDR was dead, which seemed to prove that no one man, not even Churchill, was indispensable; moreover, had Roosevelt been alive, many people in England might have voted differently on the ground that the Roosevelt-Churchill partnership, working so brilliantly toward climax, should not be broken up.

David Lloyd George was another British statesman whom Roosevelt strikingly resembled; like Lloyd George, FDR greatly modified the structure of capitalism, and as a result was hated and vilified by the "ruling" classes; like Lloyd George (and Churchill), he organized victory in a tremendous war. The Lloyd George reforms paved the way indirectly for the rise of British socialism to political power; the remark has been made about him, "He saved capitalism, but by so doing made socialism certain." A similar remark may quite possibly be made about Roosevelt some day in the long future.

A final point: Roosevelt may have been cavalier to Churchill on occasion, and perhaps he did speed up, despite him, the progressive disintegration of the British Empire; yet it cannot be denied that, the Prime Minister aside, Roosevelt deserves more credit for keeping Britain herself alive after Dunkirk than any Englishman. He was one of the best American friends Britain has ever had, and during the blackest period of the Battle of Britain he was almost as important in maintaining *British* morale as Churchill himself, which is to say a lot.

Roosevelt and Hitler

Surely no two men who played supreme roles in the same supreme drama could have been more unlike. But Hitler is worth brief mention for two reasons. (He came to power, incidentally, on January 30, 1933, which was Roosevelt's birthday, and just five weeks before the first inaugural.) First, several of the forces propelling Hitler into power were much the same as those that put Mr. Roosevelt into office—mass despair in the midst of unprecedented economic crisis, impassioned hatred of the *status quo,* and a burning desire by the great majority of people to find a savior who might bring luck. Roosevelt won in 1932 partly because Mr. Hoover was so discredited and unpopular; similarly the electorate in Germany, though of course tricked and deluded and beaten down by terror, voted not merely for Hitler but *against* the feebleness and ineptitude of the previous regime.

But, second, Mr. Roosevelt never became a dictator. He was often called a dictator, as he was called a Communist, by people too stupid, too dishonest, or too prejudiced to be able to tell good from bad, white from black, or fish from fowl. A single item, among hundreds available, serves to refute the dictatorship charge—for instance the fact that although FDR had been in power for twelve years and the country was in the midst of the greatest war in its history, he went to the electorate in 1944 in an entirely proper and free constitutional election, and beat his opponent, Mr. Dewey, by fair, open, and constitutional means— and at that had to extend himself to win. Or, to consider the "dictatorship" issue on a different level, recollect merely that some months before this election FDR had to submit to the indignant resignation of his own majority leader, Alben Barkley, when he vetoed the tax bill passed by Congress. (True, Barkley resumed the senate leadership later.)

A further point is that Roosevelt might easily have tried to make himself dictator, and moreover a dictator like Hitler, who was legally *voted* into office, had he been crudely ambitious or unscrupulous. Roosevelt had the votes; what is more he had the actual power—and chose never to exercise it. We are apt to forget nowadays the immense, unprecedented, overwhelming authority conferred on FDR by an enthusiastically willing Congress during the first hundred days of his first administration. The Reichstag did not give Hitler much more. Suppose Roosevelt had *not* been a democrat at heart. Merely by pressing the analogy to Hitler, we may toll off what we might have lost, but did not—the existence of opposition parties, a free judiciary, independence of the civil service, the rule of law, freedom of religion and education, the Bill of Rights, the Constitution itself—to say nothing of the right of Americans to think freely, talk freely, breathe freely, throughout the land.

Chapter 2

PERSONAL

Perhaps the simplest way to proceed is to describe briefly something
out of my own experience, although this was minor in the extreme—
I met the President only four or five times. But since no single clue
exists to the subtle complexities of Roosevelt, almost all clues are relevant, and almost all direct personal evidence has a certain value.

The first time I ever saw him was at a press conference on December
7, 1934, midway through the all-but-forgotten pressures and turmoils
of the first term, and seven years to a day before Pearl Harbor. I was
then the Vienna correspondent of the Chicago *Daily News,* I was home
in the United States on leave, and I was permitted as a matter of
routine courtesy to be among those present.

I had never been to a presidential press conference before. I had
never seen Mr. Roosevelt before. I was astonished and amazed. I was
bewildered. I had been used to the stuffy, useless kind of press "conference" we got in Budapest or Paris, in London and Vienna; this
was something utterly new to my experience. Here are the notes I
hurriedly, carefully scrawled afterward:

President at 4 P.M. We were lined up in a thick crowd for half an hour
before the doors opened. I was up in front and got a place directly at the
corner of his desk. It is not a very big desk and not neat. Papers all over
the place and a half-smoked can of Camels. He has a big head, very
tanned; he cocks the whole head continually, snapping his eyes this way
and that as it finishes an arc; talks with a cigarette holder clenched between
his teeth, at the extreme corner of the mouth; blinks to get smoke out of
his eyes. He just waited for a moment as we stood there. This new office is
bigger than the old one, yet not quite big enough to get everybody in comfortably. Someone said the new room was nice, but that it ought to have a
bar. "Don't you think we might have a bar, Mr. President?" FDR twinkled,

that is the only word for it, and said absolutely nothing; but everybody felt that the questioner had been satisfactorily answered, just by the twinkle. Then the President stated slowly and deliberately that he was thinking of adding a new agency to the government with a new set of initials, S.C.S. General stir and curiosity. "SCS?" "Yes, Sewing Circle Stories, to deal with all such silly questions and proposals." He uttered the single short sentence with as much elocution and pause for dramatic effect as if it had been a line from Hamlet. Of course everybody roared. Then the first serious question: "When are you going to make your next radio speech, Mr. President?" "Somewhere between now and Christmas, and if you do any guessing now, I can tell you one thing, your guess will be wrong." Laughter. FDR appreciates this; his head tilts up; the eyeglasses glitter like windowpanes flashing in the sun. "Can you make any statement as to whether General MacArthur will be reappointed Chief of Staff?" "I cannot," after a long clever pause. "We understand you are sending Hugh Gibson to Europe on a special mission." Astonishment on the President's features, pure astonishment. "Wherever did you hear that?" "From Mr. Gibson himself this morning." "But he's going to Europe to see his sick boy in Switzerland." So everybody decides that Gibson *is* being sent abroad on a special mission. "What about Ambassador Bingham's speech on naval negotiations, Mr. President?" Bland puzzlement, then the reply, "What did he say?" Someone explained. FDR smiled, "Hmm, hmm, I guess I'll have to get a copy." Laughter. A reporter then mentioned a treaty about Niagara Falls and the necessity for joint action by the United States and Canada to preserve scenic beauties, repair crumbling rocks, and the like. Long pause. "I never heard of such a treaty. Hmm. Yes, come to think of it, I do remember. In fact, when I was Governor, didn't I sign some bill opposing it? Or was I for it? Don't remember! Hmm. Very interesting. It was something about the water power there. But your question was about scenic values, crumbling rocks . . . ? Let us draw up a bill to turn the Falls on and off at regular intervals for the benefit of sightseers!" Roars of laughter. FDR blinks, takes a bow, tilts the huge head, grins sharply. Everybody in a marvelous humor by this time. "Mr. President, what do you think of this Balkan crisis?" He looked serious for the first time. "I didn't even know there was a Balkan crisis until I picked up the afternoon paper. I phoned Mr. Hull and he is telegraphing all the ministers and I expect to have information tomorrow." "Mr. President, how about the naval negotiations?" "You know as much about that as I do, I am afraid." This was the last remark. "Thank you, Mr. President, good-by Mr. President." The room emptied almost as quickly as it had filled.

In twenty minutes Mr. Roosevelt's features had expressed amazement, curiosity, mock alarm, genuine interest, worry, rhetorical play ing for suspense, sympathy, decision, playfulness, dignity, and surpass-ing charm. Yet he *said* almost nothing. Questions were deflected, diverted, diluted. Answers—when they did come—were concise and clear. But I never met anyone who showed greater capacity for avoid-ing a direct answer while giving the questioner a feeling he *had* been answered.

Stephen T. Early, FDR's press secretary, introduced me later. The President was leaning back, relaxed, with the look of an officer who has just won a minor skirmish. It was explained that I lived in Vienna, and FDR asked if I knew George Messersmith, for a long time the American consul general in Berlin, who had just been assigned to Austria as minister. I said that I knew Mr. Messersmith very well. The President suddenly broke out into laughter, "Ha, ha! That was a good joke on the State Department, wasn't it! Just think what the career boys will say! I've put a lowly consul into a diplomatic post. Ha, ha, ha!" Then came minor chitchat. My first thought as I walked out of the White House was, "Obviously that man has never had indigestion in his life."

Then I recalled a current wisecrack, to the effect that it was ridiculous to call Roosevelt a dictator—inasmuch as he sat with a broad window at his back. And indeed for anybody who lived in the atmosphere of Mussolini and Pilsudski, Kemal Atatürk and the rising Hitler, all that I had just witnessed was incredible—its open-ness, simplicity, lack of posture, lack of pressure. Nor could I avoid being impressed by the absence of fanfare in the White House itself—no trooping of the colors, no changing of the guard, no frock-coated underlings, no obsequious secretaries, no machine guns as at the Bundeskanzleramt in Vienna, no cordons of police blocking off the streets near the Wilhelmstrasse. The White House was as cozy as a porch—and indeed it was the front porch of the nation.

*

Next came a private meeting some years later. I had just returned to the United States from a long trip throughout Latin America, and Sumner Welles, the Undersecretary of State, suggested that it might be useful if I saw the President. FDR was intensely interested in Latin America, and Mr. Welles thought that I might have some impressions, news, and gossip that could be illuminating. So an appointment was arranged. But when I arrived in the Executive

Offices, General Edwin M. ("Pa") Watson, in charge of the President's schedule, told me that it was a mercilessly busy day and that I could not possibly have more than six or seven minutes. On the appointment sheet just before me were the Commissioners of the District of Columbia; FDR had to govern Washington, D.C., as well as the United States of America. After me was a member of the Cabinet. I was to be sandwiched in—and very briefly. The day was April 7, 1941. A few days before, the Germans had marched into Yugoslavia. Washington was dark with the shadow of impending catastrophes that might. well involve America; the atmosphere was that of confusion, excitement, and alarm. I waited. The Washington, D.C., Commissioners were taking a lot of time. They came out eventually. But now it was lunchtime. Pa Watson told me I would have to come back in the middle of the afternoon.

When I got in finally the President was leaning back in his big chair and Fala leapt forward and bit a doll that squeaked. FDR laughed. Miss Marguerite ("Missy") LeHand, his private secretary, picked up a folder of papers and left the room, pushing Fala along with her. The President hitched himself forward and grinned, "Hello! How are you?" (Of course he didn't know me from Adam.) I mention all this, trivial as my own experience was, because it is so typical of what happened to so many—for, in the midst of this crushing day, the President then proceeded to talk for 46 minutes without a break. I managed to get a few words in, but not many. Yet the only excuse for my being there at all in circumstances of such pressure was that I might have something useful to say.

His face, the best-known face in the world except possibly Hitler's, was hard to study, too mobile, never at rest, almost hyperthyroid, quivering with animation. I kept thinking that he looked like a caricature of himself, with the long jaw tilting upward, the V-shaped opening of the mouth when he laughed, the two long deep parentheses that closed the ends of his lips.

I tried to save time by plunging in with the remark that I had just returned from all twenty of the Latin American republics. FDR paused comfortably and then replied with amusement, "What? All twenty? Even Paraguay?" He flashed with a grimace at his own small joke, his own knowledge that most travelers to Latin America miss at least one country, Bolivia or Paraguay. In a fraction of a second the mood changed and he asked me the only direct question, so far as I can remember, that occurred during the whole talk: "What are the bad spots?" I said that Panama was the worst and mentioned the President of Panama, a remarkably polished and plausible adventurer who had gone to Harvard. "My goodness!" the President exclaimed. "Not really, is he a *Harvard* man?" He shifted quickly and mentioned two other Latin American dictators, one of whom is still in office, saying, "They're both bad men, really bad, shocking, but they've done good things."

Then began the monologue. By the time it had gone on for half an hour I was acutely embarrassed. It simply was not right that I should be taking so much time on such a busy day; it was outrageous that the President should waste these continuing precious minutes on anybody so totally irrelevant. He had no *right* to be so talkative; it was indecent and irresponsible. I made several gestures to get away, but he patted me back in my chair. I kept wishing for glue in my ears, as the bright, sharp, discursive, chatty talk went on—how he had once met President Stenio Vincent of Haiti (he called him "Stenio"); how Argentina really was a problem but that one solution might be (I shuddered) "to colonize it"; how Lend Lease was going to help all along the line because (a huge wink) "money talks"; how the President of Uruguay had once taken him for a ride through Montevideo, though assassins were supposedly waiting at every corner; how Iquitos, Peru, should become a free port; how he once told President Vargas of Brazil that he, Mr. Roosevelt, would absolutely not stand for it if he were in his place, in regard to the fact that most Brazilian public utilities were owned outside Brazil; how other countries might "buy back" their utilities debt, and how there would be a revolution in the United States if American industry was similarly controlled by foreigners; how the tourist business might be stimulated in Chile; how some silly American politicians had opposed the Pan-American Highway because it might be a route for invasion of the United States ("as if a real enemy would use *roads!*"); how I ought to have met a certain chap in Puerto Rico, he lived on such-and-such a street, he had once been married to so-and-so, and he liked very dry Martinis; how the Navy was satisfied with our present position in the Galapagos; how he often made idealistic speeches but he knew full well that what really counted in Latin America was power; and how (a hearty laugh) no Latin American knows how to sail a ship.

Suddenly a movement of the eyes, and the President had gone

to Europe. Again I felt embarrassed; it was appalling that he should be so indiscreet. He could trust me, of course; even so, he really had no business talking quite so freely about top secrets. All this is water long under the bridge by now, and perfectly harmless today; but then it was hot as firecrackers. No, we were not ready for convoys (across the Atlantic) "yet." Yes, the power of the Japanese was overestimated. Yes, we already had full plans to take over the entire Atlantic sphere, including Greenland. Yes, what was going on in Iraq was highly unpleasant, because it gave the Turks an enemy on the other side. No, it would take about two months to get effective relief to Yugoslavia. Yes, Natal was necessary, but we could have it for the asking. I find in the notes I took with great care immediately afterward that I made one remark that interested him, but for the life of me I cannot recall what authority I had for what I said. But he was talking about Russia (this was some months before the German invasion of the USSR), and I said that I thought that before the war was over the Union Jack and Hammer and Sickle would be on the same side, and that the Russian Army might "save us all." "Really! What makes you think that?" he exclaimed, and then just laughed.

The phone rang with a low buzz, and I made to go. He picked up the receiver, waving me to stay. Then began ten or eleven long minutes during which he said "Yes, Harry . . . No, Harry . . . Why, I thought that had been done, Harry. But of course it *ought* to have been done, Harry!" He looked angry and nervously, forcefully, stabbed with a pencil at a pad. "All right, I'll see to it, it's done now, thanks, Harry." I thought this must be Harry Hopkins. But now the President was leaning back in his chair, more relaxed, cupping the phone intimately to his ear, and setting off on a long discourse. I could not believe my ears. "Well, Harry, as I see it, there have been three cardinal events in the evolution of American foreign policy since 1919. One was . . . The other was . . . And the third was your doctrine on Manchuria." So this was not Harry Hopkins, but Harry Stimson! The President was telling Mr. Stimson about Mr. Stimson's doctrine on Manchuria. Then I saw a quick rather hurt expression on FDR's face, and he laid the phone down suddenly. Obviously, Mr. Stimson had cut him off. The President had completely forgotten me by this time. He turned, saw me, looked at me with some surprise, stretched out his great hand, and ended the interview with one of the most startling single remarks I have ever heard—"So long! I've got to *run* along now!" And all the time I had been having a hard time keeping my eyes off his wasted legs.

*

Next came a brief social meeting early the next year, on April 23, 1942. Mrs. Roosevelt had asked me to dinner at the White House, but through the slip-up of a secretary the invitation did not reach me. I was mortified and angry, never having been invited to a meal at the White House before, and I called up Miss Thompson, Mrs. Roosevelt's secretary, to make apologies. A day or two later came an invitation to tea. I walked up the White House driveway and was puzzled because a group of photographers stood waiting on the steps of the porch. I had a broadcast, not yet written, to give that evening, and though I looked forward extremely to having tea in the White House, I hoped the function would not last too long. I was ushered in and there, to my surprise, stood Mrs. Roosevelt herself, waiting just inside the front door. I had not looked to the right or left and, my surprise suddenly mounting, I heard Mrs. Roosevelt say, "Mr. Gunther, you know the President, don't you?" And there the President was, tucked in his wheel chair, a wrap over his legs, behind the half-open door. He was tense with what seemed to be suppressed excitement. I was so startled that I almost jumped. Then Miss Thompson whisked me through the hall and led me to the South Portico, where the paraphernalia for tea was ready. I was still bewildered. Miss Thompson proceeded to explain amiably that Prince Bernhard and Princess Juliana of the Netherlands had just arrived in Washington, and that Mrs. Roosevelt had not known they were to make their first call on the President that same afternoon, at the same hour when she had invited me. Since they were royalty, FDR had to wait for them at the door. I offered to get out at once, but Miss Thompson said to stay. Mrs. Roosevelt then walked in with Bernhard and Juliana, and the President entered in the wheel chair. What he thought of my being there I have no idea. I doubt if he knew who I was. But Bernhard remembered me from several meetings in London earlier in the war, and the group rapidly became informal. The President talked almost without interruption for a solid hour. It was perfectly obvious that he was going to charm that Dutch princess out of her skin, if he burst doing so. He went right at her. He did not wait for any countermoves. She looked somewhat baffled, and hardly said a word. Mrs. Roosevelt and Miss Thompson

and I made another pool of conversation at the other end of the table.
Mrs. Roosevelt asked me to take a trip to West Virginia, as field work
for my projected *Inside U. S. A.* Then the President was addressing
everybody. He was marvelous. He was dumfounding. One of his
generals had just confused Dutch Guiana with one of the Guineas in
Africa and FDR boomed out, "No general knows anything about
geography!" Then he pointed across the White House lawn, made
Juliana get up and look, and explained that the grass concealed an
air-raid shelter newly built in the subterranean passage leading to the
Treasury. He said that when a raid came he was going to stow Henry
Morgenthau down there ("to penalize him") and make him play poker
with twenty-dollar gold pieces. Becoming serious, he mentioned that he
fully expected "light token bombings of Washington" to occur during
the summer. The talk then turned to his secret Maryland retreat,
Shangri-La. The Dutch visitors did not understand the name, and
everybody became confused trying to explain it to them. "An Asian
name," pondered Prince Bernhard, puzzled. I came mildly to the
rescue by saying that anyway China was in the war and that Shangri-La
was pretty close to China, wasn't it? The President lifted his head and
grinned and beamed.

Presently the party ended. I scooted out of the White House, could
not find a taxi, and walked as fast as I could to my office to get to work.

*

I did not see Mr. Roosevelt again, except once in the 1944 campaign
when he spoke before the Foreign Policy Association, until the fourth
inaugural. Orson Welles, Quentin Reynolds, Mark Van Doren, and
I had done a broadcast that he liked, and so we were all asked down.
(The President always gave thanks for favors indirectly, and without
ever mentioning them.) I was terrified when I saw his face. I felt certain
that he was going to die. All the light had gone out underneath the
skin. It was like a parchment shade on a bulb that had been dimmed.
He sat alone in one corner of the big room as four or five hundred
guests passed down an informally arranged table with a somewhat
scant buffet. (Dorothy Thompson said immediately after we were
presented to the President, "Let's go out and get something to *eat!*")
One by one, guests were led forward in a long crooked file, while a
secretary whispered, "Don't hold him up. Let him finish his lunch."
He shook everybody by the hand as I recall, and the handshake was

firm enough, but I could not get over the ravaged expression on his face. It was gray, gaunt, and sagging, and the muscles controlling the lips seemed to have lost part of their function.

The next morning, January 20, 1945, we reached the White House in good time and joined the crowd, not a big crowd, on the snowy lawn. I had never been to an inaugural before. Seldom have I been so moved. We saw the White House children and grandchildren strolling and scampering around the porch, in wintry clothes—red scarves, blue mittens, bright stocking caps—while eminent dignitaries of the Republic mingled with them. Down below, we stamped our feet in the snow, moving about in small circles and craning forward to see better. The scene was like a Brueghel, with the sharply colored figures etched on the loose snow, the throng of tall men in dark clothes above, and the fluid, informal movement of the listeners. Jimmy Roosevelt helped FDR to his feet, Chief Justice Stone administered the oath, and the President delivered a short, taut speech. The absence of pomp was utter; the whole occasion might have been a high-school graduation. I kept thinking how an affair like this would be organized in one of the Axis countries, or even England. Yet the United States was the most powerful nation on earth. Maybe, I ruminated, the way this simple and colossal ceremony took place helped tell me why.

Chapter 3

SOME MAJOR QUALITIES
AND ATTRIBUTES

A man so various he seem'd to be
Not one, but all mankind's epitome.
—JOHN DRYDEN

Roosevelt had so many positive characteristics and sources of power that one scarcely knows how to begin. His good qualities far outride his bad in retrospect. Some of those bad were, I once heard it put, a kind of overburden—the price he paid to get things done.

There is no easy window into the mysteries and paradoxes of Roosevelt, but one outstanding trait, on which almost everybody would agree, is courage. I will not mention for the moment his indomitable conquest of a crippling disability, or even that he cared little for personal safety. After the attempt on his life in Miami in 1933, when Mayor Cermak of Chicago was assassinated, he was the calmest person present. Twice he insisted that his automobile stop in the very middle of the melee, so that he could render Cermak aid. The precautions imposed on him by law, and faithfully executed by a magnificent Secret Service, bored and irritated him. Obviously Mr. Roosevelt was one of those lucky ones who are born without any sense of physical fear, which is the more remarkable because most men without physical fear are unimaginative; they are likely to be among the least sensitive of the inhabitants of the earth's surface. But FDR was both extremely imaginative and sensitive to a marked degree. Even so, he had no physical fear except about one thing—fire. He hated and feared fire, and this was certainly reasonable enough, because if he were trapped in a sudden fire, his helplessness would have been complete. He was never allowed to travel except with a portable rig handy to get him out of wherever he was if a fire broke out.

There are all sorts of courage—that of bravado for instance. FDR certainly had that. There is the courage of audacity. That too Mr.

Roosevelt had. There is the slower, less spectacular courage of resolution, which he also had. Then too he had the courage to make tremendous lonely decisions, and to stick to them. Later I shall try to analyze how the President did reach decisions; let it suffice now to list a few and consider what courage it took to make them. It is perfectly true that the matter on which he had to decide was usually presented to him by expert opinion, and that often, particularly on appointments, he followed the multitudinous recommendations of others. But the ultimate responsibility was his. He took the decision, alone, to help arm Great Britain after Dunkirk; he took the decision to promote General Marshall over 34 senior officers and General Eisenhower over 366; he, alone, took the decision to spend two billion dollars on a fantasy known as the atomic bomb.

Or think of Pearl Harbor.[1] Some pretty disgraceful things happened in Washington that night; panic ran in some very high places indeed. There were men who behaved like somebody howling "Fire!" in a crowded theater, but one spot where absolute calmness and resolution reigned was the White House. People were busy and excited, yes, but Roosevelt steadied them. This was the more remarkable in that FDR knew more about the full catastrophic extent of the damage than most, and in addition he had a profoundly personal interest in the destroyed ships. The Navy was his greatest love; it was a frightful body blow. But, though strained, he was never for a moment confused or cowed. Not only did he fail to flinch at the shock itself; his compelling and instantaneous thought was of immediate counterattack, not defense at all, and he set in motion that very night the processes by which the United States soon moved expeditionary forces to Australia and Northern Ireland. But even a crisis as pivotal as this did not change the way he liked to do things. At one moment when half a dozen of his leading military and other councilors waited tensely for release to get on to their jobs, FDR leaned back and exasperated his audience almost to frenzy by telling an anecdote about lobster fishing in Maine that lasted twenty minutes.

From what did his courage derive? Pride had something to do with it, curiosity, ease of conscience, lack of self-doubt, and something indefinable called faith. FDR was primitive in some ways. He felt sincerely that if he did the right things, the right results would follow. By this

[1] More on this in Chapter 18 below.

simple process which had nothing to do with logic he freed himself from worry over the supreme enemy of courage, fear of responsibility.

Sleep: The Secret of His Serenity

A good authority has stated that in the whole time Roosevelt was in the White House he had only two sleepless nights. I asked Mrs. Roosevelt about this once, and her reply was characteristically candid and discriminating: "My husband never had a sleepless night. But it is quite true that there were two nights when he could not sleep, because of interruptions. To be sleepless is one thing. To be kept from sleep is quite another." One of these nights was early in the first term, when the banks were still closed; the other was the night Tobruk fell, when Churchill was a White House guest.

James Roosevelt, the President's eldest son, says that when he was one of his father's secretaries the rule was invariable that FDR must not, under any circumstances or for any reason whatsoever, be disturbed between midnight and eight-thirty in the morning. It was this regime that helped carry him into the third term with his health and strength unimpaired. But when the war came telephone calls poured in from Europe at all hours, particularly very early in the morning, and the President was forced to accept them. It may seem to indicate callousness, or inertness, or lack of capacity to be excited, that he should always have been able to sleep so well. But it was lucky too, for both FDR and the country.

Edward J. Flynn, one of FDR's closest friends and the most enlightened political boss in the United States, recalls that, just after the first inauguration when the entire nation was creaking and breaking at the joints with strain, he spent a night at the White House and asked FDR in the morning how he had slept. The President replied, "Why shouldn't I sleep? I had a perfect night."[2]

Once he told Hugh Johnson: "During my waking, working hours, I give the best in me. . . . When time comes for rest, I can reflect that I could not have done it better if I had to do it all over again, except for hindsight which simply does not come at the same time as the problem. There is nothing left for me but to close my eyes and I am asleep."

Sometimes, in periods of fatigue and irritation, the President

---

[2] *You're the Boss*, by Edward J. Flynn (New York, The Viking Press, Inc., 1947), p. 126, a book which contains a lot.

would complain to Mrs. Roosevelt that he hadn't slept; this usually meant that it had taken him longer than usual—say half an hour—to drop off. The mark of the true insomniac, that of waking in the middle of the night and being unable to sleep again, never afflicted him. One odd point, as recorded by Mrs. Roosevelt in her first volume of memoirs, *This Is My Story,* is that he had occasional nightmares as a young man, and even walked in his sleep. So far as I know none of his dreams has ever been recorded. It would be valuable to have them.

Mr. Roosevelt had the kind of mind that he could, so to speak, turn on or off at will. This was a considerable factor in enabling him to maintain his good temper, his serenity. He was often restless, even agitated, but once a decision was made, he seldom worried. He never took a worry to bed; when he was through for the day he was through. "He must have been psychoanalyzed by God," one of his early associates told me. He almost never showed serious dubiety, disappointment, or depression. He was full of nerves and conflicts, as Frances Perkins records, but these did not end in any "neurotic stagnation"; his buoyancy, gay resilience, and capacity to withstand shocks made him seem made of rubber. When the fighting in Africa had bogged down, Eisenhower found him almost too "light-hearted." Once he summoned Archibald MacLeish during the very worst of the battle for Guadalcanal; prophecies were grim, and the general tension desperate. But there the President sat placidly, smiling and eager, playing with his postage stamps and paying no attention whatever to the horror that must have been with him day and night.

His physical durability, his stamina, were of course much fortified by the easy way he relaxed. It all goes to show the force of an aphorism once uttered by Mr. Justice Holmes: "Even in the White House, one must keep at home with oneself." Of course he was nettled and exasperated often. Mr. Roosevelt was no mollycoddle. He had the natural irritability of men who work too hard. I have asked many people, "Did you ever see him really go off the deep end?" The answer was usually, "No, but I have certainly seen him pretty mad." He knew that when he lost his temper seriously it was a warning from nature to take a rest. Sumner Welles was a witness to one of the rare occasions when he did blow up; in the hundreds of times Welles did business with him, this happened only once. What produced the explosion was a silly—in fact hysterical—exhibition by a French dignitary whom

Welles brought in to see him early in 1941. Roosevelt was bewildered
by the man's bad behavior, and just got mad.

The Celebrated Charm

The easiest way to deal with another of FDR's most notable qualities, charm, is to tell an anecdote or two; hundreds are available.
The charm of some personalities resides in their unawareness of how
charming they really are. This was not true of FDR. He knew exactly
what charm he had, and his power of awaking response was almost
limitless. Many times people who thought that they loathed him
were won over, and if a person did not succumb to his charm it was
a serious challenge. One of his ambassadors told me once, "If he
thought that you didn't like him, he'd practically jump over a chair
to get you."

Pa Watson would say sometimes to a trusted adviser who was going
in to resist the President on some project, "Look out—this is one
of the days when he can win the bark off a tree."

General Eisenhower had never met FDR, except for one brief
impersonal contact, until he was assigned to go to England in 1942 as
commander of the American forces there. He expected some pretty
heavy strategic and military talk, but the President's opening remark
was, "I've just had to spend an hour on your baby brother. He's giving
me an awful lot of trouble." "My brother Milton?" Eisenhower
replied, startled. "Yes. Four different government departments want
him, and I have to decide which will be lucky enough to get him!"

FDR kept dozens of men from quitting big Washington jobs by
his persuasive intercession, men who wanted to get out of government because of irritation at jealous cross fires and muddle or because
they couldn't live on their salaries. Once Jerome Frank, the head of the
Securities Exchange Commission, told FDR that he could not possibly
afford to work in Washington any longer. The President dissuaded
him from leaving largely by one suave sentence, "Why, Jerry, after this
crisis is over, do you think that either of us will ever have trouble
earning money?"

Like a woman, he hated to let anybody go. Mr. Ickes tells us in
cogent detail how, on two occasions, the President talked him out
of resigning; once he said simply that they were "married" for better
or worse, and could not get a divorce. Miss Perkins wanted to resign
for years, but she could not resist FDR's appeals to stay. Ed Flynn

was another. Donald Nelson, who had been badly mauled, went in to resign one day; FDR never let him say one word for forty-five minutes, and then cheerfully waved him out; Nelson did not resign.

Not only this; his capacity to win new people was unparalleled. I recall how Frank Knox, the publisher of the Chicago *Daily News*, told me in 1934 not to bother to try to see the President. "He'll just gladhand you, kiss you on both cheeks, don't go near that son of a blank." Not so many years later, Knox himself was his loyal and devoted Secretary of the Navy. Once Knox called in an officer to serve on his staff, and the officer said, "I'm no New Dealer—that ought to be understood." Knox replied, "And what do you think I am? I fought the President with every resource at my command. But now I've squared my politics with my conscience and I'm proud to serve under so great a man." Then, laughing, he added, "At that, it's a good thing to have a couple of fellows around here who *aren't* New Dealers!"

Years before this, he met one of his most vigorous opponents, Senator Nye of North Dakota, for the first time. Nye said belligerently, "Mr. President, I've got a 100 per cent voting record against you—on banking, economy, and beer." FDR chuckled in return, "No, Senator. You were only 25 per cent against me. There were some things in those bills that neither of us liked." When Nye emerged from the charmer's den he expressed himself as being "highly elated" by the conversation.[3]

No matter what pressures were brought to his attention, FDR's touch to his own men was light. William McReynolds, one of his administrative assistants, said one day on finishing a job assigned to him, "There are a couple of things I'd like to talk over, in advance of the time when you read in the newspapers about what you did." The President laughed: "Wait till I complain, Mac."

The six New England governors came to see Roosevelt on one occasion as a group. The New Englanders are notoriously individualistic, and it was rare in those days for all to be seen together. The President greeted the delegation with the remark, "All six of you! You're not going to secede, are you?"

Some people who slaved for him till their bones ached were treated by Roosevelt with what seemed to be an almost brusque ingratitude, but almost invariably if he wanted to win them back he could. I have

[3] Edmund Wilson, "The Hudson River Progressive," *New Republic*, April 5, 1933.

asked several men if they would have felt the same power and fascination if FDR had not been President: how much came from the office, how much from the man. The answer is simple; it came from the man. In fact he made people forget that he was President. Oddly enough the famous smile was not so much an adjunct of his charm as might be thought; people would succumb even when on guard against the "synthetic" smile. A few people remained impervious to his wiles, no matter what. At Teheran, for instance, FDR took time out to win over a British official he had never met. He was like a violinist playing a dazzling cadenza, but the Englishman disliked and resented the performance. He felt (a) he was not worth that much time; (b) Roosevelt could not be "sincere," and must simply be using him to sharpen his bow on; (c) it was superb showmanship, but not quite nice.

Charm has an occasional contrary concomitant, heartlessness. The virtuoso is so pleased by the way he produces his effects that he disregards the audience. Once Dorothy Thompson came in to see FDR after a comparatively long period of having been snubbed by the White House—although she had deserted Willkie for Roosevelt during the campaign just concluded, and as a result had been fired from the New York *Herald Tribune*, the best job she ever had. Roosevelt greeted her with the remark, "Dorothy, you lost your job, but I kept mine—ha, ha!"[4]

Talkativeness and charm are both, as is well known, characteristics somewhat feminine; and they often add up to guile. Certainly there was a strong streak of the female in Roosevelt, though this is not to disparage his essential masculinity. Confidence in his own charm led him into occasional perilous adventures—almost as a woman may be persuaded, with a long series of glittering successes behind her, to think that she is irresistible forever and can win anybody's scalp.

Human Values, Popularity, and the Will to Power

Mr. Roosevelt liked to be liked. He courted and wooed people. He had good taste, an affable disposition, and profound delight in people and human relationships. This was probably the single most revealing of all his characteristics; it was both a strength and a weakness, and is a clue to much. To want to be liked by everybody does not merely mean amiability; it connotes will to power, for the obvious reason that if the process is carried on long enough and *enough* people

[4] Later he murmured to her winningly. "Let's talk about what we agree about!"

like the person, his power eventually becomes infinite and universal. Conversely, any man with great will to power and sense of historical mission, like Roosevelt, not only likes to be liked; he *has* to be liked, in order to feed his ego. But FDR went beyond this; he wanted to be liked, not only by his contemporaries on as broad a scale as possible, but by posterity. This, among others, is one reason for his collector's instinct. He collected himself—for history. He wanted to be spoken of well by succeeding generations, which means that he had the typical great man's wish for immortality, and hence—as we shall see in a subsequent chapter—he preserved everything about himself that might be of the slightest interest to historians. His passion for collecting and cataloguing is also a suggestive indication of his optimism. He was quite content to put absolutely everything on the record, without fear of what the verdict of world history would be.

Not only did Roosevelt, such a pleasant person himself, like to be liked and hate to be disliked; he genuinely liked people too.[5] This is to understate. He *loved* people. Unconsciously he obeyed one of the soundest of human laws: To get, you have to give. Moreover his love for people was not abstract, but concrete and intimate, and an important and distinctive reason for the power of his leadership. A man like Henry Wallace, say, who loves "people," may find it difficult to get along with persons; there are many humane men who are frightened by humanity in terms of individuals. But FDR was always personal in a very practical way. He set up goals in human terms that the average man could grasp for.

Nobody was too big for Mr. Roosevelt's human interest, or too small. Nothing personal ever bored him. He was interested, really interested, in the mind of Mr. Justice Holmes, and in the postman at Warm Springs who took all day to deliver the mail because he read everybody's post cards. Frances Perkins[6] records his horror when somebody, early in the New Deal, said that the depression would in time level off, and that it was just hard luck that people were suffering. He snapped, "But people aren't cattle!" Morris Ernst, the well-known attorney, once told him that several leading commentators were unex-

[5] Once as Governor of New York he said, "I *like* my opponent, the legislature." Once he answered a questionnaire from Harvard about his aversions by saying, "None."

[6] In her valuable and discriminating *The Roosevelt I Knew* (New York, The Viking Press, Inc., 1946), p. 108.

pectedly supporting him on a certain issue. "I don't care about the commentators," he replied. "What about Joe Palooka?"

Ideas meant little to him unless they were communicated in terms of people. He personalized the most epochal events; for instance Mrs. Roosevelt tells us that the night before D-Day he thought of the whole adventure, on which the fate of the world might depend, in terms of whether or not one of his former servants at Hyde Park would get through all right! Much of his welfare legislation had its springs in personal emotion. The rural-electrification program derived in part from his discovery that his electric-light bill at Warm Springs was four times what it was in New York. Similarly the poverty of veteran farmers he had known for years at Hyde Park, come on hard times, was the initial spark of the old-age insurance program, and his own trips in the West led to his later interest in irrigation, reclamation, and the like. He himself records in *On Our Way* how, even on such a matter as the gold crisis in 1933, his chief motive was to put the country back on its feet "without destroying *human* values," and that the happiest single event of his first years in Washington was the abolition of child labor in the cotton textile industry. Finally, Roosevelt's intensely personal approach was an advantage of great moment in his speeches. He was the inventor of the Fireside Chat, so aptly named. He gave the impression, on the radio, of speaking to every listener personally, like a sympathetic, authoritative, and omniscient friend; as almost every American knows, you could practically feel him physically in the room. Europeans who never heard him on the radio may be puzzled by this phenomenon. But nobody will ever really understand FDR who did not hear him talk and catch something of his magnificent delivery.

Was Roosevelt a snob? In some ways, yes. He adored kings and queens and such. Why not? He was a prince himself. He was much taken by names and titles. It is somewhat ridiculous that he should have been impressed by creatures like the Sultan of Morocco, whom he met at Casablanca, but this was part of the fun of his position. Elliott Roosevelt gives a positively regal account of this episode; he quotes his father as saying, "Make a note that the Sultan must come to dinner one night, Elliott. Find out from Murphy or whoever knows what the protocol involved is. This Nogues [the Resident-general, no less] is not to be considered."[7] Then too he was something of a snob so far as his

[7] *As He Saw It*, by Elliott Roosevelt (New York, Duell, Sloan & Pearce, Inc., 1946), pp. 88-89.

own huge family was concerned. He detested the parvenus and the international white trash of café society. Also interesting were his relations with the millionaire class, most members of which hated him so venomously. For a long time he had close social relations with Vincent Astor and various Vanderbilts; later many rich men (Averell Harriman, Nelson Rockefeller, Edward R. Stettinius, Myron C. Taylor, among others) served him with respect and even devotion. All this brings up complex issues. One reason why FDR liked to cruise on the Astor yacht was probably because it annoyed him to be called a "traitor to his class"; he was in the position of being able to say, "See, I get along quite well with men of wealth, even if most of them don't like *me!*" Needless to say, FDR never showed a shred of inferiority on these occasions; he didn't have an inferior atom in his whole being, and in fact he probably enjoyed the company of millionaires for the opportunity it gave him to show how superior *he* was. And he could certainly crack down on the rich if he wanted to. One of his most famous remarks was about the president of Bethlehem Steel Corporation: "Go tell Eugene Grace he'll never make a million dollars a year again!"

Next we should consider, in this general realm, Mr. Roosevelt's simplicity about human relationships, his informality and homeliness. One of his close associates, who must have talked to him two or three hundred times, told me that he had never once known FDR to act "presidentially."[8]

He called almost everybody by first name at first sight, as is well known. Some people resented this, on the ground that it was both false and humiliating; it was as if they were peasants, with forelock pulled, entering into the presence of the king; for instance Dean Acheson was shocked when the President called him "Dean" the first time they ever met. Sometimes FDR took too much for granted and got nicknames wrong; this caused hilarity. An incidental point is that he seldom addressed women by nicknames, even if these were used by almost everybody else; he always called Mrs. Harry Hopkins "Louise," never "Looie." He called General Marshall "George," of course, but such was his respect for him that he usually referred to him before others as "General"; after a conference he would say to his aides, "Give this to Bill" [Admiral Leahy] or "Tell Ernie [Admiral King] this," but

---

[8] His homeliness entered into his speeches too. Nothing could have better sold the Lend Lease program to the country than his famous remark that it was like lending a garden hose to a neighbor with his house on fire—even though, as the wits had it, it turned out to be an "ocean-going" hose.

Marshall was "General Marshall." Few people indeed reciprocated by calling Roosevelt "Franklin"; scarcely anybody did so with other people in the room except Josephus Daniels, whom Roosevelt himself called "Chief," and Louis Howe. Privately, not more than a dozen people out of the thousands close to him ever used "Franklin" or "Frank" after he became President; among these were Al Smith, Governor Cox, and Henry Morgenthau; Cox always addressed him in letters as "My dear Frank." This is not to say that everybody called him "Mr. President" all the time. Jim Farley and a good many others said "Governor," Missy LeHand used "F. D.," several of his administrative assistants, like Lowell Mellett, called him "Boss," Vice-President Garner said "Captain," and many compromised on "Chief." Even so "Mr. President" was all but universal. Robert E. Sherwood mentioned to me once how startled he was when on one occasion a cousin of FDR's walked into the room where he and the President were at work and called him "Franklin."

A Gentleman

Mr. Roosevelt was a gentleman.[9] This may seem only too obvious, but it is important to state; not all American presidents have been gentlemen by any means. I mean gentleman in the literal sense. He was decent; he was civilized; he was kind. He loathed anything disagreeable; he hated unpleasantness; he abhorred crudities in personal behavior. His casual letters are, one sometimes feels, almost too "nice," even effeminate; it would be a relief if he would break out, get angry, and sass somebody. But what a pleasant touch he had! Consider a little note he sent to Sam Rayburn, on the Speaker's sixtieth birthday:

DEAR SAM:
Ever so many happy returns on the day—it must be *AWFUL* to be so old—I don't get there for 23 days.

F. D. R.

Then the next year FDR called Rayburn over. "Sam," he said, "I sent for you on a very serious matter that affects you personally, and I'm worried about it." Rayburn looked blank. The President went on, "You're sixty-one!"

FDR had a deep sensitiveness to other people. Many years ago, while

---

[9] But he once told Mr. Ickes that luckily neither he nor Ickes were gentlemen, in contrast to members of the Government too gentlemanly.

cruising on the *Tuscaloosa*, a note came from a woman saying that her twin sons were sailors on this ship; Roosevelt, though tired out, gave the letter to Admiral Daniel Callaghan, with the order, "Have those boys up to see me after we've been to sea for a few days." When he called the late Cardinal Mundelein in to talk about James A. Farley's presidential aspirations, this was out of kindness to Farley, not otherwise, though Farley himself didn't seem to get the point. His considerateness was marked in the extreme. He badly wanted to keep Captain John L. McCrea as his naval aide in October, 1942, but released him to take command of the battleship *Iowa* when it became clear that continued shore duty might stand in the way of his advancement. Once Mr. Ickes, though seriously ill (the President had broken precedent by visiting him in the hospital), got out of bed to attend an important Cabinet meeting; FDR rebuked him sternly with, "But this is insubordination!" Sometimes he contrived trips and missions for men, like Hopkins, as a device to force a rest on them. His solicitude was personal on every level, though he knew no doubt what political advantages this might induce. If, say, he picked up a newspaper and noticed that some favorite column of his did not appear, he would find out why, and then, if the author was ill, send some message of sympathy. His last words to Eisenhower when they met at Casablanca were, "Can we do anything for Mamie [Mrs. Eisenhower] when I get home?" When, in the most grisly days, with every conceivable pressure assaulting him, he had to work out some administrative problem, he would somehow contrive, as Lowell Mellett once expressed it, "not to pass the agony on"; he would do everything possible to lift the pressure from his own subordinates.

Roosevelt's decency and considerateness, together with his hatred of hurting anybody who was working *with* him, became vices when carried too far; they were the main source of his deviousness, his tolerance of sloppy administration, his addiction to temporizing and delay, and his downright inability, so it often seemed, to rebuke *anybody*. It is revealing that when the children were growing up, it was always Mrs. Roosevelt who had the job of disciplining them. It was simply beyond the capacity of FDR to do so himself. He had a valet for many years named McDuffie, who had been his barber at Warm Springs and to whom he became closely attached; the time came, however, when McDuffie had to be got rid of. But the President couldn't bear to fire him and, after long delay, finally pleaded with Mrs. Roosevelt (a) to do it for him; (b) to wait till he himself was out of town before doing it.

One of his best friends told FDR when he was appointed to an important post, "Listen, Mr. President, I'm reserving to myself only one thing—the right to quit. I've seen too many people hang around here after they've outlived their usefulness." When the President did decide to get rid of anybody—it is a revealing touch—he could usually only bear to do so after deliberately picking a quarrel, so that he could provoke anger and then claim that he himself was not to blame.

Walter Lippmann said many years ago, "Mr. Roosevelt is too eager to please . . . he is not the dangerous enemy of anything." Jim Farley talks of the way "he forever put off things distasteful" (it's a well-known human failing), and Ed Flynn describes how he would promote people instead of discharging them, and if possible promote them to places far away, so that there would be no disagreeable memories close at hand. He hated so much to dirty himself in a big mudhole that he inadvertently created little mudholes all around. The way he dilly-dallied before finally dismissing one eminent Cabinet member just before the war was little short of shameful. Another important personage, who had once been extremely close to FDR, fell out of favor at about the same time. But even after he had outlived any possible usefulness and had been guilty of gross mischief the President could not bear to cut him off altogether. For an interval he would not see him, but would permit him to telephone once a week; then the telephone talks irritated him so much that he restricted communication to a weekly letter; then this was tapered off until finally all contact ceased.

It was often said that Roosevelt echoed the opinions of the last person he saw. This is not quite true. No single person ever controlled his behavior, and when he finally reached a decision he reached it alone. But he often did give the impression of agreement when in fact he did not agree. He could not bear to let people down or disappoint them when they were counting on him so highly. The reason was, again, his intense dislike of having to say No or of being disagreeable or discouraging. Besides it was his duty to listen to everything, and he could not afford to take time out for arguments. If you haven't got hour after hour to convince a person, and if he is too important to be dismissed and too stubborn to listen to reason, why, you may have to let him deceive himself. The fact remains that, for all his canniness, it never

seemed to occur to FDR that to mislead people out of kindness is one
of the worst of all forms of cruelty, whether deliberate or not.

I have said that he did have a temper, and when he lost it people
certainly knew it; the big freckled fist would bash down so that the
desk shook, and he certainly could, if pressed, get rid of people.
Nor was there anything lacking in the positiveness of his leadership,
once he was aroused; he was quite capable of laying down the law
to someone and saying, "Sign here!" None of those present, including most of the Cabinet and several financial advisers, are likely
to forget a Sunday evening during a crisis in 1933, when the President
was hot with anger at various leaks in the highest levels of the Administration. He said slowly and emphatically that if anybody wanted to
know who was running the Government, the answer was that it was he
and he alone; that he was captain, he issued the orders, and if anybody
didn't like the ship, he could go ashore. "The funny thing was," I heard
it said, "every man in the room thought that the President was after
him. They all sat and looked like schoolboys. Joe Stalin himself never
gave the Politburo more of a dressing down."

Roosevelt lost the friendship and support of John L. Lewis (he
didn't miss either very much) largely because of a secretarial slip and
Mr. Lewis's great sensitiveness. Through a fluke Lewis was not invited
to an important White House luncheon at which other labor leaders
were present, but only to a reception held later that afternoon. He was
furious. To make amends the President and Mrs. Roosevelt subsequently invited Mr. and Mrs. Lewis to tea alone. But, an hour or so
before they arrived, Mrs. Roosevelt was urgently called out of Washington on account of illness in the family. Missy LeHand was present
instead. Mr. Lewis's intricate Welsh brain somehow construed this to
be a deliberate "insult" on FDR's part, and he never forgave the fancied
"affront."

Dean Acheson, of all people, was one man of caliber at whom
Ro⸢sevelt really got furious. This was early in 1933, when Acheson was
Undersecretary of the Treasury; later Acheson rejoined the Administration and is now, of course, Secretary of State; at the end, he and
Roosevelt were good friends, and indeed FDR always had distinct
respect for him. But he certainly got angry at him—so much so, in fact,
that Acheson is one of the very few Roosevelt appointees who, when he
resigned, never got the familiar friendly letter thanking him for his
past services. The reason for this was that Acheson, a man of profound

courage as well as integrity, flatly refused to sign the order which made devaluation of the dollar legal. Acheson thought that this action should await an opinion by the Attorney General, and FDR refused to delay. Roosevelt turned to him with indignant anger, "Don't you take *my* word for it that it will be all right?" to which the imperturbable Acheson replied that it was he, not FDR, who had to put his actual signature on paper. "That will do!" Roosevelt commanded. He was so enraged that Acheson thought he might have apoplexy. A few days later William H. Woodin, the Secretary, who had been ill, told Acheson, "Look here, son, you're in terrible trouble. The President has a paper on his desk firing you. If he does, I've told him that *I'll* resign. You'd better resign gracefully yourself. Write him a nice letter in longhand, and you are not to keep a copy." Acheson said that he would resign if necessary, but that he would *not* submit to any such pressure as being told whether or not he could keep a copy of his own letter. Later Woodin, a gallant soul, without warning anybody before-hand, brought Acheson in to attend the ceremony at which Henry Morgenthau was sworn in as Acheson's successor. The President looked at Acheson thunderstruck. Then he relaxed and exclaimed, "I'm mad as hell at you, but for you to come here today is the best act of sportsmanship I've ever seen!"

During the war Roosevelt got frigidly angry on one occasion with George Earle, the former governor of Pennsylvania, who had been serving him as a special envoy in Turkey. Earle came back from Istanbul and threatened to make a statement to the American people unless he heard from Roosevelt "within one week" to the effect that "Russia was a greater menace than Germany." This, be it remembered, was in 1945 when the Russian armies were, to put it mildly, making substantial contributions to allied victory on the whole of the eastern front. FDR was certainly not a man to be threatened with an ultimatum. But Earle had slipped away out of town; only after considerable effort did the Secret Service find him, and deliver into his hand what Roosevelt wrote. Subsequently Earle was banished to Samoa. FDR's letter was as follows:

DEAR GEORGE,

I have read your letter of March 21 to my daughter Anna and I have noted with concern your plan to publicize your unfavorable opinion of one of our allies at the very time when such a publication from a former emissary of mine might do irreparable harm to our war effort. . . .

You say you will publish unless you are told before March 28 that I do not wish you to do so. I not only do not wish it, but I specifically forbid you to publish any information or opinion about an ally that you may have acquired while in office or in the service of the United States Navy.

In view of your wish for continued active service, I shall withdraw any previous understanding that you are serving as an emissary of mine and I shall direct the Navy Department to continue your employment wherever they can make use of your services. . . .

People could say No to Roosevelt, argue with him—sometimes hotly —and occasionally overrule him. Usually this happened on a high level only when FDR knew he had to give in, because his opponent was a man of principle who was indispensable and would stick to his position no matter what. Once in Tunis FDR asked Eisenhower to prepare a recommendation on French internal affairs; Eisenhower promptly replied that this was outside his jurisdiction and involved matters which could come to him only through the Combined Chiefs of Staff. Roosevelt looked embarrassed, said "Oh!" and never referred to the matter again. Once a general in Alaska refused to allow in his area a man whom Roosevelt wanted to send there; he telegraphed, "If my instructions barring civilians from this region are overruled, I shall have no recourse but to resign my command." FDR promptly yielded. He yielded too on one occasion when he asked General Marshall, through Hopkins, to block sending out to the troops one issue of a news magazine that contained an article which he thought to be scurrilous. Marshall's reply was, "I won't obey that order unless I get it in writing, and if I do, it will come back with my resignation as Chief of Staff."

Mr. Ickes fought him to a standstill on the question of giving helium to the Germans. Steve Early sometimes interrupted and corrected him at press conferences, even to the point of interjecting sharply, "Make that off the record." Admiral King, I once heard it put, could "raise holy hell with FDR." Lowell Mellett, one of his administrative assistants, would never give him an inch concerning his knowing anything about the newspaper business (the President fancied himself as a considerable expert on journalism); when Mellett left the White House, FDR gave him a photograph inscribed affectionately, "to my old associate on our City Desk, good luck!" Another point in this general connection is the frequent allegation that Roosevelt liked to surround himself with weaklings and yes men. In rebuttal think of Ickes, Leahy,

Hugh Johnson, Leon Henderson, Mr. Stimson, General Marshall, and some other corrugated titans.

The President's equanimity and easygoingness were the more remarkable in that he himself was hated so malignantly. But you can tell a good deal about a man by his enemies, and Roosevelt's were choice. One merely needs call to mind Colonel McCormick, Father Coughlin, and Gerald L. K. Smith. Even so, one is apt to forget nowadays the furtive vindictiveness of the whispering campaign against Roosevelt, the sheer defamatory wickedness of the calumny that descended on him day by day, year after year. One forgets the atmosphere of the "better" country clubs in the late 1930's, the ghoulish talk at the bankers' lunches, the burble of poisonous gossip at fashionable dinners, the army officers who, even in uniform, refused to toast the President of the United States. The "Rosenfeld" myth of Dr. Goebbels was dutifully swallowed by thousands of otherwise sane Americans. A bookstore in Boston once informed FDR's publisher that it would sell his collected speeches only "if bound in that man's skin!"

Roosevelt talked back seldom. But here are excerpts from a press conference in 1937:[10]

The President: There isn't very much news; but before we talk about news, I am going to ask you for a very few minutes to resolve ourselves into a Committee of the Whole. Off the record, wholly off the record, I wanted to tell you a story that I think you ought to know because it does affect the Press of the country. . . . As you know, I have always encouraged, and am entirely in favor of, absolute freedom for all news writers. That should be and will continue to be the general rule in Washington. . . .

There have come out, though, in the past couple of weeks two things from one news service which, in a sense, do affect the Press of the country as a whole.

The McClure Syndicate . . . sends out to about 270 papers every week these (indicating) white sheets . . . Of course it is absolutely legitimate that they should collect this news at the White House, or from Congress or from anybody else. With these white sheets for publication, there goes out at the same time, a pink sheet as information for the editor, marked not for publication but sent to the editor in confidence. Of course you and I know that that is not a news service in the strict sense of the word, but it goes out with the news service and you pay for the whole service at the same time.

[10] Rosenman, Vol. VI, pp. 200-203.

Now, there are two things in here that I think you people ought to know about. As I say, this is off the record, and just in the family. . . .

"Unchecked. A New York specialist high in the medical field is authority for the following, which is given in the strictest confidence to editors:

"Towards the end of last month Mr. Roosevelt was found in a coma at his desk. Medical examination disclosed the neck rash which is typical of certain disturbing symptoms. Immediate treatment of the most skilled kind was indicated, with complete privacy and detachment from official duties. Hence the trip to southern waters, with no newspaper men on board and a naval convoy which cannot be penetrated."

That is number one.

Number 2. "At a recent private dinner in New York an official of the American Cyanamid expressed in extreme form the bitterness towards the administration which is typical of the personal reactions of many right-wing leaders in business and finance.

"The gentleman in question asserted in so many words that 'the paranoiac in the White House' is destroying the nation, that a couple of well-placed bullets would be the best thing for the country, and that he for one would buy a bottle of champagne as quick as he could get it to celebrate such news."

That is all I wanted to tell you because, after all, all I think I have to do is to repeat that I have been in favor, as you all know, of any legitimate news reporting, no matter what its origin may be and no matter whether for friendly papers or hostile papers—it makes no difference.

Q. Is that off the record?

The President: Yes, absolutely.

Q. Is that signed?

The President: It is sent out by the McClure Newspaper Syndicate.

Q. How about that clipping?

The President: That was clipped out of another paper. It was used by a radical paper in order to point out the terrible things that are being said by the conservatives, but it has been used in the press.

Q. That is not newspaper reporting.

The President: That is just it, it is not newspaper reporting.

Q. Have you taken the matter up with the syndicate?

The President: No, certainly not.

Q. Isn't that second one actionable under law?

The President: You know, that does not make any difference at all. The President of the United States does not sue for libel and the Department of Justice does not proceed for libel.

Q. How much of this is off the record?

The President: It is all off the record; all strictly in the family and nothing else.

Did Roosevelt himself actively hate anybody? It is doubtful. He had very little venom or spleen. He said at a press conference once, "I just don't hate." But he expected decency in personal relationships, and when this was not forthcoming he was relentless; he was loath to forgive people who, he thought (Mr. Justice Black on one occasion, Governor Lehman on another, Henry Wallace on a third), put him out on a limb or otherwise let him down. Usually his anger rose slowly, and he sometimes liked to pretend that he was angrier than he really was; he cooled off quickly. But I know of one man who is never likely to forget how Roosevelt said to him, with cold contempt and scorn, "This is the last appointment you will ever have. Good-by." He had considerable affection for two of his chief political opponents, Landon and Willkie; he despised Hoover intellectually, and resented what he thought had been some wanton rudenesses on Hoover's part, but he was sorry for him on the whole. He disliked and feared Dewey, but did not hate him; Dewey (like de Gaulle) had high capacity to irritate him however. Admiral Leahy spent election night at Hyde Park in 1944. He went to bed, tired, at about ten o'clock when FDR cheerfully told him that they were over the bridge, but then woke up at two in the morning, unable to sleep. He walked downstairs to get a glass of milk, and met FDR being carried up. Roosevelt snapped, "I've been waiting four hours for that s.o.b. in New York to make up his mind and admit that he is defeated."

Normally the President took fair criticism easily—almost too easily. There were, however, times when he behaved as sensitively as a small boy. Some particular things he was always touchy about. He was bitterly annoyed at the account in a news magazine of events at Hyde Park this same election night; he counted no fewer than twenty-two misstatements of fact in it, and moreover was outraged at its general overtone of malice. It took Steve Early and others main force to dissuade the President from writing an indignant personal letter to the publisher; they had to explain that it just would not do for him to lower himself into a controversy on such a level.

Humanity Continued

Mr. Roosevelt did not become a man of the Left and a great fighting leader of the masses purely out of intellect; he was a man of the Left —or at least left of center—out of what was basically an emotional and personal approach, his sense of fellowship and profound regard for human suffering. That he should have been a man of the Left at all, considering his background and upbringing, is astonishing in itself; to say merely that he was an upperdog working for the underdog is to oversimplify an abstraction quite complex; later we will explore this whole issue fully. The fact that much of his liberalism derived from emotion rather than reasoned conviction is probably one reason why parts of his program sometimes seemed half-baked. He had a strong human impulse to help the average man get on better, to see that he got an even break ("That guy," a taxi driver once put it, "has a slant in *my* direction"), but he did not always see the full intellectual implications of what his heart told him to do.

This brings up another aspect of Roosevelt's humanity—that, like a good father, he shouldered other burdens as well as his own. It is a minor point, but of some interest psychologically, that he called himself a father to many more people than his own children. Occasionally he signed informal letters to Missy LeHand and Harry Hopkins "Papa"; sometimes he referred to himself as "Papa" in the third person and would call in his staff after a press conference and ask, "How did Papa do?" or, after a good speech, inquire, "Aren't you proud of Papa now?" Once Leon Henderson had to make six or seven major decisions on O.P.A.; if any went wrong, it would not only mean that Henderson would be bitterly attacked, but that he would be less useful to the President. FDR listened, told him to use his own judgment, and said, "If you do get into trouble, come back to Papa." Of course paternalism has its disadvantages. Far too many people evaded their own responsibilities by saying, "Well, we can't do anything more; Roosevelt will have to take care of it himself."

Finally consider the essential quality from which the other human traits derive, FDR's intense and overwhelming joy in life, and particularly joy in his job; his love of the simple fact of living and being Chief Executive was inexhaustible. Almost naïvely he said to a friend once, "Wouldn't you be President if you could? Wouldn't anybody?"

Chapter 4

FACTORS ON THE DEMERIT SIDE
AND OTHERS

I am very peaceful to myself, up to a limit.
—FRANKLIN DELANO ROOSEVELT

Let us consider now some negative traits in Mr. Roosevelt. Probably his worst quality was deviousness, lack of candor. This arose not so much out of duplicity but from the agreeableness we have already mentioned and his marked distaste for hurting friends. The fact remains that he could be devious on occasion. He went north by going south, and loved it. He was tricky for fun. In particular he was tricky about statistics. Now deviousness in a person usually derives from lack of courage, since most dishonesty is based on cowardice. But Roosevelt had the courage of a lion. Why, then, should he have been so fond of techniques and maneuvers that, to put it bluntly, verged on deceit? One answer is, I think, that he was so superclever and superconfident that he thought people would not catch on. Another is that he simply *liked* mystery, subterfuge, and indirect tactics in general for their own sake; still another is that the structure and shape of events and his titanic responsibilities compelled him sometimes to go into things backward instead of forward. It was often a necessity—even a duty—not to expose his full hand. He was devious and crafty because he had to be.

"His greatest defect," one of his best friends told me, "is that he seldom explained himself when he changed position. He was never frank about a switch." Someone who knew Al Smith and Roosevelt equally well said, "Al Smith would fight you inch by inch in conversation, and then you found he *did* agree with you. Roosevelt would give the impression of agreeing, when he didn't."

His blandness, when caught out, was impenetrable. Once, years ago when he was Governor of New York, he told one of his advisers that he was going to veto a bill, and then signed it. The adviser did not see him again till he became President, and, annoyed at the way FDR had apparently let him down, declared, "Next time I ask for anything I'll ask for it in writing, Governor." FDR gave him a warmhearted smile and murmured, "Isn't it lucky the people around here have no idea what we're talking about?"

Roosevelt hated controversy within his official family, but his methods helped to make it inevitable. Once a Cabinet member, convinced that the chief of a great government agency was poaching on his preserves, angrily brought the matter to FDR. The President listened, and then in the minister's presence scribbled a memorandum to the agency chief, rebuking him. "Blank belongs where it is. Keep off. FDR." The Cabinet member, after Roosevelt's death, told me this story, and then added quietly, "But did he ever actually *send* the memorandum to the man in question?"

The chief practical consequence of FDR's lack of candor was confusion. Consider some of the classic administrative feuds, like Hopkins versus Ickes, Woodring versus Johnson, Morgenthau versus Hull. Sometimes it seemed that FDR positively loved a muddle, so that in the end everybody would have to come back to him and say helplessly, "*You* fix it!" Over and over he distributed authority and established two or even three competing agencies, not only with conflicting powers but set up so that each chief thought he alone had most—with the result that ultimate responsibility remained where it had been all along, on Mr. Roosevelt's desk. It was as if he were saying, "Go ahead and have your fun; in the end return to me." In the whole history of the War Production Board, it was never made clear who had final authority to do what. The President always saw to it that he himself was the last judge and arbiter. He was quite frank about his idiosyncrasies in this direction; once he laughed at a press conference, "I have a single responsible head, and his name is Knudsen-Hillman!"

Once he faced an uncomfortable situation between Hull and Morgenthau; he called in an officer much junior to these two and said, "You go over and get Cordell and Henry together on this. Knock their heads together." The junior officer was appalled. "Good God, Mr. President, you want *me* to tell *them* that they're both crazy!" FDR pondered and replied, "Well, if you don't, I'm afraid I'll have to create some new board." He was perfectly serious. There are many stories of this type. Even on such a matter as arranging details of Mrs. Roosevelt's trip to the Pacific during the war, he gave two contradictory instructions about whether she should go to Guadalcanal or not.

He loved to "pull" surprises and put on a show. For instance Mr. Hull records that the tart reference to aggressor nations in the Chicago "Quarantine" speech in 1937 never appeared in the draft FDR sent over to the State Department for approval. "The President himself was responsible for this insertion. . . . I did not know the phrase was there until the President uttered it."[1] Another item in this field, again according to Mr. Hull, is that Roosevelt listened in to a telephone conversation of great urgency and delicacy between Hull in Washington and Sumner Welles in Rio de Janeiro, without letting Welles know at first that he was on the line. One dutiful government servant said to me in Washington long ago: "When five or six people with sharply different views on the same issue all leave the White House happy on the same day, you can be damned sure that someone is getting his throat cut."

Results: (1) FDR's enemies continually charged that he was not "sincere"; (2) some of his friends did not altogether trust him, particularly if they could not get contact with him direct. Roosevelt once assured a senator that the late Joseph T. Robinson of Arkansas would be given the next vacancy on the Supreme Court. Robinson said ruefully to the senator, "I won't believe it until *he* tells me." (Robinson was right; the situation changed, and he never got the seat.)

Closely allied to Roosevelt's deviousness was his almost childish love of secrecy. Of course in many instances secrecy was essential; Washington is a town notoriously indiscreet, and the President's most substantial weapon against dangerous leakages was to keep his own mouth shut. But, particularly on appointments, when no great issue was at stake, he could be secretive altogether beyond reason; partly this was because he enjoyed so much the dramatic effect on the person concerned. He never told Henderson that he was to get OPA (Henderson heard it on the radio); he never told Ickes until the very moment of the appointment that he was to be Public Works Administrator. Many people never knew that they were going to get a job until the White House telephoned to ask what state they wanted to go down from. One trusted friend said to him once, "I have only one favor to ask. Don't give me a new job without telling me beforehand."

Ed Flynn[2] has stated flatly that "the President did not keep his word

---

[1] New York *Times*, February 6, 1948. Of course FDR must have feared that the State Department would cut the phrase out.

[2] In *You're the Boss*, pp. 162-63.

on many appointments," and he was once so angry at what he thought was a double cross that he hung up on him on the telephone.

Also FDR loved to have information of his very own from private sources, and spring it unexpectedly on the State Department or elsewhere; his credulity in this regard was sometimes excessive. He trusted the reliability of some who did not deserve trust, and occasionally got into hot water as a result, because he was stubborn and vain about how much better informed *he* was than anybody else, though of course in general his judgment of people was very good.

The following might well have been written by an enemy of the President's: "He knows how to appear the aggressor when he connives, and a benefactor when he betrays, how to manage an apparent enemy and exasperate a pretended friend, how to find himself at the opportune moment of the dispute on the side of the strong against the weak, and how to utter brave words in the act of running away." Actually this passage was composed about Lord Palmerston, and its author is none other than the well-known London correspondent of the New York *Tribune* at the time, Karl Marx.

Of course Roosevelt had defects. He was, after all, a human being. There are half a dozen aside from deviousness that one might mention, and we shall allude to them from time to time. He was capable of bearing grudges, he was not discriminating, he lacked what has been aptly called "intellectual and moral precision," and he broke some promises. For instance he certainly persuaded Louis Johnson to stay on in government in 1937 by promising him the Secretaryship of War, but Johnson never got the job.[3] He ran the country as a "one-man show"; Henry Wallace once told me in 1942 that nothing whatever counted in the entire administration except "what went on inside FDR's head." He never paid sufficient attention to building up an efficient succession, he sometimes undercut those who became too conspicuous as second-men, and he killed off several potential rivals for the Presidency. He was too much of a prima donna. He was sometimes irritable; he got rid of frustrations by minor aggressions. He was, some of his advisers felt, overcautious in the Phony War period, and even timid; others thought him insanely bellicose. Even Sherwood calls him hypocritical for "taking credit for the neutrality law," which he had bitterly opposed. People sold him gold

[3] Of course many years later, under President Truman, Mr. Johnson became Secretary of Defense.

bricks occasionally, and he was foolishly misled about Ibn Saud and Palestine. He made too many snap decisions and was too fond of experimentation and trial balloons. Mr. Stimson says flatly, "Both in the December meeting of 1941 and in the following June the President made suggestions to the Prime Minister which if seriously pursued *must have disrupted the American military effort.*"[4]

Also one should mention a certain tendency to being grandiose. He once told Mr. Hull, when the Secretary of State was about to propose his health at a Cabinet dinner, "Please try to address me as the Commander-in-Chief, not as President." He behaved in some ways like a conqueror and lord of the earth when he reached Africa, giving out decorations almost as a monarch does; he talked about the French empire as if it were his personal possession and would say things like "I haven't quite decided what to do about Tunis." He could be Jovian in domestic fields too. Once he said of Senator Harry Byrd, "I have a long friendship with him, and great intimacy with Dick [the explorer, his brother], but Harry . . . hates every single thing this administration has been forced to do. He just can't help it. I have nothing against Harry, but he just can't understand. If Harry will work with me, all right. But if he wants to make trouble, he will isolate himself and *there will be nothing that I can do to save him!*"

Another of Roosevelt's defects was an occasional tendency to ingratitude. I have heard it said that he never thanked anybody for anything, if he could help it. Some good men were thrown to the dogs without any thanks at all, and he was somewhat chary of bestowing praise. Perhaps this was part of his technique of keeping everything in his own hands. Also, when he played one man against another, we should not forget that he alone always had to keep the supreme end in view.

It has been said, not without a measure of truth, that Roosevelt got along by sabotaging his friends and placating his enemies, but a man in his position of final responsibility had to remain above friendship, above purely personal considerations of any kind. His friends necessarily had to be lightning rods to deflect criticism, and buffers to keep it off. Two other points should be kept in mind: (1) as President he had to use the machinery of the democratic process; sometimes enemies *did* have to be rewarded at the expense of friends; (2) he could count

[4] *On Active Service in Peace and War,* by Henry L. Stimson and McGeorge Bundy (New York, Harper & Brothers, 1948), p. 414. Italics mine.

on his friends even if he did cuff them down. A president cannot always give thanks, because the president is an institution, not just a man.

How Mr. Roosevelt Liked To Talk, and Why

FDR's extreme loquaciousness, to which I have already alluded, was another outstanding characteristic. But, like all really good talkers, the President was a good listener too. He had to be, since so much of the work of a competent executive is listening. But exactly how and when he listened has always been a mystery to those who knew him well, because he himself seemed to be talking all the time.

Dozens of people will bear witness to the fact that, at dozens of White House conferences, it was almost impossible for them to get a word in, and people who saw him often came to adopt special techniques to deal with this phenomenon. "My own method," a well-known judge has reported, "was to let him run for exactly five minutes, and then to cut in ruthlessly." Another close friend told me, "You had to manhandle him, but politely." Vito Marcantonio once startled him by interrupting him in midstream, "Sorry, Mr. President, but you're filibustering on *my* time!" James F. Byrnes has described an occasion when FDR met General Clay: the general never got a chance to say *one* word! The simplest way to get at the President was to be invited to lunch. Then you could talk while he ate. Mr. Hull is one witness to the success of this maneuver, and Leon Henderson learned to be an adept strategist in the same domain. He would pay no attention to his own food, watch carefully for the precise moment when FDR's mouth was full, and then let fire. Mr. Roosevelt, who never missed anything, was fully aware of this; he would try to outwit the doughty Henderson and throw his timing off. Or he would murmur slyly, "Leon, what's the matter with you, you aren't eating!"

Roosevelt made good use of his talkativeness on occasion. He would stall at a conference by telling a long anecdote, with the deliberate aim of making the group more malleable. Visitors new to this technique would sometimes twitch with nervousness, fearing that FDR had forgotten why they had come. Sometimes during the very last moments of preparing a speech, when all the conferees were exhausted and the deadline was getting closer every second, FDR would burst out into a totally irrelevant story and talk interminably. Then, calmly, he would pick up the threads of his speech, make the final point, and close the conference. People left the room tearing their hair. One interpretation of this is that the President hated the irrevocability of decision; but, while he told his long anecdote, the decision was steadily working itself out, and at last he decided what he wanted; the external monologue and the inward processes of thought proceeded concurrently and concluded at exactly the same time.

Not only was Roosevelt garrulous; he was maddeningly discursive. He positively reveled in changing the subject without transition or explanation, and he could startle visitors almost out of their wits by, say, asking somebody who had never been in Latin America what was the best hotel in Peru. Of course, as Mrs. Roosevelt has pointed out in her memoirs, his discursiveness was a defense. "Franklin had a way, when he did not want to hear what somebody had to say, of telling stories and talking about something quite different."

Albert D. Lasker was summoned from Chicago to lunch at the White House once. Mr. Lasker, one of the most influential Republicans in the country, was a busy man and it was a considerable inconvenience for him to drop everything and rush to Washington at a moment's notice. His curiosity was great; the invitation came out of the blue, and had been couched in the most urgent terms. He arrived —and Roosevelt chatted amiably during a cozy lunch. That was all. Nothing whatever of importance was disclosed or discussed. The President did not even ask a question. The best hypothesis to explain this is that Roosevelt *had* wanted to sound out Lasker on isolationist sentiment in the Middle West, and then changed his mind; but he didn't feel that it would be courteous to call off the invitation. Anyway, for months thereafter, Mr. Lasker could be heard muttering, "When I get to heaven, there's only one thing I want to ask Saint Peter —why, *why*, WHY did Franklin Delano Roosevelt ask me to lunch that day?"

Gardner Cowles of *Look* once had a similar experience. The President peremptorily summoned him to lunch all the way from Des Moines—and then talked about nothing but the Harvard *Crimson*. Mr. Cowles finally got out at three o'clock—with the anteroom crowded with impatient ambassadors and such—and FDR called after him, "Haven't enjoyed a lunch so much in years!" Mr. Cowles had hardly got a word in, except to reminisce about Harvard and compare notes on the *Crimson*, of which each had been managing editor. Of course there was method in such seeming madness. Roosevelt wanted to look Cowles over carefully, with the thought of offering him a job; the Cowles newspapers, very important in the Middle West, were supporting the Administration's foreign policy, and FDR loved to pick off bright and promising young Republicans and make them his.

The President repeated himself a great deal, and this was an onerous burden to his friends. Hopkins in particular must have heard some of the same stories thirty or forty times. The President would even repeat to some dinner guest on Tuesday, say, the identical long anecdote he had told another guest on Monday, with Hopkins present on both occasions. Significantly FDR's favorite anecdotes had to do with (a) physical prowess or athleticism, (b) royalty or high figures of state, (c) social chitchat generally. Also he loved to show his desk to people he was meeting for the first time, and describe at eager length the history of the multitudinous gadgets it contained.

The cruelest sidelight on FDR's discursiveness I know is contained in General Stilwell's memoirs.[5] The general was summoned to the Cairo Conference in 1943 to discuss China, and this is his report on the way the conversation went:

F.D.R. Well, Joe, what do you think of the bad news?

J.W.S. I haven't heard yet how bad it is.

F.D.R. We're in an impasse. I've been stubborn as a mule for four days but we can't get anywhere, and it won't do for a conference to end that way. The British just won't do the operation, and I can't get them to agree to it.

J.W.S. I am interested to know how this affects our policy in China.

F.D.R. Well, now, we've been friends with China for a gr-e-e-at many years. I ascribe a large part of this feeling to the missionaries. You know *I* have a China history. My grandfather went out there, to Swatow and Canton, in 1829, and even went up to Hankow. He did what was every American's ambition in those days—he made a million dollars, and when he came back he put it into western railroads. And in eight years he lost every dollar. Ha! Ha! Ha! Then in 1856 he went out again and *stayed there all through the Civil War*, and made another million. This time he put it into coal mines, and they didn't pay a dividend until two years after he died. Ha! Ha! Ha!

---

[5] *The Stilwell Papers*, by General Joseph W. Stilwell (New York, William Sloane Associates, 1948), pp. 251-4. One should keep in mind that Stilwell was an acidulous character not very fond of FDR.

J.W.S. I take it that it is our policy to build China up.

F.D.R. Yes. Yes. Build her up. After this war there will be a great need of our help. They will want loans. Madame Chiang . . . wanted to get a loan now of a billion dollars, but . . . it would be difficult to get Congress to agree to it. Now, I'm not a financial expert (!!) but I have a plan to take fifty or a hundred million dollars and buy up Chinese paper dollars on the black market. It wouldn't take much. (!!) When the Chinese found out that these notes were being bought up, they would tend to hold them and the rate would come down. We might beat the inflation that way. And I'd share the profit with the Chinese government—I'd put the notes in escrow and when they were needed I'd sell them to the Chinese for what I paid for them. . . . Yes. Yes. How long do you think Chiang can last?

J.W.S. The situation is serious and a repetition of last May's attack might overturn him.

F.D.R. Well, then we should look for some other man or group of men, to carry on.

J.W.S. They would probably be looking for us.

F.D.R. Yes, they would come to us. They really like us and just between ourselves, they *don't* like the British. Now, we haven't the same aims as the British out there. For instance, Hongkong. Now, I have a plan to make Hongkong a free port: free to the commerce of all nations— of the whole world! But let's raise the Chinese flag there first, and then the next day Chiang can make a grand gesture and make it a free port. That's the way to handle that! Same way in Dairen! I'm sure that Chiang would be willing to make that a free port, and goods could come through Siberia—in bond—without customs examinations. . . .

J.W.S. We need guidance on political policy in China.

F.D.R. Yes. As I was saying, the Chinese will want a lot of help from us—a *lot* of it. Why, K'ung one time asked me for a loan of fifty million dollars for developing transportation and I said to him, "Mr. K'ung, that's a *lot* of money!" Then I said to him, "What are you going to use this money for?" and he said, "Construction materials," and he said, to try and influence me, "If we get this loan, we'll buy those materials right here in the United States." And I came right back at him and said, "Mr. K'ung, in your country you have construction materials already. You have cement, you have sand, you have rock— you have all those materials." Then he said, "Yes, but we need technical help—engineers and other technicians. We would pay a good engineer $100,000 a year, and give him a house and twenty servants." And I said, "Mr. K'ung, when I was governor of New York

State, I had a superintendent of highway construction named Green
—(ever know Green?)—and he was paid $15,000. And he was the
best road engineer I ever saw. But he's dead. But don't pay $100,000
—pay $15,000—no house, no servants. You don't want to pay $100,-
000. Why, there are any number of good engineers in the Army—
not the regular service, men from civil life—and you can get them
for $8,000. . . .

One way to seize the President's attention was to tell him something
he didn't know in a field, no matter what, in which he was an expert.
Former Senator Baldwin of Connecticut gained his interest once by
opening up with a discussion of cherry trees. Eleanor Roosevelt recounts the only known occasion when the President ran out of talk.
This was during the first inaugural, when FDR and Hoover drove to
the ceremonies together; the unresponsiveness of his unhappy companion was such that FDR completely dried up too and was reduced to
muttering something about the "lovely steel" in modern skyscrapers.
Final incidental irony: Roosevelt thought that Churchill was "horribly" garrulous!

However talkative he was FDR was never, or almost never, indiscreet about things important. This is remarkable. Think what
the President had to sit on all those years! I do not mean merely that,
obviously, he could not let any detail slip out in the sphere of military
security; he would not be likely to announce the date of D-Day at
cocktail time. But, hour after hour, day after interminable day, he
had to keep absolutely silent about multitudinous *small* affairs, because everything was so interlocked and ramifying that the most minor
error of the tongue could have brought disaster. One can savor, in
retrospect, what must have been behind his dead-pan countenance
when major strategy was being discussed irrelevantly and when he
alone knew what was really going on. Of course his habit of detachment was an ally. He delivered the Fireside Chat about the fall of
Rome on the very night that the invasion of Normandy was being
mounted. Nobody would have guessed from his tone that anything
special was in progress. Roosevelt *never* gave anything away—unless
he wanted to.

Why did the President talk so much? Partly because he couldn't
walk. This is of course an oversimplification; the fact remains that
conversation was his favorite method of relaxing. Normally a man
can pace the room during a tense discussion, shift in his chair, cross

to a bookcase, open a window, or beg to be excused for a moment or two—anything to shift the mood of a tight conference, take a little time out, readjust perspective, knit a group together. Roosevelt could do none of these things. So he relieved himself by gossiping, asking questions, interrupting, and telling stories. He liked to do things that didn't take too much out of him; stamps were one, and talk another. Conversation was his golf, his tennis, and his badminton.

More Sources of Power and Attributes

Now we swing back to qualities more positive, or mixed. One major trait was patience. A constituent of patience is, of course, impatience; a man will be impatient with detail in order to free himself for his real objective. FDR had a high regard for patience in the abstract; once he told Mrs. Roosevelt that she could never be a really good politician because she wasn't patient enough.[6] All manner of evidence is available about his patience, and how well this trait served him; to take just one instance, recall with what infinite care he slowly coaxed public opinion to the point where he could really count on it in 1940-41. This quality was so pronounced, in fact, that it boomeranged on occasion and became a defect. He discovered as Governor of New York that one way to settle an unpleasant, thorny problem (for instance the dispute over Mayor Walker) was to sit it out, hoping that a solution would come of itself in time. He sought to deal with the Japanese in much the same way, by "babying them along." A cruel master taught him patience—his own illness.

FDR's almost diabolically subtle sense of timing is a related characteristic. I have heard this explained by the remark that "he was in tune with history," and certainly there was something more than mere luck to it. His perceptive feeling for proportion, as well as of time, probably played a role, together with his sense of distant goals and how to reach them, which often meant not merely how, but when. Any expert politician knows what the people "want"; what counts is how *much* they want it, and at what precise time. That he could so accurately gauge the intensity and degree of feeling on a public issue, to the last ounce or millimeter, and moreover in relation to the advance scheduling of a legislative program, was one of his most powerful and

6 Incidentally, Mrs. Roosevelt thought that "the quality most responsible for FDR's success was his patience and ability to look at things historically."

useful qualities. His technique was almost that of a billiard player: ball to ball to pocket.

No president has much time out, and in more than twelve years Roosevelt hardly had a day at the White House without some crisis or other. One does not think of him as being industrious in the manner of a beaver or an automaton; he had too much variability, nervousness, and informality. Yet the amount of work he did was murderous. The mere physical bulk of material that reached his desk could be weighed by the ton, year after year. "He had to take it," someone said once, "for everybody." On one day, late in March, 1945, when he was already a sick man, he arrived at the White House from Hyde Park at 10:25 A.M. and left for Warm Springs at 3:15 P.M. In between he swore in Jonathan Daniels as press secretary; had a long consultation with Senator Barkley on man power; received a British mission; confronted a sudden crisis over a news leak revealing that the Soviet Union was going to receive three seats in the United Nations; worked like a terrier over various drafts of a communiqué about to be issued; had lunch with a member of his family; read, absorbed, and signed about thirty documents; decided that there was "a hole" in the Yalta communiqué and called two of his advisers back for another look at it; then caught the train.

"How *does* he do it?" former Senator Carl Hatch asked once. "Here we are in the Senate, each of us with one ninety-sixth of the total responsibility for what goes on just here. And half the time we are dead with strain." An assistant secretary of state told me once, "We work on a difficult decision for a week. It is on a matter so far-reaching and interlaced that two or three of us think we had better resign and go home. We take it over to Pennsylvania Avenue and confront him with our conclusion and the alternatives. And he decides in twenty minutes. Moreover this happens half a dozen times a day. It is just too much for any single man."

One of his administrative assistants put it to me this way: "All the time he had to protect himself from the strain of constantly having to absorb a *new* problem. When somebody came in with something vital it was like an iceberg, with only the tip showing; the President had to get to the rest intuitively. Day after day this would happen and it was always something new. But there is a limit to what anybody can absorb, and, remember, he always had to pretend that he liked what was going on, even if he didn't. This happens to any president, maybe; but FDR attracted more people and more problems than any other president ever did. Sometimes he was so tired after a conference it would make you weep. Then, ten minutes later, he was ready to push the whole world over. It was incredible that it could be the same man."

Roosevelt's supreme confidence was another trait and source of power. This was based on a naturally sanguine disposition, an almost defiant optimism, and his own personal superiority. Once he told a friend, "When I give my full attention to something for three hours and feel that my conclusion is right, it wouldn't change things if I studied it for three years. I know I'd still be right." What is more he had a marvelous capacity to transmit this confidence to others, to irradiate them with his own energy. He could, by a word or two, instantly lift up advisers crushed by burdens; he made them think that nothing was impossible, no goal too remote or difficult.

There was no trace of self-pity in his nature; Rexford Tugwell has recorded that he had less self-doubt than any man he ever knew. Consider the way he would risk ad-libbing in radio speeches heard by millions. At Hyde Park one may see the memorandum prepared by the Combined Chiefs of Staff for the invasion of Europe, estimating various dates and operations. Roosevelt changed them all to be more optimistic. Even when baffled, he was cheerful; he was always sure that something would "turn up." Eleanor Roosevelt says, "I never heard him say that there was a problem that he thought it was impossible for human beings to solve." Of course overconfidence led him into grave pitfalls on occasion, as at Yalta.

Roosevelt was a superb actor. Consider merely how stunningly effective was his diction. After seeing himself in a newsreel once he grinned, "That was the Garbo in me." Quite seriously he mentioned to Orson Welles on one occasion, "You know, Orson, you and I are the two best actors in America."

He was, despite occasional shifts, remarkably consistent. "Never," writes Compton Mackenzie, "was there any betrayal of the essential self." Anne O'Hare McCormick, one of the most skilled and sensitive of reporters, who saw him several times a year during the whole course of his office, was always impressed by the way he didn't change; he had, she wrote, "an infinite capacity for remaining himself."

Then again, as David Lilienthal once expressed it, he was "gloriously stubborn"; a good stout Dutch obstinacy was, in fact, one of his outstanding qualities, though he was infinitely elastic and flexible in regard to the means with which he stubbornly, obstinately, pursued his ends.

He was full of detachment and common sense. He always had his ear to the ground, and, as Dorothy Thompson put it once, "every pore in his body was an ear." Once he described to Dr. Luther Gulick, head of the Institute of Public Administration, his plan for setting up a staff of administrative assistants (at first he was going to call them "executive" assistants), and his conversation went something like this: "Let's have one man for foreign affairs. He should go out in the morning and see Hull, then go to the Treasury, Agriculture, Commerce, the Federal Reserve, and find out what was up, touching foreign relations in every field. And he would come back and tell me. Another man for business relations. Another for finance, another for welfare and conservation. You can't have just one executive secretary. The columnists would never let him alone. They're always looking for a white-haired boy." Then Dr. Gulick suggested that still another secretary might be useful for planning and general ideas. "Exactly!" FDR exclaimed. "Yes, and that would be the fellow who never went out, who always stayed right here!"

His vitality was, as everybody knows, practically unlimited. Raymond Moley records that in one campaign he traveled 13,000 miles in about seven weeks, and "made 16 major and 67 second-string speeches—not to mention innumerable back platform appearances—talked to hundreds of people who boarded the train to ride from one station to another—governors, senators, mayors, obscure county politicians, farmers, miners, mine owners, tradespeople, local bankers, newspaper owners, reporters, manufacturers, welfare workers—and never stopped having a wonderful time."[7] As President his working day averaged fourteen hours. He once wrote Governor Cox, "I *never* get tired!"

He was no stickler for presidential dignity, but he had a well-developed sense of propriety in reprisal. When the Russians threatened to make Ambassador Laurence A. Steinhardt come personally to the central telephone office in Moscow to put in long distance calls to the United States, FDR suggested to Mr. Hull that the same rule should be applied to the Soviet Ambassador in Washington.

Finally, among miscellaneous sources of power, he seldom forgot,

[7] *After Seven Years,* by Raymond Moley (New York, Harper & Brothers, 1939), p. 52.

even in his greatest days, that he had once been beaten for the sena-
torial primaries in New York State and as vice-presidential candidate
in 1920; he was forever alert and on guard to see that all political
fences were mended and secure, and above all he had a magical gift
for managing to disassociate himself from any failures, errors, and
blunders by his subordinates.

He Loved To Break Precedents

Roosevelt broke so many precedents that one can scarcely list them.
He was the first President to accept the nomination of a convention
in person on the spot, and the first to swear in the whole Cabinet en
bloc. He was the first President to invite the Vice-President to sit
regularly in Cabinet meetings, the first to leave the country in time
of war, the first to appoint a woman to the Cabinet, and the first to
fly. Innovations never frightened him, and he liked nothing better
than a new idea.

The distinguished editor of a widely circulated magazine whom the
President liked got what he thought was a fantastic idea—that Queen
Elizabeth of England might write an article. A daring man, he brought
the idea to the White House, and then blandly suggested that FDR
himself should proofread what the Queen wrote. Roosevelt was delighted! But he made one qualification—that the article would have to
come to him through Lord Halifax, the British Ambassador. The editor
promptly saw Halifax, who was of course stunned by the proposal.
But the article was prepared (whether the Queen herself actually wrote
it is unknown) and duly put into type. Then at the last minute the
British Foreign Office protested so vigorously that the magazine was
forced to cancel its publication. Roosevelt thought that this was a
shame.[8]

A Word About His Knowledgeability

The President's knowledge about things far outside his own orbit
was astonishing. After the Atlantic Charter meeting his party moved
on to his yacht, the *Potomac*, which was anchored at Pulpit Harbor,
Maine. The stout Maine citizenry saw the presidential flag aloft, and
sent some small gifts aboard; one was a swatch of wool, with the note,
"We thought you might be interested in seeing the kind of wool we
grow here." That evening FDR thumbed through his mail and came

[8] This anecdote is from Thomas H. Beck of *Collier's*.

across the bit of wool; he examined it attentively, and then said to Lieutenant Commander Francis Terry, the ship's clerk, "Please get a boat, go ashore, and ask these people to have lunch with us tomorrow." Terry did so. Typically enough the Maine folk showed no sign of being impressed by the presidential invitation. They came aboard— whereupon FDR proceeded to tell *them* all about wool.[9]

Roosevelt's memory (which derived from his quickness of perception, capacity to be interested, and ability to concentrate) was phenomenal. It was, obviously, a substantial source of power, if only from the point of view that when confronted with a problem, he could bring into focus all manner of divergent factors bearing on it; the whole of his previous experience was, it seemed, at his instantaneous command. He himself claimed that he could remember a torchlight parade at Hyde Park celebrating Cleveland's election to the Presidency in 1884, when he was two. There were, of course, gaps in detail. When he would assert, during a conference, that he could remember the whole dossier of a case eight or nine years back, his assistants would politely agree, and then, as soon as they were out of his sight, proceed to check it; FDR would turn out to be right a remarkable percentage of the time. All manner of relevant detail is to the point. Eisenhower was astonished, after the Casablanca Conference, at the President's memory for historical facts and figures; he knew the Tunisia terrain better than some of the generals did. The artist Walter Tittle records that FDR remembered particular buildings and streets in towns in Italy that he hadn't seen for forty years. He knew not merely the name, which would have been remarkable enough, but the nickname of the British ambassador to Turkey when this dignitary happened to be called to his attention at Cairo. Anna Rosenberg, who was his most valued adviser on labor during the war, has described how he told William Green of the A. F. of L. something that Green himself had told him, but completely forgotten, years before, and how, after his visit to Africa, he even remembered the names of two GI's who had been his cooks. Henry Morgenthau brought William H. McReynolds to meet him in 1933. Roosevelt said, "Don't introduce

---

[9] The printer on the *Augusta* was named Simonetti. When FDR congratulated Terry on how well the menus and so on had been handled Terry said that the credit belonged to Simonetti. "Have him here at four," the President commanded. Then he asked Simonetti all manner of pointed questions on the way printing was done on board, whether he needed any more equipment, and what his conditions of work were.

me to Mac. The last time I saw him was in the Walker-Johnson Building during World War I, when he argued with me about supplies and accounts, and darned if he didn't have his way."

The President's omniscience and erudition covered a very wide arc indeed; he knew a little about almost everything, from where to get good beer in Georgetown to which wives of Cabinet ministers gossiped most. The three subjects about which he knew *most* were politics, American history,[10] and geography in general. Nobody ever knew more about American politics than FDR; his knowledge ranged from constitutional precedents on the highest level to exactly what was going on in the First Ward in Chicago or who was postmaster in Walla Walla, Washington. His ability to keep in mind the smallest political details was "aldermanic," the late Mayor La Guardia of New York once told me. In the field of geography FDR's omniscience was even more striking. One anecdote is well known; the report came to Washington that a ship had been sunk off Scotland, either by a torpedo or by hitting a rock; Roosevelt said it must have been a rock, and at once guessed the height of the tide at the time, out of his knowledge when that particular rock would be submerged. One story has been told several times; it is to the effect that if you drew a line in any direction across the United States, FDR could name in order every county it traversed. Once Anne O'Hare McCormick saw him just after a visit to the Carpatho-Ukraine; whereupon FDR proceeded to tell *her* all about the Carpatho-Ukraine. Once he asked Sumner Welles to prepare a report on Angola; the State Department worked a fortnight on it, and then found that he knew more about Angola than their experts did. Arthur Sweetser talked to him about possible locations for the new League of Nations after the war; Roosevelt thought the Azores might be a possibility, and there was absolutely nothing he did not know about the Azores. And the way he could draw a map!

He Loved To Laugh[11]

Mr. Roosevelt's sense of humor was, as everybody knows, hearty and robust; it was a special type of humor not too easy to analyze; a good

[10] It is an interesting commentary that his four favorite characters in American history were Benjamin Franklin, Thomas Jefferson, Theodore Roosevelt, and a man whom scarcely anybody else has ever heard of, Benjamin Thompson. See Anne O'Hare McCormick in the New York *Times*, January 25, 1942.

[11] Roosevelt haters used to say that his stentorian laugh was a symptom of his "paranoia," and that he had developed "a peculiar form of insanity which led him to laugh on the slightest occasion."

enough description might be to call it archetypically "American." FDR was no great wit, and he had little gift for drawing-room repartee. His humor was seldom subtle or profound; it was somewhat heavy, smart-alecky, and based on exaggeration; his fondness for tall tales is well known; he invented anecdotes, embellished them, and finally came to believe them himself, like a bard. He told stories well, but they were seldom intricate stories; often he laughed at pretty feeble jokes. Above all he shared the national trait of being fond of heavy kidding. But what a relief to the nation in 1932 to have a President with any sense of humor at all!

Once he had to make a public appearance before the Daughters of the American Revolution. He didn't want to go, but did. The proceedings were stupefyingly formal—until FDR began his speech with the words, "Fellow immigrants"!

Early in the first term he took a southern cruise on a friend's yacht; for a brief interval he managed to leave his destroyer escort behind. Reporters on the destroyer caught up with him when he landed at New Orleans, and asked him where he had been. Blandly Roosevelt named three islands with exotic, resounding Spanish names. The story was duly printed with the names of the islands. The newspaper men then discovered that one island was off the coast of Great Britain, one in the Indian Ocean, and one beyond the Arctic Circle.

One year the President tried month after month to get rid of an adhesive minor official, by kicking him upstairs or otherwise. Then one of his assistants walked in and reported that the minor official had suddenly resigned. The President turned on his assistant an eye at once quizzical, beaming, and suspicious, with the words, "You're not kidding me, are you?" Being a great kidder himself, he liked to be on guard.

His puns were terrible. When a member of the White House mail staff, Ira R. T. Smith, was buried in an avalanche of dimes pouring in as contributions to the infantile paralysis campaign, Roosevelt sent him a note, "I hope you are having a good dime."[12]

One story related by Thomas H. Beck, chairman of the board of *Collier's*, concerns an ichthyologist, Professor Waldo L. Schmitt, whom the President asked to accompany him on a marine expedition in July, 1938. The Professor arrived for duty, and FDR asked him what his

[12] "My Fifty Years in the White House," by Ira R. T. Smith and Joe Alex Morris, *Saturday Evening Post*, January 22, 1949.

specialty was. "Burrowing shrimp." "Oh, if I had known that, I wouldn't have taken you from your work in Washington. You must run into them there all the time!"

Admiral Wilson Brown, one of the President's best friends and one of his naval aides, dropped in one day; FDR turned to him with the words, "Hello, Moses Brown!" The Admiral looked astonished. In a tone of mock reprimand, FDR proceeded: "You don't know who Moses Brown was? Run right over to Dudley Knox and find out!" (Mr. Knox, an erudite specialist in naval matters, was a mutual friend.) Knox duly told Admiral Brown that Moses Brown commanded a small man-of-war in the naval scuffling between the United States and France in 1798-1801. The explanation is that Roosevelt had just happened to receive an old portrait of Moses Brown, and thought that Wilson Brown bore him a close resemblance.

Roosevelt's humor in letters was sometimes crude, and even juvenile. He wrote his mother from London (he was about twenty-three at the time) of his arrival at Brown's Hotel.[13] "We were ushered into the royal suite, one flight up, $1,000 a day—a sitting room 40 ft. by 30, a double bedroom, another ditto and a bath. Our breath was so taken away that we couldn't even protest and are now saying, 'Damn the expense, wot's the odds?' " He loved to tease his mother—the remarkable lady of whom we shall hear much before this book is done. She was somewhat parsimonious, and he invented wild extravagances to tantalize her.

Here are two telegrams he wrote in 1937 after packing off Harold Ickes and Harry Hopkins, who had been at each other's throats over the Public Works Administration, to a holiday in Florida together.[14]

For Secretary Ickes and Administrator Hopkins: So glad you both in Everglades. Government is at last seeing the light of solvency. Bell [Acting Director of the Budget] hopes you will never come back. . . . Can't you go ashore with a tent and a month's grub? Will send occasional supplies and copies Hearst papers and Chicago Tribune. Pa [Colonel Watson, military aide] and Doc [White House Physician McIntire] hope the seas are heavy and shark will bite you both.

(Signed) F.D.R.

[13] *F.D.R.: His Personal Letters* (New York, Duell, Sloan & Pearce, Inc., 1948), Vol. II, p. 10.
[14] "My Twelve Years With FDR," by Harold L. Ickes, *Saturday Evening Post*, June 19, 1948.

For Honorable Harold L. Ickes: Greatly disturbed about alligators. As senior officer present, please insist Hopkins deliver to you Colonel Watson's bottle of bait. Pa begs whole [old?] West Point scandal be not revived at this time. His promotion depends on his affairs with the alligators being forgotten. National budget almost in balance. You both stay away another week. Debtor nations will pay war debts. We can all head for Samoa.

(Signed) F.D.R.

Once at a press conference the following dialogue took place:

Q. Mr. President, does the ban on the highways [as part of the national defense program] include the parking shoulders?

FDR: Parking *shoulders?*

Q. Yes, widening out on the edge, supposedly to let the civilians park as the military goes by.

FDR: You don't mean necking places? (*Prolonged laughter.*)

And at another, when John G. Winant was about to be named ambassador to England:[15]

Q. Have you personally made your selection for the Ambassador, Mr. President?

The President: Yes.

Q. Could you tell us ——

The President (interposing): No.

Q. Could you tell us, sir, whether he is acceptable to the British?

The President: No, I haven't even asked them; and he doesn't know, either.

Q. He doesn't know?

The President: No. Isn't that an awful mystery? You could almost write an Oppenheim novel around that—probably will, so it's all right! (*Laughter.*)

Q. A lot of people uncertain, sir.

Q. Would it narrow the matter down to ——

The President (interposing): Yes—before you finish your questions—it would. (*Laughter.*)

Q. I didn't ask the question, but close to it, sir.

The President: Don't do any guessing; because I haven't mentioned this to anybody at all—not even to myself out loud. (*Laughter.*)

Q. Will it be a surprise? (*More laughter.*)

Q. You may not realize it, sir, but we are trying to encourage you to mention it now.

The President: Down East they would say, "You don't say!" (*Continued laughter.*)

15 Rosenman, Vol. IX, pp. 584 and 710-11.

Sometimes he laughed at things other people did not think were so funny. Rexford Tugwell records that Roosevelt caught Pa Watson, who was trying to reduce, cheating by having a second breakfast at a cafeteria on his way to work; FDR's laughter could scarcely be contained. Once Frank Knox came into his office fairly bursting with anguish and frustration. "What's the matter, Frank?" the President inquired. "The admirals won't let me into my own map room!" exclaimed Knox. The President sat back and roared.

Once he opened a press conference by asking a reporter what was going on in Washington. "Only surmise," the reporter replied. "Sir who?" the President rejoined.

Once he fenced with newspaper men about the contents of a letter to Stalin he was sending to Russia by the hand of Ambassador Davies. "Did you write it in English?" he was asked. "No, Irish," the President retorted.

He loved practical jokes. For instance Rosenman describes how he "rejected" an invitation to one of his own inaugurals. His humor had considerable imagination; he once gave the code name "Rover" to Mrs. Roosevelt. Nothing was too serious for him to be facetious about, if it were necessary to let off steam. He liked to make fun; Elliott Roosevelt tells how he picked up a book in the villa where he was staying at Casablanca, and then autographed it with a magnificent flourish and stuck it back in the shelves wondering if it would ever be discovered. His irony could be sharp; for instance when General Knudsen presented him with the names of big-business men to be given jobs in the Office of Production Management, FDR turned to him with the remark, "There must be a mistake here, Bill. One of the men on this list is a Democrat."[16] Finally, he liked to have people around him who could treat serious matters with his own irreverence. Roosevelt himself describes, in his book *On Our Way*, how he broke the news to Mr. Woodin, his Secretary of the Treasury, that the United States had left the gold standard. Woodin replied, "My heavens! What, again?"

If anyone thinks from stories like these that Mr. Roosevelt was a lightweight, they are wrong. Let us continue to explore.

---

[16] Knudsen topped him by replying, "It's all right, Mr. President—I have checked on this man and found out that last year he voted for Willkie." Sherwood, p. 949.

Chapter 5

ROOSEVELT THE HUMAN BEING

Precious is man to man.
—THOMAS CARLYLE

We proceed now to discuss some of FDR's fundamental allegiances and attitudes. What, for instance, did he think of four of the major determinants that control the lives of most men—women, money, God, and fame?

Already a vast lot of apocrypha has grown up over Roosevelt; so, even on comparatively minor aspects of his character and life, it is important to pin down facts while memories are still fresh and the record open.

Attitude to Sex

FDR liked women, knew plenty about them, and had a healthy, salty attitude toward sex. His development was somewhat late and his adolescence prolonged, as is often the case with men who had masterful mothers. No record exists that he had any interest whatever in female companionship until he fell violently in love with Eleanor when he was twenty-one; he had, so far as one can tell from his letters and other evidence, no adolescent dissipations or escapades at all, even as a college boy. Sara Roosevelt, his mother, testifies in her odd little book about him[1] that young FDR was "never in any sense a ladies' man," and that, until he met Eleanor, she could not remember his ever having even talked about a girl. Of course incidents may have occurred that the elder Mrs. Roosevelt knew nothing of. It is hardly credible that any young man as handsome and full of magnetic appeal as Roosevelt could have reached his twenties without some flirtation, dalliance, or amatory adventure. But, to repeat, the record is completely blank so far as any direct evidence is concerned.

[1] *My Boy Franklin*, as told by Mrs. James Roosevelt to Isabel Leighton and Gabrielle Forbush (New York, Crown Publishers, 1933), p. 63.

Later FDR came to have a very fair sophistication about sex, though sometimes he was naïve. He liked to joke with his wife if, for instance, some lady famous for the aggressiveness or plenitude of her charms was coming to dinner; he would mutter in mock alarm, "Don't let me alone with that female!" When seeing a movie with his mother he would tease her by broad remarks about attractive points in the leading lady. Occasionally, when irritated at a Cabinet minister or some other associate who seemed suppressed about sexual matters, FDR would mutter *sotto voce* that he ought to go out on the town for a while and get rid of his bottled-up emotions. Nevertheless, even if his humor was broad and his perceptions about sex acute, Roosevelt never quite got over his Puritan upbringing, though it would be off the mark to call him a consistent Puritan.

Women liked him extremely and devotedly. Even after his illness, his physical magnetism was powerful to almost all who met him. Particularly in his later years he loved to flirt, and Mrs. Roosevelt talks with mild irony of the "lovely ladies who worshipped at his shrine." Yet he had some characteristics almost feminoid; I heard one lady say with asperity, "If he lives long enough, he'll be like Queen Victoria." Two splendid women gave the major share of their professional lives to him, Missy LeHand and Grace Tully, and both were exceptionally able, of good disposition, full of charm, and very pretty. He was very fond of several of his daughters-in-law, notably Mrs. John Hay Whitney, who was James Roosevelt's first wife. And he was the dominant note, year after year, in the lives of several other women, for instance Margaret ("Daisy") Suckley, the fine and distinguished lady (she was a remote cousin) who among other things gave him Fala, and who was with him at Warm Springs when he died, along with another cousin, Miss Laura Delano, and an old family friend, Mrs. Lucy Rutherfurd.

Both Miss LeHand and Miss Tully came to him in the first place through Mrs. Roosevelt; they had been her secretaries at the beginning, as had Mrs. Rutherfurd. Miss LeHand and Miss Tully (who was once secretary to the late Cardinal Hayes) were both of Irish descent and Roman Catholic. People who watched them carefully for years say that though Missy was much closer to FDR personally, Miss Tully was "better" for him in some ways, because more detached and business-like. Between Roosevelt and Missy the closest possible rapport existed; they were as sensitive to one another as brother and sister. I have even heard it said, "When he became President, FDR cut every really personal relationship out of his life except his love for Missy." She died during the war, after long illness, and her disappearance was one of the worst losses FDR ever suffered. It was Missy, among other things, who curbed his ebullience, tempered his occasional lapses into questionable taste, and made him relaxed and comfortable. She was (like Miss Tully) an altogether admirable personality. Few people ever "took" more for a man than she did for Roosevelt; on occasion she was cruelly—even villainously—exploited. She had almost complete authority in the White House on some social matters for many years; she would invite guests to stay, arrange dinner parties, and so on. She was much more than just a secretary. Missy had, for instance, considerable power in her management of the President's daily business routine; to have her favor was the best possible channel to his attention, and it was she who suggested several major appointments, for instance that of Homer Cummings as Attorney General. One of the President's bitterest enemies told me once, when I asked him how he accounted for FDR's alleged "decline" in the early 1940's, "The fact that Missy began to lose influence." Tribute should be paid this warmhearted, sensitive, and faithful woman; American history owes her much.

As to Mrs. Roosevelt she is, it goes without saying, a tremendous story in herself, to which we will come soon. The relation between Franklin and Eleanor was complex—as it is, for that matter, between most husbands and wives. The burden of the Presidency, to say nothing of his illness, increased their occasional difficulties. One story sometimes told is that when he was Assistant Secretary of the Navy they underwent a period of severe strain. FDR is supposed to have fallen in love with a lady of Washington society, and Mrs. Roosevelt offered him his freedom. But the vigorous intervention of FDR's mother, among other things, prevented a divorce.[2] Many years later, when he was President, FDR saw a great deal of the Crown Princess Martha of Norway; she had the run of the White House and even of Hyde Park for a long period. There was, however, no hint of anything improper in this friendship. The plain fact of the matter is that Roosevelt, all his life, genuinely *liked* women and was interested in them; he enjoyed immensely having them around.

I have seen the big blue-and-gold guest book he kept at Shangri-La;

[2] See Olive Clapper, *Washington Tapestry* (New York, Whittlesey House, 1946), pp. 238-39, which gives what is apparently an authentic account of this.

he enjoyed pretending that this retreat was a ship, and he entered a "log" for each week-end visit, as if it had been a cruise.[3] He always liked to have amiable women present, who did not tire him and with whom he could be *en pantoufles*, so to speak. Guests on the first "cruise" of 1944 were Crown Princess Martha and his beloved daughter Anna, among others; on the last were the Boettigers, Jimmy Byrnes and his wife, Dorothy J. Brady, who was Miss Tully's assistant, and Miss Suckley. Contrariwise, he never took women along on actual cruises or fishing trips.

Attitude to Money

Roosevelt was a comfortably well-off and somewhat frugal man, but he cared little for money for its own sake. He liked to watch things like the cost of long-distance telephone calls or of flowers for the dining room; he hated needless extravagance. When the Hyde Park library was being furnished the designers drew up plans for an iron grille to close off his own room, while still permitting sightseers to look into it; when FDR found that this would cost $200, he canceled the order. (Later, however, he was overruled, and the grille is there.) Mrs. Roosevelt records that, in his early days at least, he "saw no sense in spending money in a restaurant when he had a home to eat in," and that he would not pay more than two dollars for a shirt. Like his mother, he practically never threw anything away. For instance he inherited a stout tweed jacket from his father, who had received it from *his* father; he wore it for years, and it is now owned, and possibly even used, by his son James.

Sara Roosevelt,[4] his mother, tells us that as a boy he never even heard such a vulgar thing as money discussed (how "refined" the home atmosphere must have been!) and he never had an allowance. The reason for this was, she says, that an allowance "was not customary at that time"; moreover, "living as we did in the country, there was little opportunity for spending . . . there was no dashing off to the village to buy ice cream cones, there were no movies to see, and

[3] The way FDR ran things himself down to the most minute detail is illustrated by a penciled order on a slip of paper that is still interleaved in this book—"New page for each time." By this he meant that guests each week end should sign their names at the top of a fresh page. He would write in his own hand such items as "On this cruise came word of the new offensive on the Italian front."

[4] The quotations below are from *My Boy Franklin* and *F.D.R.: His Personal Letters,* edited by Elliott Roosevelt (New York, Duell, Sloan & Pearce, 1947), Vol. I.

all his books and toys were provided for him." Nevertheless his early letters show a considerable—but quite normal—interest in minor financial matters. When he was seventeen he wrote his parents, "I have ordered an extra of grey flannel trousers, awfully nice . . . and only $6.oo, I thought you would not mind." A little later he describes how a Brooks Brothers suit cost him $31, which he thought was quite a lot.

His mother doted on him and spoiled him in some ways but she was always serious with him about money. As a boy he was an easy mark for book salesmen; he loved to buy subscription sets of Dickens or Scott on the installment plan, paying some small sum down. Then, fearing his mother's wrath, he would hide these accumulations of books under his bed; she would prod with a stick to see what he had hidden, and if she disapproved of what she found, she would cut off payment of the installments due. This did not endear FDR to the book salesmen. (When, many years later, he became President, he had a number of small outstanding bills in the secondhand shops on 59th Street; nobody could ever stop him from buying books. A member of the family went down the street settling the bills before the first inauguration.)

Of course Sara pampered FDR about money on occasion, and in his letters he complains several times that his accounts are confused because she tore up or didn't cash checks he sent her. But once, when he was a very young man, she had to rebuke him for piling up petty debts:

> To my sorrow I find poor Aunt Doe has been troubled by the knowledge that my dear boy's bills are not paid, though two years old. . . . I have today been to the bankers and the bills are paid. I will say nothing, as it will do no good, only it *is* a surprise as I am not accustomed to this way of doing business my dear Franklin and if you love me you will be more careful in the future.[5]

Roosevelt would never have had to work for a living; Sara was rich, and so were other members of the family; in 1927 he got a bequest of $100,000 from his half brother James, and his father left him a considerable sum. But he was not the kind of person who would live off his family, and he worked at some job or other, or held public office, almost from the day he got out of college. He was sensible enough to know what virtues money brings in such areas as privacy,

[5] *Letters,* op. cit., Vol. II, p. 127.

mobility, and gracious living; and of course the fact that he was rich greatly assisted his political career, and above all proved to be an indispensable convenience when he was ill. On the other hand he never had the slightest interest in building up a great fortune. He was not in the least avaricious. He was not at all competitive about wealth. Every reference to money in his published correspondence deals with the mechanics of household finance and the like. He would write his mother, working out what percentage of the Hyde Park garage bill was his to pay; one elaborate tabulation ends with the notation, "Balance due me—$111.28." On another occasion he reminds his wife that he owes her "either $1104 or $1404" but cannot remember which. Another letter (to his mother), of date 1927, begins gaily with "Ever so many thanks for the check for 1/3 of the horse." Still another describes how, when he hears that the elder Mrs. Roosevelt has rented her New York house, he hopes that the tenants "are nice people and that you got at least $10,000." (The tenants turned out to be the Thomas W. Lamonts.)

In 1920, when he was running for vice-president, he wrote his mother this:

DEAREST MAMA—

You are not only an angel which I always knew, but the kind which comes at the critical moment in life! For the question was not one of paying Dr. Mitchell for removing James' insides, the Dr. can wait, I know he is or must be rich, but of paying the gas man and the butcher lest the infants starve to death, and your cheque which is much too much of a Birthday present will do that. It is so dear of you.[6]

The Roosevelts always lived well, if not luxuriously, and Eleanor has recorded many details of their financial affairs. Immediately after their marriage they put equal sums into the household account and lived on $600 per month. Later their standard advanced; when FDR was Assistant Secretary of the Navy in Washington, they had ten servants.[7] One fascinating letter describes how, during the shortages of World War I, they maneuvered to cut down the enormous amount of food required to maintain this staff. Mr. Roosevelt, among other things, taught his wife how to keep accounts; she describes how she

---

[6] *Letters,* op. cit., Vol. II, p. 486.

[7] And two automobiles, both of which were bought secondhand. At this time the combined income of the family, from salary and investments, was roughly $27,500 a year.

wrote down every detail of household expense for many years, and finally turned the account book over to their daughter Anna as an example. In the White House it was, of course, impossible to save money. FDR got $75,000 salary as President, plus $25,000 expenses; but taxes took roughly $50,000 of this, and the cost of maintaining the presidential establishment was prodigious. The food bill alone, not including official entertainment, was around $2,000 per month, because FDR had to feed the servants, who consumed roughly 90 meals a day. I have heard from a member of the family that, in fact, it cost the Roosevelts almost $175,000 a year in all to live. This figure included, of course, maintenance of the properties at Hyde Park, Campobello, and Warm Springs. But the Warm Springs establishment was so modestly set up that the President's cottage did not even have an electric refrigerator. The Hyde Park payroll was about $3,000 a month, and it cost a lot of money to build firebreaks and keep the roadways in repair. Think of such a minor matter as the number of Christmas presents the President had to give, not only to the family itself, but to officials, servants, and staff; think too of the fantastic amount that had to be spent on entertainment not chargeable to the government. The most scrupulous tabulations were made daily, down to the cost of single meals. It is revealing that Mrs. Harry Hopkins was assessed 50 cents per day for the keep of her old brown poodle, Suzi.

Roosevelt seldom carried money in his own pocket—few heads of states do—although, when he died, he had $133 in his clothes. If he needed cash suddenly, he would borrow from anybody close at hand. He always worked out his own income-tax return, and Miss Tully[8] records that he would spend hours to trace a missing nickel.

Even if Roosevelt liked money he disliked many of the rich, particularly the newly rich. If a man of good family lived on a comfortable income, deriving from a fortune made a generation or so before, it was all right with him; but he detested the "upstart" rich, the overnight millionaires, the gamblers, speculators, and promoters. Nor did he think that anybody ought to be *too* rich; he genuinely felt that a man in private life ought to be able to get along on $25,000 a year. How such considerations played a role in the New Deal and some of

---

[8] Grace Tully, *F.D.R., My Boss* (New York, Charles Scribner's Sons, 1949). Miss Tully also mentions that he never speculated while he was President.

his subsequent legislation is well known. Once I heard it said, "FDR was radical because he had always been rich enough to be scornful of those richer."

Roosevelt left life-insurance policies worth $562,142 to the Warm Springs Foundation, and in addition a gross estate of $1,940,999, the net value of which was $1,085,486. He bequeathed the great bulk of this to Mrs. Roosevelt; after her death it passes to the five children. A small income was left to Missy LeHand, but she died before he did. Of this fortune a large amount—$920,115—came from his mother's estate, which he never touched. All in all his estate included $103,855 in real estate, $353,855 in stocks and bonds, $197,543 in cash or its equivalent, $29,726 in insurance aside from the policies for Warm Springs, and $105,208 in house and personal effects. Among the investments he held were 800 shares of General Electric, 735 of National City Bank of New York, 300 of Lehman Corporation, 200 of Reynolds Tobacco, 100 of Standard Oil of California, 84 of du Pont, 59 of Electric Bond and Share, and 1 of Safeway Stores. He had bought a good deal of worthless stock; the itemization includes about 2,600 shares in 13 issues. Also he held roughly $65,000 in United States Treasury bonds. Among current bills at the time of his death were $8.88 for newspapers at the Hyde Park drug store, $48.53 from the neighborhood bakery, $44.86 to the telephone company, $786.07 for miscellaneous farm expenses, $46.20 to Mrs. Roosevelt for expenditures at Campobello, $72.96 to a philatelist in England, and $368.58 to a London bookseller.

Roosevelt's estate was substantially greater than that left by any other president. Taft left about $475,000, Wilson about $250,000, and Coolidge roughly $500,000.

Attitude to Religion

FDR's feelings about God and religion were direct, personal, and simple; he felt that God helps those who help themselves. He was not, as we know, at all introspective, and problems of dogma were miles outside his province; he never explored the why of things, even the giant why of belief itself. He disliked the institutional side of religion; his basic approach was ethical. Mrs. Roosevelt worried about what instruction to give the children as they grew up; FDR said, in substance, that what he and she had learned as children had hurt them little, and why not give the youngsters more of the same?[9] He was completely open-minded on most aspects of religion. If he felt confidence that his soul was immortal and would have life everlasting, he seldom made it known; on the other hand, he had little fear of death. Death, like life, was a process intensely interesting. Somebody asked him once what he thought of spiritualism. His reply was that he didn't know any reason to disbelieve *anything*, until it was proved untrue. If one put to him such a stock question as, "Do you believe that a purple elephant is flying at this minute around the top of the Empire State Building?" his reply would probably have been, "It *might* be true—let's go out and see."

FDR was christened in the St. James Episcopal Church in Hyde Park; the joke was that "this is Roosevelt's church, once God's." He had a strong neighborly feeling for it all his life, attended services in it hundreds of times, became a vestryman in 1928, and eventually the senior warden, as his father had been before him. He took the duties of this position with complete seriousness. As the presidential years wore on, however, he went to services less often; the Secret Service did not like him to go to any kind of church, and it became increasingly difficult for him to handle his leg braces in the narrow wooden pews. Incidentally, like twelve other American presidents, he was a Mason.

Roosevelt's favorite passage from the Bible was the 13th chapter of I Corinthians; his two favorite hymns were "O God, Our Help in Ages Past" and "Faith of Our Fathers." I do not know what his favorite prayer was, but he read to the nation one of the finest and most stirring of all modern prayers on the eve of D-Day in 1944. Some passages of this are:

God of the Free, we pledge our hearts and lives today to the cause of all free mankind. Grant us victory over tyrants who would enslave all free men of nations. . . . Our earth is but a small star in the great universe—yet of it we can make—if we choose, a planet unvexed by war, untroubled by hunger or fear, undivided by senseless distinctions of race, color, or theory. Grant us that courage and foreseeing to begin this task today, that our children and children's children may be proud of the name of Man. . . . Grant us patience with the deluded and pity for the betrayed, and grant us the skill and valor that so cleansed the world of oppression and the old base

[9] In her autobiography Mrs. Roosevelt describes how she asked the President if he believed in all that he himself had been taught, and he replied amazingly enough, "I really never thought about it. I think it is just as well *not to think about things like that too much!*" (Italics mine.)

doctrine that the strong must eat the weak because they are strong. . . . We are all of us children of earth—grant us that simple knowledge. If our brothers are oppressed, then we are oppressed. If they hunger, we hunger. If their freedom is taken away, our freedom is not secure. Grant us a common faith that man shall know bread and peace . . . an equal opportunity and an equal chance to do his best, not only in our own lands but throughout the world, and in that faith let us march toward the clean world our hands can make. Amen.

He had, it goes almost without saying, complete tolerance for men of all faiths provided they themselves were tolerant, and sometimes even if they weren't. He had a great number of close Jewish friends, like Felix Frankfurter, Samuel I. Rosenman, and Henry Morgenthau; and a great number of close Catholic friends, like Missy LeHand and Miss Tully, to say nothing of Thomas G. Corcoran, William D. Hassett, and the Irish-descended bosses, Farley, Hannegan, Flynn, Frank Walker, and many others. It is a little-known point that Roosevelt, an Episcopalian, actually assisted in the deathbed conversion of his dearly beloved friend, Pa Watson, to Catholicism. Watson, whose wife was Catholic, had for a long time wanted to join the Church; when he was dying en route home from Yalta, Roosevelt encouraged him to do so, and the ceremony was performed by a Catholic chaplain aboard the ship.

When Roosevelt voted in 1944 he accidentally locked himself in the voting booth at Hyde Park (after his familiar identification of himself to the electoral officials as a "tree grower") and was heard to utter a mild expletive. He called out to a friend, "The damn thing won't work," when the lever broke. As a matter of fact FDR seldom swore in any loud or gaseous manner. But the story got around that on this occasion he had said "goddamned thing"; he took the trouble to deny this indignantly. Never, he insisted, would he take the name of the Deity in vain. Americans are the most profane people on earth (next to Spaniards, Australians, and a few others), but FDR did not share this national trait.

Attitude to History and Fame

Roosevelt had a keen sense of history and his own place therein. He was not, however, at all vainglorious about it. He collected a complete newsreel history of himself, running to hundreds of thousands of feet of film, but he seldom had any of it shown. We will see presently what an astounding mass of personal material he assembled at Hyde Park; yet his actual will never mentions his private or public papers. Perhaps the best analysis would be to say that he had a passionate adhesive interest in history of any kind, and was therefore naturally interested in his own. He was always easily accessible to people who wanted to write about him, but he scoffed at the idea of an official biography while he was still alive. "Let's wait a hundred years," he would say cheerfully. He never read carefully any of the books about him that appeared in his lifetime, though he may have thumbed through one or two, making wisecracks about the authors if they were, or had been, friends.

A few weeks before his death I asked several members of his family what FDR was proudest of. One answer was that, in all his years as Governor and President, he had never once called up or used troops to deal with any civil disturbance. Another was that he had been able to arouse the United States (such a far cry from Wilson in 1919!) to the point of joining firmly an international organization to keep the peace. He was not at all sure that the new world league would work, but his hopes were high, and he was intensely proud of his role as educator, elucidator, and popularizer to this humane end.

What was his chief ambition? It lay precisely in this same field, to create the beginnings at least of a functioning world machinery to keep peace in perpetuity. I have heard it said that, if he had finished out the fourth term, he would have been the happiest man alive to take on some such job as that held now by Trygve Lie, Secretary General of the United Nations. Of course he had other ambitions too, and they provide still another sidelight to his copious character. He wanted (a) to be editor of a country newspaper, (b) to grow trees in Hyde Park,[10] and (c) to build a hurricane-proof hut on the Florida Keys where he could fish with Harry Hopkins.

Among Friends

One of FDR's most heart-warming qualities was his almost illimitable gift for friendship, which arose out of his idealism, his innate delight in life, and his generosity. His friends were of the widest possible variety, from formidable old crustaceans like Admiral King to courageous, incisive women like Anna Rosenberg to columnists like Walter Winchell.

[10] When he met King Ibn Saud of Arabia the first thing he said was, "I'm a tree farmer."

It is suggestive that two of his best friends for years were almost utterly unknown to the public at large, Lathrop Brown, his roommate at both Groton and Harvard and the best man at his wedding, and the New York attorney, Henry S. Hooker. Probably, in the whole course of his life, the person he was fondest of, outside his family, Missy LeHand and Hopkins, was Pa Watson. In some cases Roosevelt wore his friendships out; he exhausted his loves, and passed on to others. Yet consider the durability of his regard for a host of devoted men and women who stayed close to him for twenty years or more. The pages to follow will be studded thickly with the names of friends.

His friendships outrode any political criterion. Watson was a conservative; so was Admiral Leahy; he *liked* them just as much as he liked liberals. But even in the field of friendship he could calculate; one reason he was so fond of Watson was that Pa had no enemies whatever, and hence was doubly useful as an aide. The only time he ever asked Vice-President Garner a favor was when he said, "Jack, if anything should happen to me, I want you to take care of Pa Watson and make him Ambassador to Belgium."[11]

Roosevelt, with his God-given amiability and warmth, got on well with both Republicans and Democrats, Southern conservatives and Northern radicals, automobile tycoons and labor organizers, tough urban bosses out of political machines and spirited intellectuals out of universities, military folk and pacifists, old-school men of the world and young-school men of the streets. Thus arose the intricate structure of personal relationships he had to juggle; perpetually he had to smooth over jealousies, relax tensions, and unlace snarls among his followers. One Cabinet member would have catfits if he didn't do something, another if he did, and he would have to try to influence Mr. A through Mr. B through Mr. C. He once told Miss Perkins, "Stick with Hugh [Johnson]. Keep him sweet for me." He even kept up amicable contact with his enemies, so far as that was possible. During the most violent days of the New Deal a social worker could go to lunch at the White House and find himself cheek by jowl with a polo-playing millionaire.

The whole subject of FDR's personal relationships is so fascinating (to the present writer at least) that it might still have a further word. Some people close to him didn't actually "like" him. For instance a

11 *What Manner of Man?* by Noel F. Busch (New York, Harper & Brothers, 1944), p. 37.

Cabinet member told me once, "There are two groups around FDR—those who are fond of him but do not respect him, and those who respect him but are not fond."

But most were fond—even bedazzled—and that was all there was to it. Sometimes a close adviser would consider it to be his burning duty to keep FDR from doing something he felt to be ill-advised. "I *can't* let him make this mistake, no matter at what cost to myself," was a familiar attitude. It became accentuated when two rivals competed for his attention. One would moan, "But that other advice was wrong! *I've* got to tell him what is right!" Then the secretariat would have to try to straighten it out. He had, of course, the best possible relations with this secretariat; he controlled the "outer office" absolutely—an important source of power—and never became its creature, which fate has often been the ruin of lesser men.

The way Roosevelt chose people often left a good deal to be desired. Elmer Davis once said that his own theory on this was that FDR imitated the farmer with a batch of newborn puppies—he took them out for a row, dumped them overboard, and then kept those who managed to swim back to shore.

Leon Henderson is, so far as I know, the only man alive who ever called the President a son-of-a-blank to his face and got away with it. The occasion was a dispute during a fishing trip over the size of the catch—and as is notorious nothing is so likely to produce muscular language and spicy altercation as a group of close friends fishing.

A great many maxims and proverbs are untrue, like "No man is a hero to his own valet." Roosevelt, at least, was a hero to his. These are some of the things his man McDuffie said about him after his death: "He complained as little as any man I ever saw. When he was sick he didn't say a murmuring word. . . . He wasn't a man to be in a very serious mood over a thing that's gone under the bridge. . . . I know that the triumph of his whole life was that he could throw off anything." McDuffie even testifies that he did not take the attempt on his life in Miami seriously. "He believed what was to be would be." Once the President heard that McDuffie's wife, who also worked in the White House, said that she believed in reincarnation and wanted to be a canary bird. Mrs. McDuffie weighed about 190 pounds. FDR looked at her, began to laugh, and burst out with, "I love it. I love it. I love it."[12]

---

[12] From an Associated Press dispatch from Washington, June 7, 1945.

McDuffie's successor, Prettyman, offers this testimony: "He was just about the most cheerful man you ever met in your life. I guess maybe he figured that there was no sense making everybody else feel bad, just because he had so many headaches."

Another point in this general connection is the way Roosevelt, great himself, lifted so many of his friends to greatness. Nobody, except possibly Napoleon, has ever contributed so much to the fame of so many others. Napoleon created marshals; Roosevelt created men.

Howe and Hopkins

Of all the multitudinous friends Roosevelt had, the two most valuable were Louis Howe and Harry Hopkins. Both were frail men physically who had long periods of ill-health; both were sharp, honest as the day, and tenaciously loyal; both, a minor point, loved race tracks and the lighter things of life; both were jealous of others close to the throne; both gave up their whole lives to Roosevelt without thought of reward except the not inconsiderable reward which came from membership in the inner circle of power; both died exhausted by their labors in his service. But there were striking differences too. Howe was, one might say, interested *only* in FDR and making him President; he had little concern with the merits of issues, policy in the abstract, or affairs outside his own orbit; if FDR had come out for the Devil, it wouldn't have mattered to him much. But Hopkins had a deep, vital, unshakable *belief* in principles and issues. In the early days it was Howe who taught Roosevelt, and told him like a Dutch uncle how to do things; conversely it was Roosevelt who was the teacher, the mentor, so far as Hopkins was concerned. Roosevelt may have loved Hopkins more, but he paid more attention to Howe. I have heard one of FDR's sons say, "The most fascinating man in father's entire life was Howe." His only ambition was to be "manager" of the man whom he genuinely thought to be the greatest human being history had ever produced. All he wanted was to be secretary to the President; probably he is the only man in Roosevelt's whole career whose ambition, from first to last, remained so modest. Certainly Hopkins had deeper ambitions, not necessarily for himself, but for mankind as a whole. Hopkins was a broader human being, he had a more decisive grip and intellectual capacity, and he moved, after the war at least, on a much more imposing stage. He had more power than Howe ever had, and he loved power. Probably Howe said No to FDR more often.[13] Hopkins could say No but he seldom persisted in opposition or resistance to the President over a prolonged interval. Howe would stick his No out—even his neck. Hopkins would delay and conciliate and finally come along.

Hopkins operated almost like an equal, whereas Howe was always an underling, the assistant. Hopkins and Roosevelt became twins, as it were; they made a unity, a body with two heads; Howe was an extra pair of hands. Hopkins was the companion at the fireside, Howe the watchdog at the door.

Howe became close to Roosevelt earlier than Hopkins; he was eleven years his senior, whereas FDR was eight years older than Hopkins. Roosevelt first became conscious of Howe, who was then the Albany correspondent of the New York *Herald,* in 1912; he became his source for political background, then his adviser, then his friend, then the manager of his first campaigns. He lived with the Roosevelts for years, and had his own quarters in the White House. More than anybody except Mrs. Roosevelt, as we shall see, he was instrumental in getting FDR back to political life after the paralysis attack. Howe became an invalid after 1933, and died in 1936. During most of this period there was no day when Roosevelt did not pass by his room to see him, have a word, and cheer him up.

One of Howe's great usefulnesses was his unerring instinct for detecting men with axes to grind, chiselers; he had second sight about politicians who were promoting nothing but themselves. He loved to reminisce about FDR, particularly when he was ill, almost in the manner of an affectionate but critical old friend discussing the vagaries of a gifted youngster still with a lot to learn. "There Frank sits," Howe would mutter. "He sits there all day and spins out ideas. Don't take 'em too seriously. He's just punching you up. Maybe nine out of ten ideas aren't so hot, but that's a pretty good average for anybody who has to be President all the time he isn't thinking."

He was a gadfly, a hair shirt, implacable in his demand for blind unquestioning loyalty to FDR. Once he gave these instructions to a group of recruits helping in the 1932 campaign: "Remember this; you're nothing. Your face means nothing. Your name means nothing. . . . I don't want to catch you or anybody else trying to crowd into a photograph. . . . All you have to worry about, night and day, day and

[13] Former Vice-President Garner has written in *Collier's,* February 21, 1948, that Howe's last words to him, on his deathbed, were "Hold Franklin down!"

night, is this man Roosevelt, and get him to the White House no matter what."

Hopkins entered the scene much later. He came to FDR's attention largely through Mrs. Roosevelt. He was an extremely charming person, and Roosevelt, a charmer himself, liked charming people. He was an admirable, patient listener. FDR could talk to him as if nobody was in the room. He had great sensitiveness to the President's own moods, and FDR liked him for his habit of irony, his irreverence, and the way he could laugh and banter and give a humorous touch no matter how serious the situation. This is not to say that he was frivolous. Far from it. Churchill called him "Lord Root of the Matter"; his mind was stubborn and penetrating to an advanced degree. Also he knew everything; he was a bottomless well of news and gossip. He brought Roosevelt gaiety and scuttlebutt. Then too FDR liked him because he *did* things, and for the way he would say, "To hell with the cost, let's go ahead." Hopkins himself always divided people with whom he came into contact into talkers and doers; what he admired most in the President was FDR's own capacity to get things done. Once a distinguished editor asked the President what Hopkins' function was. FDR replied, "I can answer that with a single illustration. We've just had a cable from the British asking for 375,000 75mm. shells. The army said, 'Sorry, but we haven't got any.' I turned the thing over to Harry. He found 100,000 shells at Fort Bragg left there since 1919, and another 150,000 in Manila. Then he got five manufacturers to produce 10,000 more apiece."

Next to Felix Frankfurter, Hopkins brought more men into the Administration than any other person—Stettinius, David K. Niles, Robert E. Sherwood, Elmer Davis, Vannevar Bush, are examples. Probably too he was the main factor in persuading Roosevelt to make George Marshall Chief of Staff; he was certainly Marshall's best avenue to the White House, and also Stimson's. Then consider Hopkins' role as agent-in-chief for so many years between Roosevelt and Mr. Churchill. The British Prime Minister told an American friend after his first meeting with Hopkins, "I *love* that man!" Hopkins' role as intermediary for Roosevelt with the Russians is a more complex story. An American diplomat who admired him extravagantly in some respects said to me once, "The trouble was that Harry only knew two things about the Soviet Union. The first was that they had had a bad Czar in Russia named Ivan the Terrible. The second was that Russia was the first country to recognize the United States after 1776."

Roosevelt, by the magical power of his will, helped to keep the ailing Hopkins alive year after year. Like many men who recover from a disastrous illness, he himself thought that any illness could be conquered, and he was convinced that he, and he alone, could protect and thus save Hopkins. And indeed Hopkins, though critically ill during all the last years of his life, outlived him by a year.

Collector's Instinct

Roosevelt loved to collect things; he even "collected" birdcalls; he even wanted to keep the Army mess kit he used at Casablanca. The impulse to collect is a phenomenon known to everybody, but in FDR it was pronounced to an exceptional degree; the psychologists have all manner of explanations for this, one somewhat dire. By and large to be a collector means that a man has a strong acquisitive and competitive instinct, a lack of originality perhaps, a delight in the concrete, a healthy capacity for fun, and a subconscious tendency to revert to childhood.

Roosevelt's postage-stamp collection was a vivid reflection of his character. Both his father and mother collected stamps; indeed FDR's own collection was based largely on Chinese and Hong Kong issues his mother gave him when he was about ten. He remained avidly interested in philately for the rest of his life, and it would not be fanciful to say that his interest in foreign affairs—to say nothing of his erudition about matters geographical—derived to a considerable extent from stamps. The Roosevelt collection contained about 1,250,000 stamps in all; of these roughly a million had little value, but the others, bound in 150 or more albums with almost every page interlined with notes in his own hand, brought approximately $250,000 at a public sale in 1946. This figure may seem large, but there are at least a hundred stamp collections in the United States much more valuable; that of the King of England is supposed to be worth $6,000,000.[14]

During his whole Presidency there was scarcely a day when FDR did not spend at least a few minutes on his stamps. They were his favorite relaxation; in fact they came close to being what one writer has called

[14] See "The Great Philatelist," by Eugene Kinkaid, *New Yorker*, March 30, 1946, which is my source for most of the details in this section. The appraised value of the Roosevelt collection was only $80,000. But eager philatelists boosted prices way up because the stamps were the President's.

"occupational therapy." They took the load off, and gave him strength for the rigors of the day. Particularly just before he went to sleep he liked to have an uninterrupted period of total ease with the stamps, and when he traveled, even on the trips to Yalta and Teheran, several bulky volumes always went along.

Roosevelt was a true collector, and cared comparatively little for financial values; he just loved stamps. He shared the idiosyncrasy of many zealots in hoarding vast numbers that had little or no importance, and he hated to throw duplicates away. He got stamps from every possible source, and he knew at sight practically every important stamp in the world, but he seldom paid large sums for any single specimen; $10 was his limit, more or less. (Professional collectors have, of course, paid thousands of dollars for a single stamp.) When he became President the State Department and other government agencies sent him any unusual items arriving in the mails, and the first sheet of any new issue of American stamps was always presented to him; there were 225 of these during his Presidency. He suggested the subjects for many new stamps himself, argued about them with Farley or Frank Walker, inspected the drawings and proofs with scrupulous care, designed several himself, and changed the design of others. For instance he insisted on adding a mustache to the face of the businessman on the stamp commemorating the National Recovery Administration (he was afraid the portrait looked too much like himself), and took off the hat, which he thought was "stuffy."

Many foreign governments made him elaborate gifts of stamps, and toward the end of his life they took to issuing sets with his name and portrait; 23 countries honored him with 85 issues in all. Numerous American officials, particularly ambassadors, carefully watched for new issues abroad and dutifully sent them off to the White House, hopeful that Roosevelt would appreciate the favor. The most valuable items in the President's collection were engravers' die proofs of all American stamps issued since 1894; these brought $52,955. Roosevelt, though dead, was severely criticized by those who hate his memory for having included these in his estate, since they had been presented to him by the government. But there was nothing at all wrong in this; every president has been presented with stamps by the Bureau of Engraving and Printing, and they have always been considered his private property.

One item making the auction interesting was a miscellaneous assortment of envelopes addressed to Roosevelt that he had carefully preserved, called "Brickbats and Bouquets." The total lot only brought $525, however. Among the bouquets were communications with nothing on the envelope but "To the Greatest Man in the World" (it reached him all right), "God's Gift to the U.S.A.," and "My Friend, Washington, D. C." Among the brickbats were "Dishonorable Franklin Deficit Roosevelt," "F.D. Russianvelt, President of U.S.A., C.I.O.," "Benedict Arnold 2nd, Washington D. C.," "Rattlesnake Roosevelt," "Plutocrat F.D. Roosevelt, Owner of 4 Estates and Member of 13 Clubs," "President of the U.S.A., care of 327 Secretaries," and "Chief Shooter at the Moon, White Father of the Pretty Bubbles."

Ships, Sailing, and Other Joys

As basic as anything in FDR's temperament was his love for water. The first letter he ever wrote, at the age of five, is illustrated by an elaborate drawing of a sailboat; even as Governor of New York, he had a boat and prodded into all manner of out-of-the-way spots by canal. He learned how to sail as a child (one of his instructors was the father of Cass Canfield, the publisher), and he had his own 21-foot knockabout when he was fourteen. At sixteen, when he was a student at Groton, he sailed a yawl alone all the way from New York to Eastport, Maine, no small feat; when he was at Harvard his father got him the *Half Moon*, a 40-footer, and this in turn gave way to the *Half Moon II*, an 18-ton auxiliary cruiser originally named the *Brynlys*. Steadily his knowledge of seamanship increased. He loved sailing, not merely for what relaxation it might bring, but as a strenuous and exciting sport; nothing pleased him more than dirty weather, or to try to outguess a fog in rough water. He helped in the navigation of the *George Washington* when it was returning to the United States in 1919, as it entered Newfoundland waters which he knew like a book, and he once brought a destroyer safely through the treacherous narrows between Lubec, Maine, and Campobello Island. He liked to get off Vincent Astor's big yacht, the *Nourmahal,* and scoot around in the small speedboat that it carried. Any kind of boat aroused him, and he loved the challenge of the sea.

As President he had the use of the *Potomac,* which was often described inaccurately as a "yacht." Actually it was a former Coast Guard patrol boat named the *Electra,* refitted modestly for the President's use.

It could only make 16 knots, and a much faster ship usually accompanied it, carrying the Secret Service men and staff.

FDR's love for ships pervades large areas of his character; for one thing seamanship taught him tactics. A sculptress of unusual discernment, when asked to portray him, suggested that she should make a statue of his hands on a wheel, because they seemed to tell so much of his nature—one hand firm, the other flexible almost like that of a violinist. All manner of further relevant detail may be cited. He liked naming new ships in the Navy, and always chose the names with great care. He liked the Naval Hospital at Bethesda, Maryland. He was always fond of admirals, like McCrea, Callaghan, and a host of others; he chose one ambassador to an important post almost entirely because he was an admiral. He urged appropriations for a bigger Navy from the moment he became President. He loved naval gadgets, and called the Navy "we." Naval records and diaries were his favorite reading matter, and when he went to Casablanca he insisted on crossing the Atlantic in a Clipper, a seaplane, though a land plane would probably have been safer.

In the summer of 1943 he took a hush-hush holiday in the Great Lakes region; this is an episode little known. Tired out, he thought that the only thing to refresh him would be a touch of water. But the Navy and Secret Service would not let him cruise off the Atlantic shore or even in the Caribbean area, for fear of German submarines. He cast about for a place to go, and at the suggestion of several friends chose an almost totally inaccessible spot on Lake Huron near Georgian Bay. Here he spent some days loafing, sunning himself, and sailing. Extraordinary precautions were taken to ensure the secrecy of this particular vacation—his special train stood by for a week—and a special small dock was built where a friend's boat waited. His absence from Washington at this time, brief as it was, gave rise to a fancy flood of rumors, one of which was that he was meeting Stalin.

Many years before, when Roosevelt was Assistant Secretary of the Navy, he met Dudley W. Knox, in charge of the office of naval records. Knox did a job for him having to do with old naval prints, on which FDR was a real expert. He knew the value of most prints to the dime. A few weeks after the first inaugural he called Knox in. They had not met for seven years. Roosevelt picked up the conversation at the exact point where it had broken off and then (a familiar trait) spent an hour cross-examining Knox on the work of his office. Out of this grew a project to prepare and publish a series of documentary volumes covering American naval operations at the time of the Barbary Wars and later. Knox went to work. The budget officer of the Navy complained. Roosevelt intervened with an order, "Give Dudley Knox all he asks for!" Finally the work was done, and FDR signed his name in the first volume, "For Dudley Knox—in appreciation of a dream of yours and mine come true."

In 1938 Roosevelt took a 5,888-mile cruise on the *Houston* from San Diego to Pensacola with the main object of collecting marine specimens. Ports of call included the Galapagos Islands, the Cocos Islands, Clipperton Island (a French possession), and Old Providence Island off the coast of Colombia. The ichthyological collection resulting from this cruise was of first-class scientific importance, according to Dr. Schmitt, the curator of marine invertebrates at the Smithsonian Museum. Some thirty new species, subspecies, and varieties were discovered, some by FDR himself. Half a dozen were named for him, like *Thalamita Roosevelti*, a crablike creature; *Eulaelaps Roosevelti*, a parasitic mite; *Neanthes Roosevelti*, a kind of annelid; and five different new molluscs and sponges. Also a new type of royal palm seen in the Cocos Islands was named *Rooseveltia Frankliniana*.

Roosevelt loved to fish, but he was the kind of fisherman who didn't care much what he caught.[15] To be invited to accompany him on a fishing trip was a substantial proof of his regard. He was always proud of having caught near-record specimens of two kinds of fish, the rainbow runner and blue crevally.

FDR seldom went to plays, because his physical affliction made entrance into a theater difficult. He liked movies, but not violently; his interest would be apt to lag halfway through a picture. His favorite stars were Myrna Loy and Walter Huston. He liked baseball if it was a lively game full of slugging; a pitcher's duel bored him. Cards interested him, particularly an almost viciously difficult type of solitaire, and he was a bold and expert poker player. He called himself "Pa" in the score sheets, always wanted to be banker, and loved games like seven-card stud with one-eyed face cards wild. He stowed away his chips in various pockets, so that he would always have a "reserve." He seldom played for high stakes, and a White House game in which any-

---

[15] He told a press conference once (Rosenman, Vol. VI, p. 197) that he took cruises mainly to get perspective on the scene in Washington. "I don't give a continental damn whether I catch a fish or not."

body won or lost more than $100 was unusual. But Roosevelt hated to lose at any game. He was definitely a bad loser.

Finally in this general sphere we should mention Fala, or, to give this celebrated Scottie his full name, Murray the Outlaw of Fala Hill. Roosevelt knew a lot about dogs, and had a fine knack with them, as he had with children. His favorite interlude in the day was the half hour at cocktail time, when he would feed Fala tidbits. Fala (he is still alive as of the moment of writing) became a nuisance on occasion if only because, no matter what precautions the Secret Service took when FDR traveled, the presence of the dog would become known and give away the fact that his master was in the neighborhood. Fala was very useful to Roosevelt; at least he was the occasion for as effective a passage in a speech as any he ever wrote. Probably, though not for this reason, the President loved him as much as he ever loved any but a handful of human beings.

No Lucullus at the Festive Board

Roosevelt once said that he had "a digestion like ten oxen" and he knew how to cook (at least when he was a very young man); but as he grew older he did not care much about refinements in food. Mostly he liked a few fairly simple, nourishing, standard dishes, and he seldom overate; he was neither a glutton nor a gourmet, if only because he could not afford the time. Few really busy men are ever gourmets. He did, however, love game, and he wanted it rare to the point of being bloody; his theory was that a duck, for instance, should be cooked "by chasing it under the fire." Then too he was fond of out-of-the-way country cheeses; in the early days Vincent Astor used to please him by sending him unusual varieties. One strange thing he liked was fish baked in mud; he once told a press conference just how to prepare it. At Quebec with Mr. Churchill, he talked about the "excellent eating qualities of the Quebec trout." To the end of his life he yearned intermittently for a few special dishes, but for some reason or other he seldom got them—oyster crabs with whitebait was one of these, and so was peach cobbler made out of biscuits with thick fresh cream. "I just don't see why I can't have some oyster crabs!" he would mutter.

The White House cuisine was, to put it mildly, undistinguished. Mrs. Roosevelt had little interest in food as such, though Henrietta Nesbitt, the housekeeper, has printed in her fascinating *White House Diary* a long memorandum by her called "Foods for the President." Among the dishes Mrs. Roosevelt recommended were "roast beef pink juice running," "pork loin or crown only once in a great while, veal legs the same," and "all kinds of cold cereals—Wheatena served hot." Other items are, "Use condiments very little," "Sanka coffee at night," and "the President does not care for either cocoanut or anise flavoring."[16]

Guests who stayed in the White House for long periods have told me that they could predict by the days of the week what they would have for lunch or dinner. The monotonous routine was like that of a boardinghouse—tongue with caper sauce on Mondays, boiled beef without any sauce at all on Tuesday, and so on. Lest this be thought the fault of the domestic staff on Pennsylvania Avenue it should be added that the kitchen at Shangri-La, which was the President's own responsibility, was even less distinctive. The food there was in charge of the Filipino mess boys from the *Potomac*. One lady told me once that on three consecutive evenings the dessert at dinner was the same —a slice of pineapple decorated with two cherries and a walnut, in a puddle of weak whipped cream.

Roosevelt loved to carve. He was one of the most accomplished carvers of his time. Perhaps this was, in a way, compensation for the loss of his legs; he always liked to do things skillfully with his hands. His touch was almost excessively precise and delicate. He could serve dexterously fifteen to eighteen people from one side of a large turkey— the slices were thin as paper—and in smaller birds he would manage to scoop out tiny fragments of meat from underneath the smallest bones. One of his idiosyncrasies was the way he ate corn at Hyde Park. Before him would be the ear of corn, a razor-sharp grouse knife, and two bowls, one containing melted butter, the other warm milk; like as not he would mention to the company the name of the very cow the milk came from, and then explain that his mother had taught him to eat corn this way. First he would cut down each line of kernels precisely in the middle, and scrape them into the bowl of butter; then he pared off what bits of corn remained on the ear and dropped them into the milk; finally he would mix the two bowls into a mash.

As a rule Roosevelt sought to conserve himself at the dinner hour; he disliked elaborate parties, and much preferred to dine alone with some close friend or member of his family, like Anna Boettiger. He

[16] Occasionally FDR would send irascible orders to Mrs. Nesbitt himself, like "No more sweetbreads till October first!"

almost never asked anybody to dinner; that was the function of Mrs. Roosevelt, Anna, or Missy LeHand in the early days. When guests assembled Mrs. Roosevelt was apt to say (particularly at Hyde Park), "I think we should go in to dinner now. The President may be late, but it doesn't matter if we have to wait two or three minutes. After all he *is* the President." Then when the guests were seated he would roll in on his wheel chair. But at formal dinners at the White House FDR was usually seated at the table first, before the guests came in. They would assemble elsewhere and greet him when they entered. After dinner they would leave when he put his napkin down; he would then be wheeled out, and rejoin them in another room later. After his illness, he practically never dined out. It was a mark of the most extreme favor for him to go to somebody else's house. But he liked to dine with Harold Ickes occasionally, and he spent the D-Day week end in 1944 with Pa Watson.

Robert E. Sherwood and Archibald MacLeish were working on a speech with FDR one evening. Sherwood had been asked to dinner at the MacLeishes but begged to be excused. MacLeish went home alone, and then came back to the White House. At about eleven P.M. there came a lull in the work and MacLeish said to Sherwood, "Well, you missed some wonderful fried chicken." Sherwood replied, "If there is anything I like better than hot fried chicken it is cold fried chicken." Roosevelt, at his desk, put in emphatically, "So do I!" and suggested forthwith that he send a White House car to the MacLeish home to fetch whatever chicken remained. Mrs. MacLeish, dumfounded, went to the icebox when the chauffeur arrived and found, to her horror, that nothing remained of the chicken except half a wing and one leg. Not enough for three hungry men still at work! The car returned empty. The next day Sam Rosenman, hearing the story, sent her a telegram, "Can I put you in touch with some poultry dealers?" Then the President ripped an advertisement from a newspaper, extolling the virtues of bigger refrigerators and frozen foods, and sent it to her with a note making pointed jokes about her depleted larder.

The President liked to drink, but seldom drank much. There were never any drinks on the picnics, and even on a fishing trip or cruise, when most men let down, he never drank anything at all during the day, and nothing after dinner. During Prohibition when he was Governor of New York no liquor was ever served in the

Executive Mansion. At the White House, as a rule, drinking was concentrated in the twenty minutes or so of cocktail time, which was FDR's best opportunity for social relaxation. Generally he had two cocktails, not more. They were fairly stiff. One legend is that two kinds of gin were stocked, one for favored guests, one for those less favored. A good many people will testify to the fact that the Martinis, at least, made of Argentine vermouth and a substandard gin, were pretty terrible. The President went in occasionally for exotic drinks, like Danziger *goldwasser* and Demerara rum, and he liked some strange mixtures, like gin plus benedictine.

Roosevelt Luck

People often talk about how "lucky" Roosevelt was, as if he were perpetually favored by a friendly star; actually he seemed lucky mostly because of his acute sense of timing and the way he could foresee eventualities; he made his own luck, like most lucky people. Nevertheless the fact that he was *thought* to be so lucky played a considerable role in his political fortunes; a great many people voted for him, particularly in 1932, because they felt that he was an extremely lucky man in contrast to Mr. Hoover, who was unlucky. One point is that, throughout most of his career, FDR did have wonderful luck with weather—so much so that the phrase "Roosevelt weather" became a cliché. Once, when he was touring the Dust Bowl, he was saluted as "Roosevelt the Rainmaker," because after months of drought the rains started to pelt down when he arrived.

Like most people with good luck, FDR was moderately—not excessively—superstitious. He hated Friday the 13th, he would never start an important trip on a Friday if he could help it, and he disliked sitting down with 13 at dinner.

Some Trivial Items Not Necessarily Trivial

What did Roosevelt like most? Going on a trip, building things, charts, trees, archives (as contrasted to mere records), politicians of every sort (even bad politicians), pre-Revolutionary Dutch architecture, gadgets, a challenge, the principle of first things first, islands, donkeys, seersucker bedcovers, the word "pipelines," the statue of Puck in front of the Folger Library, and the future.

Dislike most? Air conditioning, mollycoddles, gloves, big words when small ones did just as well, to be hurried, the term "bureaucrat," and all enemies of progress.

Chapter 6

THE HOME, LIBRARY, AND COLLECTIONS

I confess that I am of an impatient disposition.
—FRANKLIN DELANO ROOSEVELT

Anybody curious about the way Roosevelt lived can satisfy the curiosity easily, because the family house is open to the public, just as Monticello and Mount Vernon are, with little changed. FDR didn't quite know what to do with Hyde Park after his mother's death in 1941. He wanted to keep it in the family; but he was fully aware of what inheritance taxes would do to the property, and how expensive it would be for his sons to maintain. There was also the question of who would live in it, and Mrs. Roosevelt didn't want to. For a time FDR flirted with the idea of making the estate a corporation. Finally he decided to give part of it to the nation, with the proviso that, after his death, his widow and children should have the right to live there during their lifetimes. No other president except Roosevelt has ever bequeathed his home to the nation. Congress duly accepted the gift, which included 33.23 acres of property; then after the President died Mrs. Roosevelt and the children waived their interests, and the nation took full title to the area. The formal opening of the home took place on April 12, 1946, the first anniversary of FDR's death. It is administered today by the National Park Service, under the Department of the Interior, as a national historic site, and it draws visitors in great number from all over the country. Since April, 1946, well over a million sightseers have gone through the house, and many more have seen the grave; on a single day as many as 11,000 people have visited the grounds. Thousands more have had to be turned away, because only about 70 people can enter the house at a time; there is only one staircase, and the old timbers won't take more.

We shall describe in Chapter 9 the way the Roosevelt family acquired this property, and tell something of its history. The house lies on a green rise about half a mile from the Hudson; the old families almost always built some distance away from the actual river, in order to avoid the New York Central railway tracks.[1] The atmosphere, even so, is somewhat dank. Shallow steps and a broad porch, under a colonnaded portico, lead into the front hall. At once you see an almost bewildering collection of Rooseveltiana—naval prints, ancient knick-nacks and mementos, family portraits, trifles, and even a large case containing the birds FDR collected and stuffed as a boy. This display of dusty ornithological specimens has stood there for something like fifty years. None of the Roosevelts ever threw anything away. When, after Franklin's death, Eleanor went through the house, she found bolts of China cloth and bits of string and ribbon tucked away in the attic by the elder Mrs. Roosevelt that had been there half a century or more.

Few Roosevelts had much aesthetic interest, and the house is pretty much of a horror from an artistic point of view. In the entrance hall is a statue of FDR by Prince Paul Troubetzkoy made in 1911; it is of a man sitting down, but without legs. The story has been told that the sculptor, while at work, said that Roosevelt's torso was so magnificent that he would leave the legs out, which is interesting enough in view of FDR's subsequent affliction. Portraits of FDR's mother and father dominate another passage; that of the mother is well worth studying for its portrayal of a woman surpassingly beautiful and imperious. The expression on her husband's face is vaguely supercilious; old Mrs. Roosevelt accounted for this by saying that the artist had caught her husband in the act "of looking down on the Oyster Bay Roosevelts." The south wing of the ground floor is a large, cheerful living room, hung with bright flowered curtains and packed with plants, lamps, books, and pictures; one fireplace is comfortably flanked by the two high-backed leather chairs Roosevelt used as Governor of New York State, one for each term; above is a Gilbert Stuart portrait of an ancestor. Also on the ground floor is a small room, hardly bigger than an anteroom, which in 1932 was transformed into FDR's office; it became world-famous as the "Summer

---

[1] But an old spur line leads to a siding directly on the property; it was used in former days for deliveries of coal and so on. FDR seldom used it; he preferred to leave the train further down, and arrive by automobile. But occasionally the siding was called into action when guests like Queen Wilhelmina came to Hyde Park. See Olin Dows, *Franklin Roosevelt at Hyde Park* (New York, American Artists Group, Inc., 1939), p. 130. This book, charmingly illustrated by the author, is full of fascinating material about Roosevelt and the neighborhood.

White House." Here Roosevelt liked to broadcast the last speech of each campaign.

Like his mother, FDR hated to change the old order of things. The face of the nation he could transform; but not his house. After his illness he could not, of course, climb stairs, but he refused to permit the installation of what would have been an obvious convenience, an elevator to connect the living room with his bedroom directly above. He said that it would spoil the architecture. So he used an old fashioned hand-drawn elevator, which looks like a big dumb-waiter and behaves like one, in the hall leading to the servants' quarters. In this, two or three times a day, he would haul himself up or down, and it is still the only elevator in the place. A ramp was, however, built along the stairs, with a handrail above. The rail was for the President's mother, who suffered from arthritis in her later years and who found it more difficult to walk on the ramp than on the steps.

On the second floor the interest tightens. One room is, of course, that in which FDR was born, with its heavy walnut bed and armoire. Then comes his boyhood bedroom, still hung with pennants and trophies he collected in his schooldays; a placard marked "Harvard Crimson" hangs above the door. The old-fashioned brass bed is narrow; the schoolboy desk is small. By tradition, as FDR himself raised a family, this room always went to the eldest of his sons in residence at the time; if no sons were at Hyde Park, the eldest grandson used it. On the other side of the long corridor are guest rooms; here the King and Queen of England slept, sharing a bathroom between two bedrooms. The three main bedrooms are in the south wing, side by side. Sara Roosevelt had one. Eleanor the second, and FDR the third. The mother's room is large and heavily furnished; Eleanor's, sandwiched in between, is small and sparse, with the simplest furniture and hangings.

The President's bedroom, in the southwest corner, looks out on a magnificent bland view of the Hudson. The room is more or less as he left it: here are his quilted bathrobe, thrown across the bed; a pair of scuffed bedroom slippers, with the socks tucked inside; and the navy blanket on which Fala slept. The telephone was a direct line to the White House. There are several snapshots on the walls; one is casually speared onto the molding with a hatpin. The only picture of FDR himself shows him, curiously enough, with Al Smith; others are of

Eleanor in Paris and of Woodrow Wilson. On a bed table are a couple of yellow pencils, a tube of dental floss, and a half-used box of Red Top matches. Near the window are some books and magazines—copies of *Time, Collier's, McCall's,* a volume of anonymous political reminiscence called *Not To Be Repeated,* a life of Mussolini, a report on the St. Lawrence river, and two or three detective stories. (On Eleanor's bedside table in the next room is a Marquand novel.) On one wall is the flag Admiral Byrd carried on his Antarctic expedition, with a framed letter starting out "My Dear Franklin," and nearby is the narrow armless wheelchair.

The President didn't like closets, preferring old-fashioned armoires. Most of the closets were, in fact, torn out to make room for bathrooms, of which there are five on this floor. But one closet, adjoining the bedroom, is still there, and is still hung with FDR's clothes—his naval cape (which was so much easier for him to put on than an overcoat), a sweater, two ancient tweed jackets, two summer suits, and the battered fedora hat he wore—for luck—in all four presidential campaigns. FDR cared little about clothes. His favorite color was blue. Once he "invented" a costume that served him for both day and evening wear—a double-breasted dark suit which he wore with a black bow tie—so that he would not have to change into a dinner jacket at night.

Library and What It Holds

The Franklin D. Roosevelt Library is a low stone Dutch colonial structure a few hundred yards northeast of the house, designed by the President himself. It is administered not by the Park Service but by the National Archives, and it contains Roosevelt's papers, the whole immense documentary record of his life; the bulk of this is, as we shall see, almost unimaginably staggering. Years ago FDR began to work on the problem of what to do with his public papers; he decided to leave them to the nation, and the library and its museum are the profuse result. None of this cost the government anything. FDR's mother donated the land, 16 acres, and money for the building was raised by voluntary public subscription; some 28,000 donors contributed roughly $400,000. Congress voted by joint resolution to establish the library as a Federal agency, Roosevelt laid the cornerstone on November 19, 1939, and the institution has been functioning ever since. The government pays part of the upkeep; the rest comes from admission fees. Something over 500,000 visitors a year pay 25 cents each to get in, and they certainly get their money's worth.

This whole procedure, the donation of a president's papers to the public at large, is unprecedented, and it brought up peculiar problems. The library, like the house, is a unique institution; no other president ever left the whole record of his life to the Federal Government. From the beginning of our history, it has been considered that a president's papers are his own personal property, for him to deal with as he sees fit; some presidents took their records home, some destroyed them; the documents of most are widely scattered, so that scholars have to work for years assembling them. All Americans know how, even today, new Lincoln material crops up year by year, and how much in the lives of several presidents is still mysterious or lost. Roosevelt wanted to avoid all this. Moreover, it seems, he wanted the historians to go to work on him at once; never before have a president's papers been available for research so soon after his death. But it is unlikely that he realized quite what an arduous task he was leaving to posterity, however much he wanted to simplify it. As soon as the library was built he began sending it material. But hundreds of crates of documents have not even been unpacked as yet; at least fifty *tons* of papers are not yet opened.

In 1943 Roosevelt appointed a committee of three persons, Judge Rosenman, Grace Tully, and Harry Hopkins, to the job of reviewing the sum total of all his papers, with the view of seeing what records were strictly personal and should go to the family, what should be made available for research at once, and what should become public in years to come. This memorandum includes the proviso that a few of his altogether personal letters to certain eminent personages, like the Pope and King George of England, should never be made public at all. Meantime the Rosenman-Tully-Hopkins triumvirate had difficulties. Hopkins died, and even preliminary screening would have taken Miss Tully and the Judge several hard uninterrupted years of toil. So the job devolved on the National Archives, and detailed operations began in 1949. All the papers, be it remembered, are the property of the nation. The work of winnowing was ticklish; Roosevelt is still a hot subject. Most of the letters and memoranda, reports of press conferences and the like, are innocent enough, and are to be made public in 1950. Yet everything had to be screened rigorously for obvious reasons. The library took the decision to exclude from public availability, for the time being, any material to or from Roosevelt in the following categories: (a) comments on the character of individuals tending to cause personal embarrassment and anything bearing unpleasantly on anybody's family life; (b) confidential material prepared by investigators of people seeking jobs; (c) material derogatory to security and national defense; (d) material prejudicial to friendly relations with foreign governments. The line is, of course, hard to draw. Suppose Roosevelt, in an off-the-cuff remark or memorandum, should have said, "I think Mr. Blank is far too weak for this job," or even, "The French are a frightfully stingy race." Should such material be excluded? Suppose he is on record as having said something fairly unpleasant about a politician now in the public eye. Which is the more important to history—the President's contemporary estimate or the sensitiveness of the politician? Anyway, the library decides. Something like 15 per cent of the total material is being withheld as of the moment; eventually everything will be made available.

One substantial group of documents, from the White House Map Room, has never reached the library at all, having been held back at President Truman's personal request; it includes most of Roosevelt's interchanges with governments on military and political matters during the war. Mr. Truman took the decision not to release this material, not only on security grounds, but because much of it bears directly on problems still current, and the files have to be on hand for reference.

The Roosevelt family has nothing whatever to do with the library, except that, like anybody else properly qualified, its members may do research there. The library officials, and very courteous and competent they are under the direction of Herman Kahn, are servants of the Federal Government, and maintain a strictly detached and neutral view on any controversial material that turns up. They are not partisans, but custodians.

The range of material is enormous beyond belief, but there are still some gaps. One reason why the bulk is so great is that the Presidency itself changed so dramatically under Roosevelt; the White House ceased to be merely the residence of the Chief Executive, and became a massive department of the Government itself, with its own files and administrative records. As to gaps, FDR did a large amount of business by scribbling a word or two on a letter or memorandum submitted to him and then sending the letter back, and he wrote out thousands of quick longhand chits. It has been difficult to recover these, because no carbons were kept at the White House and the originals lie buried in the files of the departments concerned. Another problem has to do with the hundreds of thousands of letters *to* Roosevelt in the library; the writer of a letter holds the copyright, and would have to give permission if a historian wanted to use it; this tends to inhibit a comprehensive publication program. Incidentally the term "memorial" is never used in connection with the library: FDR himself hated this word, and the purpose of the institution is not to "memorialize," but to be a research center.

Indeed a good many students and professors are in attendance, and all manner of work is going on. Judge Rosenman recently completed the last four volumes of FDR's public papers and addresses, and Elliott Roosevelt and a team of researchers are preparing a final volume of personal letters. Arthur Schlesinger, Jr., made the library his temporary headquarters for his forthcoming *Age of Roosevelt,* and a number of graduate students from Harvard, Princeton, Vassar, Ohio State, and other universities are at work on various theses; among the subjects are Roosevelt as State Senator, FDR as Governor, the vice-presidential campaign of 1920, the psychology of the Fireside Chat, Roosevelt and the Navy, and FDR versus Tammany. Other historians are working on material associated with FDR indirectly, since his papers will presumably throw light on all manner of other topics, from the Dust Bowl to the Red Cross. Finally, the 840-volume diary of Henry Morgenthau, Jr., is in the library, and other friends and associates of FDR are being encouraged to concentrate their papers in this one spot.

Looking Around, Inch by Inch

I went into the library. I was appalled. I was stupefied. Here are 16,000 books, 34,000 pamphlets, 15,000 photographs, 275,000 feet of movie film (FDR appeared in about 30 newsreels every year), 300 sound recordings, 14,000 file containers and speech cases, 12,000 museum objects, and 4,500 rolls of microfilm. Not less than 4,400 cubic feet of papers have been processed so far, which is the equivalent of 1,200 three-drawer filing cabinets. The correspondence marked "Personal File" alone is subdivided into 9,000 different folios; no fewer than 14,000 "sections" comprise the "White House" file. One major classification is of American naval items—letters, logbooks, prints, manuscripts—and another is of material on New York State.

FDR was a member of the Dutchess County Historical Association for 31 years. The total number of individual items in all categories is supposed to be about fifty *million*.

Roosevelt took, of course, an eager interest in the library; he maintained an office there and spent hours cataloguing and classifying the material as it began to arrive, studying and checking this or that. Aisles in the stacks were broad to provide easy access for his wheel chair. One point of considerable political interest is that FDR laid out the building on the presumption that he would only serve two terms; it bulges at the seams today, largely because nobody thought that there would have to be room for more than eight years of White House papers.

Signal logs from German cruisers in World War I; check stubs of various banks dating back many years; family account books going back to 1852; a red-bound series of diaries written by Rebecca Howland Roosevelt, his father's first wife; a six-page longhand letter from Churchill to Bonar Law, without a word crossed out or altered; a card index of 75,000 White House guests; dog-eared copies of ancient magazines; Louis Howe's old bank statements; a set of ten new dollar bills with Henry Morgenthau's autograph—there are hundreds of such items. Roosevelt's zeal for collecting became, at times, plain silly. For instance several drawers hold a selection of the Christmas cards he got each year, and others hold an immense accumulation of birthday greetings. Six or seven large boxes are required for one totally minor classification—"Postcard Protests, 1940-41, Against Convoys." One collection is of "Lithographs Typical of the 1880 Period," and they are horrors. The White House staff clipped about twelve newspapers daily, and every Roosevelt item was preserved; this meant that, in many cases, whole pages of each paper had to be pasted up, day after day, week after week, year after year; these scrapbooks, covering three months each, are eight inches thick and a yard square, and they fill a whole bank of special cases. Another set of scrapbooks is just for cartoons.

FDR had a positive mania for writing his name in books, like a schoolboy. I even came across several books of my own, which I had inscribed to him; doggedly scrawled over my handwriting was his own signature, "F. D. Roosevelt." As if anybody would not know what books belonged to him! Even the most casual and frivolous pamphlets are signed. He was rather chary of giving autographs, and he knew accurately what they were worth; but he certainly must have signed his name in four or five thousand books. I picked up what seemed to be a copy of one of his own early volumes, *On Our Way;* it was blank, a dummy. And duly written on the flyleaf, in the President's own hand, are the words, "This is the dummy of the book." Next to it is an actual copy, and I found the words, "This is one of the first copies off the press. See errors. FDR."

Later I spent an hour or two listening to recorded sound tracks of people who knew Roosevelt well. George Palmer of the Park Service, the superintendent of the house, had the fruitful idea of getting dozens of Hyde Park neighbors, family friends, and particularly servants to record for posterity their recollections of the President. About fourteen hours of material have been put on wire so far, and the work goes forward steadily. I heard the reminiscences of Moses Smith, a local farmer who was one of FDR's best Hyde Park friends; of William A. Plog, who joined the Roosevelt staff back in 1898 and who is now eighty; and of Robert McGaughey, whom Sara Roosevelt hired many years ago, and who was FDR's houseman from the time he became ill.[2]

One wing of the library is the museum, which is a wonderful hodgepodge indeed. FDR worked on it himself even to such details as deciding what pictures should go on what wall. It does not, to put it mildly, follow modern ideas in museum technique, which holds that exhibits should be arranged to tell a consecutive, documented story. Roosevelt conceived it in a much more old-fashioned pattern; he wanted it to be a place where people could roam around freely, without too much printed tutelage, and enjoy themselves. The displays are constantly rotated, since space exists only for about one tenth the material available; the rest is stored upstairs. Distinguished visitors sometimes arrive and vex the directors by demanding to know why something they gave the President is not on show.

Here are some things I saw:

The cradle FDR used as an infant, his baby shoes, and the garment in which he was christened; also Mrs. Roosevelt's christening dress, which was sent out to California last year to be worn at the christening of her newest granddaughter.

---

[2] Most of the code names Roosevelt picked for distinguished personages during the war were suggested by Hyde Park people. General Marshall became "Plog" and Churchill was "Moses Smith." Sir Stafford Cripps was "Mrs. Johansen," who ran a gas station near the Roosevelt property. See Sherwood, p. 606 and Dows, p. 177.

A gold watch and case used by Jacobus Roosevelt, one of his ancient forebears.

Two bejeweled swords given him by King Ibn Saud of Arabia; one is said to be worth $100,000.

A four-foot fountain pen, a gift from one of his inveterate opponents, Senator "Pappy" O'Daniel of Texas.

Cuff links, watches, trinkets, medallions, cigarette boxes, medals, and similar mementos by the hundred; also gold membership cards in a dozen organizations, and a gold pass to the circus.

A 200-year-old manuscript Torah, rescued from a burning synagogue in Czechoslovakia during the Nazi occupation, presented by the National Council of Young Israel.

A cigar humidor as big as a trunk, from ex-President Batista of Cuba.

Thirty-two different academic hoods.

An aquamarine as big as a small cake of soap (it measures five inches by three and a half, and weighs 3,500 carats) from Brazil; and a musical score from El Salvador.

His favorite ship model, the USS *Constitution*. (He rerigged it himself.)

One of the bullets fired at him at Miami.

His birth and baptismal certificates, some of his schoolboy themes, pictures of himself (with goatee) as an actor at Groton, and his Harvard textbooks.

A buffalo coat from an animal shot by his father.

A *halat* (robe) of blue and gold, from the government of the Uzbek Soviet Socialist Republic, brought back by Henry Wallace.

But this is by no means all. Downstairs is a collection of what might be called heavy equipment—a 48-foot iceboat that belonged to his uncle, a huge model of the movable ports used in the Normandy invasion, a sleigh given by Napoleon III to Alexander II of Russia (bought by his father in Paris for $15), an early nineteenth-century carriage owned by the Suckley family of Rhinebeck, his father's bicycle, and his own famous blue Ford with license plate *New York 3,* equipped with hand brake and clutch so that he could drive it himself. Next door in the basement is what FDR called the Chamber of Horrors, but which is now known by the more sedate term Oddities Room. Here repose all manner of outlandish souvenirs and freakish gifts, like a portrait made of postage stamps, a huge papier-mâché mask of the Sphinx in his image, the United States Constitution written on a post card, oversize keys, an elephant's tail, airplane models, and a totem pole.

The President's own room. his office in the library, is of moderate size, and is maintained exactly as when he last used it, on March 28, 1945, even to a crumpled pack of Camels on the desk. In the bookshelf are a line of juveniles he read as a child, together with some early texts; on the floor is a carpet given him by the Shah of Iran. The last thing the President brought into the room is a standard bearing the flags of the four chief United Nations (as of that era), the United States, the Soviet Union, China, and Great Britain. On one mantelpiece is the silver baby cup given him by his grandfather Warren Delano in 1882 (again and again we see the emphasis on childhood), and a cup he won at golf before illness struck him; surrounding the fireplace are old Dutch tiles on marine subjects which he himself searched out. The books he had been assorting include a large volume of Cook's voyages, a twenty-volume edition of the Book of Knowledge (bound in 7,000 different pieces of leather), a bird guide, a volume of H. G. Wells, and several books on Wilson. In the case is a sumptuous set of first editions of Winston Churchill, presented to FDR by the author, bound in red leather and adorned with the Roosevelt crest. The inscription in the last volume is "A fresh egg from the faithful hen, Quebec, 1944."

The Grave

Between the house and library is the grave, set in a rose garden with a border of myrtle, behind a hundred-foot old hemlock hedge. FDR wrote a memorandum in 1937 setting forth his wish about the tombstone, and his instructions were followed to the letter:

A plain white monument—no carving or decoration—to be placed over my grave, east and west, as follows: Length, 8 feet; width, 4 feet; height, 3 feet. Whole to be set on marble base extending 2 feet out from monument all around—but said base to be no more than 6 inches from the ground.

I hope that my dear wife will on her death be buried there also and that the monument contain no device or inscription except the following on the south side:

FRANKLIN DELANO ROOSEVELT
1882–19—
ANNA ELEANOR ROOSEVELT
1884–19—

Thousands have been moved visiting this grave; FDR's friend Archibald MacLeish once wrote a poem about it:

So this was what we had to learn—
That jackal with his treacherous claws
Will dig the lion up to earn
The dog's forgiveness and the crow's applause.

And this was what we had to know—
That where, upon the new laid stone,
The dog, the jackal, and the crow
Rejoice, there buried greatness lies alone.

Further Glimpse of These Scenes

Much else of Roosevelt still flavors the Hyde Park area. One scarcely needs mention the St. James Church, the Reformed Dutch Church (built in 1794) which had his warmest sympathy, and the chapel the family used in winter; also the Town Hall where he voted and the James Roosevelt Library, set up by FDR's mother as a memorial to her husband. Then a few miles from the village is Val-Kill (Valley Stream), the cottage where Eleanor Roosevelt lives today; it was built during the depression to house a small furniture factory, which she hoped would relieve unemployment by reviving hand crafts; the venture dwindled off, and she converted the building into living quarters. Next door is Stone Cottage, used nowadays as a guest house; FDR designed this building, did the contracting himself, and was very proud of it. A small swimming pool adjoins. Then, up the hill, is Top Cottage, once know as "Roosevelt's Dream House," where his son Elliott lives now, and which is a small story in itself.

Unbelievably enough FDR never had a house really his own except in Warm Springs. Hyde Park was, of course, his mother's, the Executive Mansion in Albany belongs to New York State, and the White House to the nation; in Washington, before he became President, he and Mrs. Roosevelt lived in rented houses. Top Cottage was to be FDR's *own* house, built to his own specifications and design; here he intended to live quietly after 1940, writing his memoirs, superintending the farm, and raising Christmas trees. He had no professional license to practice architecture, and so his friend Henry J. Toombs of Atlanta bore the responsibility for the blueprints and so on, but the President made the sketches, and superintended the work to the smallest technical detail.[3] How good a job FDR did with Top Cottage

---

[3] FDR strongly fancied himself as an architect. Several other buildings in the neighborhood, in particular the Rhinebeck Post Office, are essentially his. See Dows, *op. cit.*, and "F.D.R. As Architect," New York *Times*, December 8, 1940.

is dubious. The ventilation is faulty and the bedrooms are too small. He wanted to take full advantage of the soul-filling view (from the front porch you can see across to the Catskills, forty miles up the river and thirty down) and so he cramped everything in favor of the large living room with its big windows and vaulted plaster ceiling. There was only one bathroom as he designed the house, no closets, and no telephone. He thought that modern people had too many bathrooms, "that the young generation was just washing itself away." One irony is that after Top Cottage was completed, FDR never spent a night in it. This was not because it disappointed him; indeed he loved it; but the physical arrangements for his sleeping and so on were easier in the big house down below. But any time an important visitor came to Hyde Park, Roosevelt would take him to see Top Cottage first. He would set out in the Ford, double back through the woods, and try to lose the Secret Service men in their big black Cadillacs behind.

Top Cottage is, as is inevitable, still crammed with Rooseveltiana. No one lived in it till Elliott took it over, and it was furnished in part from things at the big house. Among items I saw were a landscape by Winston Churchill, given to the President after the Casablanca conference; the green White House chair Roosevelt used from 1933 to 1941; blue Chinese screens that call up the Delano inheritance; some saucy *New Yorker* cartoons that he greatly enjoyed;[4] and a choked array of books, which of course he catalogued himself, marking some "Rare" in his own handwriting, or with notations like "First American Edition—?" One collection is of miniature books, which interested him greatly, almost as if he were still a child—a *Bijou Almanac,* Homer, a *Compleat Angler,* and, of all things, the autobiography of Calvin Coolidge, none of them much bigger than a match box.

The reader may be surprised, or even shocked, by the extreme miscellaneousness of FDR's collections. But this is as nothing compared to that of collectors who, after his death, are voraciously pursuing every known type of article relating to him. An organization exists in Chicago, the Franklin D. Roosevelt Collectors' Association; it publishes a magazine, and has members all over the world. They seek autographs, holographs (a good letter in the President's handwriting can bring $300), and even such items as scarce campaign posters and

---

[4] FDR's favorite cartoon was of a girl who scrawls his name in the snow and is rebuked for using such a dirty word.

the like. About 2,500 different campaign buttons, to name just one item, are known to exist. One specialist has a collection running to six or seven thousand objects. The complete issues of foreign stamps honoring him are eagerly sought, and so are copies of the forty-one popular songs associated with his name, from "Our Boy Roosevelt He'll Go In" to "F. D. Roosevelt Jones."

Chapter 7

MORE ABOUT FDR THE MAN

You'll find me just the same, and I'll wear the same size hat.

—FRANKLIN DELANO ROOSEVELT

Roosevelt was like a cornucopia; one can draw out of him inexhaustibly. We turn now to the structure and make-up of his brain, his mental processes. Sumner Welles believes that he was one of those peculiar men whose subconscious works by day rather than at night, and that he did his best intellectual work between nine in the evening and midnight. The day was good enough for routine; the night was for creative thinking. Time and time again he would evade decisions in the morning; after dinner, they came out sharp and clear.

The plain fact of the matter is that Roosevelt did not *like* to think. He almost never analyzed anything, and almost never explained, even to himself, what made him determine on a course. Nor did he like to tackle a subject premise by premise; he reached his conclusion in one big jump, a pounce. All this is by way of saying that he was intuitive rather than logical, and that he worked by intuition and hunch rather than by ratiocination. This is one reason why he often seemed inattentive. But his brain was an extremely powerful instrument, even if not delicate. He was impatient of elaborations and always more interested in the major end than the precisions of approach. But there was nothing wrong with his perspicacity.

His mind had defects; nobody would deny this. He had, as we know, little taste for philosophical abstraction; he was "a broker of ideas rather than an architect of systems," as Harold Laski once pointed out. He got stimulus from conversation, not from meditation. Another blemish was that he didn't like debate. I asked one of his oldest friends, "*Could* he argue?" and the answer was, "He certainly didn't like to." Then again he had an exaggerated disposition to compromise. For instance consider the following anecdote from Mr. Hull. The State Department agreed to settle for $3,000,000 a claim against Canada having to do with excise taxes paid by Canadian distillers during Prohibition. But Mr. Morgenthau, at the Treasury, insisted that $6,000,000 should be the figure, and Hull had to go to the White House for a decision:

> I told Mr. Roosevelt the facts in the case.
>
> "What do you think our claims are really worth?" he asked.
>
> "Frankly," I replied, "they're probably worth nothing legally."
>
> Without saying more, the President picked up the telephone and got Morgenthau at the other end.
>
> "Henry," he said, "Cordell is in my office about the whisky claims against Canada. I'd like to have you do a little figuring for me. Can you put a piece of paper and a pencil before you? All set?
>
> "Now put down on the left side of the paper what you say the claims are worth. That's $6,000,000. Now opposite that, on the right side of the paper, put down what Cordell has settled for. That's $3,000,000.
>
> "Now under your own figure I want you to put down a figure I'm going to give you. This is my own estimate of what the claims are worth. Are you ready? All right, put down zero. Now draw a line below your figure and mine, and add them together. What do you get? $6,000,000. O.K., now that is the sum total of what you and I think the claims are worth. Now take the average. Since there are two of us, divide by 2. What do you get? $3,000,000.
>
> "Well, that balances exactly with what Cordell settled for. How about settling for that?"
>
> There was a moment of silence. Then the President laughed and hung up. He turned to me.
>
> "It's O.K.," he said.[1]

Certainly FDR was never afraid of figures. It makes one shudder to learn that when he decided in 1933 to raise the price of gold, he chose 21 cents as the amount, partly because "That's a lucky number —three times seven." Sherwood records two instances of FDR's debonair manner with colossal figures. In 1942 he "arbitrarily" boosted production estimates upward, on his own responsibility and just before going to Congress, to a degree that frightened even Hopkins— estimates that included such items as 75,000 tanks and 100,000 aircraft. He said, with his supreme confidence in the capacity of America, "Oh, the production people can do it if they really try." And they did. In a speech in Chicago in 1944 he wanted to make a prediction about postwar employment figures. The highest estimate submitted by ex-

[1] *The Memoirs of Cordell Hull* (New York, The Macmillan Company, 1948), Vol. I, pp. 206-207.

perts was 57,000,000 jobs. He said, "Let's make it a good round number," and changed the figure to 60,000,000.

Roosevelt once stated that "to accomplish anything worth while . . . there must be a compromise between the ideal and the practical." Blandly he wrote Mr. Stimson during the Supreme Court fight that the "truth" was probably halfway between Stimson's position and his own! When half a dozen men worked independently on a single piece of legislation, it was sometimes difficult even for such a magician as FDR to "weave" the results together. Particularly was this true in the realm of economics, a subject in which the President had little training or intrinsic interest. Mr. Justice Jackson recalls an occasion early in the New Deal when it was pointed out to FDR that the principles of N.R.A. were completely irreconcilable with the antitrust legislation he was fostering at the same time. He was put out and irritated. Similarly when he was pushing the great automobile men to increase production of munitions in 1942 he gave orders, "Never mind about prices—just iron out all those hills and valleys," without considering that until the question of price was fixed nothing else could be "ironed out" at all.

Roosevelt was one of the supreme brain pickers of all time. A genius is, by one definition, someone with infinite capacity to make use of everybody and everything, and FDR was certainly a genius by this as well as other reckonings. Moreover he had an unerring instinct to take the best of what was offered him. Raymond Swing got a telephone call from the White House one night, asking that he send over the text of a broadcast he had just delivered on the Darlan crisis; Mr. Swing was of course happy to do so, and a few days later heard his sober and judicious remarks followed almost word for word in the President's own message about Darlan. Roosevelt encouraged everybody to tell him everything, but he had a kind of filter in his mind; he seldom took advice without checking it. Later as he became an oracle he could not pick brains as obviously as he did at first. What he heard from people, especially at round-table discussions, became so inextricably involved with his own thought that it was sometimes difficult later to tell what came from whom, and sometimes he even gave back to somebody as his own an opinion or idea he had heard a few days before from the same person. Another characteristic was the way he loved to try out on one person an idea he had just heard from another. One morning during the financial crisis of 1933, Ambassador

Laurence A. Steinhardt saw him just after he had talked to a radical professor of economics, who had urged him to issue government bonds without maturity date, and bearing no interest, as a measure to finance public works. Immediately the President put the idea up to Steinhardt, who replied, sapiently enough, (a) such bonds would be the exact equivalent of currency; (b) workers and others would nevertheless be tempted to sell them at a discount; (c) according to Gresham's law, bad money inevitably drives out good. Awarely the President cocked his eyebrows, and exclaimed, "Just what *I* had been thinking!" But Steinhardt could not be sure whether the President had, in fact, already rejected the idea, and was simply using it to test *him*, or whether he was flirting with the notion of adopting it.

On another occasion Mr. Steinhardt got a remarkable insight on the way the President's subtle mind worked. Home on leave from Istanbul, he asked FDR for a decision on a critical difference then developing between ourselves and the British on Lend Lease in Turkey. The Ambassador stated his case. Roosevelt hardly appeared to be listening, and brushed him off with a ten-minute monologue on, of all unrelated things, three impending appointments to the Federal judiciary in New York; FDR wanted one judgeship to go to a Catholic, one to a Protestant, and one to a Jew. He had made up his mind on the first two, but not the third. The Democratic National Committee was supporting one Jewish candidate, the state chairman another, and a powerful senator still another. FDR himself favored a fourth man, and he asked Steinhardt, with his wide experience of the New York bar, if he knew anything against him. "No," the Ambassador replied. Roosevelt then waved him out cheerfully, adding almost as an afterthought: "Oh— on that Lend Lease matter, see Hopkins." By this technique FDR had killed several birds. He avoided making a decision himself on the Lend Lease dispute, which was already the cause of a serious tussle between Hopkins and Sumner Welles. Moreover, by sending Steinhardt to Hopkins rather than Welles, he implied that he favored the Hopkins view, while not actually taking sides. Finally, he had obtained Steinhardt's opinion on an entirely different matter; the Ambassador had said no more than the single word "No," but Roosevelt was quite capable of using this so that, if anybody did oppose the man he favored, he could claim that Steinhardt had supported him.

Consider now some of Roosevelt's more positive intellectual qualities. He had limitless curiosity·and an immense, magnificent practicality as well. During the worst of the London blitz he repeatedly asked Ambassador Winant to report to him on various social phenomena far removed from immediate tasks; he knew how important these might be in the future. Of course curiosity is an extremely useful trait, in that it often produces new avenues to problems and breeds optimism. His mind cut to the bone; he could seize at once the basic reality of almost any issue, and then set about realizing it; he was one of the greatest cutters of red tape ever known. He was always willing to experiment, to try a thing out, if a practical result could be attained. His attitude was, "If we can't do a thing one way, let's try another."[2]

Roosevelt had an extraordinary ability to concentrate, not merely on one thing at a time, but on many; the way he could compartmentalize his mind was almost inhuman. For instance on the Monday after Pearl Harbor he was keenly interested in the results of a luncheon conference that had been scheduled a long time ahead, and which, of all things, dealt with WACs and birth control. Similarly Rexford Tugwell records that on December 8, 1941, he asked for a report on— Puerto Rico!

He was quick as lightning in sizing up a complex situation or report. The late Josephus Daniels once told me that of all Roosevelt's qualities he put agility of mind first, even ahead of charm and courage; this nimbleness was not merely useful in rescuing him from sudden conversational holes, but demanded qualities of sure judgment, courage, and omniscience. When he took a quick decision on an important matter, he had usually to reckon with alternatives that were almost literally boundless. He liked work to go forward quickly too. Once, after much commotion, the decision was taken to merge six important Government agencies into one. FDR reached for a piece of yellow scratch paper, scribbled out a brief executive order in longhand then and there, and told his staff to go ahead; he hated to hold up the work even by the few hours it would take to get a formal order written.

He had enormous ingenuity and imagination. Sometimes both these factors came into play at once, as, for instance, when he casually sug-

[2] It disappointed him that the new executive offices, which he thought would be big enough for the workings of the Presidency for a quarter of a century, turned out to be too small after a year or two. But he told a friend, "It doesn't matter much. I can move the files and machinery over to State, and build a tunnel!"

gested in the late summer of 1941—to the bewilderment of his subordinates at first—that the United States ought to buy up all the wool
available in neutral countries. His line of thought was (a) perhaps the
Russians will hold the Germans after all; (b) if so, a winter campaign
is inevitable; (c) winter is always hard on an invading army in Russia;
(d) the Germans will need a great deal of wool for uniforms; (e) keep
them from getting it.

His mind was almost always flexible and hospitable to new ideas;
he would take a suggestion from anybody anywhere. He said once,
"You sometimes find something pretty good in the lunatic fringe. In
fact, we have got as part of our social and economic government today
a whole lot of things which in my boyhood were considered lunatic
fringe, and yet they are now part of everyday life."[3] Nor was he ever
afraid of confessing ignorance or asking that something be explained
to him over and over again if he could not understand it. Ernest
Lindley describes how FDR once sent Tugwell to Chicago to attend a
meeting of agricultural economists and check on new developments.
Tugwell telephoned him to explain some ideas that had come up on
surplus crops. FDR listened, rang off, and then called back. "I don't
understand it yet. Put it in a telegram."

As soon as he saw the Sahara he wanted to irrigate it. As soon as he
got to Teheran he was full of ideas—good ideas too—for improving
the lot of the Iranese. His imagination touched every field; he was
capable of thinking out the "shelter belt" of trees to check erosion in
the Dust Bowl and of playing with ideas for a new world unit of currency to be called the "Dimo" and for "Free Ports of Information" to
disseminate impartial news all over the world. Once on a tropical
cruise he flamed up with the sudden notion that bamboo might be
used for armor in warfare. He invented the title "Expediter" for
Averell Harriman when Harriman was put in charge of Lend Lease
and said happily, "This doesn't conform with anything anybody ever
heard before." Once he wrote a memorandum for action by whoever
should be president in 1956, and he once sketched what he thought
would be the world picture in 2057.

"That fellow in the White House," I once heard Wendell Willkie
say, "is just too smart to live." Some eminent Republicans put it less
politely: "FDR has the guile of a serpent." The President's cleverness
was, indeed, almost maddeningly acute. He never missed a trick or a

[3] Rosenman, Vol. XIII, p. 147.

shadow of a trick. His cleverness grew out of his omniscience in part; for instance the fact that he once said the first prerequisite for a European settlement was that no German should ever be permitted to wear a uniform shows how well he understood the German character. He was a great feeder-out of rope. He never gave away his hand. He calculated every inch. He spent a few days with Eisenhower on what seemed to be little more than a sightseeing trip before the Cairo Conference in 1943; what he was really doing was sizing up Eisenhower finally before giving him the supreme command.

In 1944 he called Robert Hannegan to the White House (Hannegan had been Collector of Internal Revenue in St. Louis) and asked him to make out his income-tax return, explaining that the President of the United States could not afford a mistake in his return, and that he "needed a good man to make it out for him." Hannegan came back the next day with a tax expert. But the President insisted on seeing him alone, and they worked out final details of the return together. Of course FDR was not even faintly interested in Hannegan's abilities as a tax man. But he was thinking of making him chairman of the Democratic National Committee, and he wanted to be with him a few hours, test him, and feel him out.

The President's mind was, of course, exceptionally good at detail, and this is doubly impressive when one considers how enormous was his area of action. He had an arrow in every quiver. When a campaign itinerary was being worked out, he wanted to be sure of every whistle stop. His love of detail was such that he liked, as a joke, to write his ambassadors about what was really going on in *their* countries. Once Frank Graham of the War Labor Board and Robert Patterson, Undersecretary of War, took opposite sides as to whether the Army should or should not take over an aviation plant, and Graham insisted on going to the President himself for a decision. FDR received him at 10 on a hot evening, in shirt sleeves, drowned with work. Graham discovered that Roosevelt not only knew all about the basic issues involved in the case, but the names of the lawyers, the detailed line of the rival arguments, and the nickname of the man who owned the plant.

Once a week for years Morris Ernst sent FDR a brief list of suggestions and notations, called tidbits, which the President dutifully answered point by point, accepting some, rejecting some, and reserving others for future action. Mr. Ernst has let me go through this correspondence; its range and variety are astonishing. Roosevelt expressed himself—I choose a few items out of many—on Litvinov, how to get on with the New York *Daily News*, a "silly business" involving a government figure in a divorce case, the type of underwear worn by a celebrated woman publisher, Coca-Cola, a book on the Four Freedoms, the Nuremberg trials, how Dorothy Thompson shouldn't take such and such a line, impending legislation in New York State, a military job for La Guardia, the kind of emblem the U.N. ought to have, and the isolationist fight in 1920. Roosevelt's point-by-point comments included "Chase this," "Let me handle this one," "I have a slightly different approach," "Time not ripe," "I will get in touch with Morgenthau on this," "Lay off," "Go ahead," "Keep these tidbits up," and "I am starting the ball rolling on No. 3."

Finally in this general field of the mind, there is a consideration above the mind—Roosevelt's sixth sense, his supernal sensitiveness to hunches, his delight in proceeding not by the book but by the spirit, and his wariness. Like a horse in quicksand, he had a highly developed sense of self-preservation and instinct for solid soil. No matter what he put his foot in, he could get it out. Oscar Cox, one of his advisers, mentioned once that if you put eight or nine memoranda on his desk at the same time, he would almost always catch instantly which one was tricky and ought to be put aside for later judgment. Roosevelt, as it has been aptly said, "played everything by ear." Of course he always banked on his luck, like any accomplished gambler. He felt that if you trusted chance, it came your way; that if you believed firmly enough that things would turn out for the best in the end, they did. Temperament is fate, according to the old apothegm; character is destiny.

The Central Belief

What did Roosevelt believe in most? First and above all, the people. The core of his belief was simplicity itself—he believed in the fundamental goodness and decency of man.

What, to summarize it as succinctly as possible, did he stand for politically? The base of his philosophy was to be human-minded, and above all social-minded.[4] In the early days at least he preferred to be

[4] " 'Social-mindedness' is the term he uses to describe the philosophy which extends the nineteenth century concept of political democracy to fit the mechanized, tightly interwoven pattern of twentieth century civilization. He defines it as freedom conditional on mass production and the new tempo of change and limited by social responsibility, a freedom much more difficult to maintain now than in the simpler, roomier world of the past."—Anne O'Hare McCormick in the New York *Times*, August 15, 1937.

called a "progressive" rather than merely a "liberal." During the whole of the "Long Presidency," as an Italian philosopher has called it, he worked continuously within the orbit of the most formidable single problem of our time, the interrelation between liberty and security. Liberty of thought, liberty of movement and expression, liberty of political mechanisms and procedures; security against want, security against revolution, security against aggressions both foreign and domestic—these were the two irreconcilables he sought to reconcile. The whole gist of his twelve years in office can be expressed by the proposition that he did succeed in giving the people of the United States a fuller measure of security than they had ever known before, without any sacrifice whatever of liberty and civil rights.

This is an extract from one of his later speeches:

I am everlastingly angry at those who assert vociferously that the Four Freedoms and the Atlantic Charter are nonsense because they are unattainable. If those people had lived a century and a half ago they would have sneered and said that the Declaration of Independence was utter piffle. If they had lived nearly a thousand years ago they would have laughed uproariously at the ideals of Magna Carta. And if they had lived several thousand years ago, they would have derided Moses when he came down from the mountain with the Ten Commandments. We concede that these great teachings are not perfectly lived up to today. *But I would rather be a builder than a wrecker, hoping always that the structure of life is growing, not dying.*

Sometimes, in 1950, we are apt to forget the way a President could make words sing in 1945.

Books, Reading, and Things Literary

Roosevelt played with books a great deal, but he did not read very studiously. His erudition in some fields was, as we know, remarkable, but there is no record of his ever having read a line of any of the seminal thinkers who have conditioned our whole epoch—Darwin, Hegel, Marx, Freud, or, on a different level, Tolstoi, Proust, Croce, Spengler, or even Henry Adams.[5] Yet, when the practical implications of Dr. Einstein's celebrated formula were brought to his attention, he acted instantly. Mostly what Roosevelt read was (a) American history,

[5] Once he gave Mrs. Roosevelt a complete set of Willa Cather as a birthday present.

(b) nautical records and books about ships—for instance he practically memorized Mahan when he was a child—(c) trash.

Newspapers, however, he read voraciously; he went through six or eight different papers every morning with the utmost care; he read the whole paper, not just clippings selected for him as most other presidents did. He liked to be alone while reading them, he read quickly, and he could tear the guts out of a newspaper like a combine eating up grain. His ability to assimilate swiftly and remember anything he ever saw in a newspaper was astonishing. Radio did not interest him so much, and he was a comparatively infrequent listener. Occasionally he liked to listen to recordings of his own speeches.

Poetry he cared little for; there was not much poetry in his nature. If he did read poems, he would choose Kipling or Rupert Brooke rather than Yeats or Spender. He liked narrative poems with a swing. Almost never did he quote Shakespeare; when he did, however, it was with great effect, as when he used Mercutio's phrase, "A plague on both your houses," in reference to John L. Lewis. Nor did music interest him much, though he played the piano a little as a child and sang in the Groton choir. In fact he had little taste for the aesthetic, except in the field of architecture. He did love to draw and design things; for instance at one time or other he designed the special type of case to hold files of his speeches in the Hyde Park library, one of his bookplates (it has a naval motif), some of the family china, a square coin, a watch he once gave Mrs. Roosevelt, and the tie clasp he presented to the ushers at his wedding. He did some of the work on design for new aircraft carriers laid down during the war, worked out the plans for a vault to contain the most confidential of his papers, and drew the first sketches for the naval hospital at Bethesda, where he once spent one of the most critical days of his life. Once Lowell Mellett showed him the plans for the new Government Information Office to be built in Washington. FDR grabbed a red pencil and moved the entrance booth and changed some other details. "It's the best new building in this town," he said later with satisfaction.

Roosevelt was certainly the first President in a great many years who had a working knowledge of three foreign languages. His German was not practiced or fluent, but he could read it; he liked to think that he "knew" Spanish, and would say that "he had the feel for it," though he was by no means expert. His French was quite good, and he was probably the first President ever to be able to make a speech in French, but he would often grope for words. Once in conversation with a group of Haitians he could not remember the word for "truck," and stumbled until someone rescued him by saying *camion*.

FDR was no great stylist. He did not write much except speeches and letters. Of course there were plenty of these. Harvard sent him a routine questionnaire on one occasion, asking him what he had written in recent years; his answer was, "Too much!" He started to keep a diary two or three times but only once did the good resolution last long; the "diaries" terminate on January 4th or 5th. He wasn't diary-minded. (The scraps of diary he did keep are in the stacks of the Hyde Park library.) Sometimes he scribbled poems—doggerel—for fun. They are pretty terrible. He had the idea, during his convalescence from illness, of writing a novel based on the life of John Paul Jones, but never got very far with it; and Miss Tully records that he once wrote a sketch for a movie on the theme of *Old Ironsides*. It was actually submitted to a Hollywood studio, but never produced. During the twenties he occasionally wrote book reviews; I have one before me now, that appeared in the New York *Evening World* on December 3, 1925, and which discusses in adulatory terms Claude G. Bowers' *Jefferson and Hamilton*. It has no great distinction. FDR's choice of words was often somewhat effusive and even effeminate, and his prose has little sustained pace or rhythm. He was much addicted to using words and phrases like "fearfully," "horrid," "perfectly splendid," "terribly," "awfully nice," and above all "thrilled." He was "thrilled" at the achievements of the Red Army in 1943, and "thrilled" by getting autographed copies of books by Mr. Churchill. He uses exclamation points a great deal, and his paragraphs are usually short, as in a newspaper. The best index of Mr. Roosevelt's literary style is his letters. These—especially those to the family—are warmhearted, optimistic, extremely agreeable, loaded with clichés like "lots of love," affectionate, and seemingly written from the top of his mind, without much thought, as if in the performance of a not unpleasant duty—in a word, letters like those that millions of good people write to wives, children, or in-laws.

The President took some aspects of his literary work with great seriousness. He had intense interest in the volumes of his public papers edited with such discernment and efficiency by Judge Rosenman. His preoccupation was keen, not merely with the text and the explanatory passages which, so far as possible, he wrote himself, but with the bindings, type face, and every detail of physical layout. The production of the book was expensive. Everything that FDR thought might be useful was put into type *before* editing, so that the cost of the overset (sufficient for three additional volumes!) in the first five volumes alone was something like $5,000. Roosevelt had exaggerated hopes for the sale of the series (he and Rosenman were to divide the royalties, if any) and Bennett Cerf of Random House, his first publisher, thought that, to save disappointment later, he should warn him that these inflated hopes might not be fully realized. This was in 1937, when the depression was still heavy; moreover anybody rich enough to spend $15 for a set of books was probably a Roosevelt hater. A celebrated anecdote describes how Mr. Cerf sought tactfully to warn the President that he might *not,* despite his eminence, turn out to be a runaway best seller. First the publisher explained that a similar work by Mr. Hoover had only sold 1,700 copies. "Why, if Hoover sold 1,700, I'll sell a million!" Roosevelt exclaimed happily. Mr. Cerf instantly chose a new and different approach, and told the President that the advance sale of his book in Washington, D.C., where it might have been expected to do particularly well, was only 334 copies. Roosevelt started to scratch on a pad. He was calculating the ratio between 334 and 600,000, the population of Washington, and thus estimating what he would sell, if this ratio held good, in the whole of the United States. Mr. Cerf then expostulated, "But, Mr. President, you forget that there are states like Mississippi, where nobody has bought a book for years!"

The first series of volumes sold, as a matter of fact, quite badly. Cerf printed 25,000 copies; the total sale was only 4,000. After swallowing this important loss for a considerable interval Mr. Cerf and his partners decided to "remainder" (i.e., dispose of at a sharply cut price) the 20,000 sets still lying in the warehouse. Roosevelt, when he heard about this, was furious. So was Rosenman, who did not think that books by the President of the United States should suffer the indignity of being remaindered. FDR had always been more than cordial to Cerf up to this time. Now he cooled sharply, and Mr. Cerf never got a Christmas card from him again.

How He Wrote a Speech

The way Roosevelt wrote speeches was a riot. This process has been described so plentifully by Sherwood and others that we do not need to go into it at any length. A speech by the President was, to put it mildly, almost always a composite phenomenon. The list of his literary helpers, from first to last, includes a great number of people—Charles Michelson, Ernest Lindley, Sumner Welles, Moley and the whole Brain Trust, Stanley High ("to take care of the spiritual side," as FDR once expressed it), Archibald MacLeish, Tom Corcoran, Basil O'Connor, Bob Jackson, and above all Rosenman and Sherwood. Some short speeches on ceremonial occasions, for instance at dedications of museums and the like, were written in their entirety by MacLeish. General Hugh Johnson in 1940 quoted two sentences from a speech Roosevelt made at Pittsburgh in the 1932 campaign, one of which was, "Taxes are paid in the sweat of every man who labors." Then Johnson, who was no longer on good terms with the President, went on to say that it was a damned good speech. "I know. I wrote it."[6]

FDR was perfectly candid about the way he utilized his eminent ghosts, and in fact joked about it often. Mr. Sherwood one day met in the White House an old friend who did not know how close he had become to Roosevelt, and who exclaimed, "Bob! What are you doing here?" Mrs. Roosevelt, who walked into the room at that moment, answered, "Mr. Sherwood has just finished writing the President's message to Congress." Early in the war Harry Hopkins took Sherwood, after a hard bout of work, into the White House bedroom where Mr. Churchill was a guest. The Prime Minister shook hands, and proffered the remark, "The President tells me that you write everything, so that he can't say anything at all any more unless he ad-libs it!" After one speech written largely by Sherwood FDR got an innocent telegram of congratulation from Mrs. Sherwood in New York. The President could not resist answering her on the spot, "Bob and I are awfully glad you liked it."

Rosenman too was an indispensable associate. Sherwood, like MacLeish, was sometimes too "literary" for the President. But Rosenman, more than anybody, had the knack of expressing FDR's own thought in just the words he himself would have chosen.

In the early days each of two or three advisers would prepare a long speech, after getting FDR's ideas. Then, facing a manuscript that would have taken four or five hours to deliver, the President would intermix the best points together and get it to manageable length. Next the advisers would consult again, and cut further. Once more FDR would go over it brutally, and it would finally be trimmed to fit into

6 Mark Sullivan in the New York *Herald Tribune*, July 20, 1940.

the proper time. Later this procedure became much more elaborate. Sometime in December, say, Missy LeHand or Miss Tully would gently prod the President into recalling that his annual message on the state of the Union was due early in January. FDR would groan, "What— already? Very well, let's start tomorrow night at nine." Then relevant material would be assembled from the State Department, the Treasury, the Navy, the War Production Board, and whatever other government agencies were involved. The President, dictating to Miss Tully, would then outline his own conception of what the speech should eventually contain. Sherwood and Rosenman would go to work furiously on this draft, often with subghosts assisting them. The President's manuscript was by no means sacrosanct. The boys would, in fact, tear it to pieces, muttering phrases like, "He'll forget that he ever said this—it's terrible —let's cut it out." But they were extremely careful to maintain his mood, his pace, his major trajectory, his essential theme. Soon (Rosenman was chief drafter) a provisional script would be submitted to the President. He would as often as not blow up, exclaiming, "I never said that!" or "What are you trying to make me say?" Then it would be pointed out, "But Economic Warfare wants that in," or, "The Pentagon asks specially that you make that point." Work would go on till midnight, and then after FDR went to bed, until two in the morning, three, four, or even six. After three drafts, which would take three or four days to prepare, the advisers had what they called a "ground floor." Then the President himself added walls and rooms. After six or seven drafts FDR would be apt to say, "We're getting along fine now. Let's go back to the beginning and start all over."

The remarkable thing was that, in spite of these mazes and confusions, the speech when finally delivered *did* have the indisputable imprint of the President himself. Always he blew his own vitality into every passage. His own gigantic personality colored the whole. He made every sentence his own, particularly by his manner of delivery. I did not appreciate how much work he did himself until I visited the Hyde Park library, where most of the important speeches are carefully preserved draft by draft. Seven or eight drafts were not unusual; sometimes there were eleven or twelve. The President's handwritten interlineations, excisions, and corrections were abundant. In particular he sought to make the phraseology as simple as possible, to give a homely touch, to eliminate anything awkwardly stated or artificial, to cut surplus wordage. Once when a complex statement on some financial matter had been prepared FDR shook his head and said, "That won't go down with Moses Smith! Let's simplify it."

Anybody, moreover, who thinks that the President could not write or speak singlehanded is severely deluded. He loved to extemporize from his written text, and the Rosenman volumes are packed with words he delivered off the cuff; the press conferences are, in particular, a proliferating treasure of original material. Perhaps his single most famous remark of this type was the "stab-in-the-back" reference to Mussolini in a speech in June, 1940. The State Department did not approve.

Some of the phrases indelibly associated with FDR were his, some were not. "A little left of center" was his own, so were the Four Freedoms, so was "nothing to fear but fear,"[7] and so was "a day that will live in infamy." Moley suggested the "Forgotten Man"; apparently this phrase was first used in an address by Walter Hines Page in North Carolina in the 1890's, from the title of an essay by William Graham Sumner. The origin of "New Deal" is obscure aside from the fact already mentioned that it derives both from Wilson and TR. Stuart Chase published a book called *A New Deal* in 1932, but I do not know whether FDR ever saw it or not; Moley says that he, Moley, was the originator. Many years before Mark Twain had used the phrase in *A Connecticut Yankee at King Arthur's Court*.

How original the President was as a phrasemaker does not matter much in the perspective of today. If you go through a big book of quotations carefully you will find disconcertingly enough that practically everything has been said at one time or other by somebody else a century or so ago. What does matter is the obvious fact that the President's speeches and Fireside Chats, so magnificently delivered, gave continued sustenance and affirmative leadership to the nation during the worst trial in its history. Roosevelt had a supremely effective vitalizing gift. His eloquence was more than a matter of mere words; it was a contagious manifestation of his own strength, glow, energizing quality, and spirit. He could epitomize in a phrase the national mood, and give, as it has been well expressed, "release, climax, and coherence" to what almost everybody in the country felt.

[7] In January, 1932, an editorial in the *Ladies' Home Journal* used the phrase "There is nothing to fear—except fear." (*The Age of the Great Depression*, by Dixon Wecter, p. 44.) But whether FDR ever saw this is more than doubtful.

Chapter 8

THE PRESIDENT AT WORK

Occasionally I think that I am a bit shell-shocked.
—FRANKLIN DELANO ROOSEVELT

He liked to take things fast, cut corners, and work informally. When people came to him with elaborate memoranda, his first request was, if possible, "Boil it down to a single page." When he was particularly interested in a memorandum he liked to read it back aloud to the person who submitted it. Unlike most heads of state, he almost never made notes following a conversation of importance with some foreign emissary or other political personage; he trusted to his memory. He did a great deal of business with informal scraps of paper. Hamilton Fish Armstrong, the distinguished editor of *Foreign Affairs,* came to see him on one occasion when, for some unaccountable reason, approval by the State Department of the credentials of a new ambassador from abroad had been delayed. Mr. Armstrong showed him a telegram expressing alarm from the ambassador concerned. FDR simply took the telegram, wrote on it, OK FDR, and the matter was settled then and there.

He did a great deal of business on the telephone; perhaps a quarter of his working day was spent telephoning. About a hundred people had the privilege of being put through to him without the intermediation of a secretary; Miss Perkins and others record that he was usually very accessible and easy to get on the telephone. But few people ever abused their right of contact; if they did, they were ruthlessly cut off the list. Bob Sherwood has said that in the hundreds of hours he spent with the President in the evening working on speeches he could count on the fingers of two hands the number of times telephone calls came through. But of course this was at night, when FDR was never disturbed except for something of major interest.

Roosevelt's technique with mail was marvelous. Millions of letters came to the White House; a superlatively efficient staff winnowed and classified them with signal promptitude. The number of letters of reply that FDR dictated and signed (and some were scribbled longhand) is almost beyond belief. He never missed *anything* important. A minor example of his methods is that he dictated acknowledgments of Christmas presents while they were being unwrapped. His last work at night was, as a rule, getting grimly (but amiably) to the bottom of the great wire baskets always mercilessly filled with documents. Sometimes—Mr. Roosevelt was human—he would shuffle these papers over and over again and keep putting at the *very* bottom some item that perplexed or bothered him. He never lost an opportunity to say a graceful word of thanks, cultivate a friendship, or keep in touch with anybody interesting. Once Cass Canfield, the publisher, wrote him a brief longhand note congratulating him on a minor matter. Within twenty-four hours a letter from FDR had come back thanking Canfield with a personal touch and saying that he got few letters that he appreciated more. And this was on a day when the White House mail might easily have totaled eight thousand items.

The routine of appointments was handled with great skill. Mr. Roosevelt was almost always under temptation to give a visitor too much time, and so the schedules had to be made elastic. The day was set up so that he would have gaps. The staff knew well that most visitors fell into a few definite categories—those who asked favors, those who had no real business being there, those who overstayed their FDR in order to impress the newspapermen outside, and those who were long-winded no matter what. Anybody who wanted to win the permanent gratitude of the secretariat had only to stay with FDR *less* time than had been assigned. Intelligent visitors knew that Roosevelt, too, appreciated this; an easy way to impress him was to leave him two or three minutes before the time set, no matter how he himself protested, and say firmly, "Mr. President, I stayed only sixteen minutes out of my twenty, so you are four ahead."

FDR is often criticized for being a bad administrator, but this is largely because the circumference he tried to embrace was so limitless; so far as running his own office was concerned he was somewhat eccentric and his executive methods were catch-as-catch-can; of course he had the unendingly faithful cooperation of a first-rate staff. That he was able, year after year, to retain such devotion from a widely variegated and numerous group was, of course, a substantial tribute to his personal power. The White House executive staff numbered

687 men and women in 1944. Everybody knows the names of Watson, Early, and the chief secretaries and administrative assistants; not so many know about the loyal and efficient work as term rounded into term of men like Rudolph Forster and Maurice C. Latta, the chief executive clerks, and Miss Louise Hackmeister who ran the switchboard and who is one of the best telephone operators who ever lived.[1]

Roosevelt, like most unconventional executives, loved to do certain things himself. Nothing gave him greater pleasure than wasting a few minutes by thumbing through the *Congressional Record* to see how senators had voted, or writing some unexpected instruction in longhand, or telephoning somebody himself without warning. Once, early in the first term, he suddenly decided to visit the State Department in person to check up on reports that the building was so crowded with archives that nobody could get proper work done. Without telling Mr. Hull or anybody he had himself wheeled over at five in the afternoon and made his way to the office which he had used as Assistant Secretary of the Navy. He asked a young (and startled) attaché to let him in, and then amiably demanded to know what the filing cabinets contained. The attaché said that they held important current papers. FDR said, "Pull one open." The attaché hesitated, and Roosevelt opened it himself. The drawer contained archives on China of no possible use and dating many years back. Later FDR asked his staff, "Don't you think that my popping over there served a useful purpose? By nine o'clock tomorrow morning every man in Washington will think that I may come rolling in at any moment."[2]

One peculiarity in FDR as an executive was that, in certain fields, he disliked and distrusted so-called experts. Certainly he had reason to be suspicious of many of these in the State Department; yet even his friends thought that he was carrying things too far when he went to Cairo, for the crucial series of meetings with Chiang Kai-shek, without taking with him a single specialist on the Far East.

He gave assignments like a benevolent city editor to the men he liked and trusted, let them have free rein, and saw them seldom. His

[1] Sometimes the White House routine slipped up. For instance Rosenman describes how, just before the ceremony of signing the United Nations Declaration in January, 1942, no fountain pen could be found—and then the text of the document itself was momentarily mislaid.

[2] But this was the only time in more than twelve years that FDR visited the State Department. Had he been able to walk he would, of course, have been much more active in such informal tours of inspection.

men had to guess a good deal as to what he wanted in detail. Leon Henderson, "operating" for Hopkins in one agency and working directly for FDR in another, felt that he was out in the dark on one occasion and so he complained, "I'd like to see the music I'm supposed to be playing, Mr. President." Roosevelt responded with a laugh, "You're on key."

Sometimes Roosevelt made terrible appointments. He shopped for ambassadors, it seemed, like a housewife choosing among apples over the telephone. But let us remember (a) that he had to think in terms not merely of hundreds of appointments but of thousands; (b) he had to work with what talent was available; (c) there were always political difficulties. For instance Mr. Ickes has described what a complex myriad of nuisances had to be gone through before FDR felt safe in offering a Supreme Court justiceship to Felix Frankfurter. This is one example out of hundreds. Roosevelt had to have, let us say, the vote of Senator Blank in order to be sure of a majority in the Senate for the Dumbarton Oaks proposals. Therefore it was imperative that he let Senator Blank have his way on the postmastership of Senator Blank's home town. It was always a business of playing off one factor against another, of having to sacrifice a minor point to gain something more important. He had to buy his legislation through. Jesse Jones, it was said, had "ten votes in the Senate and forty in the House." So it was difficult to refuse Jones favors. One reason he found Bernard M. Baruch so useful was that Baruch had such prestige among the Southern senators. One of the signal paradoxes of democracy is that, to achieve it, a president often has to use somewhat undemocratic means. The American system, Mr. Stimson said once, is a "terribly wasteful instrument of human endeavor." Then there was always the point that if Roosevelt let somebody bad go, he might get someone even worse. Perhaps his chief defect as an executive was that he never trained a whole cadre, a group, to form a permanent matrix of government, as the British do. But the exigencies of American politics are such that he never had the opportunity.

The President's method of conducting government was so individual and even haphazard that subsidiary confusions were inevitable. Late in the war a devoted and experienced public servant, whom I had better call Mr. X, assumed that he had FDR's consent to proceed on a project of high consequence. Then, the next morning, "someone got through

to FDR while he was shaving," and the President reversed himself.
Mr. X heard the news through a private pipe line, informed Knox
and Stimson (it was a serious matter), and put his own forces into
action. His motive was quite unselfish; he felt that the President had
been badly advised and that the resultant procedure would be a tragic
error. Knox, Forrestal, and Mr. X rushed together to the White House
to see what they could do. The President said that he would not see
them, inasmuch as he had made his decision and was going to stick to
it. Mr. X protested. Harry Hopkins was assigned to mollify him,
which he proceeded to do with the words, "Why, you presumptuous
louse, how can you have the nerve to try to get the greatest man in
the world to change his mind after he's made it up!" Mr. X then
turned to Pa Watson, asked if a secretary were free, and proceeded
to dictate a memorandum then and there. This, he insisted, must go
through to the President at once. He then spent several hours getting
in touch with Mrs. Roosevelt, with Mr. Stimson again, with six or
seven lesser but important figures, and in particular with everybody
who was on the appointment pad to see the President that afternoon.
Toward 6 P.M. FDR reversed himself again, and Mr. X had won.

The President continually was forced into the position of making
people innocent victims of trial balloons, and turning them into
whipping boys. Once he said to a confidential adviser, "Get out of
here for a while and put some pressure on me from the left. I can't
stay in the middle unless I get a prod from the other direction."

FDR had a perceptive eye for anybody who got too big for a job,
anybody who exceeded his authority, and anybody who interfered in
jurisdictional quarrels not his own. The administrators he liked best
were those who (a) never bothered him, and (b) got along well with
Congress. Sometimes he delayed a decision because of confidence in
his own ability to placate; sometimes he enjoyed pulling a rug out
from under somebody without warning. He had a wonderful knack
for playing one person against another so as to get the best out of
both. This and other artifices arose partly because he could not get
around physically himself; he had to trust to what came to him. Sometimes he would confidentially receive a bitterly critical memorandum
on a person; his usual technique was to send it immediately to the
person involved!

Did members of his secretariat often disagree with him? Yes—but
only when it was important. He did not mind it at all when people

said No if the circumstances justified it, and a friend could tell him almost anything, though sometimes the friend would get a mildly dirty look. Of course the secretariat did everything possible to protect him and not break his stride. Sometimes an aide, conscious of his own responsibilities, would feel that he should have pressed a matter harder; the aide would leave the room, sighing to himself, "I won't be so considerate of *him* next time!" One of his closest advisers told me recently, "Only now do I begin to realize what a force he was, and appreciate how well he did business. What does it matter if he was not a good organizer? He was dealing all the time with things that you could never put on a chart. And I am convinced now that one of his greatest sources of power was the way he put *trust* in all of us."

Always, too, he sought to educate his own circle. When he asked somebody to do some research for him on, say, Russia, what he was really doing was to ensure that the person concerned should learn something about the subject.

Probably his greatest single source of power—next to his resolute faith in democracy and his identification with the people at large— was his extreme political dexterity and capacity for political maneuver. He almost always contrived to present a new issue so that it was not a shock; one of his masterly qualities was the way he could, so to speak, contrive so that the people at large, particularly the great mass of independent voters, would appear to be forcing him on to a spot he himself had already chosen. Then, when he acted, it seemed that he was responding to an overwhelming popular demand. He could create the disposition to listen and agree, by siphoning a problem out to the people, just as on a conversational level he could phrase a question so that the only possible answer was to say Yes.

Once Dr. Luther Gulick told him, "I don't think that Mr. Z has a single taint of New Deal enthusiasm." Roosevelt replied, "Right. But I can keep him useful. You know a man will do a lot of right things for the wrong reasons."

Roosevelt was a prodigious politician—consider how his own loftiness emerges in comparison to almost all the other politicians he dealt with year after year—and also a prodigious educator. Even such an inveterate antagonist to the President as Professor Beard once wrote, "He has discussed in his messages and addresses more fundamental problems of American life and society than all the other Presidents combined."

The columnist Samuel Grafton wrote the following appreciative note a year after his death: "One remembers him as a kind of smiling bus driver, with that cigarette holder pointed upward, listening to the uproar from behind as he took the sharp turns. They used to tell him he had not loaded his vehicle right for all eternity. But he knew he had stacked it well enough to round the next corner, and he knew when the yells were false, and when they were real, and he loved the passengers. He is dead now, and the bus is stalled, far from the gates of heaven, while the riders hold each other in deadlock over how to make the next curve."

How He Ran a Cabinet Meeting

Here too Roosevelt's technique was informal. Of course, as time went on, he paid less attention to the deliberations of his actual Cabinet; what interested him more was the opinion of men slightly under Cabinet level, like Marriner Eccles of the Federal Reserve, or the heads of the great administrative agencies. The President liked to deal with individuals, not with a group. Besides most men in the original Cabinet had been picked for predominantly political reasons; they were there because they kept fences mended, to pay off debts, or because it would have been dangerous to FDR's influence in Congress to keep them out. One Cabinet member told me, "A Roosevelt Cabinet was a delightful social occasion, where nothing was ever settled." Another member of great renown actually snubbed the President for six or seven months, by never even appearing at Cabinet meetings. One reason for this was that he had had a bitter quarrel with Hopkins, who, he said, had "influenced" FDR so that the President would not see him by himself. Everybody wanted to get to FDR alone.

In the later years a Roosevelt Cabinet meeting was not a policy conference at all, but simply a series of staff reports. Only seldom did serious debate take place, and only rarely were the members polled. FDR seldom confided in the group as a whole, if only because he feared leaks (especially by Garner in the first two terms), and when the war came the meetings of the Joint and Combined Chiefs were much more important, though FDR never attended these in person.

Roosevelt usually opened Cabinet proceedings by turning to Mr. Hull and saying cheerfully, "Cordell, what's the news from abroad?" Hull's stock answer was, "Not very encouraging." If Sumner Welles was present in place of Mr. Hull, the reply would be swift, precise, and comprehensive. FDR must have wished at least ten thousand times that Welles, not Hull, was the actual Secretary. But he could not possibly get rid of Hull because of his pivotal power in the Senate and his prestige in the country at large. Roosevelt liked and even admired Hull, but he was impatient at his fussiness, slowness of grasp, and mountaineer conservatism. He was his own Secretary of State— or Hopkins was. Then too Hull was a somewhat vindictive old man, and the President did not like this; perhaps it was a hereditary trait, for Hull's father had once tracked down and killed a man in cold blood in a Tennessee blood feud. Finally—though he persistently invited him after 1940 to run with him as Vice-President—FDR must have been aware of the intrigues whereby the Farley-Garner clique hoped to oust him from the White House with Hull's help. Farley reports that Hull once referred to Roosevelt as "that fellow!" At any rate the Secretary of State was gradually frozen out of control of his department and of intimate participation in affairs; one of the reasons why the President kept his team small at the great international conferences during the war was that this gave him an excuse to leave Hull out. Henry Morgenthau records that when he, Morgenthau, had a talk with Hull on what was to follow Teheran in 1944, Hull gasped and said, "Henry, this is the first time I have ever heard of this. . . . I have never even been permitted to see the minutes of the Teheran conference!"

After hearing Mr. Hull at a Cabinet meeting, FDR would turn to Henry Morgenthau. Roosevelt, quite aside from his penetrating affection for Morgenthau, always felt closer to the Treasury and was more interested in it than any other Government department except the Navy. Morgenthau has been described by former Vice-President Garner as "the most servile" of the ministers, and he thought that he had "a divine right" to lunch with the President alone every Monday, according to Mr. Ickes. Morgenthau seldom spoke much at Cabinet meetings; he would seek to reserve his energies for private talk. Roosevelt liked him so much not merely because he was an old Dutchess County neighbor but because he was relaxed and soothing and never argued. He would call him up and say, "Henry, come on over and hold my hand!"

Mr. Stimson, when he became a Cabinet member, was universally respected; next to the President, he had by far the widest vision of anybody in the room. Knox blustered, seldom had an original idea, and was often incapable of thinking a proposition through. Jesse Jones played his own close game; his mind was acute, practical, and powerful. The other members were inclined to distrust or fear him. Wallace was affable, frustrated, and somewhat secretive as a rule. It is a striking point that he was against, not for, Roosevelt's recognition of the Soviet Union when this matter was first broached in 1933. Ickes, because he would say No and talk back, had the President's great respect—incidentally FDR had never met him until he offered him a Cabinet post—but at 60 per cent of Cabinet meetings Ickes never said a word. Roosevelt knew that he could rely on him utterly. And FDR never lost his admiration and affection for Frances Perkins.

Mr. Garner records a colloquy purported to have taken place during the crisis over sit-down strikes in 1936:

"I said to Miss Perkins," Garner said, " 'Do you think the sit-down strike is right?'
" 'Yes,' she replied.
" 'Do you think it is legal?'
" 'Yes,' she answered.
"I asked the President:
" 'Do you think it is right?'
" 'No,' he replied.
" 'Do you think it is legal?'
" 'No,' he replied."

Garner left the meeting under the impression that Roosevelt would issue a statement excoriating the sit-down strike. But the statement did not materialize.[3]

Not only were there bitter and implacable feuds within the team; several members were disloyal to the President himself. Miss Perkins has recounted in conversation how, on one occasion, FDR was summoned out of the Cabinet room by a telephone call that he wanted to receive privately. (He often took ordinary telephone calls during a Cabinet meeting, and used the telephone frequently while they were in progress, but this is the only time Miss Perkins can recall when he left the room.) He apologized, and said that he would be back in five minutes. The instant he was out of sight the pent-up private emotions of these trusted advisers burst forth, and a fierce bout of backbiting began. It was the first time that members of the Cabinet had ever been alone together as a group without FDR, and it was clear by the time

[3] "John N. Garner's Story," by Bascom N. Timmons, *Collier's*, February 28, 1948.

he returned that only two people there besides Miss Perkins were really on his side, Morgenthau and Hopkins.

His Relations with the Press

Of course Mr. Roosevelt was a genius. In some respects he was a supreme genius, as for example in the field of his associations with newspapermen and the press. From 80 to 85 per cent of the newspapers of the country consistently opposed him; yet he retained the most cordial possible relations with all the men who covered him in Washington and elsewhere. In the 1940 campaign there were six states in which not a single newspaper supported him;[4] in the whole of New England only five small papers took his side, and in many one-newspaper cities all over the country the paper was anti-Roosevelt; in some metropolitan centers like Boston *every* newspaper was against him in each campaign. Of course I am referring to the ownership and management of these papers. It is notorious that even on Hearst papers and the McCormick-Patterson press, many members of the staff and employees were vigorously (if secretly) *for* FDR. Also of course we must take note of the fact that the President was always a "story"; everything he did down to his smallest whisper for more than twelve years was news. The newspapers had to print what he said whether the bosses liked him or not, and even if, like so many, they hated his very guts. Even so the paradox is remarkable that the President, twice a week for year after year, sat down with men who worked for other men who loathed him, established the most friendly contact, won them over, became their friends, and made his partnership with them of highly effective value to the nation.

FDR always had acute interest in journalism and the newspaper business; for instance he once wanted to start a national tabloid with a central office in Washington, D.C., that would print all the news but without any editorials. As fascinating a bit of dialogue as may be found in any of the press conferences is his advice to John Boettiger, his own son-in-law, when Boettiger became publisher of the Hearst newspaper in Seattle. ("He has old man Hearst as a boss, which is no joke either.") That FDR had a wonderful instinct for publicity is of course obvious; he was never caught napping on even the most minor opportunity for improving his press relations. I remember

[4] Delaware, Louisiana, Maine, Maryland, North Dakota, and Vermont. See "The President and the Press," by Walter Davenport, *Collier's*, February 3, 1945.

being present at a small testimonial dinner given in the Middle West in 1934 for an inconspicuous foreign correspondent; a telegram of congratulation arrived from Mr. Roosevelt on the split second that the guest of honor rose to speak, without any warning or intimation that the President even knew the dinner was taking place. He always watched out carefully for the interests of newspapermen assigned to the White House, fathered them, and protected them. Once, on a cruise, he offered to write dispatches for members of the party who were seasick. He was furious at the time of the Atlantic Charter when it became known that the British had two correspondents present in the guise of "historians," whereas the Americans had none. This had nothing to do with coverage of the story so far as he was concerned himself; he was angry because the American press had been let down in principle.

He almost never attacked a newspaperman by name, no matter what the provocation. We have noted above his mention at a press conference of inflammatory rumors about his health, but such talk was very rare. In a moment of bad temper he once launched out at Drew Pearson (but this was mostly to protect Mr. Hull), and on one occasion he permitted himself to get annoyed at Arthur Krock. Early in 1940 he said at a press conference that only "one person" among important leaders in the United States whom he had asked for help in the prewar period had refused to serve, and somewhat reluctantly he revealed his name later—Roy Howard.

Once he made some mildly critical remarks about columnists. Elizabeth May Craig, the well-known Maine newspaperwoman, interjected, "But, Mr. President, you've got one in the family!" FDR—and the whole room—shook with laughter.

Mr. Roosevelt's press conferences were like nothing else ever seen in Washington before; as a matter of fact, until Theodore Roosevelt, reporters were not even admitted to the White House. There were 998 FDR conferences in all. Sometimes a hundred men were present, sometimes two hundred. The President knew most of those who attended regularly on first-name or nickname terms; he was like a friendly, informal schoolmaster conducting a free-for-all seminar, and indeed the chief function of the conferences was educational. The President would explain an issue, take it apart, and present it over and over again from a new angle; he tackled the exposition of a difficult piece of legislation almost like an engineer demonstrating a new model of some machine. Also FDR could refresh the whole nation by the atmosphere he gave out at a press conference. The first one he ever held as President came on March 8, 1933, when most of the banks were still closed and the entire nation was prostrate and quivering with panic. Within two minutes the newspapermen, whose words would reach the ends of the earth in an hour, were rocking with healthy, hearty laughter. A photograph taken of FDR on this occcasion tells much about his character; he was the very epitome of robust vitality, cheerful assurance, and solid optimism.

Nobody talked back to the President, and he could be sharp ("No cross-examination, please!" was a famous early remark), but discussion at a press conference was often lively. This is an example. The date was October 6, 1937, and the subject of discussion the Quarantine speech he had recently delivered:[5]

Q. I had two major things in mind. One was what you had in mind with reference to quarantining—what type of measure. Secondly, how would you reconcile the policy you outlined yesterday with the policy of neutrality laid down by the Act of Congress?

The President: Read the last line I had in the speech. That gives it about as well as anything else. (*Looking through New York Herald Tribune of October 6.*)

Q. I don't believe that paper carried it. (*Laughter*)

The President: Here it is: "Therefore America actively engages in the search for peace."

Q. But you also said that the peace-loving nations can and must find a way to make their wills prevail.

The President: Yes?

Q. And you were speaking, as I interpreted it, you were speaking of something more than moral indignation. That is preparing the way for collaborative ——

The President: Yes?

Q. Is anything contemplated? Have you moved?

The President: No; just the speech itself.

Q. Yes, but how do you reconcile that? Do you accept the fact that that is a repudiation of the neutrality ——

The President: Not for a minute. It may be an expansion.

Q. Is that for use?

The President: All off the record.

Q. Doesn't that mean economic sanctions anyway?

[5] Rosenman, Vol. VI, p. 422-25.

The President: No, not necessarily. Look, "sanctions" is a terrible word to use. They are out of the window.

Q. Is there a likelihood that there will be a conference of peace-loving nations?

The President: No; conferences are out of the window. You never get anywhere with a conference.

Q. Foreign papers put it as an attitude without a program.

The President: That was the London *Times*.

Q. Would you say that that is not quite it, that you are looking toward a program as well as having an attitude?

The President: It is an attitude, and it does not outline a program; but it says we are looking for a program.

Q. Wouldn't it be almost inevitable, if any program is reached, that our present Neutrality Act will have to be overhauled?

The President: Not necessarily. That is the interesting thing.

Q. You say there isn't any conflict between what you outline and the Neutrality Act. They seem to be on opposite poles to me and your assertion does not enlighten me.

The President: Put your thinking-cap on, Ernest [Lindley].

Q. I have been for some years. They seem to be at opposite poles. How can you be neutral if you are going to align yourself with one group of nations?

The President: What do you mean, "aligning"? You mean a treaty?

Q. Not necessarily. I meant action on the part of peace-loving nations.

The President: There are a lot of methods in the world that have never been tried yet.

Q. Do you agree or disagree with what apparently amounts to the conclusion of the British, that sanctions mean war?

The President: No. Don't talk about sanctions. As I said to Jimmie, don't get off on the sanction route.

Q. Is a "quarantine" a sanction?

The President: No.

Q. Are you excluding any coercive action? Sanctions are coercive.

The President: That is exactly the difference.

Q. Better, then, to keep it in a moral sphere?

The President: No, it can be a very practical sphere.

This is part of the dialogue when Hopkins was being sent abroad on a job:

Q. Mr. President, will Mr. Hopkins be a dollar-a-year man?

The President: No, he will not.

Q. Will he be an Administrative Assistant then, sir?

The President: No, I don't know what he will be.
Q. Will he get paid? (*Laughter*)
The President: Yes, sure. He's a Democrat! (*Loud laughter*)

In 1941 there came a discussion about the patrol system newly instituted in the Atlantic.

Q. Mr. President, if this patrol should discover some apparently aggressive ships headed toward the Western Hemisphere, what would it do about it?
The President: Let me know. (*Loud laughter*)[6]

Sometimes he could be mildly irritable. In 1937 he was heckled severely when it became known that Justice Hugo Black had been a member of the Ku Klux Klan:[7]

The President: Anticipating what you are going to ask and in order to save time (*laughter*), I know approximately what is on your minds and I want to be helpful if I can. Therefore I am going to give you this statement for direction quotation. Get out your pencils. (*Reading*) "I know only what I have read in the newspapers. I know that the stories are appearing serially—not seriously, I said 'serially'—and their publication is not complete. Mr. Justice Black is in Europe where, undoubtedly, he cannot get the full text of these articles. Until such time as he returns, there is no further comment to be made."
That is all.
Q. Has Mr. Justice Black been communicated with by you or any member of your Administration?
The President: No.
Q. You said, "No"?
The President: No; I said, "No."
Q. Have you any information as to the time of his return?
The President: No.
Q. Prior to the appointment of former Senator Black, had you received any information from any source as to his Klan membership?
The President: No.
Q. May we ask, if it turns out that he is a member——
The President: That is an "if" question.

This is the opening of the press conference at which the bill to "pack" the Supreme Court was announced:[8]

[6] Rosenman, Vol. X, pp. 116 and 135.
[7] Rosenman, Vol. VI, p. 352.
[8] Rosenman. Vol. VI, p. 74.

Q. Can you tell us what the Senators have been telling you about your Judiciary reform bill?

The President: You don't want to be here all day, do you? (*Laughter*)

Q. Are you surprised at the reaction to your Judiciary bill?

The President: It depends on which paper you read. (*Laughter*)

Newspapermen loved to try and trip FDR up. Once, late in 1939, he was asked if the new American neutrality policy (he had been talking about our "maritime" frontiers) reached the Rhine; he replied that he was concerned only with "salt water." Once Mrs. Craig asked him something about Stalin, and his reply was, "May, I don't write no social column." During the discussion on applying Lend Lease to Russia he was asked if the defense of the Soviet Union was the defense of the United States. Roosevelt brushed it off with, "How old is Ann?" He loved to tantalize and tease. He opened one of the greatest of all press conferences, the one at which he laid out the scheme for Lend Lease, by turning idly to Early and saying, "We haven't got a darned thing today, have we, Steve?" He sometimes ended a conference with some such remark as, "You've got a mouthful, better run."

How Roosevelt Traveled

Roosevelt traveled immensely more than any other American president, and probably more than any other chief of state who ever lived. I do not know if any total exists of the number of miles he went by boat, automobile, and airplane; in 1944 alone, including all methods of conveyance, it was 50,000 miles. The total mileage merely of his railway travel during the Presidency was 544,864 miles in 399 separate trips. Interestingly enough, the 400th trip taken by his special train was that which brought his body back to Washington from Warm Springs after his death.

Roosevelt was always keenly interested in any trip, and he loved trains. He took maps with him, and watched the route. He liked to travel slowly, not merely so that he could watch the country by day, but because he couldn't use his feet to brace himself, as everybody with a normal pair of legs does unconsciously. His favorite speed was 35 miles an hour. At night the presidential trains made up time by going fairly fast; it is doubtful if he knew how fast they sometimes went.

Daniel Long, who was in charge of travel arrangements at the White House, had a staff of seven men, all experts in railroad transportation, with offices in an upper floor of the Executive Mansion; later men from the Signal Corps supplemented this group. FDR, when he planned a trip, always called Mr. Long in first, and then Michael F. Reilly of the Secret Service. The route was as a rule chosen so as to give competing railroads an equal chance to carry the President, and the operating vice-president of the company would be aboard; his word was law so far as any railroad procedure was concerned. There would be a complete change of crews and porters, selected on a seniority basis, when a new line took over. A pilot train usually ran one mile ahead of the President's special and no train followed until after a "reasonable" interval.

On campaign trips the President's train ran to sixteen or even eighteen cars; on the runs between Washington and Hyde Park or Warm Springs they averaged eight. They were equipped with a direct, instantaneous telephone circuit between the President's car and the engineer, and had an automatic device so that no matter what happened, the cars could not slip backward at campaign stops and hit anybody in the crowd. Also radio equipment maintained direct contact with the White House. The train was, as a rule, broken up after each trip, but early in 1944 it stayed intact for the month that the President was visiting Mr. Baruch's plantation in South Carolina; there was no telephone in the house, and the train, parked eight miles away, became his office. Until 1940 the President used any of various private cars owned by the Pullman Company. Then a new car, especially designed for his use, was built; it is the property of the United States Government, and, being heavily armored, weighs about twice what a normal Pullman weighs. Its name is Ferdinand Magellan.

All the President's trains had to carry a ramp until about 1940, when Navy engineers worked out an elevator device. The ramp meant that FDR's car always had to be "spotted" where the incline would not be too steep. Usually when the President left Washington on a trip publicly known, he would insist, no matter what the effort cost him, on walking the length of the ramp rather than being wheeled or carried.

During the war arrangements for Roosevelt's unprecedented trips to Casablanca, Teheran, and Yalta produced fantastic problems. The need for security was, of course, doubly imperative. The Casablanca journey, in January, 1943, included a trip by train from Washington to Miami, the flight across the Atlantic in a Clipper operated by Pan-American Airways for the Navy, the flight up to Morocco itself from Dakar by a land plane operated by the Air Transport Command of the United States Army Air Forces, and the return to Washington by the same process. The departure from Washington was arranged with the utmost (and necessary) secrecy. The names of the Pullman cars were painted out, and the special train, on leaving the capital, headed north as if it were on an ordinary trip to Hyde Park, and then turned around at Baltimore to go south. Filipino mess boys replaced the ordinary porters, and these were forbidden under pain of court-martial even to mail a letter from Florida when they got there; then the train was broken up, hidden for a few days on a deserted siding near Jacksonville, and finally sent north again.[9]

Once aboard the Clipper on the Casablanca flight FDR might have noticed that one face among the Secret Service men was new. A special agent named Hipsley was aboard who was an exceptionally powerful swimmer; it was his job to keep the President afloat if the plane crashed in the ocean.

The President did not like to fly, because there was nothing to look at and he could not relax as easily as on a boat or train. The flights he took to Casablanca were the first he made since becoming President. I have been given access to the pilot's navigation reports on all his wartime expeditions, and they make engrossing reading. On January 3, 1943, high personnel in the Atlantic area were warned that a flight of such importance was about to take place (they were not told what it was) that "all other operations must cease during this period." FDR's plane was preceded by another plane, and followed by still another; they kept about an hour apart. General Arnold himself piloted the President's Clipper during the first part of the trip, over a route just skirting the coast, and even inland on occasion, to avoid possible antiaircraft fire from German submarines which still prowled on the surface of the Caribbean. There was no untoward incident except that the ground crews in Puerto Rico were not alerted; high-ranking officers on the presidential plane stood fire guard themselves while it was being refueled, holding small hand extinguishers taken from the cabin. Once across the ocean there were other problems. To fly across the Atlas Mountains meant going higher than the President's medical advisers liked, and care was taken to avoid Spanish territory, out of the fear that if FDR had made a forced landing there he might have been "interned." The President was much impressed by the C-54 that carried him in Africa and, on arrival, he showed it to Mr. Churchill with great pride.

[9] My source for most of the above is a private White House memorandum.

Teheran was a more formidable adventure. The President traveled from Hampton Roads on the battleship *Iowa*, and arrived at Oran, Algeria, on November 13, 1943. He then flew under ATC auspices to Tunis, Cairo, Teheran, and back. By this time he had his own C-54 (the type of Douglas craft known in civilian terms as a DC-4) which had been converted to his use with a special galley, two berths, a space roomy enough for a small table, and leg rests.[10] General Arnold asked him if he wanted any particular pilot, and FDR said, "Yes, get that little fellow who flew us to Casablanca." This was Major Otis Bryan, a veteran of the domestic airlines, who had become vice-president of Transcontinental and Western Air. Arnold drew him back to active duty, and he was commissioned a lieutenant colonel for the trip.

In the plane besides FDR and Prettyman, his valet, were Hopkins, Leahy, Rear Admiral Wilson Brown, Pa Watson, Dr. McIntire, and four Secret Service men. A special "knockdown" ramp had been built. The agents hated the big 30-foot ramps that were normally put into position when he was expected anywhere, because of course they imperiled security by giving notice to anybody that something special was going on. The flights went off without a slip. But at Tunis a small plane landed on the airstrip directly ahead of the President, ignoring the red flares shot at it in warning; also three P-39's of FDR's fighter escort had to peel off and warn away a French plane that approached too close while the C-54 was aloft near Cairo. General Eisenhower was a passenger, and sat in the copilot's seat. "A close call for that Frenchman," was his comment. Roosevelt wanted badly to circle over a battlefield in Italy, but this was not permitted, nor would the Secret Service men let him visit Naples.[11]

[10] FDR himself, according to Byrnes (*op. cit.*, p. 23) had not been consulted about this and did not approve that a plane should be remodeled for his own use, because of the expense involved.

[11] This is part of Colonel Bryan's log:

Date	Departed GMT	From	For	Arrived	Elapsed Time	Mileage
18 Nov. 43	1035	Oran	Tunis	1305	3.30	635
21	2125	Tunis	Cairo	0740	10.15	1,851
27	0435	Cairo	Teheran	1130	6.55	1,310
2 Dec.	0610	Teheran	Cairo	1240	6.30	1,270
7 Dec.	0615	Cairo	Tunis	1445	8.30	1,571
8	0700	Tunis	Malta	0855	1.55	310
8	1200	Malta	Sicily	1310	1.10	164
8	1425	Sicily	Tunis	1535	1.10	155
9	0530	Tunis	Dakar	1810	12.40	2,460

The trip to Yalta (Mission Number Seventeen was the code name) was the most complex and difficult of all. The project demanded a great deal of skillful organization; the job was to move the President and 135 Very Important Personages and between 300 and 350 other personnel by air to a remote spot in the Crimea over routes never flown by the Air Transport Command before, and skirting German-held islands in the Aegean. It was, in fact, a major operation; some 325,000 miles of air service were involved. It is not generally known that Colonel Ray W. Ireland of the ATC and his staff spent three weeks in the Crimea scouting out the whole project before it was finally approved; the "advance crowd" (i.e., the Secret Service) also got there early, and a survey ship went in from Tunis; later mine sweepers, patrol boats, and destroyers were stationed along the route. The President's party arrived in 14 C-54's; they came into the Saki airport ten minutes apart, and not one was more than sixty seconds off schedule, after a 1,400-mile flight from Malta. Then a courier service was maintained daily to Cairo. The operation as a whole took 31 big transports; 16 fighters (P-38's) comprised the escort. Only three planes were given this guard, those of the President, General Marshall, and Admiral King. The President's own plane was not the first to land, but came in fourth or fifth. Six "shop" airplanes were brought along, filled with spare parts in case anything went wrong, and between 60 and 70 pilots were on duty. There were minor worries because Russian gasoline has a smaller octane rating than ours, and one engine on the President's plane broke down and had to be replaced by another the night before he flew back.

FDR's pilot on this occasion was a well-known young officer, Lieutenant Colonel Henry T. ("Hank") Myers, who, as commander of the *Sacred Cow* and later the *Independence,* has probably flown more eminent personages more miles than anybody in history. One thing that interested Myers highly was the "dry run" he took to Yalta, a few days in advance of the President's own flight, to scout out the route and see what the landing fields were like, and also to arrange liaison with the Russians so that FDR would not be shot down by error. (A British plane *was*, incidentally, shot down near Sebastopol, by accident of course; it crash-landed and nobody was hurt.) The actual trip with the President went with perfect smoothness. "It was the first time I had ever flown him," Myers told me later, "so I took it pretty easy. I was glad it was sunny. You don't want to drag the President of the United States through a lot of clouds."[12]

The President's plane, the *Sacred Cow,* now contained a secret elevator, so that there was no need to have ramps ready. "The darned thing didn't always work," Myers has said. "We sure were worried about that elevator. Every time we showed it to General Arnold, it got stuck. Soon as Arnold's back was turned, then it worked again." I asked Myers if FDR had a parachute. "No. Someone cuts your tail off at three thousand feet, there's no time to get back to the President and get him in a chute." Nobody on board had a chute, in fact, and strange as this may seem, nobody was armed. In the Roosevelt party were Leahy, Admiral Brown, Dr. McIntire, Dr. Howard G. Bruenn (a heart specialist assigned to the President), Mike Reilly, Prettyman, and Anna Boettiger. The President boarded the plane at Malta at about 10 P.M. the evening before the take-off, and went right to sleep. He did not even wake up when the huge craft took off.

How Roosevelt Was Guarded

All presidents are protected carefully; Roosevelt presented some unique problems because in the event of an attempted assassination he could not move quickly, and he had continually to expose himself in great crowds. (Two people were accidentally killed in a melee in a Pennsylvania city on one occasion when the crowd around him got unmanageable.) On the other hand he was, in some ways, less trouble to the Secret Service than other chief executives, in that he was almost always in a fixed spot. Several agents lost pounds in weight when Mr. Truman became President, since they had to follow his spry figure on foot a great deal.

Perhaps it is not generally known that FDR's armored automobile weighed almost 8,000 pounds (it was sent by ship all the way to Yalta but could not be used there because it was too heavy), that the FBI and Secret Service even checked distant relatives of the White House grocer and butcher out of fear that the President might be poisoned, that the special trains and planes carried their own milk and water, that the White House was equipped with Geiger counters and an X-ray machine for inspecting packages, that during the war an anti-aircraft battery was stationed on the roof of the Executive Mansion,

12 Colonel Myers is one of the few men alive who has a short-snorter roll of bills (it is 35 feet long) containing signatures of FDR, Churchill, and Stalin.

and that the bomb shelter was built out of what had been a vault where the Treasury sequestered opium. But, until the war, the White House never gave the impression of being closely guarded. I know one newspaperman, a young European, who walked in one day and attended press conferences for six months before he was ever asked to present a credential.

There was considerable fear that some crazy person might get hold of an airplane and bomb the White House, Hyde Park, Warm Springs, or Shangri-La, and even that there might be an attack by Axis parachutists or kidnapers. Mike Reilly, head of the Secret Service detail, has disclosed some fascinating details of the precautions taken in this regard.[13] A highly complex agenda was worked out. "At the White House, the Secret Service and the Army Signal Corps maintained a twenty-four-hour watch on an intricate telephone land line and on a frequency modulation radio communication system which was in direct two-way contact from the White House air raid shelter and three isolated points in Washington. . . ." A number of other points, including the President's train, his room in Hyde Park, and all Secret Service field offices throughout the United States, were linked up in this system, and every unidentified plane was spotted all the way from Greenland to the Straits of Magellan! In case of a raid on the White House, the President was to be moved either to the shelter under the lawn, the Treasury vaults, "one of ten secret buildings in the suburban area of Washington," or to an army bomber always held in position and alerted at an isolated airfield.

So far as I know the President used a dummy only once, at the time of the Atlantic Charter meeting, though other heads of state use them sometimes. To throw people off the scent FDR's yacht steamed slowly all day through the Cape Cod Canal, with a man conspicuously sitting on deck dressed like Roosevelt and resembling him, while Roosevelt himself was far away at sea.

FDR is believed to have been somewhat annoyed on one occasion when it was discovered that his own telephone was being tapped. A night watchman with a bent for electricity did it to amuse himself. Evidence exists that after the war began all conversation at his desk was secretly recorded, of course with his knowledge and consent.

Strangely enough, the President once came near to being blown

[13] *Reilly of the White House*, by Michael F. Reilly and William T. Slocum (New York, Simon & Schuster, Inc., 1947), pp. 235-37.

up by a ship of his own Navy. He was aboard the *Iowa* en route to the Teheran Conference, and a torpedo was accidentally discharged from the *Thompson*, one of the destroyers in the escort. But Captain McCrea, on the bridge of the *Iowa*, and other officers saw it coming, and after frantic maneuvering the battleship turned sharply and steered swiftly away just in time. The torpedo missed it by about twenty yards. A seaman was court-martialed later; apparently he fired the torpedo by mistake, and was not punished. The *Thompson*, an unlucky ship, was sunk later in the Pacific war.

The Mystery

We face, finally, the central problem and mystery we have posed before. What *made* Roosevelt what he was? What, despite all the negative qualities we have mentioned, turned him into one of the supreme creative characters of history? How did he become a man of the Left? In the deep core of his personality, why did certain forces come out on top, and what transformed a somewhat effete and shallow young man into the cryptic giant who won two wars at once? What made him not merely a national figure but the embodiment and symbol of *world* democracy? What was the Roosevelt secret? *Why* was he what he was?

Several factors might be mentioned:

1. He was one of those persons with the good luck to grow up slowly; he held traces of the adolescent all his life, and he was always fresh, youthful in mind, and receptive to new ideas. Till the end of his days, he was as eager as a boy.

2. His boldness, his contempt for precedent, the continual advancement of his curiosities and satisfactions, probably had some roots in the fact that his father was a very old man; consequently he grew up with little fear of authority.

3. The central point of his character as a youth was that he was a "good boy." Later, as the psychologists would say, he overcompensated for this by a delight in being unconventional and daring, by upsetting applecarts though almost always in a well-bred way.

4. That he was rich played a powerful role. There have been plenty of poor men who were idealists, but a solid background of wealth and privilege makes idealism easier if the impulse is there. Roosevelt had enough assurance never to be afraid of being radical.

5. He was an extremely superior and confident person; then came

the attack of infantile paralysis which caused an almost complete temporary disintegration of personality. Nothing of his character or career can be understood without reference to his illness. For three years "he rolled in the gutter with Death."

6. To make up for the fact that he was paralyzed he developed the tremendous drive, exuberance, and radiating energy that carried him into the White House. (This, however, is something of an oversimplification, as we shall see below.)

7. The single clue that is the best common denominator to all the multifarious paradoxes of his character is his love for action. He resolved most confusions by the simple process of doing something, *acting*.

*

Against this broad backdrop we proceed now to the story of one of the most commanding lives the world has ever known.

Chapter 9

THE BACKGROUND OF HYDE PARK

Man is his own star . . .
—JOHN FLETCHER

The Roosevelts were newcomers to the Hyde Park region comparatively speaking; some of their neighbors, of the old river families, have roots much deeper. FDR's distant forebears were, in the main, metropolitan folk who lived and worked in New York City. When people use the term Hyde Park in connection with Roosevelt, they generally mean a house originally called Springwood, which was built in 1826. It was remodeled from time to time; various owners added wings to the frame and clapboard structure, and gave it a late Georgian stucco front. FDR's father James bought it in 1867 for $40,000, with 110 acres of "water lots" worked by tenant farmers; later the total family holdings came to about 1,300 acres. It is not a particularly elaborate house, and Roosevelt hated to have the property described by any such imposing word as "estate," but the old trees and smooth grounds, sloping down to the Hudson, have impressive quality; the house was his mother's for decade after decade, it became the inner citadel of the family, and it was here that he was born.

Hyde Park, the village, is a mile and a half to the north; the vigorous city of Poughkeepsie is four miles south. The area as a whole is about eighty miles from New York City, and the Albany Post Road (US 9) and the swift new parkways sweep close by. Hyde Park (population about 1,200) was originally named Stoutenburgh in honor of its first settler, Jacobus Stoutenburgh, who came in 1741. Several of the towns nearby have Dutch names, like Rhinebeck and Red Hook (Roode Hoeck); families like the Van Wycks and Beekmans go back to Revolutionary times. The region is rich in Dutch background and eighteenth-century history; four houses still standing on Roosevelt property date back to the 1760's. The signposts and markers in Dutchess County are more historic, if less spectacular, than those in Montana say; this valley knew Hendrik Hudson, Rip van Winkle, and engagements and forays without number between colonists and Indians, French and British.

The Hudson Valley squirearchy was, in some respects, the nearest thing to a landed gentry the United States has ever had. The river families grew up here, intermarried, and intermingled behind their own stockade; even as recently as in the days of FDR's youth, they were all but segregated. "They never fell in love except with cousins," I heard it said, "because they never met anybody outside their own families." Merits—and demerits—attended their way of life. Many were extremely parsimonious in their living habits—or let us just call them plain skinflints. Yet they had a marked sense of *noblesse oblige*; not only did they perform obvious good works like endowing churches and taking care of orphans, but they founded music schools, established courses in domestic science, or otherwise sought to pay, in part, their obligation to society. They were sound and sober, and often dull; they were dutifully brought up on strict ethical standards and, in theory at least, on the principle of undeviating good citizenship; they understood tradition and believed in it, because it helped fix them immovably—so they hoped—in a world that would never change. They believed in decorum and convention. Above all they believed in order. Members of some families were distinguished for that type of idiosyncrasy which is apt to crop out in bourgeois civilization at its most refined. In one house near Hyde Park the dining-room table and chairs were all bodily moved by servants three times a day to different rooms, so that one view of the Hudson might be enjoyed at breakfast, another at luncheon, and a third at dinner. One lady whom the Roosevelts knew always carried with her a kind of wheeled sled when she went into New York by train, so that she could haul her own luggage out of the station and thus avoid tipping the porter.

"All that is in me goes back to the Hudson," Roosevelt wrote once. Indeed the Hudson dominated the community, not only because it is one of the most majestic and beautiful rivers in the world, but because it symbolized the fixity of these old families, their continuity, their undisturbed superiority and gentility. They, like the river, had an eternal flow—or so they thought.

Today the patroon atmosphere is largely obliterated. Roosevelt himself did as much to kill it as any man. I do not mean merely that an ice-cream parlor juts out on the road just opposite the library, or that

Hyde Park (it is still a very pleasant village) has neon lights. But the big families have lost their grip; the estates have shriveled up. They have smaller properties, because of relentless taxation; they have fewer children, and the children tend to move into New York City or elsewhere rather than stay on the ancestral domains. When, many years ago, Roosevelt's own father sold part of his holdings to the State (which built thereon what is now a hospital for the insane), he inadvertently set a pattern. Much nearby property has been bought by the Catholic Church; for instance, directly south of Hyde Park, a Jesuit school occupies what was once an old river estate. The Ogden Mills properties are now a State park, and the Frederick W. Vanderbilt château is now a national historic site. Incidentally it was this house that was originally called Hyde Park; in fact the village took its name from it, and as recent a publication as the New York State volume in the American Guide Series uses "Hyde Park" to identify the Vanderbilt house, not Roosevelt's.

FDR, let us keep in mind, belonged to the landed gentry, and was brought up like an English "county" gentleman. The wealth he inherited came mostly from shipping and the land; it was not in large part industrial wealth, and did not accrue in the first instance from the mass exploitation of labor. A characteristic of the landed gentry is that it has a persistent tendency to side with the townsmen, and thus indirectly with the working class, against those interlopers who make colossal new fortunes out of machines. Here is one clue to Roosevelt. He had little personal experience of the abuse of labor, and so never came to hate labor out of greed or bad conscience; he grew up in the atmosphere of a direct paternalism that made him feel intimate personal responsibility for those afflicted with hardship or insecurity.

Also, compared to their really wealthy neighbors the Roosevelts were pretty small potatoes—not at all magnificent, ornate, or regal.

Family Tree and Trees

The Roosevelt family was founded by a certain Claes Martenszen Van Rosenvelt who set sail from Holland to Nieuw Amsterdam in the 1640's. What caused this worthy citizen to leave the Old World for the New at this precise juncture is unknown. He was, so far as we know, the first Roosevelt to come to America. Claes was probably a peasant; his name means "son of Martin," and he was ironically nicknamed Kleytjen, or "little one," because he is supposed to have been a very large man physically. The name "Roosevelt" derives from the locality where Claes lived, Rosen Velt (Field of Roses), on the island of Tholen, near Zeeland. Some Roosevelts still live in Holland today. The last male member of the Dutch line, H. W. F. Van Rosevelt, works in a Chinese restaurant in Haarlem, and gets $18 a week; his wife has a job in a hosiery shop, and his father is a dockhand.

In 1935, some three centuries after Claes, Franklin Roosevelt wrote a friend who had inquired whether any basis at all existed for the Nazi charge that he had Jewish blood:

I am grateful to you for your interesting letter. . . . All I know about the origin of the Roosevelt family in this country is that all branches bearing the name are apparently descended from Claes Martenszen, who came from Holland sometime before 1648—even the year is uncertain. Where he came from in Holland I do not know, nor do I know who his parents were. . . . I have never had either the time or the inclination to try to establish the line on the other side of the ocean before they came over here, nearly three hundred years ago.

In the dim distant past they may have been Jews or Catholics or Protestants. What I am more interested in is whether they were good citizens and believers in God. I hope they were both.[1]

Claes Martenszen had a son, who became known as Nicholas Roosevelt, who married a woman named Heyltje Jans Kunst. They had two sons, Johannes (b. 1689), and Jacobus (b. 1692); from these all the contemporary Roosevelts derive, one line having produced Theodore, the other Franklin. As a matter of fact FDR was, the genealogists tell us, related to no fewer than eleven other American presidents; old Claes himself was the direct ancestor of five.[2] Roosevelt always liked to think of himself as a Dutchman, but actually the family proliferated so widely that, in the course of three centuries, it picked up all manner of other bloods; for instance it has the right to wear a Scots tartan, the Murray plaid. It has been calculated that FDR was only about 3 per cent Dutch; the really predominant strain was English, and other admixtures came from Flanders, Germany, Italy, France, and Sweden.[3] Naturally the Roosevelts married women more and more Anglo-Saxon as time went on: in the Jacobus branch, these were successively named

[1] Rosenman, Vol. IV, p. 96.

[2] The eleven are Washington, both Adamses, Madison, Van Buren, both Harrisons, Taylor, Grant, TR, and Taft.

[3] The family motto is *Qui Plantavit Curabit*; the coat of arms is three roses on a silver shield.

Hardenbroeck, Hoffman, Walton, Aspinwall, Howland, and finally Delano; in the Johannes branch, Sjoerts, Bogard, Van Schaack, Barnhill, and Bulloch. TR married a Lee, and then a Carow; FDR married another Roosevelt. Indeed members of the family intermarried practically like Hapsburgs or white mice. It was all very tribal. Not only was Eleanor Roosevelt Theodore's niece and goddaughter and FDR's fifth cousin once removed; her father Elliott (TR's only brother) was Franklin's godfather. Or to go further—Theodore Douglas Robinson, the son of TR's sister Corinne, married Helen Rebecca Roosevelt, who was Franklin's half niece. The Robinson children and FDR's children are at one and the same time sixth cousins, second cousins, and half first cousins once removed.[4] A second cousin of Alice Longworth, TR's daughter by his first marriage, by name Philip Roosevelt, married Jean, the daughter of John Roosevelt, who was also Alice's second cousin. FDR's father had a son, James Roosevelt Roosevelt (Rosy), by his first marriage, who married Helen Schermerhorn Astor; they had two children who were older than their "uncle," FDR!

Roosevelt was inveterately interested in his own lineage from the time that the family settled in America; one of his early themes at Harvard dealt with the Roosevelts in New Amsterdam. He wrote his mother in 1901: "I have been in the library constantly looking up old records, but nothing much is to be found. Do please copy for me all the extracts in our old Dutch Bible and send them to me." Eleanor Roosevelt once told me that FDR knew far more about her branch of the family than she did, and that his mother's knowledge was encyclopedic beyond belief. His own approach was more than just snobbish; what appealed to him was that he came of a breed of seafarers, adventurers, and revolutionaries. His forebears took the American side in the Revolutionary War, not the British. In a speech in 1938 he told his audience vigorously, "Every one of my ancestors on both sides—and when you go back four or five generations that means thirty-two or sixty-four of them—every single one, without exception, was in this land in 1776. And there was only one Tory among them."[5]

But until the last generation the Roosevelts were not overly conspicuous. We think nowadays of "Roosevelt" as a classically great name; actually it was not. It was a good name, but not great; outside a

[4] "Roosevelt Family Album," by Joseph Alsop and Robert Kintner, *Life,* September 9, 1939.
[5] Rosenman, Vol. VII, p. 259.

limited circle, few Americans had ever heard of it, and it had nothing of the glamour it has now. The historian Gerald W. Johnson has some cogent words on this point. The whole Roosevelt record, for generation after generation, was colorless from any really large point of view, he points out: the family never produced an artist, a fanatic, or a madman. Skeletons are rare in Roosevelt closets. The central mystery remains. "Here is a race that for three hundred years remained consistently unremarkable. The only amazing thing about them is that for six generations they never startled anyone. They were all respectable, reasonably industrious, reasonably able, reasonably prosperous—only one or two in the long list ever got into the millionaire class, but none ended in the almshouse—and, to be brutally frank, all were dismally dull. Then, in the seventh generation, this dynasty of the mediocre suddenly blazed up with not one, but two, of the most remarkable men in American history."[6]

The Paternal Line

FDR's great-great-grandfather on the paternal side, by name Isaac, son of Jacobus, was born in 1726 and died in 1794—most Roosevelts are long-lived. This Isaac was a weighty citizen: he lived in Wall Street, married a woman from the frontier (i.e., Dutchess County), made a fortune in rum, joined the Continental Congress, helped finance the American Revolution, served in the New York Senate, assisted in writing the State's constitution, and became the second president of New York's first bank. His son James, born in 1760, went to Princeton and followed his father into banking; he has been described as "a highly respectable gentleman of the old school," and was the last member of this wing of the family to hold public office until FDR; he was a New York City alderman, and marched in George Washington's victory parade. He died at eighty-seven. But the most interesting thing about him from the point of view of what happened later was that he was the first member of the family to settle in Dutchess County. James had very large properties indeed in Manhattan; he owned, in fact, a 400-acre tract that covered half of what is now Harlem; it ran from 110th Street

---

[6] From a review by Gerald W. Johnson of *The Amazing Roosevelt Family 1613-1942*, by Karl Schriftgiesser (New York, Wilfred Funk, Inc., 1942) in the New York *Herald Tribune*. See also Johnson's book *Roosevelt: Dictator or Democrat* (New York, Harper & Brothers, 1941), and the Shriftgiesser volume, which is the most complete study of the Roosevelt family yet written, and which is my source for several biographical details.

to 125th Street, and from Fifth Avenue all the way to the East River. Had he held on to this immense property the Roosevelts would, of course, have become much richer than they ever were. But James loved the Hudson Valley and wanted to get out into the country, and so he sold his Manhattan holdings. It would be interesting to know what price he got.

James's oldest son, FDR's grandfather, was Isaac Roosevelt II, born in 1790; he was "almost a queer duck, singularly ineffectual," who also went to Princeton; he became a physician, but never practiced because, so the story goes, he "could not stand the sight of human pain." He turned to botany as a relaxation, married a socially prominent woman, and lived most of his life as a Dutchess County squire. He built a home near Poughkeepsie, called Rosedale, about a mile from his father's, which was named Mount Hope. *His* son, James Roosevelt II, was FDR's father.

Meantime the Johannes wing of the family that produced TR followed a similar development. Every male member of the family was born on Manhattan for generation after generation. But these Roosevelts tended to settle on Long Island near Oyster Bay, and became staunch Republicans; the Hudson Valley–Dutchess County Roosevelts were Democrats. The TR branch was, on the whole, somewhat the richer, and if possible even more staid; but it was more vigorous, and produced more distinguished men during the nineteenth century, like James Henry Roosevelt, a well-known philanthropist, Nicholas Roosevelt, an inventor of some note, Latrobe Roosevelt, who had a lively career in the Navy, and Robert Roosevelt, a civic reformer, author, and naturalist.

Word About the Delanos

Turn now to the Delanos and FDR's maternal lineage, which was of the most vital force in shaping his character. In some ways he was more a Delano than a Roosevelt; his mother's strain was very strong indeed, and in fact she was wont to say, "My son Franklin is a Delano, not a Roosevelt at all!" The American branch of the Delano family derives from Philippe De La Noye, who arrived in Plymouth in 1621; until FDR, only five other presidents had Pilgrim blood. But the Delanos go back much further than that; the family was of mixed French and Dutch descent, and traces its ancestry all the way to William the Conqueror.

Philippe's son Thomas married the daughter of Priscilla Alden in 1667; this was, according to one historian, "the first shot-gun wedding in American history."[7] The old records of Plymouth colony show, at least, that a certain Thomas Delano was fined ten pounds "for having carnal copulation with his *now* wife before marriage." Another of Philippe's sons, Jonathan, married Mercy, the daughter of Richard and Elizabeth Warren; the Warrens have been an important factor in the Roosevelt ancestry ever since. Elizabeth died in 1673; "an aged widow aged above 90 years haveing lived a Godly life came to her grave as a shok of Corn fully Ripe." Five different lines of descent passed down to FDR's mother from this fine old lady.[8]

The Delanos and Warrens grew and spread out almost as the Roosevelts did, but they lived in New England rather than New York; they were wealthy, cosmopolitan, and politically more conservative; they had wide shipping interests, and flourished in the China trade. Roosevelt haters today like to say that the family fortune came from opium. Captain Amaso Delano was a famous seafarer in the early 1800's, Jane A. Delano was a well-known philanthropist and Red Cross worker, another Delano woman was Grant's mother, and still another married Junius Brutus Booth. Colombo Delano was a Cabinet member under Grant.

In about 1880 Franklin Hughes Delano, who lived in Fairhaven, Massachusetts, married Laura Astor, the aunt of the Helen Astor who married FDR's half brother. Miss Astor was rich; her husband retired from business and they set up houses on Lafayette Place in New York City and at Steen Valetje, an upriver estate near Hyde Park. These Franklin Delanos were childless, and part of their fortune passed to their niece, Sara Delano, the President's mother.

Franklin was named for this uncle, which is why he is worth mention. But only by a fluke did FDR escape being named Warren Delano Roosevelt; in fact this *was* to have been his name, in honor of Sara's father. It happened, however, that an infant son of one of Sara's brothers, named Warren Delano, had just died, and the brother protested that "he could not bear it" if the name were used again. Also the President was almost named Isaac Roosevelt. But Sara finally

<hr>

[7] *Franklin Roosevelt and the Delano Influence*, by Daniel Webster Delano, Jr. (Pittsburgh, James S. Nudi Publications, 1946), pp. 40-41.

[8] *Mr. Roosevelt*, by Compton Mackenzie (New York, E. P. Dutton & Company, Inc., 1944), p. 23.

settled on Franklin Delano, partly because she liked the name, partly because of the uncle. FDR was the first Roosevelt ever to be called Franklin.

Father and Mother

James Roosevelt, FDR's father, was born in 1828; it may seem incredible that a President in our own lifetime should have been born of a man himself born in the Presidency of an Adams. The easiest way to describe James Roosevelt is to say that he was an old-fashioned county gentleman, a "museum piece." He wore heavy muttonchop whiskers and almost always carried a riding crop; portraits make him seem faintly ridiculous, though his face has a fine gentility. His nickname was "Poughkeepsie Jimmy," and he was an enormous snob; members of the family joked with him unmercifully because he thought that only dukes were really proper company. A member of the family once told me, "He tried to pattern himself on Lord Lansdowne, sideburns and all, but what he really looked like was Lansdowne's coachman."

Be this as it may, James Roosevelt had quality. No weakling, no oaf or dullard, could possibly have interested any woman so brilliant and beautiful as Sara. Nor was his career without merit. He went to Harvard Law School. When in Europe as a young man he enlisted in Garibaldi's legions and fought for the freedom of Italy. He managed his fortune with great prudence, and made the Springwood property into a paying proposition. Young FDR's letters contain numerous references to shipments of milk and the like from the family farm.[9] For some years James was a vice-president of the Delaware and Hudson Railroad, and a director in half a dozen other companies. Once Grover Cleveland offered him the fairly important post of American minister to The Hague. He and Sara went to Europe every year, and they became familiar figures in the society life of the Continent of that era.

James Roosevelt married twice. His first wife was Rebecca Brien Howland; they were married in 1853, and she died in 1876. By all accounts she too, like Sara, must have been a remarkably pungent woman (as was one of her sisters who lived in Paris and belonged to the circle of Marcel Proust). Their only son, James Roosevelt Roosevelt (Rosy), was born in 1854, and thus was not less than twenty-eight years

---

[9] One letter, written by FDR at Harvard, tells his father not to worry about the loss of a butler, because "there are always plenty of butlers."

older than FDR, his half brother. About Rosy there could be much to say, had we the space; he was one of the most dashing young bloods of his time. He married Helen Astor, worked in the diplomatic service in Vienna and London—if you could call it work—and cut fashionable capers all over Europe and America. He was very fond of FDR, but never influenced him much. He died in 1927, aged seventy-three.

After Rebecca's death James Roosevelt spent some years as a widower, and then met the fascinating young debutante Sara Delano at a dinner party given by Mr. and Mrs. Theodore Roosevelt, Sr., on 26th Street. James was fifty-two, Sara was twenty-six; he was exactly twice her age, and she was exactly the age of his son. At the time James was described as a "tall, middle-aged gentleman with a hearty, infectious laugh, and a fund of fascinating stories." "He smoked his cheroot with a fine flourish." James and Sara discovered that they were sixth cousins—just as Franklin and Eleanor, years later, discovered that *they* were cousins—and fell in love; the courtship was brief, and they were married at Algonac in the Hudson Valley on October 7, 1880. They went to Europe for their honeymoon, and then set up housekeeping at Hyde Park.

More must be said of Sara, FDR's mother, the only woman in American history ever to see her son inaugurated as President. She was the seventh child (that both the Roosevelts and Delanos were prolific in the extreme is another trait) of Warren Delano II, and a lady named Catherine Robbins Lyman; five of the children were girls, and they were known as the "fascinating Delano sisters." Sara was born in 1854—it is continually refreshing to note how deeply FDR's roots go back into the American past. Her father was a prosperous merchant, who lived for many years in the Far East; he even had a house in Hong Kong, and here one catches a glimpse of the far horizons that contribute so distinctly to the Roosevelt heritage. Before she was ten, Sara had had a remarkable adventure; her father was wiped out by the crash of 1857, and he sailed for China to recoup his fortunes. The family joined him there; Sara, her mother, two nurses, and six little brothers and sisters all set sail on the perilous, 125-day journey half-way around the world; the ship was the celebrated square-rigged clipper *Surprise*. Sara has recorded some details of this fabulous experience:

> To go to China! Even today I suppose a child of eight would be thrilled at the prospect. . . . I suppose it was altogether terrifying to my young mother

to give up her beautiful home and its peaceful security for perhaps the rest of her life. . . . The *Surprise* was a fine, sturdy ship, and one that had made the voyage many times. . . . Our lives were regulated just as they had been at home. We had our lessons, our sewing, our reading aloud and talks with our mother. . . . There was a cow on board, and chickens. . . . You know, I have always been a great believer in heredity, and Franklin's wanderlust can be attributed directly to my own love of ships and distant horizons. . . . The Delanos have always been associated with the sea.[10]

The family returned in due course and Sara's life became a crisscross between Algonac and trips to Europe. She met Dr. Oliver Wendell Holmes and Ralph Waldo Emerson on this side of the Atlantic, and on the other saw the Empress Eugénie ride in Paris.

One more word about James. Despite the disparity of their ages it was an extremely happy marriage. He died in 1900, when she was only forty-six and still a woman of magnificent beauty with a handsome fortune; it is striking that she never remarried.[11] Of course all the power and force of her attention went to Franklin, who was then eighteen. For her husband she must have had great devotion. For her only son, something more than that.

Fact of Birth

On January 30, 1882, James Roosevelt wrote in his diary, "At quarter to nine my Sally had a splendid large baby boy. He weighs ten pounds without his clothes." So Franklin Delano Roosevelt was born. His mother has recorded that both she and her infant son almost died in childbirth because of an overdose of chloroform. Of such hairbreadths is history made.

FDR's Relation to His Father

At the cost of upsetting chronology we must digress here. James Roosevelt was fifty-four when Franklin was born, and hence the boy never knew his father except as an old man; he might have been his grandfather. Some psychologists have suggested that this may have been an influence on FDR in such affairs as the struggle to pack the Supreme Court; he hated the nine old men because they were images of his

---

[10] *My Boy Franklin,* by Mrs. James Roosevelt, pp. 7-9.
[11] His will had an unusual provision: "I do hereby appoint my wife sole guardian of my son Franklin Delano Roosevelt, and I wish him to be under the influence of his mother."

father's dotage. Actually, so far as we can tell, young Roosevelt had little marked emotion toward his father one way or other, aside from filial respect. James gave him his first gun, and taught him to ride, shoot, and sail. FDR recognized that his father's health was delicate; it was he, it seems, who helped protect him from overexertion and strain, in exact reversal of the usual role between father and son. I have heard it said on high authority, "What Franklin admired most in his father was his father's control of his mother, who controlled *him*." Of course Roosevelt had an Oedipus complex as big as a house. He passionately adored his mother. An Oedipus complex is usually the result of resentment by a boy at his father's love for his mother; he becomes a subconscious competitor for his adored mother's favor, with consequent jealousy and torment. But James was almost too old to be an effective rival or barrier. There is, at any rate, no record of any hostility between James and Franklin. Had James been younger, the story could have been quite different, and Franklin might have turned into a very neurotic and unstable child, which he wasn't.

More About a Great Lady

The first thing to say about the President's mother was that she was beautiful—extravagantly so. She was a tall woman, almost five foot ten, with luminous dark eyes, heavily arched brows, and a spoiled lustrous mouth; her head rose like a flower from a throat that can only be described in terms of cliché—it was that of a swan; her presence and carriage were imperious. One of her grandchildren has told me that the impression she made on him was ineffaceable; she wore ankle-length flowing dresses, and always looked cool, though vivacious; she was a veritable queen even in repose.

If her looks were impressive, so, to put it mildly, was her character. The reader of her strange, artless little book on FDR might be led to assume that she was a gentle old thing; she was not. Of course the very tenderness of her devotion softens the book. But a member of the family, on reading it, was impelled to burst out, "Granny wasn't like that at all!" In actual fact, behind the most courtly of exteriors, she was a *grande dame* in the grand manner, a dowager of tremendous will, and a tyrant. Wherever Sara was, even when her son was President, she was boss; she sat at the head of the table, not he. I asked one of her old servants if Hyde Park changed much year by year. Reply: "In the house of such a lady, nothing ever changed!"

Sara Roosevelt was close about money; her ambition was to leave her whole fortune (she inherited $1,338,000 from her father) to Franklin intact. She did not mind spending the interest, but she would not touch the principal. She was apt to be slow paying bills, as Roosevelt was. The tale is told around Hyde Park that just before the visit of the King and Queen of England, she decided that the toilet seat their Majesties would use ought to be replaced, and the plumbing in that bathroom overhauled. Months later the bill came from the local plumber; she considered it too high and refused to pay. The plumber— according to local legend—thereupon descended on the house, took the toilet seat away, and hung it for some weeks in his shopwindow, with a placard attached, "The King and Queen Sat Here."

When the Hyde Park library was being built, old Mrs. Roosevelt liked to cross the lawn to watch. It scandalized her that the carpenters and other workmen had their own cars, and she asked why they didn't walk. They replied that they came from Hyde Park village, a mile and a half away. "When I was your age," she replied tartly, "I was fully capable of walking a mile and a half twice a day, and I did so many times to get the mail!" Sometimes she would cock her eye balefully at the workmen and mutter in a clucking undertone, "You're all in clover . . . clover . . . living off the fat of the land!"

The old manner of society was obviously breaking up before her eyes (and her son was conspicuously responsible for this), but she would not believe it. When one of her sisters was momentarily stranded in Europe in 1939, she asked the President to send a battleship across the Atlantic to fetch her; it horrified her when he said he couldn't quite do so. Several of her sisters, it should be noted, had almost as much strength of character as she; one, Mrs. Price Collier, and a niece named Mrs. George St. George, were fibrous and conservative enough, despite all family considerations, to oppose FDR stubbornly on nearly every measure, and to vote against him vociferously every time he ran.

Sara Roosevelt was resolutely old-fashioned. For instance she refused to allow herself to be photographed kissing FDR, even during campaigns. She was packed with salt and spirit. Once she said to her granddaughter Anna, whom she adored, "There is no excuse for ever being bored. If you are ever bored for even five minutes, it is your own fault." She abhorred the uncouthness of many politicians who visited Hyde Park; she always spoke her mind and never cared who heard what; a famous anecdote describes how she hissed, only too audibly,

"Who is that terrible man sitting next to my son?" when FDR was entertaining Huey Long at lunch. Nor did she like some of the people Eleanor Roosevelt brought home. "Where does she *get* those people?" she would grumble. Once a political group assembled on the Hyde Park porch and she said just loudly enough for everybody to hear, "Why, they look like a lot of gangsters!" She turned to Ed Flynn on one occasion and asked him to identify a young lady talking to one of the President's sons. "Why, it's your new granddaughter-in-law to be!" Mr. Flynn replied. "You don't say!" rejoined the dowager Mrs. Roosevelt, astonished. Finally, she had supreme confidence. When someone asked her, in 1932, if she were not surprised that her son was in the White House, she replied with some acerbity, "Certainly not. It is what I have always planned."

The following excerpt from a letter to "Dearest Franklin and Dearest Eleanor" gives insight on her character:

. . . I am sorry to feel that Franklin *is* tired and that my views are not his, but perhaps dear Franklin you may on second thoughts or *third* thoughts see that I am not so far wrong. The foolish old saying "noblesse oblige" is good and "honneur oblige" possibly expresses it better for most of us. One can be democratic as one likes, but if we love our own, and if we love our neighbor, we owe a great example, and my constant feeling is that through neglect or laziness I am not doing my part toward those around me. . . . Do not say that I *misunderstood*, I understand perfectly, but I cannot believe that my precious Franklin really feels as he expressed himself. Well, I hope that while I live I may keep my "old fashioned" theories and that *at least* in my own family I may continue to feel that *home* is the best and happiest place and that my son and daughter and their children will live in peace and keep from the tarnish which seems to affect so many.[12]

Several of her grandchildren have talked to me of this wonderful old woman. They thought of her, rather than of their father, as the real head of the family; Hyde Park was her house, not theirs. They called her "Granny" (FDR and Eleanor called her Mamá), and knew well how formidable she was. (Incidentally the servants distinguished between the two Mrs. Roosevelts by calling Sara "Madame," Eleanor "Mrs. Franklin.") Granny spoiled them, but she was made of iron. Still, one of the boys told me, "She was the source of all the good things in life when we were little kids, if you knew how to handle her."

It has been written, "The men of the Delano clan were cast too

---

[12] *F. D. R.: His Personal Letters,* Vol. II, pp. 274-75.

much in the mold of women to be men." The elder Mrs. Roosevelt, to the end of her life, even after FDR had been President for years, treated him almost as if he were a boy. When he went to Harvard, she took a house in Boston to be near him. When he became Governor, she said with proud joy (he was forty-six at the time), "Now Franklin has grown up and is the Governor!" Visitors to Hyde Park almost always had some story to tell about the old lady's incessantly watchful interest in her son. "Help my boy!" she whispered to Jim Farley once. She would keep close to FDR's study and chat with callers, or, after a conference, hover in the background, with words such as, "I like to hear about the important things on which Franklin is working." Once she whispered to a visitor, "Franklin is busy with the Mayor of Poughkeepsie, and they are both very angry, I can hear them through the door." She said to an artist painting him, "You will have trouble with his jaw; it is just like mine." And when she was eighty-two and the President fifty-six she told a visiting newspaper man, "I will not let Franklin go to church tomorrow, because he is so far behind on his mail."

The old lady had, of course, great charm and winningness, qualities which (needless to say) her son inherited. Shortly before FDR became President she wrote him:

DARLING SON: May 8, 1932

Just 51 years yesterday, the 7th, I came to visit [Hyde Park]. . . . If I had not come then, I should now be "old Miss Delano" after a rather sad life!

May 11, 1932

. . . In writing you I said 51 years. It is really 52 since I came to visit in May. I am not famous as a mathematician.[13]

Sometimes FDR was irritated by his mother. He was only a very moderate drinker, but she detested any drinking at all; while he was convalescing after the paralysis attack he was reduced to the subterfuge of hiding a bottle behind the books next to his chair, so that she would not know when he took an occasional nip. She became convinced, during one period, that he ought not to drink at all, but she knew full well how much the cocktail hour meant to him socially; so she would contrive, by various seemingly innocent devices, to announce dinner abnormally early, so that he could not mix more than one round of

[13] From *Franklin Roosevelt at Hyde Park*, by Olin Dows, p. 2.

drinks. Some years ago at the family table, FDR's young son John used the word "damn"; Sara did not approve, but held her tongue. Later FDR himself said "damn." The old lady could contain herself no longer. She announced: "Little Johnny learns his language from the stable, and Franklin learns it from his ten-year-old son." Roosevelt was put out and angry.

Napoleon said once, "The future destiny of the child is always the womb of the mother," and nobody would deny the permanent massive influence Mrs. Roosevelt had on FDR. But another profoundly important contributor to Roosevelt's life entered the scene—his wife. About the relations between the two Mrs. Roosevelts historians will write much, and we shall mention later how Sara tried to prevent or at least delay her son's marriage. Eleanor Roosevelt won. She won, too, in the supreme crisis of the future President's career, his illness. It is a matter of surpassing interest, in fact, that so much of FDR's life should have depended on the outcome of a struggle between two women both of whom loved him, wife and mother. For years the elder Mrs. Roosevelt dominated the younger, along with her son; but gradually both threw off her zealous and loving domination. Step by step, little by little, FDR became free. In a sense it was the paralysis that cut the cord. But this is to get too far ahead of our story.

In September, 1941, Bernard Baruch was visiting FDR, and asked how his mother was. "All right," FDR replied. Baruch said that he, an old man, knew how deeply elderly people yearned for attention and affection, and suggested that the President spare a little more time for her, though she had certainly not been neglected. Roosevelt picked up the phone then and there, called her at Hyde Park, and had a chat with her. She died a few days later. She was eighty-six, and had outlived her husband by one and forty years.

Chapter 10

THE BLOOM OF YOUTH

There is no cure for birth or death save to enjoy the interval.

—GEORGE SANTAYANA

Roosevelt had an abundantly happy childhood; the grim, biting distresses that afflict most children passed him by. There were few, if any, abrasions from the outside world—he was as sheltered as if behind a Chinese wall—and few harassments or discontents at home. So far as we know today he was never severely punished; he lived in an atmosphere almost totally devoid of conflict. Perhaps this helped give him his confidence in later life, and perhaps too it may have contributed to his touchiness and sensitiveness to criticism.

One can trace his early development through pictures recently unearthed: the infant with blond curls and a pancake hat, the boy with the delicate narrow face, tiny mouth, and eyes too close; then the skinny young man rather pert, smug, and springy—even at Harvard he never weighed more than 150 pounds. He was a lonely boy, with an affectionate disposition and few playmates; he was taught by tutors, and never went to school until he was fourteen; this may account for his subsequent gregariousness. One story seems to indicate that he learned assurance early, but it is the type of story told of almost every bright youngster. His mother perceived that he was ordering other children around in a somewhat arbitrary way, and she told him, "My boy, don't give the orders all the time. Let the other boys give them sometimes." "Mummie," responded Franklin, "if I didn't give the orders nothing would ever happen."

Another story recorded by the elder Mrs. Roosevelt describes her concern when, at five, he seemed very depressed and moody. She became alarmed, and asked if he were unhappy. He thought this over seriously and then replied, "Yes, I am unhappy."

She asked him why and he was silent. Then, with a gesture com-

167

bining impatience and entreaty, he exclaimed desperately, "Oh, for freedom!" She was deeply shocked.

As an infant, his mother tells us, he was "plump, pink, and nice." She proceeds: "He was born right here in this house, of course—one never went to hospitals in those days. . . . I realize how much more scientific hospital care is, but I am old-fashioned enough to think it's nicer for a baby to be born in his own home. I've passed the door of that sunny, upstairs room many hundreds of times in my long life, and oh! so often I've remembered that there my son first saw the light of day. . . . I used to love to bathe and dress him. . . . Franklin's early care would, I am afraid, be considered very unscientific by modern standards. We never had a formula."[1]

The family tone and mood may be gathered from this report of a toast offered by one of his uncles to young Franklin on Thanksgiving Day, 1882, when he was ten months old:

He [the uncle] wished to propose the health of one member of the family who, although the last to arrive in the world, would, he was certain, not prove to be the least in worth. He wished for him all health and happiness in his career and hoped that when the November days of his life should come he could say what his grandparents certainly may say, that his children and children's children rise up and bless him, and he hoped that the last of those November days might be, as in this year, days of Thanksgiving.[2]

One story sometimes told is that his father took him, aged four or five, to visit President Cleveland in the White House. The troubled, busy Cleveland said, "I have one wish for you, little man, that you will never be President of the United States."

Many anecdotes that Sara Roosevelt records so lovingly might easily be told of any boy of similar background. He was "rather introspective," but "consistently enjoyed himself." Once, when she asked him where his obedience was, he replied solemnly, "My 'bedience has gone upstairs." A little later he announced that he would be ashamed of himself if he were not capable of "doing two things at once." He liked mischief moderately, played with a treasure chest, had a pony, and cut ice on the Hudson. His father gave him his first gun at eleven, and his prowess collecting specimens was so considerable that, when he was twelve, his grandfather Warren Delano gave him a life membership in the American Museum of Natural History.

[1] *My Boy Franklin*, pp. 12-13.
[2] "A Dutchess County Boy," by Michael Straight, *New Republic*, April 15, 1946.

One more anecdote from his mother's book:

One day Franklin came in from the river side of the house looking for his collecting gun. He did not seem in any particular haste, so I asked him why he wanted it.

"There's a winter wren way up in one of the big trees down there," he said. "I want to get him."

I laughed at him. "And do you think that wren is going to oblige you by staying there while you come in and get your gun to go back and shoot him?"

He looked surprised but quite unperturbed. "Oh, yes," he said confidently, "he'll wait."[3]

Intellectually his progress was somewhat spotty. His reading was restricted but he had a lively curiosity, and one legend is that, at the age of nine, he read a whole dictionary from cover to cover. His mother protested at the rigor of this feat, and he replied, "But the dictionary is so interesting!" His governess—he had regular school hours at home—was for some years an able and discerning Swiss woman, Mademoiselle Sandoz; here is a written examination she gave him in 1892, when he was ten.

Q. La date de la grève de Waterloo?
A. 1815
Q. La date de la grève de la Crimée?
A. 1854
Q. Pourquoi cette dernière a-t-elle eu lieu?
A. Les Russes voulaient d'avoir la Turkey. Les autres pays n'ont pas voulu.
Q. De quelle parenté était Georges II à Georges III?
A. Petit-fils. (Grandpère!)
Q. Quelle était la cause de la guerre entre les Américains et les Anglais?
A. A cause des taxes.
Q. Qui a sauvé la France après la révolution?
A. Napolion Bonaparte.
Q. Qu'était ce "Bill de Reform" que l'on a passé dans le régime de William IV?
A. Que les grandes villes pouraient envoyer des membres au Congress.[4]

Young Franklin traveled a good deal; his father took him to see the World's Fair in Chicago, in his private railway car, and he crossed the Atlantic for the first time at the age of two. Every year between the ages of seven and fifteen he went to Europe with his parents; he even

[3] *My Boy Franklin*, pp. 15-16.
[4] "A Dutchess County Boy," *New Republic*, April 15, 1946.

attended a *Volkschule* in Nauheim for a time, where his father took the cure, and began to learn German. These firsthand childhood glimpses of the Continent had a good deal to do with shaping Roosevelt's attitudes toward things European, as was only natural. In a single remarkable day, when he was bicycling through the Black Forest in Germany, he and his tutor were arrested no fewer than four times by the Kaiser's police, for minor "crimes."[5] It is not altogether fanciful to imagine that FDR gained from these incidents impressions of German character that never left him.

His mother meticulously preserved every scrap of letter FDR ever wrote and as a result the student can trace his development in the most minute detail. The following was written when he was under six; his mother explains that "he knew his letters but was told how to spell the words:"[6]

> Hyde Park, N.Y.
> Telegraph Station, Poughkeepsie
>
> MY DEAR MAMA
> we coasted! yesterday nothing dangerous yet, look out for tomorrow!! your boy.
>
> F.

By the time he was ten he wrote like this:

> Feb 27th, 1892
>
> MY DARLING MUMKIN AND PAP!
> Good morning. I hope you have used Pear's Soap and are flourishing now. I am dying of school fever and you will be horrified to hear that my temperature is 150°. But really I have got a "petit rhume" only. I am in the hands of the celebrated Dr. Sandoz. . . . We got 12 eggs yesterday and there is no clocking hen. I can't write any more, so Good bye. Your afectionate
> Roosevelt Delano Franklin

Roosevelt left the womb of Hyde Park at fourteen, when he was packed off to Groton. But the influence of this early childhood environment was ineradicable, and to the end of his days he loved every tree he had known as a youngster, every rise of meadow, ripple of lawn, and fall of brook. Most of us, the psychologists tell us, are stamped forever with the imprint of our own childhood; FDR was no exception.

---

[5] Knocking over a goose, picking cherries, parking bicycles in a railway station, and cycling after sunset.
[6] *F.D.R.: His Personal Letters*, Vol. I, p. 6.

Peabody and Groton: The Last Spartan

Most people think of Groton as a very old school but actually it was founded as recently as 1884, and its first alumnus, George Rublee, the well-known Washington lawyer, is still alive; when FDR entered, it had only been in existence a dozen years. It is not a big school compared to Andover, Exeter, or even Deerfield; when Roosevelt was there the total enrollment was only 150, with about 25 students in each of six forms. Nor—again contrary to familiar belief—is Groton particularly expensive compared to other New England schools in the same category; in FDR's day the total fees were only $500 a year, and the amount today is around $1500. But Groton had, and has, some provocative distinctions. It was strongly British in spirit, and it was devoted largely to Christianity, character, and muscle. Today Groton has broadened out and takes poor boys and scholarship students, but in FDR's time its clientele was very restricted indeed. It was the school which, above all, accepted only the accepted. To be rich or a "swell" was not enough. Its basic root was the old Boston and New York society; it was where the parvenu millionaires sent their boys, if they could somehow manage to get them in, to join the sons of older, more respectable millionaires. Phillips Brooks, the Bishop of Massachusetts, was chairman of the first board of trustees; a mere member was J. Pierpont Morgan.

By far the most remarkable thing about Groton was the person of its headmaster, the Reverend Doctor Endicott Peabody. He founded the school in his own image, which was dictatorial, Spartan, and immaculate, and he ran it uninterruptedly for fifty-six years until his retirement at eighty-four. As salary he would take only $1200 a year. He was called "The Rector" by his awed students; he had in some respects a singularly sweet nature, but shafts of Puritan fire could burst from him like jets of lightning. His prestige was that of Jehovah, and he was a fearsome snob. Yet what the estimable Dr. Peabody admired most, next to God, was public service. It has been said loosely by several commentators on Roosevelt that he became what he was in spite of Groton. But the opposite is more nearly true. In his squeaky voice Dr. Peabody preached daily, almost hourly, to his young flock the theme of the reformer, that it was the hale duty of the privileged to enter into the public arena and fight to elevate the standard of those less fortunate. Dr. Peabody taught service. It was not at all extraordinary that a

Groton boy should have gone into politics, if you measure politics in terms of righteousness versus corruption, enlightened reform (to a degree) versus satiety. In fact Groton, considering what a small school it is, has contributed to American public life an astonishing number of men of high caliber—one need only mention Sumner Welles, Dean Acheson, Averell Harriman, Newbold Morris, Francis Biddle, and Roosevelts by the half dozen, to say nothing of men who have made progressive records in private fields, Motleys, La Farges, Osborns, Whitneys, Alsops, Davisons, Cushings, Curtises, and so on without end.

In Roosevelt's day—and the manner of tutelage has changed little— "Grotties" slept in a doorless cubicle, rose before seven, had to take a cold shower every morning, washed in a tin basin, had no privacy or luxury whatsoever, studied under a master's eye in the barest kind of room, were forced to work almost as hard at athletics as at studies, went to chapel twice on Sunday and once every weekday (in addition to participating in evening prayers in the classroom), and said an individual good night to both the Rector and Mrs. Peabody when, after dinner in their stiff white collars, they retired to their cells for the night. All this was, of course, the expression of a mechanism for perpetuating the virtues of the ruling class. So does superiority entrench itself. A "Grotty" was, only too manifestly, elite of the elite, and to the advantages already bestowed by wealth and position, Dr. Peabody sought to add the iron of an almost intolerably rigid discipline.

Young FDR didn't like Groton much, and it didn't like him. He was not a success there. He entered in the third form, and so had the handicap of joining his class two years late. Of his twenty-one classmates (all but two went on to Harvard incidentally—in those days almost all "Grotties" chose Harvard, or had it chosen for them) not many became prominent in later life. Blagden, Bradley, Chadwick, DeKoven, Greenough, Robeson, Thayer, Thorndike . . . these are names on the class roll. As a matter of fact the boys who were the best "Grotties" usually turned out to be nonentities later; boys who hated Groton did much better. The explanation of this probably lies in the fact that the boys who became successes were not conformists; hence they were apt to be excluded from the compact group that made the core of each class. Sumner Welles was asked once if he had had a good time at Groton, and he replied, "Oh, Lord no, I was a worm."

FDR was not disliked; it was simply that he went unnoticed. One point of some interest is that he was the only Democrat in the entire student body. He confessed to a classmate years later, "I always felt hopelessly out of things." One of his fellows has recorded (how ironic may be the processes of history!) that he was "nice, but completely colorless." His nickname was "Uncle Frank." Probably FDR, like most pampered boys, missed horribly the devotion he was used to at home, and hence made himself recessive. It is revealing that when he arrived at the school, he was hazed by being made to dance alone in a corner while his classmates hacked at his ankles with a hockey stick. He took it so well, submitting to this indignity with such good grace, that the hazers simply gave up in disgust and let him alone. He was still very much a Mama's Boy. His letters to his mother during this period, written two or three times a week and beginning as a rule "My Darling Mama," or "My Dearest Mummie," are almost embarrassingly affectionate.

Groton set its mark on Roosevelt in several other ways. A great many people, even including presidents, have overcompensated in later life for slights and slurs undergone in school days. Also Groton probably contributed something to FDR's "insincerity" in that he was taught in the British manner always to cloak unpleasant emotions and never to be disagreeable. Most "Grotties" wear a mask.

His scholastic record was nothing much, although in his first term he ranked fourth in a class of nineteen; he fell off later, and in his third year failed in Greek; generally, he was somewhere between sixth and tenth. The three or four outstanding boys in each class became prefects; FDR never became one. His first report card is reproduced in the first volume of his letters, and shows that Dr. Peabody, at least, regarded his promise as satisfactory: "Very good. He strikes me as an intelligent and faithful scholar and a good boy." His last report gives him B's in Latin and English, a C in physics, and a "good" in social studies. His chief academic distinction was, according to old copies of the *Grotonian,* something quite odd and striking; for three years—a dutiful boy!—he won the annual prize for punctuality. Nor was his athletic record distinguished, though on one occasion he won an event no longer in existence—something on the sissy side called the high kick—and in his senior year he was the manager of the baseball team.

He took part, so the records tell us, in three debates: he talked against restriction of immigration into the United States, against the annexation of Hawaii, and for the independence of the Philippines. Here, quite markedly, is a foretaste of his liberal attitude. In the

Hawaii debate (Januair 19, 1898) he mentions the importance of Pearl Harbor, and talks about how "a little inexpensive dredging" could transform it into a valuable base; this, in its way, is much the same kind of fascinating premonitory nugget that we get in Winston Churchill's early novel, *Savrola,* which forecasts a naval attack on the Dardanelles. Also in this debate Roosevelt said: "The United States and Russia are the only countries no part of whose territory can be cut off by a naval enemy." He adds that if we annexed Hawaii, we would acquire such a vulnerable point for the first time—but goes on to say that Japan has disclaimed any ambition to seize the Islands, and that any invading armies there would be as lonely as "Robinson Crusoe." This in 1898!

Suddenly toward the end of his Groton years FDR's interests began to broaden. The young patrician was rubbing his wings against certain externals for the first time. He developed, for a "Grotty" of that era, a very strong original streak indeed: for instance he became conscious of Jews (though there were certainly none in the school as of that day), and he went to a lecture by a Negro on the lack of Negro education in the South. He became intensely interested in the struggle of the Boers against the British in South Africa; he took the Boer side wholeheartedly, and even raised money for their cause. Also when the Spanish-American War broke out he plotted to escape from Groton and enlist, but a sudden attack of measles kept him from being able to run away.

Finally another word on Dr. Peabody. He was not only the most powerful personality FDR had ever met aside from his mother; he was probably one of the three or four strongest influences in the whole course of his career. Mr. Roosevelt maintained the most cordial and respectful relations with the great headmaster till the end of his life; it was Dr. Peabody who officiated at his marriage, and by immutable tradition he was a guest at Hyde Park every New Year's Eve; what is more, FDR summoned him to Washington to conduct a private service before each inauguration, and also to officiate at a special ceremony when he entered into his tenth year as President. FDR did not do this, as I have heard it put, "merely because Peabody was a nice old man who needed a ride on a train." Roosevelt's emotion for him was, I am sure, partly sentimental; yet it had deep roots—for instance FDR saved for forty-three years every card of birthday greeting the Rector sent him. Looking at it from the other side, think what a problem Roosevelt must have been to Peabody, when the President tossed out of the window, from the economic point of view at least, almost everything that Groton stood for. But he loyally defended Roosevelt and always stood up for him when other Grotties called him a "paranoiac," "a traitor to his class," and so on. It is a matter of interesting record that Peabody's last words, just before he died, were, "You know, I think Roosevelt is an absolutely sincere man."

Cambridge and the Yard

FDR went up to Harvard in 1900, and had four happy years of broader, more relaxed horizons. His college record is somewhat mixed. He was a tolerable enough student, and finished the undergraduate curriculum in three years instead of four, spending the fourth nominally as a graduate student; this was not, however, too much of a feat as of that day, since Groton boys had such a good scholastic grounding that they often clipped a year off any college course. Roosevelt majored in American political history and government. He failed in several examinations, and never got much better marks than B. One of his professors—a rabid Roosevelt hater—has told me that he was a lazy student, arrogant and careless, a judgment probably based on the rankest prejudice.

FDR's classmates recall him today as a boy not particularly popular; he was a mixture of affability, marked sensitiveness, and superiority. His desire to be universally liked repelled some of his fellows, who called him "two-faced," but even in those days he must have been a good politician, because he won his first "election" at Harvard—he was chosen permanent chairman of his class committee, no small honor. His efforts in athletics were halfhearted. He went out for freshman football, but failed to make the team; the only other sport he took up was the highly fashionable one of rowing, which attracted many of the Gold Coast boys. He stroked several minor crews. On the other hand he was managing editor and then president of the college newspaper, the well-known *Crimson*.[7] This really meant something. To be president of the *Crimson* signified, then as now, a great deal of drive, ambition, and executive ability. He had lively gifts as an editor; he campaigned for better standards in the class elections and for such things as more adequate fire escapes in the dormitories. On one occasion he achieved minor fame by daring to ask President Eliot how he was going to vote

[7] He was also president of the Political Club one year, and a member of the Hasty Pudding and others.

in the presidential campaign then going on; Eliot told him, and the story was a scoop. Generally, as editor, he had the reputation of being an aristocrat who played with the masses, but not on vital issues. He gave a sense of caring quite genuinely about the interests of the people at large, but all within an orthodoxy of the most gentlemanly kind.

FDR lived all four years at one of the most choosy of the Gold Coast dormitories, Westmorly, and he belonged to numerous organizations and clubs, in particular the Fly. Much has been written about the fact that he was not elected to Porcellian, the most famous and exclusive of the "final" clubs. "The bitterest moment of Franklin Roosevelt's life came when he was passed over by Porcellian," a relative once told me. But this hardly seems credible because in Roosevelt's day several clubs were neck and neck in social priority, and the Fly was certainly one of the top three or four; to be in the Fly was not what you would exactly call being an outcast. But Theodore Roosevelt was a member of Porcellian, and perhaps Franklin was disappointed in not following his illustrious cousin. The reason he did not make Porcellian, which was a club with no damned nonsense about merit, was simply that he was not "swell" enough. The boys in the Fly met in a red brick house with a white portico on Mt. Auburn Street. All the clubs, no matter how exclusive, maintained a discreet façade of respectable shabbiness; they were organized on a semisecret basis, and not everybody knew who was in which. I have seen a list of FDR's fellow members in the Fly; all were boys from St. Marks, Groton, or similar schools, and not one reached serious prominence in later years. Anybody who has gone through the social hocus-pocus of American college life must recall, with a relieved sigh, how enormously unimportant were the things that seemed so enormously important at the time.

Young FDR went to Europe with a classmate[8] the summer before his senior year, and had a surpassingly good—if conventional—time in London, Interlaken, and elsewhere. His letters have a vivid bounce and gaiety. But in retrospect several passages sound odd. One to his mother says, "The President's tendency to make the executive power stronger than the Houses of Congress is bound to be a bad thing." Another tells her not to worry, that he always lands "on his feet."

Roosevelt liked Harvard, but it never meant as much to him as Gro-

[8] Roosevelt's class was not particularly distinguished, but among men of his year were the late Arthur Davison Ficke, the poet, Arthur A. Ballantine, who was Hoover's Undersecretary of the Treasury, and the well-known lawyer Laird Bell, president of the board of trustees of the University of Chicago.

ton; the influences in Cambridge were much more diffuse and gentler. His life was pleasantly luxurious and otherwise unexceptional. Between terms he went to Hyde Park or Campobello; he developed his hobby of naval history and became an expert craftsman with boats; he took courses in things as various as paleontology, Renaissance art, and public speaking; he dined with all the blue bloods; he kept a trotter and a light runabout at Cambridge, for forays into Boston; he browsed in books about whales and eagerly read the *Scientific American* and the London *Sphere*; he saw his mother steadily, and all in all seemed destined to become an archetypical example of a privileged, attractive youngster with nothing whatever facing him except the most conventional style of worldly life. But, already, mysterious seeds were sprouting. His letters illustrate some heady intellectual developments. He took the lead on the campus for the rights of Negro students and he campaigned vigorously for Bryan—though TR was running for Vice-President on the McKinley ticket.

While he was still at Harvard something else happened to young Franklin, and his adult life began. Her name was Eleanor.

Chapter 11

LADY WHO BECAME FIRST LADY

A spectacle unto the world, and to angels.
—I CORINTHIANS 4:9

The luckiest thing that ever happened to Franklin Delano Roosevelt occurred on March 17, 1905, when, aged twenty-three, he married his twenty-one-year-old fifth cousin once removed, Anna Eleanor Roosevelt, an orphan whom he had known since childhood. The wedding was a very brave affair. As I have already mentioned, Eleanor's uncle, President Theodore Roosevelt, gave the bride away, and guests at the ceremony were so excited and impressed by him that they scarcely paid attention to the nervous bride and groom.

Franklin, according to his mother, was almost late at the altar. She records that he, Lathrop Brown, his best man, and Dr. Peabody were so deeply engrossed in conversation while waiting for the bride "that they did not realize until the wedding procession was well under way that the music had actually started." But they caught up quickly and "met the bridal party in the approved fashion"; nobody suspected how close they had come "to missing their cue."

The ceremony took place at the twin houses of Mrs. Henry Parrish, Jr., and Mrs. E. Livingston Ludlow at 6 and 8 East 76th Street. This is from next day's account in the New York *World*:

Owing to the immense crowds that surrounded these houses the entire block was closed and seventy-five policemen were employed to keep order. . . .

When the open landau stopped in front of the awning women at neighboring windows cheered and waved handkerchiefs. The President half arose from his seat and waved his silk hat. But the President's smile was not so expansive before he entered the house as when he reappeared, and when he gave away his only brother's daughter his face wore an unusually solemn expression. . . .

The cousins were married under an enormous bouquet of pink roses containing 450 flowers.

Miss Roosevelt walked down the improvised aisle with the President. The bride's gown was white satin with a court train and a trimming of lace. The lace veil was an heirloom. The bride was lavishly jewelled. She wore a dog collar of pearls, a diamond bowknot and the veil was fastened with a diamond crescent, which had been worn by the late Mrs. Elliott Roosevelt. . . .

Some of the guests were asked only for the reception. Mr. and Mrs. Charles B. Alexander were among the reception guests, and when they arrived too early they sat on a vacant stoop nearby to wait. Finally one of the Parrish servants asked them to come in.

At 5 o'clock the Roosevelt party was ready to leave. The carriage turned toward Fifth Avenue from Seventy-sixth Street. At one corner a vacant lot is screened by a tall fence, and the top of this fence was black with small boys. From them the President received three cheers, and the President tipped his hat to them. "Three cheers for Teddy! Ain't he the real thing?" came from a hundred youthful throats, and then the President shook his fist playfully at the boys. In his excitement one small youth fell backward. . . .

At the Roosevelt-Roosevelt wedding the following families were represented: the Burdens, the Sloanes, the Vanderbilts, the Baylisses, the Chanlers, the Winthrops, the Riggses, the Alexanders, the Mortimers, the Belmonts, the Crugers and the Van Rensselaers.

Eleanor Roosevelt, the youthful bride, was born in New York City on October 11, 1884, the eldest of three children of Elliott Roosevelt, TR's brother, and Anna Hall. Her mother, like Franklin's mother, was a woman of distinctive beauty and strength of character; her photographs show her to have been almost as beautiful as Sara. The family home, called Oak Terrace, was at Tivoli, twenty-six miles up the Hudson from Hyde Park; it was part of the old Livingston estate. Eleanor had a suppressed and thoroughly unhappy childhood—in acute contrast to that of her husband. Her brother, whom she adored and whom she describes as "angelic," died of diphtheria when she was about eight, and so did her beloved mother. Two years later her father died, and her maternal grandmother, Mrs. Valentine G. Hall, took charge of the young orphan. Her upbringing was austere in the extreme. She was a lonely prisoner of all the stiffest conventions of the time. Then for some years she went to a school called Allenswood in England; from its headmistress, a forward-looking woman named Mademoiselle Souvestre, she got the first inkling that people existed in the world who were not a formidable combination of Victorian and Tory. For some years—nobody would believe it now!—she suffered from curvature of the spine, and had to wear a brace. It was no more rigid a clamp than the environment which grasped her spirit.

Her father, Elliott Roosevelt, a man of the utmost amiability and weakness, had to be "exiled" from his children because he drank. It was stated in a legal action some years after his death that "for three years . . . prior to his decease, his mental condition had been such that he was to a very considerable extent unable to manage his own affairs." His disintegration at the end was tragic; this is one reason why the surviving family took care that Eleanor should be brought up in such a straight-laced fashion. Her brother, G. Hall Roosevelt, who died in 1941, also drank. Mrs. Roosevelt herself, be it noted, perhaps as a result of this family history, scarcely ever touches a drop of alcohol. Perhaps I should explain that mention of these details is no improper invasion of family privacy; Mrs. Roosevelt has written about them herself in the most explicit and familiar detail. For instance she says of Hall in *This I Remember*, with deep affection and concern, "By the time he realized that he could not just stop drinking whenever he wanted to, he had been through so much that he no longer wanted to stop." Never has the ill fortune of the alcoholic been more acutely stated. Why, one may ask, should Mrs. Roosevelt have felt impelled to disclose details and dilemmas of this sort? Partly I imagine it is because she is such a tremendously honest woman that it simply would not occur to her not to tell the truth. FDR, incidentally, was extremely fond of Hall, and treated him as long as he lived like a younger brother; he lived year after year in the FDR-Eleanor periphery.[1]

Franklin first met young Eleanor when she was about two; it is a family legend that, aged four at the time, he carried her piggyback around the halls of Hyde Park. Then, apparently, they had a remote cousinly relationship for many years, but seldom met. Once, when he was at Groton, he wrote his mother suggesting that his cousins Teddy Robinson and Eleanor Roosevelt should be invited to a house party; he said "they would go well and fill out chinks." A couple of years later, he and his mother were in the Pullman car of a train en route to Hyde Park, and he saw her in the adjoining coach and asked her to join them, and they talked a while. Subsequently they met at occasional dances and family parties.

[1] But Hall never had much to do with the President's political life. Farley records that he was present when FDR first discussed the Supreme Court bill with his secretaries Early and McIntyre; this is one of the rare instances of such activity. Also Governor Frank Murphy of Michigan once gave him a job in Detroit.

Obviously he was attracted to her and began to be fond of her. When she was eighteen she spent some of her afternoons teaching and helping out at the Rivington Street Settlement House; she taught, of all things, "calisthenics and fancy dancing" to the slum children. A serious young lady! On one occasion she allowed Franklin to meet her there and take her home. "All the little girls were tremendously interested," she has written, "and the next time they gathered around me demanding to know if he was my 'feller,' an expression that meant nothing to me at that time!"

Young Roosevelt was still at Harvard. Presently he found himself in love with Eleanor. He kept this passion a great secret, however; he did not even tell his roommate, Lathrop Brown. Late in 1903 he asked her to marry him, and she at once accepted. She writes, "Though I was only nineteen, it seemed an entirely natural thing and I never even thought that we were both young and inexperienced. . . . My grand-mother, when I told her, asked me if I was sure I was really in love. I solemnly answered, 'Yes,' and yet I know now that it was years later before I understood what being in love was or what loving really meant." Then, "I had very high standards as to what a wife and mother should be and not the faintest notion of what it meant to be either a wife or mother, and none of my elders enlightened me. I marvel now at my husband's patience."[2]

But first there was an obstacle to get over: Franklin's mother. FDR was only twenty-one. His mother, in the most patient and tactful way, set out to break the engagement, or at least defer for as long a time as possible the actual marriage. It was not that she disliked Eleanor— quite the contrary—but simply that she could not endure that her precious and beloved son, at the beginning of his maturity, the very springtime of his youth, should marry *anybody*.

This is what FDR wrote his mother immediately upon becoming engaged:

Dec. 4, 1903

DEAREST MAMA—I know what pain I must have caused you and you know I wouldn't do it if I really could have helped it—*mais tu sais, me voila!* That's all that could be said—I know my mind, have known it for a long time, and know that I could never think otherwise. Result: I am the happiest man just now in the world; likewise the luckiest—And for you, dear Mummy, you

[2] *This Is My Story*, p. 111.

know that nothing can ever change what we have always been and always
will be to each other—only now you have two children to love and to love
you—and Eleanor as you know will always be a daughter to you in every
true way[3]—

Then two days later:

Dec. 6, 1903

DEAREST MAMA—

Yours of Friday came yesterday and I have been thinking over what you
say about next Sunday—I am so glad, dear Mummy, that you are getting
over the strangeness of it all—I knew you would. . . .

Now if you really can't see the way clear to my staying in N.Y. of course
I will go to H.P. with you—but you know how I feel—and also I think that
E. will be terribly disappointed, as I will, if we can't have one of our first
Sundays together—It seems a little hard and unnecessary on us both and I
shall see you all day Saturday which I shouldn't have done had the great
event not "happened."[4]

Meantime Eleanor wrote Mrs. Roosevelt:

DEAREST COUSIN SALLY,

I must write you and thank you for being so good to me yesterday. I know
just how you feel and how hard it must be, but I do so want you to learn to
love me a little. You must know that I will always try to do what you wish for
I have grown to love you very dearly during the past summer.

It is impossible for me to tell you how I feel toward Franklin, I can only
say that my one great wish is always to prove worthy of him. . . .

With much love, dear Cousin Sally,

Always devotedly,
Eleanor[5]

Mrs. Roosevelt, an extremely determined lady, persuaded them to
delay official announcement of the engagement, and then in the
spring of 1904 resorted to another artifice; she hustled FDR away on
a Caribbean cruise with Lathrop Brown. But Franklin did not forget
his fiancée; indeed he contrived to rush back to the United States as
soon as possible, and Eleanor met him in Washington where they
dined at the White House with Uncle Ted. Next, Mrs. Roosevelt
went to Joseph Choate, the American Ambassador to the Court of
St. James's, and asked him to take her son back to London as his

---

[3] *Letters, op. cit.* Vol. I, p. 518.
[4] *Ibid.*, pp. 519-20, and for excerpts from the honeymoon letters below.
[5] *Franklin Roosevelt at Hyde Park,* by Olin Dows, p. 63.

secretary. But Choate refused on the ground that FDR was still at Harvard and ought to finish his education. In June, 1904, Sara and Eleanor attended his graduation together, and all three spent most of the summer in Campobello. "Franklin came down to get me, and we made the long trip by train," Eleanor records. "Of course, I had to have my maid with me, for I could not have gone with him alone!" Finally, in December, 1904, after a year, Mrs. Roosevelt submitted to the inevitable, and official notification of the engagement at last took place.

Students of personality should find much to interest them not only in the subsurface struggle between Sara and Eleanor, but in the emphatic similarities between these two remarkable women. In many ways Eleanor resembled her future mother-in-law; perhaps Franklin fell in love with her partly out of craving to be associated with a woman of markedly strong character. Also of course he liked her open-minded, alert intelligence; one reason for their deep attraction was that they were intellectually so companionable.

Nowadays it is customary to take at face value Eleanor Roosevelt's description of herself in those remote days as a bereft, miserable "ugly duckling." Actually the truth is far different. Photographs of the time show her to be, if not beautiful, certainly attractive in a very individual and striking way; one, taken when she was at school in England, is particularly lovely, and so is one of her in her bridal dress. Her hair and eyes were always magnificent. Nor was she a bad match by any manner of means. Her breeding was distinguished in the extreme; she was honest, intelligent, and dutiful; she was the favorite niece of the President of the United States; and she had $5,000 a year or more in her own name. It was highly intelligent of Franklin to fall in love with Eleanor. Testimony of the day shows, in fact, that in general it was he who was thought to be more deserving of congratulation than she; people wondered why a young girl with such brilliant prospects should have wanted to marry *him*, a minor Roosevelt with no great prospects at all so far as one could see.

Honeymoon

The young Roosevelts had, in fact, two. First they spent a week in Hyde Park; this was all the time FDR could afford, since he was now studying law at Columbia. After this they lived in the Hotel Webster in the West 40's, where Hall stayed with them; later they went to Hyde Park again—family-bound people!—where the caretaker watched over them, and so, as Eleanor records, she "did not have to display the depths of her ignorance as a housewife." Then, in June, 1905, they went to Europe for several months for their real honeymoon.

Eleanor Roosevelt's own account of this, in the first volume of her autobiography, is of the greatest fascination. She was badly frightened as they set sail on the RMS *Oceanic*. "How terrible to be seasick with a husband to take note of your suffering, particularly one who seemed to think that sailing the ocean blue was a joy!" They began their grand tour with London, where Brown's Hotel confused Franklin with TR and gave them the royal suite, which they couldn't afford. Eleanor grew gradually out of her intense shyness; the record is almost that of breaking out of a cocoon. She learned that FDR was very good at games, that he bought books all the time, that he liked to bargain, and that he spoke quite good French but poor Italian. They called on various aunts and uncles all over Europe, bought some red damask in Venice which was made into a dress that Anna Roosevelt Boettiger still wears, fed the pigeons on the Piazza San Marco, saw an extremely "French" play on the Champs Élysées, and wandered in the Dolomites. Indeed the whole picture is one of the most conventional honeymoon bliss. But——

"My husband," she wrote in *This Is My Story*, "climbed the mountains with a charming lady, Miss Kitty Gandy. She was a few years his senior and he did not know her very well at that time, but she could climb, and I could not, and though I never said a word I was jealous beyond description and perfectly delighted when we started off again and drove out of the mountains. Perhaps I should add that Miss Gandy has since become one of my very good friends!"

The young couple wrote long letters to the elder Mrs. Roosevelt with religious regularity (one of the bride's ends with "Ever and ever so much love my Dearest Mummy from your devoted Eleanor") and some of FDR's are worth quoting. On the boat going over he met some Japanese. "I have had several interesting talks with them though their English is not voluble and I find myself giving out more information than I receive." They went shopping in Paris. "Today we went to various dressmakers, at one of which I distinguished myself by going to sleep. Eleanor got a dozen or so new dresses and two more cloaks. I am getting Eleanor a long sable cloak and a silver fox coat for myself." Of course this was a joke. They visited picture galleries. "We went to the Acedemica de Belly Arty—a few Paul Veroneses and

Titians, and so forth—chiefly indecent infants sitting on, or falling off, clouds—or scared apostles trying to keep the sun out of their eyes." They took a drive in the Tyrol. "It was very dusty and the horse flies were so bad that I had to get out my revolver to shoot several brace. I only skinned the horse once and shot one fly off the driver's nose without scratching him." In Paris they met a fortune teller. "E. is to inherit a fortune . . . and will live to be 105 in the shade, and I am to be President of the U.S. or the Equitable, I couldn't make out which!"

Meantime Sara Roosevelt had furnished a house for them at 125 East 36th Street and engaged the servants, so that all would be comfortable on their return. FDR's letters are full of queries about the plumbing, and such sentences as "if there is a telephone please don't let it be taken out and is there a safe in the house?"

But Eleanor[6] wrote:

Franklin and I have been discussing the electric light question. Of course we would rather have it than gas and you are a dear, sweet Mama, to want to put it in for us, but we are pulled in two ways for we will only have the house two years and it seems hardly wise if it is very expensive to put it in for so short a time and besides if you really want to give us something we would rather have something we can keep, such as furniture. F. says dining room furniture, chairs, etc. are quite unnecessary, but I fear he will want them more when we get into the house. *In any case* he says *not* to put in electric light. You see he has come to a decision since I began this sentence.[7]

On their return—Eleanor was pregnant with Anna—she found that she was going to be "completely taken care of by her mother-in-law." Sara set up their establishment down to the last dishpan and curtain rod; she dominated every aspect of her daughter-in-law's life. Presently the young Roosevelts moved to a house of their own on East 65th Street. Of their own? Hardly—because the elder Mrs. Roosevelt bought and furnished it; moreover she herself moved into the house next door, and the two adjacent brownstones became a single ménage, with a vestibule in common and interconnecting rooms upstairs. Eleanor has recorded that, after several of her children had been born and when FDR became ill, she did not even have a room of her own. Even at Campobello it was impossible for the Roosevelts to escape from the

[6] I mean no disrespect by calling Mrs. Roosevelt "Eleanor" at times. It is a matter of euphony, particularly when "Sara" is being mentioned too. There is a limit to the number of times an author can use "Roosevelt" in a paragraph.

[7] *Letters, op. cit.*, Vol. II, pp. 68-69.

adhesive affectionate attentions of the old lady, if they had wanted to, because there too their house was side by side with hers.

For many years Eleanor Roosevelt was completely dutiful under this regime. She never dreamed "of asking for anything" which would not meet with her mother-in-law's approval. But by imperceptible degrees she began to gain confidence and independence, as did FDR himself. Presently she began to resent being dominated, particularly after they were settled on 65th Street. She was beginning to be uncomfortable and to revolt:

> That autumn I did not quite know what was the matter with me, but I remember that a few weeks after we moved into the new house . . . I sat in front of my dressing table and wept, and when my bewildered young husband asked me what on earth was the matter with me, I said I did not like to live in a house which was not in any way mine, one that I had done nothing about and which did not represent the way I wanted to live. Being an eminently reasonable person, he thought I was quite mad and told me so gently, and said I would feel different in a little while and left me alone until I should become calmer.[8]

Shortly after this FDR entered politics and Mrs. Roosevelt's life became public property, as the whole world knows.

Mrs. Roosevelt: Essentials of Her Character

We must pause to pay tribute to this extraordinary woman who, thirty-odd years later, was to become the First Lady of the World, and allude at least in passing to the relations between this most famous husband and wife of modern times. What Franklin thought of Eleanor, as the years wrote their way along, what she thought of him, will occupy chroniclers for years to come; their story is as dramatic as that of the Brownings, and they made a team, a partnership, that has scarcely been rivaled since Ferdinand and Isabella. No matter what human anguishes and torments may at times have afflicted them, their marriage was certainly one of the most productive in all history.

The line of Mrs. Roosevelt's courage, democracy, unselfishness, and devotion to principle is straight and consistent from first to last. It is the same woman who told an interviewer many years ago, "I always looked at everything from the point of view of what I *ought* to do, rarely from what I wanted to do"; the same woman who, in her sixties,

[8] *This Is My Story*, p. 162.

said to a friend, "Think! I am over sixty, which means that I only have fifteen years left for useful public service!" and the same woman who, immediately after her husband's death, when Mr. Truman asked if he could do anything for her, responded, "Tell me what we can do for *you!*"

Politics first began to interest her when her husband became State Senator, almost forty years ago. As the children grew up she found herself with time on her hands, and few people have ever made more exhaustive and efficient use of time. Nowadays her calm imperturbability before a complex pyramid of tasks has become a commonplace; we accept the fact that she does twenty things at once and does them extremely well; what we forget is that she has been doing exactly this for a quarter of a century or more. An article about Mrs. Roosevelt written when FDR was Governor of New York tells us that in a brief period she (a) visited Ellis Island, a Christmas sale for the blind, a girl's camp at Bear Mountain, miners' homes in West Virginia, the International Flower Show, the New York legislature, the Dutchess County Horse Show, the bonus camp at Huntington, Virginia, the Lee home at Stratford, her son at Groton, and friends in Los Angeles; (b) attended a community singing benefit for a New York infirmary, a political reception, the annual frolic of the Women's National Press Club, a Paderewski concert, a ball for unemployed women in New York City, another ball for a girls' canteen, the silver anniversary of the Congressional Club, and a dinner of the National League of Women Voters; (c) addressed groups all over the country, from the Prudence Penny Institute of Home Economics to a matinee audience at the Metropolitan Opera House; and (d) edited a magazine (*Babies, Just Babies*), served soup to the jobless in Grand Central Terminal, inspected her son Franklin's room at Harvard, helped open the Mid-Hudson Bridge, flew with Amelia Earhart, inspected ships, police stations, and Washington slum homes, wrote some verse, laid various cornerstones, and joined the New York League of Business and Professional Women. Also, while her husband was Governor, she organized the Val-Kill furniture factory, taught three days a week at the Todhunter School for Girls, was chairman of the women's advisory committee for the Democratic National Committee, and edited the *Women's Democratic News*. All this before FDR became President! Her subsequent activities through the years are too well known to need mention, from the column "My Day" to her monthly magazine article for *McCall's*, from her various lecture trips (she has traveled some 400,000 miles in the United States) to her work in innumerable charitable causes and the hard, exacting job she does today on the American delegation to the United Nations.

Not all this came the easy way. Mrs. Roosevelt had to train herself through strict disciplines. Once she reminisced to an interviewer:

When I first tried to make speeches, Louis Howe impressed on me the fact that I could be of great help to Franklin if I handled them well. He came and sat in the back, and sat and sat. Afterward he would say to me, "You were terrible. There was nothing funny—why did you laugh?" That laugh of mine was only nervousness, of course. I've managed to control it, but now and then I lapse, and every time it happens, I remember Louis Howe.

He said to me, about speaking, "Think out what you want to say, and when you've said it, sit down. Write out your first sentence, and your last. Never write down anything in between. Just talk." I still do it that way.[9]

She began to write "My Day" in 1936, and has kept it up ever since. Usually she dictates it to Miss Malvina Thompson, who has been her competent chief secretary, almost her alter ego, for more than twenty-five faithful years. (She has always been masterfully astute in picking secretaries.[10]) The column is, as everybody knows, comparatively easy to parody; Mrs. Roosevelt is sometimes humorless, complacent, and gullible. But how few serious indiscretions she has made in so many years! The column became suddenly fresher and more vital after the President's death; she herself knew as well as anybody the reason for this, namely that she was freer to express what she thought without fear of embarrassing FDR or intruding on matters of high policy. Nobody, despite her seeming artlessness, can turn a pointed phrase better than Mrs. Roosevelt. Nobody, least of all Cardinal Spellman, is likely to forget how, with perfect dignity, she pungently rebuked that eminent dignitary in the controversy over religious instruction last year. James A. Farley wrote in his autobiography that she told him that FDR "found it hard to relax with people who were not his social equals." What she had really said was that the President sometimes found it uncomfortable to be with people who did not share

[9] Kathleen McLaughlin in the New York *Times*, October 8, 1944.
[10] Once, according to the *New Yorker*, Mrs. Roosevelt picked up the telephone and a voice asked for her secretary. "I'm sorry," she said, "Mrs. Roosevelt's secretary isn't in now, but this is Mrs. Roosevelt. May I take the message?"

his social objectives and ideals. Her reply to Mr. Farley was, in part, "I am deeply grieved to find that Mr. Farley was not the person I thought him; or perhaps it would be better to say that I am grieved to find that Mr. Farley allowed himself to be made the kind of personality that Mr. Trohan, of the Chicago *Tribune*, would inevitably make him." (Trohan helped Farley write his book.)

Her simplicity, her composure, and her assurance are all powerful weapons. Sometimes she seems almost too simple. Here are a few excerpts from the question-and-answer book, *If You Ask Me*, which was compiled from her contributions to the *Ladies' Home Journal*:

Did your husband notice a new dress or hat when you wore one, or was he like so many other men who never even see a wife's new clothes?
I think my husband was too preoccupied, usually, to notice my clothes, but sometimes he would suddenly look up and say he liked something I had been wearing for two or three years!
Have you any good friends who are Republicans?
I hope so.
Have you ever said to yourself, "If only I were a man"? Or are you quite content with being a woman?
No, I have never wanted to be a man. I have often wanted to be more effective as a woman, but I have never felt that trousers would do the trick!
Is there anything you have always longed to do, and never quite gotten around to?
I have always wanted to try to write fiction, but I have never had the time.
Are you afraid of mice?
I do not like them, but I do not shriek when I see one.
What do you think of the increasing tendency of today's novelists to use so many "four-letter words" not spoken in polite society?
I did not know there were any words left that were not spoken in polite society.

Mrs. Roosevelt, it has been said, was much more a Roosevelt than Roosevelt. Like most Roosevelts, she has great drive and will to power. She wrote once, "I had painfully high ideals and a tremendous sense of duty . . . entirely unrelieved by any appreciation of the weaknesses of human nature." She has always been quite willing to concede her errors, though sometimes her method of acknowledging these is oblique, as was the President's. Once she declared, "I have never been a very great partisan." She took a position markedly to the Left for many years, and was always more Leftish than her husband; several people duped her. Nowadays she hates and despises the Communists, particularly the American brand—because she found out they were lying to her—and her experience on the UN has shown her that the Russians are by no means what she once thought them to be. Recently in Paris the Soviet Ambassador congratulated her on how fresh and unfatigued she looked after an exhausting session of the Human Rights Committee. "Ah, Mr. Ambassador," she exclaimed with gracious irony, "You may be tired of course, but *I* belong to the decadent democracies!"

Today, in the autumn of sixty-five, Mrs. Roosevelt looks wonderfully well. She is a bit deaf; that seems to be the only toll the merciless years have taken. (And they were merciless; no woman has ever been more savagely attacked.) It is an odd point that Mrs. Roosevelt, like her friend Dorothy Thompson, is one of those women with the misfortune to photograph badly. But the camera is one of the most blatant liars of our time, and in real life she is hearteningly good to look at. Her indefatigability is undiminished, and the demands on her time and favor continue to be relentless. Her position today is much more considerable than when her husband was alive, and for the asking she could have almost any job in the world. Her incessant search for good works and her inflexible liberalism, the gentility and wisdom that come from within her own great heart, have made her something akin to the conscience of the nation.

Husband and Wife

"FDR is nine parts mush and one part Eleanor." This remark, once supposed to have been made by a caustic friend, is of course nonsense. But it reflects, in a distorted way, what is certainly a correct impression —that Mrs. Roosevelt was of great consequence to her husband's career and character. One simple thing to say is that, after his illness, she became his legs.

Also she was his eyes and ears. Her gargantuan travels and excursions, her curiosities and researches into almost every phase of the national life, brought him a great deal of first-hand information. Moreover he taught her how to inspect, how to see, just what to watch out for, how to weigh evidence. Then too the firmness of her convictions sometimes helped set the tone of policy; on any high ethical question, he gave more weight to her opinion than to anybody's. She provoked him to interest in new fields, and she was useful in launching trial balloons. She soothed him often, particularly in the early days. Finally, she was something of a problem in that she shared the presidential aura, but without responsibility.

All manner of stories are to be told in this general connection. Mrs. Roosevelt was, only too obviously, a person extremely close to the President; therefore almost everybody sought her favor or intervention. She probably did not actively want FDR to run for President; when he did, she became—it went without saying—his most scrupulously loyal advocate. She had a certain veto power on some of his decisions, which she used sparingly; when she thought he had done something wrong, she frankly told him so—for instance she disapproved strongly of several of the assistant secretaries of state who went into office with Stettinius. Sometimes she did not like the men closest to him, but she held her tongue as a rule. She thought that Tom Corcoran was too "radical" and that he and Missy LeHand sometimes gave the President bad advice; on some grounds she disapproved of Harry Hopkins. There was considerable rivalry, in fact, between Mrs. Roosevelt and Hopkins for a time.

Occasionally, but not often, she was a positive force in suggesting appointments. But she never pressed them hard; she would consider her duty done if she brought a person to the President's attention. "She'd launch the ship, then they'd have to get themselves across the ocean," as I heard it put.

Leon Henderson was a witness to one occasion—they were rare— when she tacitly rebuked the President. This was after his shilly-shallying over Loyalist Spain. She said, "You and I, Mr. Henderson, will some day learn a lesson from this tragic error over Spain. We were morally right, but too weak." She turned then to FDR as if he were not there. "We should have pushed *him* harder." The President said not a word.

What did she think of him, in her inmost heart? One gets a curious sense from her two books, which are so largely concerned with him, that, in a strange way, she did not know him altogether well. They tell us a great deal about herself, but comparatively little about the President except in externals. The Roosevelts, I have said, made a "team." But probably they were never quite so cohesive a team during the White House years as we are likely to assume in retrospect. Perspective pulls them closer together than they really were.

What did FDR think of her? He adored her of course; he loved to tease her; on occasion she bored and irritated him; he was exasperated by many of her friends. But he never ceased to respect and admire her, and for many years there is no doubt that he was passionately in love with her. She says with almost startling candor in *This I Remember*, "He might have been happier with a wife who was completely uncritical. That I was never able to be, and he had to find it in other people. Nevertheless, I think I sometimes acted as a spur even though the spurring was not always wanted or welcome." Then comes an astonishing sentence: "I was one of those who served his purposes!"

His early letters are models of spirited devotion. In correspondence he always called her "Babs" or "Babbie"; he would address her as "My own Dearest," and usually signed himself, "Ever your devoted F."[11] Here is a segment from a letter written when he was Assistant Secretary of the Navy in 1917; he was urging her to stay in Campobello:

. . . I really can't stand that house all alone without you, and you were a goosy girl to think or even pretend to think that I don't want you here *all* the summer, because you know I do! But honestly *you* ought to have six weeks straight at Campo, just as *I* ought to, only you can and I can't![12]

Of course she embarrassed him by her public activity and got in his way sometimes. The following is a colloquy from an early press conference:

Q. Mr. President, I want to apply for a White House job.
The President: Good.
Q. I want to be Coordinator of White House Press Conferences. You have one at a quarter to eleven and Mrs. Roosevelt has one at eleven.
The President: The trouble was the Canadian Prime Minister came in. What are you going to do about that?
Q. Haven't you any influence with Mrs. Roosevelt to get her to postpone hers? (*Laughter.*)
The President: Ask the Canadian Prime Minister.
Q. To ask Mrs. Roosevelt to have hers at a different time?
The President: Yes.[13]

[11] To others he often referred to her casually as "Eleanor," sometimes "Ma," and often "the Missus." Once he told Morris Ernst, who was en route to England, "If you run into the Missus, tell her I'm fine."
[12] *Letters*, Vol. II, p. 347.
[13] Rosenman, Vol. VII, p. 601.

No marriages proceed for forty years without occasional squabbles and fracases. Sometimes Mrs. Roosevelt would leave the Hyde Park table abruptly in the middle of a meal, because of some pressing engagement; the President and his mother would be hurt or angry. During one small dinner party she was curious about some talk going on at his end of the table and called out to be included in the tête-à-tête; he replied sharply, "The conversation remains at *this* end of the table!" But if anybody else rebuked her, he was furious. Robert E. Sherwood sat with him in the Oval Room one evening, listening to the radio; they heard a commentator bitterly attack Mrs. Roosevelt for her trip to the Pacific front. The President reached over and turned the radio off, an expression of acute pain and anguish on his face. It was as if he felt that perhaps she *was* open to criticism in some respects, and he could not bear to hear it.

During one of the worst periods of the war in 1942, when the Germans were at the gates of Cairo and the Japanese on the borders of India, Mrs. Roosevelt became obsessed by a case concerning a Negro named Waller, a tenant farmer who had been sentenced to death for the murder of his landlord. This was, it might have been thought, of absolute unimportance compared to Rommel's threat, the disastrous campaign in Burma, the U-boat menace, and a severe domestic crisis over man power. But not to Mrs. Roosevelt. She sought to intervene with the governor of the state where the murder occurred, and then asked the President to do so. Then FDR, though he had quite a lot else on his mind, wrote a "very strong letter" to the governor requesting him to commute Waller's sentence to life imprisonment.

The following memorandum from Harry Hopkins, which has not been published before, carries on the story:

The Governor had given six different reprieves and the President felt that he could not interfere again. He thought the Governor was acting entirely within his constitutional rights and, in addition to that, doubted very much if the merits of the case warranted the Governor's reaching any other decision.

Mrs. Roosevelt, however, would not take "No" for an answer and the President finally got on the phone himself and told Mrs. Roosevelt that under no circumstances would he intervene with the Governor and urged very strongly that she say nothing about it.

This incident is typical of things that have gone on in Washington between the President and Mrs. Roosevelt ever since 1932. She is forever finding someone underprivileged and unbefriended in whose behalf she takes up the cudgels. While she may often be wrong, as I think she was in this case, I never cease to admire her burning determination to see that justice is done, not only to individuals but to underprivileged groups.

I think, too, in this instance Mrs. Roosevelt felt that I was not pressing her case with the President adequately, because in the course of the evening he was not available on the phone and I had to act as a go-between. At any rate I felt that she would not be satisfied until the President told her himself, which he reluctantly but finally did.

Mrs. Roosevelt, in one of her books, mentions a trick that her mother-in-law sometimes indulged in: if the President steadily refused to meet somebody whom she thought he *ought* to meet, she would invite the person to a meal without telling FDR beforehand. It is striking that she herself should make a point of this; because time and time again she resorted to the same gentle stratagem. Once Aubrey Williams, the head of the National Youth Administration, which was one of Mrs. Roosevelt's favorite projects, had an urgent problem. He wanted to see the President but FDR was so totally occupied with top-level military affairs that he could not possibly give him an appointment. Mrs. Roosevelt thereupon invited him to dinner. Mr. Williams, a gentleman, protested that he did not want to abuse the hospitality of the White House by any such device, but Mrs. Roosevelt thought the matter under consideration to be so important that it was his duty, no less, to take it up with the President himself. So the dinner took place; FDR liked Williams, but was somewhat surprised to see him at the table.

Then, at the beginning of dinner, some devil possessed Mrs. Roosevelt to tell the President that he *must* at once see a young Chinese student who had just arrived in Washington; this young man, she insisted, would transform his whole point of view on China. FDR replied that he simply could *not* take time to talk to any such student at this particular time. Eleanor pressed him. FDR said that he could not receive any lone young Chinese student if only from the point of view of protocol. Eleanor continued to press him. FDR, irritated, finally burst out, "Send your Chinaman over to the State Department!" Eleanor replied, "Franklin, you know perfectly well that the State Department is on the other side politically so far as China is concerned, and it will be useless in the matter!" Roosevelt said in despair, "Have the damned Chinaman see Hopkins!" Eleanor said, "Hopkins is too busy." Finally FDR refused to do anything at all about it. Eleanor thereupon declared, "Well, I will ask him to dinner as my guest," whereupon the President at last blew up, exclaiming, "Just remember, I want dinner to be a relaxation, not an excuse for doing business!"

Meantime Aubrey Williams had been listening to all this open-mouthed, and he could not resist bursting into laughter. The President snapped at him, "What's on your mind, Aubrey?" Williams then had to explain why he himself was there. The President looked chagrined for a moment, then saw how funny the whole thing was, regained his temper, gave a resounding laugh, and listened with great care and interest to Williams' problem.

As the war went on the President and Mrs. Roosevelt saw less of one another; sometimes he did not even know whether she was in the White House or not. She seldom went to Shangri-La, and FDR never saw her New York apartment on Washington Square till late in 1944, though she had been trying to get him to look at it for years. "Mother and Father were in such a state that he simply couldn't talk to her on some things," one of the children told me once. For a time Mrs. Roosevelt could not easily get through to him on the telephone without the intermediation of Miss Tully. Then—during his last visits to Warm Springs—she once or twice exasperated him by long telephone calls from Washington on matters that he thought had no great consequence.

But the depth, the solidity, the fruitfulness, the fine permanence of the love these two illustrious citizens bore for one another could not be invalidated by the inevitable occasional frictions caused by fatigue, illness, and the strain of war. It tells a great deal that when Mrs. Roosevelt went to England during the Blitz and a high-priority dispute took place as to how she should return, the President impatiently telegraphed to his staff in London, "I don't care how you send her home, just send her."

A Word About the Children

The Roosevelts had six children; there are seventeen grandchildren today, and one great-grandchild. Anna Eleanor, the eldest child, was born in 1906. Then came James (1907), and Franklin Delano, Jr. (1909), who died when he was eight months old; Mrs. Roosevelt records that he was "the biggest and most beautiful" of all the babies. Elliott was born in 1910, less than a year after the first Franklin's death; then in 1914 came another boy, who was also given the name of Franklin, Jr., and finally in 1916 the youngest child, John Aspinwall, was born.

Anna has married twice, James twice, Elliott three times, John once, and Franklin, Jr., twice. There have been six divorces so far, with another impending as these lines are written. This accumulating series of matrimonial breakups was, it goes without saying, a disappointment and a bitter grief to both parents. "In each case," Mrs. Roosevelt records, "he [the President] did what he could to prevent the divorce," but although he knew that many of his opponents would attempt to make political capital out of these personal disasters, "it never occurred to him that the children should subordinate their lives to his interest."

Mrs. Roosevelt, who has always defended her children like a tigress, but who knew well how high-spirited and strong-willed they were, blames herself to a certain extent for the divorces but not on the ground that she neglected the children. What she feels is that, perhaps, she was too rigid a mother, not the opposite, and also that she was overzealous in protecting them. It was almost always she who had the task of disciplining them, since, as mentioned in a chapter above, FDR was constitutionally incapable of doing this himself; moreover when she did inflict punishment, he would be apt to ruin everything by letting the guilty child dissolve in tears on his shirt front. The children talk about her today with great tenderness. They remember her, as they grew up, as the most loving and solicitous of mothers, sweet and thoughtful always, but sensitive and with a strong sense of right and wrong.

Mrs. Roosevelt's own views on divorce were once stated in her question-and-answer book:

Divorce is something which should never be taken lightly, but I think the real emphasis should be laid upon the seriousness with which we undertake marriage in the first place. Sometimes even when a marriage begins with every apparent prospect of success, people develop differently and find themselves, over a period of years, unable to live together in harmony. When that happens it seems to me that there is nothing to do but resort to a divorce.

Certain religions do not recognize divorce, and of course I am not talking about people who belong to those religions. . . .

It is better, I think, to make the inevitable adjustment and separate, hoping that both people involved may find companionship and love with someone else, or that one can make of life alone something worth living. For two people to live unhappily together seems to be bad for them and for the children, if any.

The Roosevelt children grew up with the sense that they were part of a large family with special privileges and prestige and a copious tradition, but except by their grandmother they were not particularly spoiled. They moved around a great deal between New York, Washington, and Hyde Park, and James told me once that he always felt "rootless" as a child. They were given very little money as children, and the elder Mrs. Roosevelt thought that they should get none at all. Young Franklin's first allowance was ten cents a week, of which five cents had to go into the church plate; at the age of ten he was raised to a quarter, of which the church collection took a dime. If he did not have cash ready for this, "all hell broke loose." Several details attending the financial circumstances of the children are curious. They were given tidy sums when they went off to boarding school and college, but FDR thought that the boys should fend for themselves after their graduation and Elliott, for instance, was never given any money at all after he finished Groton. One of the manliest letters I have ever read came to FDR from James at Harvard, in which James explains politely but very explicitly how his college career will be ruined if he has to pay more attention to earning his keep at various jobs than to his studies.

Young Franklin's first memory of his father is of the way he would rush up the four flights of stairs in the Washington house, rub him affectionately on the back of the neck, and murmur, "I hope you're as snug as a bug in a rug." Elliott's first recollection goes back to the time when he was about six; FDR loved to take the boys swimming and teach them to race model boats, and another vivid and persistent memory is of his father reading aloud on Christmas Eve. James's chief memory is of being spanked—if only because this didn't happen often.

The parents usually called Anna "Sis," Elliott "Bunny," and John "Young John." Elliott called FDR "Pops," Anna called him "Father" as a rule, and the rest used "Pa." Probably Anna was his favorite among them; she was much closer to him politically than any of the sons. Mrs. Roosevelt's favorite was probably Elliott, if only because he was ill much of the time as a young boy, and yet had such a rambunctious spirit. *"All* those kids," as I heard it put, "were handfuls."

Here is a homely touch in Mrs. Roosevelt's first book, describing an occasion in 1919:

Before I knew it, all my five children and my husband were down with the flu, and three of the servants. We succeeded in getting one trained nurse from New York . . . who was put in charge of Elliott, who had double pneumonia. My husband was moved into a little room next to mine, and John, the baby, had his crib in my bedroom, for he had bronchial pneumonia. There was very little difference between day and night for me, and Doctor Hardin, who worked as hard as he possibly could every minute of the time, came in once or twice a day and looked over all my patients. He remarked that we were lucky that some of us were still on our feet, for he had families with nobody able to stand up.[14]

Mr. Roosevelt had a wonderful touch with children, and he loved his own deeply. He called them his "precious chicks," and was violently proud of them. Two circumstances interfered, of course, with his behavior as a normal father: his illness and his accession to the Presidency. When he became paralyzed he had perforce to give up most of the outdoor sports he shared with them, but there was never any question of his physical superiority; he could sit or crawl on the floor, wrestle with the boys, and overcome them by the power of his arms and shoulders. When he became President it was impossible for him to see as much of the children as he would have liked, but the old arguments continued at family dinners, he wrote them dutiful letters whenever they were away, and both James and Anna had arduous periods of service in his secretariat. And always, if possible, one of the boys stood by him holding his arm on ceremonial occasions.

We have not the space to tell the story of the children's own lives. It might be mentioned that all four boys earned, by their own intrepidity and merit, very good war records indeed; if young Franklin had been British he almost certainly would have won a Victoria Cross for one exploit saving the life of a comrade. It is interesting to note such little-known facts as that John, the stablest of the lot, once worked for a while under an assumed name in order to avoid any possible intimation that his own name was favoring him; that James was packed

14 *This Is My Story*, p. 270.

off as a youngster to a lumber camp and then to Sweden to broaden his education; and that Anna once wrote a book for children called *Scamper, the Bunny Who Went to the White House.*

Elliott has always been the most difficult and rebellious of the boys; perhaps he subconsciously resented his father, and hence was given to bad behavior. He deliberately failed in an examination rather than go to college; he wanted to get out into the world at once, and prove himself. For a time he worked for Hearst and he actively opposed FDR in Texas politics on one occasion. His various failures in business and the affair of his dog Blaze certainly did not add to White House prestige. On the other hand his good and useful qualities are many. At present he operates a big agricultural enterprise in the Hyde Park region, Val-Kill Farms, and is helping his mother on a television program. James has been politically active and ambitious all his adult life, and he has overcome the most severe handicaps of illness to take part in fruitful public endeavor. He is running this year for Governor of California. The boy who resembles FDR most is young Franklin; he is, in fact, the spitting image of his father. His brilliant success in beating Tammany and winning Sol Bloom's Congressional seat in 1949 gave him an auspicious entrance into politics, and there are many who think that it will not be long before another Roosevelt is Governor of New York and perhaps, in the future, President of the United States. Young Franklin has *élan*, guts, almost too much charm, vigorous liberal principles, and the full magic of the family name.

*

Now, after this long interlude, we return to FDR's own career, and see him off on the first great adventure of his life.

Chapter 12

NOVITIATE OF THE YOUNG PATRICIAN

We don't buy headaches, unless we have to.
—FRANKLIN DELANO ROOSEVELT

Roosevelt entered politics at the age of twenty-eight, in 1910. This was a comparatively passive year in the history of the world; much that happened then seems as remote today as Fabius Maximus. It was the year after Blériot flew the Channel, and the year before a forgotten war between Italy and Turkey. The stout and placid Taft was President of the United States, the Emperor Franz Josef still ruled a patchwork Austria-Hungary, and England was basking in the sun of Asquith. Hitler was an angry youth in Linz, unknown to history or fame, and Mussolini a village anarchist.

Roosevelt's baptism into politics deserves a good deal more space than we can give it here, if only because the details have been so largely forgotten; the tremendousness of the presidential years blots out what went before. But we must be brief.

The young Roosevelts were living in the 65th Street house, week-ending in Hyde Park, and spending their summers at Campobello. FDR could never, in the frank words of his wife, quite break with his mother and make a real home of his own. But life was pleasant in the extreme. His letters to Mrs. Roosevelt in this period—when he happened to be away on a hunting trip or brief cruise—are full of lively affection, and he adored the children. The Roosevelts went to Washington often, and stayed at the home of Mrs. William S. Cowles (Aunty Bye), one of TR's sisters.[1] One measure of Franklin's youthful interest is that he was an enthusiastic member of the volunteer fire department at Hyde Park, and he continued to be an ardent sportsman. He could handle almost any kind of boat, and once he sailed with

[1] They attended TR's inaugural in 1905 as guests of the President; Mrs. Roosevelt tells us (*This Is My Story*, p. 123) that she never expected to see "another inauguration in the family!" Much later they rented the Cowles home, when FDR was Assistant Secretary of the Navy. It was located at 1733 N Street, and in those days was called the "Little White House," because TR had lived there too.

Eleanor up to Nova Scotia, in search of buried treasure. He rode and hunted, played good tennis, and became a passionate devotee of golf. Golf meant more to him than any sport, and this interest was to mount for the next ten years. Quite aside from the fact that he was exceptionally good looking, FDR had a vibrant physical grace in those days; one of his biographers calls him a "young Apollo." An English friend met him at a family picnic at about this time, and told me years later that he had never forgotten the sight of young Roosevelt leaping across a brook "like some amazing stag."

FDR studied law at Columbia after leaving Harvard, but he never graduated or took a degree.[2] Frankly, further school work bored him. But he managed to pass the state law examinations in 1907, and was admitted to the bar. He went to work for the old and distinguished firm of Carter, Ledyard and Milburn; this company was trustee for J. P. Morgan, and it represented such interests as the Astor estate and the American Express Company. Roosevelt, however, did not have much to do with clients on this level; he was employed in a very junior capacity indeed. But presently he became head clerk in charge of municipal court cases, and then for a time worked in the firm's admiralty division, which suited his talents better. He chose the law as a profession for a number of reasons: his father, who died while he was at Harvard, wanted him to be a lawyer, as a preparation for handling the family properties, and the law was, in any case, the path of least resistance for a young man of his position. It was the natural thing to do. Roosevelt's experience at the bar was useful in that it enlarged his horizon greatly; for the first time in his life he was rubbing shoulders with people far outside his own milieu. He himself has said that he was merely an "office boy," but he learned a good deal about judicial procedure in minor courts and how to handle witnesses. "His early interlude as a fledgling lawyer was his first real introduction to the various classes of society not encompassed by his heritage and education."[3] However this may be, Roosevelt never gave much sign of talent for the bar, and it did not hold him long.

By 1910 young FDR was a popular and civic-spirited member of the Hyde Park community. Everybody liked him, and a group of Dutchess County politicians got the idea of running him for State

[2] One of his classmates was William J. ("Wild Bill") Donovan. General Donovan thought at the time that his chief characteristic was "daring."

[3] *Letters*, Vol. II, p. 139.

Senator. They asked him to drop in at the Poughkeepsie headquarters, and he arrived in riding clothes. They surveyed him with some curiosity, and one said, "If you run, you'll have to take off those yellow boots and put on pants."

Why did the Poughkeepsie leaders want Roosevelt? (1) The local mayor had his eye on him for some time; (2) Roosevelt was a terrific name politically, since TR was the dominant personality of the nation, and a *democratic* Roosevelt would be a dramatic drawing card; (3) FDR was rich, and would pay his own expenses and perhaps contribute to the campaign at large; (4) it didn't matter anyway, since the seat was traditionally Republican.

Why did Roosevelt agree to run in what appeared to be a hopeless race? (1) He had had, ever since Harvard, a sneaking desire to try himself in public life; (2) he loved being a politician; (3) he was bored with what he was doing; (4) the race was a challenge.

Perhaps we should interpolate here one word on why FDR was a Democrat. The most truthful answer would be that he never thought to be otherwise. His whole family had been brought up that way, although his father deserted Bryan in 1896. Far behind that, the Dutchess County Roosevelts had always been Democrats. Young Roosevelt admired TR, especially his progressivism, but he opposed him on a good many issues; in particular FDR was much more liberal on tariffs, the American "imperialism" of that epoch, and foreign affairs. In any case it was lucky that he should have been born and raised a Democrat, since, after decades of oblivion, the Democratic party was coming to the fore with a rush.[4]

State Senator

Roosevelt's race for the State Senate, his fledgling run, foretells much of the future. He stated straight away, "As you know, I accept this nomination with absolute independence. I am pledged to no man; I am influenced by no special interests, and so I shall remain. In the coming campaign, I need not tell you that I do not intend to stand still. We are going to have a very strenuous month."

Only four weeks remained until election day, and strenuous they indeed were; the three counties that comprised the constituency had never seen such a campaign before. FDR hired an open red Maxwell,

[4] See "The Governor," by Milton MacKaye, *New Yorker*, August 15 and 22, 1931, for much valuable material on this period.

and hour by hour, day by day, visited every inch of the area, making speech after speech not merely in the towns and villages but at the isolated crossroads and literally from the top of haystacks—wherever, in fact, he could find a listener.[5] His ambition was to call personally on every farmer in the entire district. This was the first time anybody had ever campaigned in New York State by automobile. It was a daring innovation. The car reached the terrible speed of twenty miles an hour, and frightened cattle and horses leaped over fences as it roared past. FDR's zeal was such that on one occasion he overshot the New York frontier, and found himself haranguing crowds in Connecticut that couldn't vote for him anyway. Moses Smith, his old neighbor, tells us that his most effective talking point was advocacy of a 96-quart standard barrel for apples; the farmers had no such standard in those days, and they wanted one. This homely touch is a forecast of much that FDR did in later campaigns.

Roosevelt won, to almost everybody's surprise, and he became the first Democratic senator from this district since 1856, with the exception of one who had squeezed in as a result of a three-cornered race in 1888. Perhaps FDR took the whole thing as a lark, but it was a well-earned and handsome victory. The result was close; he won by only 1,140 votes.[6] Had those 1,140 votes gone the other way, what might have happened? Would FDR have dismissed the interlude as an adventure, gone back to law, and never tried his hand at politics again?

As State Senator in Albany Roosevelt became well known overnight —not in any big way, but enough so that his name was printed in newspapers all over the State, and even beyond. To attentive politicians everywhere he became a marked man. This was because of the affair, once celebrated but now forgotten, of William F. ("Blue-Eyed Billy") Sheehan.

In those days, early 1911, the grip of Tammany Hall on Democratic politics in New York, both State and City, was strangulating; the boss of Tammany, Charles F. Murphy, was a complete dictator. Federal senators were chosen at this time by the state legislatures. Murphy decided that the Democratic candidate to fill the seat about

[5] Mrs. Roosevelt listened to his first speech and was terrified that he might not acquit himself well.

[6] The local press either ignored or attacked him during the campaign, incidentally. The leading Poughkeepsie paper, an ardent Republican organ, only mentioned his name twice. Did FDR ever recall this to mind in later years?

to be vacated in Washington by Senator Chauncey Depew should be a Buffalo boss and Tammany subchieftain, William F. Sheehan. All that was necessary to achieve this was approval of Sheehan in the Democratic caucus. Young Roosevelt decided to oppose Sheehan. This was a remarkable decision for a new senator to take in his first days of office. What is more FDR summoned a group of "reform" Democrats to meet in the house he and Mrs. Roosevelt had taken in Albany, at the precise time the caucus was taking place. The result was that Sheehan lacked ten votes for approval. It is difficult to appreciate nowadays what a storm this provoked. "Roosevelt bolted," a commentator of the day expressed it, "before his seat was warm." That an absolute novice should defy the full might of Tammany and lead an insurrection was unprecedented; that he should be permitted to get away with it was intolerable. Tammany marshaled its forces, and the fight went on for ten solid weeks. But FDR and his splinter group held the balance of power, and they won in the end on the sixty-fourth ballot; Sheehan withdrew his candidacy and a compromise candidate more or less acceptable to both sides, James A. O'Gorman, got the nomination. This was Roosevelt's first political victory within the party, and it shows, as is only too clear, several of his traits—leadership, heterodoxy, a courage bordering on audacity, adhesiveness, and a dramatic sense of timing. It was also important in that it aroused sentiment for the constitutional amendment which led presently to the direct election of senators, and in a remote way it influenced the choice of Woodrow Wilson as Democratic presidential candidate in 1912.[7]

At about this time Roosevelt went down to Trenton to call on Wilson. The first recorded mention of FDR by Wilson came in a conversation Wilson had with one of the Pennsylvania bosses, Joseph F. Guffey.

Wilson said, "The young man just elected as state senator from a safe Republican district in New York will bear watching. His name is Roosevelt."

Guffey replied, "Professor, I thought that all Roosevelts were Republican."

"No, Guffey, this one comes from the Democratic branch of the family, and he is the handsomest young giant I have ever seen."

[7] I have followed *Letters*, Vol. II, pp. 160-64 for most of these details about Sheehan.

Roosevelt ran for reelection to Albany in 1912, and won this time with a nice majority after a campaign he described as "joyous." He did not, however, more than begin to serve this term, because great events seized him suddenly and he became Wilson's Assistant Secretary of the Navy.

FDR's record as Senator, the Sheehan episode aside, was nothing to shake the world apart, but the experience was interesting. His education began in earnest, and so did Eleanor's. He was chairman of the Forest, Fish, and Game Committee, and he became deeply interested in conservation. He came out for woman suffrage. He shocked the orthodox by refusing an appropriation for his own county on the ground that it wasn't necessary. He took a strong line against the utilities lobby—which took courage—and for farm relief. He learned a great deal of the practical ins and outs of political maneuver; Mrs. Roosevelt records that he showed a predisposition for the "science" of government, rather than its "philosophy." The Roosevelt house burst with politicians day and night; the atmosphere was a far cry from 65th Street, Dutchess County, and the waters of New Brunswick. Above all, he made strong friendships with such men as Robert F. Wagner, Al Smith, and Louis Howe.[8]

The Roosevelt personality made a sharp imprint even at this time, when he was about thirty. Frances Perkins records that he seemed "arrogant"; Mrs. Roosevelt's explanation of this is that he was shy. He became a "news" name almost at once; people talked of "the second coming of a Roosevelt" to the legislature, and one Tammany sachem declared, "Well, if we've caught a Roosevelt, we'd better take him down and drop him off the dock. The Roosevelts run true to form, and this kid is likely to do for us what the Colonel is going to do to the Republican Party, split it wide open."[9]

The first article ever written about FDR, so far as I know, is a sketch by W. A. Warn in the Sunday section of the New York *Times* on January 22, 1911.[10] The first political cartoon portraying him appeared in the New York *Herald* at about the same date; it em-

---

[8] Wagner was a fellow senator at the time, Smith an assemblyman.

[9] *Franklin D. Roosevelt, A Career in Progressive Democracy*, by Ernest K. Lindley (Indianapolis, The Bobbs-Merrill Company, 1931), p. 78.

[10] Mr. Warn asked him if he had heard from TR recently; Roosevelt replied, "No, I have had no word from Uncle in a long time . . . but who can help but admire him?" The Warn article contains FDR's oft-quoted remark, "There is nothing I love so much as a good fight."

phasizes the jut of jaw and delicately adjusted pince-nez, as millions of caricatures were to do in later years.

Here are three pictures of the Roosevelt of that day. Mr. Warn's:

Roosevelt is tall and lithe. With his handsome face and his form of supple strength he could make a fortune on the stage and set the matinee girl's heart throbbing with subtle and happy emotion. But no one would suspect behind that highly polished exterior the quiet force and determination that now are sending cold shivers down the spine of Tammany's striped mascot.

From the New York *World,* as reprinted in the second volume of letters:

A distant cousin of Colonel Roosevelt, he is 32 years of age, of spare figure and lean intellectual face, suggesting in appearance a student of divinity rather than a practical politician. Gold-bowed spectacles loop his long thin nose, and a frock coat drapes his figure. He is wealthy, possessing, according to his friends, a fortune of considerable size, and is able and of pleasing personality.

And from Mrs. Roosevelt in her first volume of autobiography:

He looked thin then, tall, high-strung and, at times, nervous. White skin and fair hair, deep-set blue eyes, and clear-cut features. No lines as yet in the face, but at times a set look of his jaw denoted that this apparently pliable youth had strength and Dutch obstinacy.

One friend in this remote period says that Roosevelt's favorite phrase was "Yes, of course"—indicating that even if he didn't understand or agree with what was being said, he felt "the social compulsion to maintain a pleasant exterior." Another testifies that he was a "fine extrovert"; his chief physical mannerism was that he walked with head tossed back, and "his eyes were never on the pavement." Still another, who visited him at Campobello, says that what struck him most was his voracious curiosity. "He was alert, cheerful and tremendously ambitious. He had few opinions himself, but he sucked people dry with questions."

Apparently the first person who thought in those salad days that FDR would ever be President, and who was willing to bet on it, was Thomas Lynch of Poughkeepsie. Mr. Lynch, a close friend and political associate, put down two bottles of champagne on the wager in 1911; twenty-two years later they were duly opened, amid festivity.

Assistant Secretary of the Navy

In June, 1912, FDR went to Baltimore to attend the convention that was to nominate Woodrow Wilson for the Presidency of the United States. He was not a delegate, and even if he had been his vote would not have counted, because the unit rule prevailed in those days and the New York delegation was pledged to Champ Clark, the Speaker of the House. It is significant that this did not deter Roosevelt from aggressive activity on Wilson's behalf; he made private contact with all the delegates he could reach, and organized young college men into Wilson teams. When the proceedings opened Wilson's chances seemed slim, but the great party bosses were split and he won on the forty-sixth ballot, after one of the most agitated conventions ever known to American politics up to that time. FDR was jubilant, and he wired Mrs. Roosevelt in Campobello, "Wilson nominated this afternoon all my plans vague splendid triumph."

Mrs. Roosevelt had accompanied him to Baltimore, but she left after a few days. FDR was extremely busy, and had no mind for anything but politics. She records that she "decided that my husband would hardly miss my company, as I rarely laid eyes on him."[11]

Roosevelt made several lifelong friendships at this convention which were highly important to his career. He met William G. McAdoo, Joseph E. Davies, and Henry Morgenthau, Sr., who were among the Wilson floor managers. He met Josephus Daniels. And he met the Baltimore publisher Van Lear Black. It is always risky to calculate what might have happened in a man's life if such and such had not happened, and vice versa; nevertheless be it noted that had he not met Mr. Black, it is just possible that he might never have got infantile paralysis, for it was after a cruise on Black's yacht that the attack came. Also Black gave him the insurance job that tided him over financial troubles in the early 20's. When Black saw Roosevelt in Baltimore for the first time, he exclaimed: "This is the most attractive man I have ever met."

A witness describes FDR's first meeting with Josephus Daniels as follows: "An extremely handsome man came into the Wilson headquarters, and said that he was heart and soul for Wilson even though he couldn't vote for him, and could he do some work." John Jenkins of the press division presented him to Daniels, who did not catch his name. FDR repeated it, and Daniels then introduced him to McAdoo and Cordell Hull. "Young Roosevelt appeared to be in high spirits at being in the company of these men."

Later Daniels, as Secretary of the Navy, offered the Assistant Secretaryship to Roosevelt, but first he talked this over with the veteran statesman Elihu Root, who had served TR. When Daniels mentioned FDR's name "a queer look" came into Root's face.

Root: "Aren't you afraid of doing that?"

Daniels: "Why?"

Root: "The Roosevelts always like to ride ahead."

Then Daniels went to Wilson, saying that if the President did not have anybody in mind for the Assistant Secretaryship, he would like to suggest someone. Daniels describes the ensuing colloquy in his *The Wilson Era*. Wilson said, "You are quick on the trigger. Whom have you in mind?"

Daniels said, "Young Roosevelt. As I am from the South, I think the Assistant should come from another section, preferably New York or New England."

The President said, "How well do you know Mr. Roosevelt? How well is he equipped?"

When Daniels broached the matter to FDR himself Roosevelt replied: "It would please me better than anything in the world. I'd be glad to be connected with the new administration. All my life I have loved ships and have been a student of the Navy, and the assistant secretaryship is the one place, above all others, I would love to hold."

Why did Daniels choose young Roosevelt? First and foremost he liked him; he even records that it was a case of "love at first sight" between them. Second, it probably flattered him to have a Roosevelt working for him. Third, he was sure he would do a good job.

Why did Wilson approve the appointment? Mainly because Daniels was a pacifist and he felt, therefore, that the Assistant Secretary should be someone more actively interested in the Navy, one who would get along well with the admirals and so on. It is worth mention, perhaps, that Daniels himself only got the Navy Department by the narrowest of margins. Wilson wanted him to be Postmaster General, but at the last moment gave him the Navy instead, partly on the ground that Daniels, in the Post Office Department, would be swamped by thousands of requests for postmasterships from people who had helped him as press director of the campaign; Wilson feared that he might not be able to cope with these because he was so softhearted. One may be permitted to point out how fortuitous are the chains of history. The whole course of Roosevelt's life, like almost anybody's, is based on a sequence of unpredictable "ifs." If Wilson had not been so high-minded Daniels might not have been Secretary of the Navy. If Daniels had not been Secretary of the Navy, Roosevelt might have been buried in some less conspicuous post. If Roosevelt had not decided to come to Baltimore, he might never have met Daniels in such favorable circumstances. If he had not beaten Sheehan and been a successful State Senator, he might not have visited Baltimore. And so on with "ifs" beyond computation.

Of course Roosevelt was a coming man; people so manifestly gifted do not crop up every day of the week, and several politicians had their eyes on him. For instance William G. McAdoo offered him two different jobs—Assistant Secretary of the Treasury and Collector of the Port of New York—before Daniels got him. But Roosevelt was crazy for the Navy. It is revealing that at this time, when he was only a little over thirty, he had already collected no fewer than 9,878 books and pamphlets on naval matters. Of these, he once told an interviewer, he had actually read all but one.

So FDR became Assistant Secretary, the youngest man to hold this post in the Navy's history. In 1910, Roosevelt was utterly unknown outside family and friends. In 1913, he held a nationally important job in Washington, with World War I soon to come. It was a quick rise for three years. He was sworn in on March 17, 1913, a date which happened to be his eighth wedding anniversary; that same evening he wrote his mother as follows:

DEAREST MAMA

I am baptized, confirmed, sworn in, vaccinated—and somewhat at sea! For over an hour I have been signing papers which had to be accepted on faith—but I hope luck will keep me out of jail.

All well, but I will have to work like a new turbine to master this job—but it will be done even if it takes all summer.

Your affec. son
Franklin D. Roosevelt

Mrs. Roosevelt's reply shows something of her character:

MY DEAREST FRANKLIN—You can't imagine the happiness you gave me by writing to me yesterday. I just *knew* it was a *very* big job. . . . Try not to write your signature too small, as it gets a cramped look and is not distinct. So many public men have such awful signatures, and so unreadable. . . .

The Roosevelts and their young children moved into Aunty Bye's house, and Eleanor records how Sara, "as usual," helped her to get settled. Later the family rented a more commodious house nearby, at 2131 R Street, and this was their home for some years.

Roosevelt remained Assistant Secretary until 1920, and nobody could say he did not do a good job. This was his first important period of proof, and he indubitably proved himself. He set out at once to establish good relations with the admirals (whereas Mr. Daniels "never believed anything that any admiral ever told him"), and turned his eye, at the other extreme, to such details as that many enlisted seamen did not know how to swim, which state of affairs he sought to remedy. He was quite frankly a Big Navy man, and he did his utmost before 1914 to put the fleet in a full state of preparedness. In particular he renovated the shore establishments; this was his major contribution before the war. Also he showed considerable prescience about the future value of air power. Emotionally, he took sides at once when war came; he made no secret of his passionate hope that the allies would win. He wrote Mrs. Roosevelt, "I feel hurt that the Emperor William has left the U.S. out—he has declared war against everybody else," and "I just *know* I shall do some awful unneutral thing before I get through!" As the war progressed his responsibilities grew enormously; he got used to working —for the first time in his life—a long and grueling day, and his resilience increased, too, as the burdens became stiffer. After 1917 most of his work was in the unheroic field of procurement, contracts, labor relations, and the like, which gave him good experience. But also he was responsible in part for two developments in the strictly military field; he worked out and set up a scheme for fast submarine chasers that helped defeat the U-boats, and he was part author of the bitterly disputed plan to wall off a 240-mile stretch of the North Sea with a new type of mine barrage, to keep the German fleet bottled in its home waters.

One admiral, quoted by Ernest Lindley, has recorded that he had never in his life been watched so closely as by Roosevelt in his first three months of office. "Then he decided that I was all right, and we got along famously for six years."

Sara Roosevelt tells us that FDR was so successful in getting material for the Navy that Wilson himself had to chide him on one occasion, "Mr. Secretary, it seems that you have cornered the market on supplies. I'm sorry, but you will have to divide up with the Army."

FDR himself described in a speech many years later how a delegation came to him from the Brooklyn Navy Yard when he had been in office just a week. The spokesman said, "You know, as Assistant Secretary, you have statutory charge of all labor matters." FDR replied, "That is fine; I did not know it." The spokesman went on to complain that a board of naval officers had usurped the function of determining the wage scale in the great navy yards, and that its decisions had been arbitrary and unjust to labor. Within three days Roosevelt got Daniels to sign an order specifically putting wages under his own jurisdiction; he set up what he called a "perfectly practical example of collective bargaining"; as a result seven and a half years passed without a single labor dispute in any American naval yard.

Roosevelt's yardstick was common sense and practicability, not the narrow letter of the law. Here too is a glint of the future. To get something important done, FDR would cut through all manner of red tape and violate almost any precedent or regulation. Several times he pushed urgent contracts through before Congress had passed the requisite appropriations; he himself took the responsibility, and persuaded suppliers to undertake large projects involving hundreds of millions of dollars purely on his own word. He said frankly (in the 1920 campaign) that he broke enough laws and regulations during his Secretaryship to "go to jail for 999 years," and was proud of it, because everything he did was for one purpose only, to help save American lives and win the war.

FDR's relations with Daniels have been the cause of much subsequent comment. That he was loyal to Mr. Daniels is beyond question, and old Josephus loved him till the end of his life; nevertheless he irritated and vexed FDR a good deal and there were times when the Assistant Secretary thought that his chief was an old fuddy-duddy. This was particularly true at the very beginning of the war. FDR wrote Mrs. Roosevelt in August, 1914, "I am running the real work, though Josephus is here! He is bewildered by it all, very sweet but very sad!" Again, "Mr. D. totally fails to grasp the situation and I am to see the President . . . to go over our own situation." What amazed Roosevelt was that Daniels, like Bryan, was so full of "idealistic nonsense" as to be unable to appreciate the fact that the greatest war in history (as of that date) had broken out, and that, sooner or later, the United States was bound to be drawn into it. Roosevelt's own grasp of these realities was acute, as his letters show. One reason why FDR was a success in the job was, of course, that the service officers knew that he was on their side. Sometimes senior officers would wait till Daniels was out of town, and then come to Roosevelt for a signature or a decision. This, naturally enough, made Daniels angry. But no split ever occurred. In fact Daniels and Roosevelt complemented one another nicely; their very differences made them a good team. Also Daniels taught Roosevelt a lot about politics. He was a genius at handling recalcitrant senators and congressmen, and wheedling appropriations through committees. The Navy was helpless without money, and Daniels knew far better than young FDR how to get it.

His seven years as Assistant Secretary gave Roosevelt experience that was of profound value all his life in several fields: (a) labor relations, (b) the detailed day-to-day management of a giant Government department during warfare, (c) naval strategy in general, (d) problems of logistics and supply, (e) the art of handling men. Also he got to know personally a multitude of officers and civilians who were to serve him as Commander in Chief in World War II.

Politics and Such: First Defeat

All this time Roosevelt was an active politician. He stumped New York for Wilson, and handled much of the President's patronage there, though patronage is often a brutal and tawdry business. The reason for this was that when Wilson reached the White House, anti-Tammany Democrats in New York found themselves in a peculiar position; Wilson was President, but they themselves were out in the cold, because the Democratic senator was O'Gorman, with whom Wilson was not friendly. So jobs and appointments had to be slipped past O'Gorman, who would have tried to block any Wilson man. Roosevelt did much of this work. When a deserving upstate Democrat needed support on a local issue, it was young FDR whom he came to see, not O'Gorman. Roosevelt in turn operated through an assistant postmaster general who later became one of his own cabinet members, Daniel C. Roper.

Not one person in ten thousand knows it, but FDR himself ran for the New York senatorship in the Democratic primaries in 1914, and was badly beaten. This is one of the least-known episodes in his entire career. It was also the first, last, and only time he ever lost a direct election. (True, his ticket was defeated when he ran for Vice-President in 1920, but this was a defeat in a different category.) He took this beating for several reasons. For one thing his job in Washington held him too tightly to permit effective campaigning in New York, and many voters thought he was too young, thirty-two, to be a Federal senator. He had not looked over the scene carefully enough; this was one occasion when his tendency to snap judgment got him into trouble. Also the vested interests in the party opposed him with all the vigor at their command; Tammany and the Sheehanites wanted their revenge. Roosevelt's opponent was the distinguished diplomat James W. Gerard, then American ambassador to Germany. Gerard did not even return to the United States for the campaign.[12] He beat FDR by 133,000 votes to 68,000. Roosevelt at once cabled him an offer of help in the election to follow, provided Gerard declared "unalterable opposition to Murphy's leadership and all he stands for." The defeat does not appear to have damaged FDR's moraie or reputation to any great extent. He told his friends, "Never mind; we have paved the way."

Four years later Tammany had become conscious enough of FDR's power to beg him to run for Governor; he refused.

What did people think of FDR in these early days? He had become a national figure; even so, newspapers would occasionally fail to identify him, or even give him the wrong first name; he came out "Carl" Roosevelt in one story in 1915. By this time, however, several friends had joined Mr. Lynch of Poughkeepsie to think that he would be President some day. One was certainly Louis Howe. And Mr. Daniels describes a scene when he and Roosevelt were photographed looking down on the Executive Mansion from their offices across the street. FDR smiled, and Daniels asked him why:

"Franklin, why are you grinning from ear to ear, looking as pleased as if the world were yours, while I, satisfied and happy, have no such smile on my face?"

He said he did not know of any particular reason, only that he was trying to look his best.

"I will tell you," I answered. "We are both looking down on the White House and you are saying to yourself, being a New Yorker, 'Some day I will be living in that house'—while I, being from the South, know I must be satisfied with no such ambition."[13]

---

[12] Old Mr. Gerard, the only man alive ever to beat Roosevelt in a straight election, was in the news as recently as November, 1949, when he took a strong prolabor stand in the steel strike then going on.

[13] Josephus Daniels, *The Wilson Era* (Chapel Hill, N. C., University of North Carolina Press, 1944), p. 129.

FDR's personality had pretty well developed into the mold that became famous by this time; his letters boil and bubble with just the kind of remark he used so often later. There is a quality of insouciance, even of naïveté, and he is perpetually in a state of excitement about something or other. When Wilson was reelected in 1916 he telegraphed Eleanor, "Dearest Babs, the Most Extraordinary Day of My Life!" In one letter occurs the remark, "I hope to God I don't grow reactionary with advancing years." He was an enthusiastic member of the Common Council Club, composed of liberals devoted to the Wilson cause; one of its members and a devoted friend, Franklin K. Lane, the Secretary of the Interior, said, "Young Roosevelt knows nothing about finance, but he doesn't know that he doesn't know." His appearance too solidified into something close to the Roosevelt we knew later, though he was still very lean. Caricatures of the time disclose almost all his later mannerisms, and people began to notice what a fine voice he had. For a time, briefly, he wore a mustache. Observant people noted that his eyes were not precisely the same size, and he developed the beginnings of a characteristic that runs in the family, heavy blue shadows under the eyes. His hands—this too was a family trait—had a slight tremor.

One interviewer of the day, quoted by Lindley, says that the key word to describe him as Assistant Secretary was "he-man," yet photographs taken about 1915 or 1916 show a certain delicacy, a frailness. Nevertheless his physical magnetism—as well as charm—were strongly marked, and he was the darling of the Washington *salons*. The late Margot Oxford, who met him at about this time, told a friend years later that he was the most "desirable" man she had ever seen. He and his friend William Phillips (later to become his first Undersecretary of State), who was also a highly attractive person, went to San Francisco together on one occasion; they entered the house of a lady of society, who reported, "They were the two most magnificent young men I ever saw. I had no idea that the Democratic party ever recruited that type of person!"

As the war reached its climax Roosevelt wanted to enlist, and he has been criticized for not having done so. He was only thirty-five in 1917. But Daniels emphatically clears him of any intent to avoid military service; he tells us, in fact, that FDR was so determined to resign and join the armed forces that he, Daniels, had to go to Wilson about it; Wilson's orders were, "Tell the young man his only and best war service is to stay where he is." Wilson was Commander in Chief, and FDR could do no more. He did manage to get to Europe and visit the front in 1918, as leader of a mission; he was the first American civilian of Cabinet rank to see the war firsthand, and a vivid record of his impressions—from dinner parties in London and talks with Clemenceau to what the trenches looked like—may be found in his letters. After the armistice he went abroad again on official business, winding up naval contracts, and took Mrs. Roosevelt with him. They returned on the *George Washington* with Wilson, who had gone to Paris for the peace conference. Wilson presented him with the desk on which he wrote the Covenant of the League of Nations; Roosevelt treasured this highly, and it may be seen in Hyde Park today.

In 1920 Roosevelt resigned from the Navy job, and was nominated as Democratic candidate for Vice-President. Let us see why.

The 1920 Run, and After

The Democratic convention met in San Francisco in circumstances of the most agitated gloom. Wilson had had a stroke, and was scarcely alive; the Senate had rejected the peace treaty; the full wash of reaction against eight years of a Democratic Administration had set in; the delegates were frustrated and divided among themselves, especially on whether or not to continue Wilson's fight for the League. James M. Cox of Ohio became the candidate largely because such wary mastodons as McAdoo, Wilson's Secretary of the Treasury, refused to run. Al Smith was put in nomination (and Franklin D. Roosevelt, no less, was one of his seconders), but had no chance; he was just concluding his first term as Governor of New York. Cox was a good candidate because the party bosses thought that the League of Nations would be a losing issue, and Cox had never been closely associated with the Wilson policies. Also he was a wet. Young Roosevelt got the nomination for Vice-President (and one of his seconders was Alfred E. Smith, no less) for precisely the opposite reason. The bosses thought that they should prudently play both sides against the middle and that, having chosen Cox to lead the ticket, it would be sensible to have as second man somebody who *was* a Wilsonian, and who might bring to the campaign all those supporters of the League whom the Cox candidature would conceivably repel. Cox himself wanted FDR badly, though the two men had never met. Roosevelt was popular, a New Yorker, and had a splendid name.

He was nominated by acclamation, and his choice was a complete

surprise to a lot of people. The New York *Herald* printed on the day
the convention opened a list of thirty-nine possible candidates; FDR
was not even listed.

One sensation of the convention was a scuffle in which Roosevelt
took a leading part. When a large painting of Wilson was unveiled on
the stage the entire assemblage rose to cheer except the New York
delegation. FDR grabbed the New York standard from the Tammany
chieftain who was hugging it, wrested it away, and stormed down the
aisles bearing it aloft.

Curiously little evidence is to be found either in his letters or elsewhere as to Roosevelt's attitude to his nomination. Probably he was
too busy to have much thought about it one way or the other. One
point not without interest is that he asked Cox, if they were elected,
to let him sit in on Cabinet meetings as Vice-President.

Cox and Roosevelt made a vigorous campaign; FDR himself made
no fewer than 800 speeches. One story has been told by several commentators on FDR. Cox and Roosevelt made a formal call on the
stricken Wilson, who sat muffled in an invalid's chair, and Cox, as a
gesture of respect, said, "Mr. Wilson, I have always admired you for
your fight for the League of Nations." The President summoned a last
spark of vitality, and whispered almost inaudibly, "Cox, the fight can
still be won." Then, as this legend goes, Cox turned to FDR and exclaimed impulsively, "Roosevelt, we will make the fight on the
League after all!" Actually this story, though it contains the substance
of the truth, is not quite correct. Cox affirms in his book *Journey
Through My Years* that, even though the Democratic high command
opposed him, he had decided weeks before the meeting with Wilson
to make the League the major issue of the fight.

Cox and Roosevelt were, as everybody knows, beaten decisively by
Warren Gamaliel Harding and Calvin Coolidge. Apparently Roosevelt
thought right to the end that his party had a good chance of winning.
No one ever accused him of underconfidence. This, incidentally, was
the first presidential election in which women voted, and Mrs. Roosevelt accompanied FDR through most of the campaign. FDR's speeches
show a steady broadening of interests; for the first time he had to touch
on basic national issues; his speech of acceptance, delivered at Hyde
Park on August 9, 1920, was the first important speech he ever delivered from his own front porch, and was a model of its kind. It is, in
fact, one of the best speeches he ever made. He said that the people

must oppose "mere coma" in the national life. The student of history may be impressed that among things he demanded were complete overhaul and reorganization of the Federal Government machinery, the end of all pork-barrel legislation, and devotion to the idea that "the effectiveness of the national government should . . . at least approximate that of a well-conducted private business." And note these words:

Some people have been saying of late: "We are tired of progress, we want to go back to where we were before; to go about our own business; to restore 'normal' conditions." They are wrong. This is not the wish of America. We can never go back. The good old days are gone past forever.

Another point important to FDR's future career was that the campaign gave him opportunity to build up what became a permanent secretariat. Missy LeHand, Miss Tully, Stephen Early, and Marvin McIntyre all entered his service at about this time, and Henry Morgenthau, Jr., became a friend. Those closest were members of the "Cuff-Links Club," and wore gold cuff links FDR gave them; this inner circle stayed cohesive for more than twenty years.

After his defeat Roosevelt took a well-earned rest. His vitality was, for the moment, low. He wasn't discouraged, but he felt the need of change. He took a hunting trip with Hall Roosevelt to Louisiana, and wrote letters to Eleanor ending with lines like "Kiss the chicks and love to Mama and oceans for yourself." (All the Roosevelt children were born by this time.) Returning to Washington, he cleaned up some last remaining Navy Department work, and then set himself up in business in New York.

Years before, he had left his first law firm and helped organize a new one, Marvin, Hooker, and Roosevelt, which in turn became Emmet, Marvin, and Roosevelt. Also his friend Van Lear Black made him vice-president and New York representative of the Fidelity and Deposit Company of Maryland at $25,000 a year, which was by far the largest salary he had ever earned up to this time. So he had two jobs, both as a lawyer and insurance man.

Roosevelt, so far as we can judge, was intensely happy during the early months of 1921. But this is the period of his life we know least about; there are some gaps still to be filled. He began to enjoy life and its delights as a private citizen; he worked fairly hard, and essayed various adventures in making money; he browsed in books and tinkered with his collections; he developed and indulged new friendships, played golf, flirted; in short he set about the business of thorough relaxation after seven uninterrupted years of demanding public service. But he was not forgotten politically, nor did he ever forget politics. Most of his friends thought that this was the merest interlude before he resumed a splendid, dazzling career. The most radiant of lives seemed to stretch out before him.

In August, 1921, FDR went up to join the family in Campobello on Van Lear Black's yacht, the *Sabalo*. Shortly thereafter he was struck down by a disaster of unprecedented magnitude.

Chapter 13

DISASTER

A Man is a God in ruins
—RALPH WALDO EMERSON

Roosevelt had a fairly wide though not unusual experience of illness before paralysis struck him. He was capable of feats of exertion over short periods that amazed his friends—for instance he could tire out a horse on rough mountain trails—but in a curious way his vitality was mercurial; he could vault over a row of chairs at the San Francisco convention and play golf within two strokes of a course record, but in those days he was not what would be called a "strong" man. He was graceful rather than muscular; taut, not solid. His body was a sensitive mechanism, and photographs of the time give him a look almost fragile. He radiated energy, as a consumptive may do, but he sometimes burned himself out in doing so; time and again his resistance weakened, and he fell prey to minor illness.

Measles, as I have already mentioned, kept him from enlisting in the Spanish-American War; also at Groton he had a severe attack of scarlet fever. He had recurrent lumbago during his honeymoon, and several attacks of hives. In 1912 he had a long bout of typhoid fever; it kept him in bed during his second run for State Senator, and Louis Howe had to make his speeches for him. A stomach complaint afflicted him in 1913, and two years later came an operation for acute appendicitis. Lumbago troubled him again in 1915, and he began to have stubborn head colds and sinus attacks. He had a serious throat infection in 1916; he spent several weeks in Atlantic City recuperating, and then had some dental trouble. The throat infection recurred the next year, and he spent a week in the hospital. Then, returning from Europe in 1918, he had double pneumonia and was so ill that he had to be carried from the ship on a stretcher. Following this came a severe attack of flu.

One should not, of course, exaggerate the importance of these illnesses; perhaps all they indicate was that he was working too hard.

Nothing at all was wrong in any deep organic sense, though his letters mention that he had trouble keeping his weight up; he weighed 170 at about this time, which is not a great deal for a man six feet two. It is a striking irony that just before poliomyelitis struck him, he had a brief period of exceptionally brilliant and vibrant health, even though he had not had a real holiday for years. Another irony is that he had an almost morbid fear that infantile paralysis might strike some member of his family.

Several members of the Roosevelt circle had illnesses which, in the light of his own experience, have considerable interest, though there is no connection. We have already noted that Eleanor wore a brace as a child, and his mother had a form of osteoarthritis so severe that for long periods she could only walk on crutches. Warren Delano II, FDR's grandfather, became paralyzed in old age and spent some years in a wheel chair. Mrs. Cowles (Aunty Bye) had curvature of the spine so badly that she was almost a hunchback, and Elliott Roosevelt, the President's son, wore leg braces as a child.

The Gray Death

Poliomyelitis, one of the most mysterious of the scourges that torment mankind, is a disease peculiar to the brain and spinal cord; it is caused by a virus, or several viruses, of unknown nature, and it induces paralysis by attacking the nerves which control muscular action. Nobody knows what leads it to single out a particular human being, how it is spread, why it chooses children as especial victims, or why its highest incidence is in summer. Almost everything about this disease is arcane. In some persons its incubation period is a few days; in others, three weeks or even longer. Polio is often difficult to detect in its early stages, since the major symptoms are familiar to so many less serious diseases—headache, sore throat, and fever. Thousands of men and women in the United States may have had mild cases without ever knowing it.

If the attack is severe the patient may have nausea, stiff neck and other muscular symptoms, a sharp fever, and acute localized pain. The culminating period varies markedly, depending on the patient; so does the degree of residual paralysis. The disease attacks with great discrimination, and hits two points in the body only: (a) the bulbar portion of the brain; (b) the anterior horn (motor) cells of the spinal cord. Most fatal cases are those that afflict the brain, since paralysis of the respiratory muscles follows. But even patients who recover from this type of polio have perfectly normal brains; the cortex and thought processes are never involved at all. Whether the results of a polio attack will be drastic or not depends on the amount of nerve involved; half of one leg may be paralyzed, or one hand below the wrist. No physician can give much of a forecast in this respect until the acute period is over, and even then estimates may be way off the mark.

Much less was known of polio when Roosevelt got it than now; particularly doctors were mystified when it hit adults. Roosevelt's attack came in 1921, when he was thirty-nine. Sister Kenny was unknown, and her celebrated treatment, which has had enormous beneficial effect in countless thousands of cases, was of the future. Had her methods been available at the time, his legs might have been saved.

Catastrophe Strikes

On August 10, 1921, Roosevelt took his wife and their sons for a sail on a small craft which he was teaching the boys how to handle. Returning to Campobello he saw a forest fire on the nearby shore; the whole family landed for the strenuous fun of fighting it. To cool off, he decided to take a swim in a nearby lake, Glen Severn, though he had been complaining for several days of feeling tired; then he and the children jog-trotted the mile and a half home. Later FDR wanted another swim, and he jumped into the ocean from the beach. The Bay of Fundy is ice-cold even at this time of year. Back in the house again, he found that a batch of mail had arrived; he sat down in his wet bathing suit and went through it for half an hour. Thereupon he had a sudden chill, and Mrs. Roosevelt persuaded him to go to bed. (Interestingly enough he had had a chill the day before, as a result of slipping and falling overboard.)

Thus the attack began—though nobody can know when, where, or under what circumstances the polio virus first entered his system. The first intimation to FDR himself that something might be wrong with his legs was a tenderness in the forepart of the thighs.

The next day, August 11, he had a high temperature and acute pain in the left leg. Mrs. Roosevelt acted promptly; she sent the children away to a nearby camp, and summoned the nearest physician, Dr. E. H. Bennett of Lubec, Maine. Bennett got there by 10 A.M. He was puzzled. FDR could walk, but had severe pains throughout his back and legs. On August 12 difficulty in walking supervened, and Mrs.

Roosevelt and Bennett thought they ought to consult another doctor. It happened that a famous Philadelphia diagnostician, Dr. W. W. Keen, was summering in the neighborhood; he examined Roosevelt on the 13th and again the next day and decided "that a clot of blood from a sudden congestion has settled in the lower spinal cord temporarily removing the power to move though not to feel." Nobody thought then in terms of infantile paralysis. But Keen knew that this was a serious matter; he thought that recovery might "take some months." Roosevelt got worse in the next few days, not better. Keen changed his mind, discarded the clot theory, and decided that FDR must have "a lesion" in the spinal cord. Also he sent Mrs. Roosevelt a bill for $600. By this time FDR's bladder and the rectal sphincter were paralyzed. Mrs. Roosevelt insisted that a specialist in poliomyelitis from Boston, Dr. Robert W. Lovett, be called in. Lovett saw FDR on August 25, made a correct diagnosis, and stopped the massages which Keen had ordered. Roosevelt was in the fiercest kind of pain during all of this, and was completely helpless. He had to be catheterized until September 8, and the paralysis spread to affect—temporarily—his arms and back as well as legs.

Sara Roosevelt was away in Europe, about to return home. The whole brunt fell on Eleanor. She did all the nursing. Her letters to the family[1] during this period are models of clarity, courage, and cool restraint. She wrote Rosy, FDR's half brother, on August 14th: "We have had a very anxious few days as on Wednesday evening Franklin was taken ill. . . . I have wired New York for a masseuse and . . . in the meantime Louis [Howe] and I are rubbing him as well as we can. . . . I have only told Franklin he [the doctor] said he could surely go down [to New York] the 15th of September . . . but it may have to be done on a wheel chair. . . . Do you think you can meet Mama when she lands? She has asked us to cable just before she sails and I have decided to say nothing. No letter can reach her now and it would simply mean worry all the way home." A few days later, again to Rosy: "I have asked Dr. Keen to try to get Dr. Lovett here . . . to determine if it is I.P. or not. Dr. Keen thinks *not* but the treatment at this stage differs in one particular and no matter what it costs I feel and I am sure Mama would feel we must leave no stone unturned to accomplish the best results." Then to Sara: "Dearest Mama, Franklin has been quite ill and so can't go down to meet you on Tuesday to his great

[1] *Letters,* Vol. II, p. 524 *et seq.*

regret, but Uncle Fred and Aunt Kassie both write they will be there so it will not be a lonely homecoming. We are so happy to have you home again dear, you don't know what it means to feel you are near again." This is as brave an upper lip as has ever been set against catastrophe. FDR with polio! It was unbelievable! Yet it had to be believed, faced, and fought through to a finish.

Meanwhile Louis Howe, a house guest, insisted that there should be as little publicity as possible and that, for the time being at least, the newspapers should not know that FDR was paralyzed. Dr. Lovett gave permission for the trip to New York in mid-September, with the prognosis that there was "a good possibility of considerable improvement." Frederic Delano, FDR's uncle, got a private railway car, and Howe worked out a stratagem whereby Roosevelt was slipped on the train with only a few people aware of what was going on. But getting him off the island to a launch, down a steep rough slope to the beach, then transferring the stretcher up the dock on the mainland and onto a baggage cart, then into the railway car through a window, was one of the grimmest jobs Howe ever had to tackle. Mrs. Roosevelt and all the children came along. The doctors had assured her that they could not catch the illness at this date.

Young Franklin, who was about eight at the time, was in an ecstasy of terror and excitement when the stretcher finally got through the train window. Previously the children knew that their father must be sick, very sick, because the shades in his bedroom window were always drawn. But of course they did not know what he had. "Once we were told not to go to church, but to wait around the house, so we knew how serious it must be," young Franklin has told me. "I have a vague memory that one of my brothers said that it must be a heart attack. But then I saw Father on the stretcher, being carried down to the beach head first. His head was lower than his feet, but he managed to wave to me, and his whole face burst into a tremendous sunny smile. So I decided he couldn't be so sick after all."

In New York Roosevelt was taken to the Presbyterian Hospital on Park Avenue, and one of Lovett's associates, Dr. George Draper, a brilliant young specialist who had known FDR well at school, became his doctor and took charge of the case. Through all the agony that followed, Draper and Mrs. Roosevelt were the closest allies; Draper, more than anybody except Eleanor and Howe, should have the credit for saving Roosevelt. Again we see the long and intricate chain of cause and effect that controls the seeming fortuitousness of human lives. Had not Draper, a friend, happened to be on hand, with exactly the right combination of technical skill and personal force, it is extremely doubtful if FDR would ever have recovered to the extent he did.

I have had access to the medical records of the Roosevelt case, including the hospital chart, none of which have ever been published before. His temperature was spotty, varying from slightly subnormal to 102.1; the pulse was between 60 and 100. The diagnosis was of acute anterior poliomyelitis. On September 23 the record shows that "the patient still shows definite signs of general C.N.S. [Central Nervous System] prostration. This is very marked. Otherwise the situation is progressing favorably." An examination on October 2 showed that the fear of bladder or prostate infection had passed; the prostate was "not enlarged, practically symmetrical, with marked median furrow and prominent lateral lobes," and the patient was voiding "good amounts of urine without difficulty and without urgency." Medicaments included urotropin, pituitary extract, and 25 per cent adrenal residue. Much of this record is too technical for useful inclusion here. On the date of discharge, October 28, 1921, the bleak record says, "Not improving."

Howe decided that the newspapers must be told something, and on September 16, the New York *Times* carried a front-page story with the following headline:

F. D. ROOSEVELT ILL
OF POLIOMYELITIS
Brought on Special Car from Campobello,
Bay of Fundy, to Hospital Here
RECOVERING, DOCTOR SAYS
Patient Stricken by Infantile Paralysis
A Month Ago, and Use of Legs Affected

The first paragraph says that Roosevelt had lost the use of both legs below the knee "for more than a month." But one doctor is quoted as saying that "he definitely will not be crippled. No one need have any fear of permanent injury from this attack."

Dr. Lovett wrote Dr. Draper this hitherto unpublished letter:

With regard to Mr. R. I was called to see him in Campobello. There was some uncertainty about the diagnosis, but I thought it perfectly clear so far as the physical findings were concerned and I never feel that the history is of much value anyway.

He had I thought some facial involvement, apparently no respiratory, but a weakness in the arms, not very severe and not grouped at all. There was some atrophy of the left thenar eminence. . . . There was a scattered weakness in the legs, most marked in the hips when I saw him, very few muscles were absent, and in those that were recovering there was a pretty fair degree of power at the end of two weeks. No deformities were present, and the general aspect of the thing was a mild, rather scattered attack without excessive tenderness, coming on promptly and not in a sneaking way, with spontaneous improvement beginning almost at once and progressing.

It seems to me that it was a mild case within the range of possible complete recovery. I told them very frankly that no one could tell where they stood, that the case was evidently not of the severest type, that complete recovery or partial recovery to any point was possible, that disability was not to be feared, and that the only out about it was the long continued character of the treatment. It is dangerous to speak from impressions at the end of the second week, but my feeling about him was that he was probably going to be a case where the conservation of what muscular power he has may be very important, and it looked to me as if some of the important muscles might be on the edge where they could be influenced either way— toward recovery, or turn into completely paralyzed muscles. I was as noncommittal as I could be about who should conduct the treatment, and I asked them to put themselves in your hands and follow your advice.

But things were not to go as well as Lovett hoped. In fact Draper thought presently that FDR might never be able to sit up again, much less stand or walk. On September 24 he wrote Lovett the following letter, which has not been published before:

Just a line to report to you about Franklin R. I am much concerned at the very slow recovery both as regards the disappearance of *pain*, which is very generally present, and as to the recovery of even slight power to twitch the muscles. There is marked falling away of the muscle masses on either side of the spine in the lower lumbar region, likewise the buttocks. There is marked weakness of the right triceps; and an unusual amount of gross muscular twitching in the muscles of both forearms. He coordinates on the fine motions of his hands very well now so that he can sign his name and write a little better than before.

The lower extremities present a most depressing picture. There is a little motion in the long extensors of the toes of each foot, a little in the perinei of the right side, a little ability to twitch the bellies of the gastrocnemii, but not really extend the feet. There is little similar power in the left vastus, and on both sides similar voluntary twitches of the ham-string masses can be accomplished.

He is very cheerful and hopeful, and has made up his mind that he is going to go out of the hospital in the course of two or three weeks on crutches. What I fear more than anything else is that we shall find a much more extensive involvement of the great back muscles than we have suspected and *that when we attempt to sit him up he will be faced with the frightfully depressing knowledge that he cannot hold himself erect.*[2] It has occurred to me that it might be possible for you to devise some kind of support for him which we can put on while he is in bed, just preparatory to getting him up in a chair for the first time, so that he will not realize too suddenly that his back will not hold him.

I feel so strongly . . . that the psychological factor in his management is paramount. *He has such courage, such ambition, and yet at the same time such an extraordinarily sensitive emotional mechanism that it will take all the skill which we can muster to lead him successfully to a recognition of what he really faces without crushing him.*

My thought was that as soon as the tenderness has left completely so that you could move him about as you please . . . you would come to New York to see him. At present I feel that we should not get the greatest value from your presence because of the impossibility of manipulating him.

I have studiously refrained from examining his upper extremities because he believes them to be untouched by the disease. It is fortunate that one does not have much opportunity in the recumbent position in bed to call upon the deltoids or the triceps—the biceps are fortunately pretty good so that he is able to pull himself up by the strap over his head and so help himself to turn in bed. This of course gives him a great sense of satisfaction.

Lovett replied that he would of course come to New York at any time, and recommended immersion in strong saline baths and the "use of electric light." He predicted that the involvement in the arms would clear up, which indeed it eventually did.

In November Draper wrote to Dr. Bennett:

First of all, let me ask your forgiveness for having delayed so long in sending you any word about Franklin Roosevelt. He has done exceedingly well ever since his arrival, although his progress has been slow. There is still a little tenderness in the muscles and, of course, practically no return to power in any of the affected ones, but his general condition is very much better and he has come out of that state of nervous collapse in which all these cases find themselves for some little time after the acute attack. He is now at home

---

[2] Italics mine, here and below.

and able to get about in a wheel chair into which he is partially lifted and partially swings himself by means of a strap and ring hung from the ceiling. He is cheerful and hopeful and his general morale is very high.

As soon as we can, we propose to get him on crutches with braces to make his legs rigid.

I am ordering sent to you one of the little books on poliomyelitis that I spoke to you about and likewise enclosing the two dollars which you so kindly provided for tipping the ambulance men.

During all this period Roosevelt of course suffered the most harrowing agonies, mental as well as physical. When did it first become unequivocally clear to him that there was no prospect that he would ever walk again? Was he told? Or did he guess it for himself? Did he ever know with full consciousness that his back and arms were in jeopardy too—that he might never be able to sit up again, never even regain the full use of his hands? Who broke it to him that leg braces would be necessary? Of course nature provides a cushion for shocks so grievous as these; the very fact of his complete nervous depression probably helped him, and mercifully he was under mild opiates a good part of the time.

There were excruciating ups and downs, as in all serious illnesses. On November 19–20 he had a mysterious relapse; his temperature went up to 101, and his eyes began to hurt. Momentarily it was even feared that, as if fate had not mutilated him enough, his eyesight might become affected. Later the tendons of the right knee tightened, bending the leg like a jackknife, and both legs had to be put in plaster casts as a remedial measure. The pain of this was the worst in the whole experience. Day by day, for several weeks, a wedge was tapped into each cast, a little deeper each time, to force the legs to become unlocked. But two items of good news compensated for this torture. First, the arms began to recover. Second, the "great muscles of the back" that Draper was so worried about resumed their normal function. He could sit up!

His mother wanted him to come to Hyde Park immediately after his discharge from the hospital, but he and Eleanor insisted on going to the 65th Street house in town. In his later convalescence, of course, he did spend much time at Hyde Park. Mrs. Roosevelt has recorded the "somewhat acrimonious" disputes that attended the decision to stay in New York City. This is to understate. What really happened during these agonizing months was a battle to the finish between these two remarkable women for Franklin's soul. Harsh words were seldom spoken; the intensity burned beneath the surface; the struggle was fierce just the same. Sara wanted FDR to submit gracefully to the disaster, and live out the rest of his years in vegetative retirement as an invalided country squire; Eleanor wanted him to continue active participation in every realm of life so far as this would not impede his recovery. She would not give an inch to the illness. She thought in fact that active re-entry into politics would assist him to get well. She was right, and in any case she won.

Anybody who has ever known and loved a person helplessly ill will understand the peculiarly harrowing nature of what Mrs. Roosevelt went through—the jagged alternations between hope and despair; the necessity of giving blind trust to a physician even when the physician, cruelly pressed, could scarcely trust himself; the fearsome responsibility involved; above all the unpredictable oscillations of mood in the patient himself, which had to be ministered to with the utmost firmness, subtlety, and tenderness. Only once, so far as is known, did Mrs. Roosevelt break down. The house was crowded to bursting, and she slept in a cot in one of the boys' rooms. FDR seemed no better, the worried children were on edge, and one day, while reading to the two youngest boys, she started to sob, and could not stop. Eventually, she records, she pulled herself together by going into an empty room in Sara's house next door; it was the only time in her whole life she ever went to pieces. Of course she herself was enlarged and steeled by the very intensity of an experience so grievous, no less than was her husband. They both came through the ravaging horrors of the ordeal with their characters—far from being diminished—magnificently enhanced.

The Beginnings of Recovery

By the spring of 1922 FDR was substantially better, though he could not walk, and by early autumn, a year after the illness first struck, he was able to do some work, and to hobble around on crutches. That he was able to make such progress was a triumph of pure grit, the conquest of flesh by will and spirit.

Now we must go into quite explicit and painful detail, because no appreciation at all of Roosevelt's later life is possible without concrete realization of what he went through. Dr. Draper taught him to "walk." Actually, though he himself might have disputed this, he never truly walked again. From the moment the illness struck him, he was "a goner below the waist," as one of the doctors put it. The major leg muscles never came back. Nor could he even *stand* (unless supported by someone's arm) without a prop, and even with braces he was like a man on stilts, because, being unable to flex with his toes, he had no balance. The braces were heavy, cumbersome, and a perpetual nuisance to manipulate. He could not put them on or take them off himself, and he "hated and mistrusted them." Without braces his helplessness was almost complete. Until the end of his life, he could not rise from a chair or sit down, even with the braces on, without help or at the cost of the most strenuously fatiguing effort. To get up he would have to lift out one leg with a hand, snap the brace tight, do the same with the other leg, then, with his legs absolutely stiff, as stiff as the legs of a pair of dividers, push himself up from the arms of the chair by the sheer power of his arms, wriggle, hold himself completely rigid from shoulder to ankle, tilt forward and upward slowly, very slowly, and then hope not to tip too far and fall.

Louis A. Depew, who became Mrs. Sara Roosevelt's chauffeur in 1918 and who still works at Hyde Park, has recorded some details of the terrible months of trial and error during convalescence. It was Depew who brought FDR back to Hyde Park for the first time after the illness in April or May of 1922. A set of bars had been erected in the garden, about ten feet long and fixed in a round base; the lower bars were hip-high, the others higher. On these Roosevelt tried to walk, riding on his hands. Then a trapezelike contraption was arranged above his bed, whereby the legs could be pulled up and down for exercise, as well as an exercise board, a traction frame, and a mechanism by which FDR could try to hoist himself alone out of the bed and into a wheel chair close by. (But the chair itself had to be held.) Sara got from Europe an electric tricycle which she thought might be useful, but it did not work and he tried it only once. Also when summer came he tried to swim, both at Vincent Astor's and in a small pool near his own house. He would crawl up to the side of the water, then slide in; Mr. Depew or somebody would stand on the edge, ready to haul him out. He would remember the Bay of Fundy and pant, "Water got me into this fix, water will get me out again!" These were, in a way, prophetic words.

For relaxation he liked to sit in an easy chair on the east porch with Louis Howe, making ship models. Sometimes he would be alone; he would drop a knife or tool, and then, if it fell any distance away, be unable to pick it up again. To sail the models, he would go rowing in the Hudson; that is, Howe would get in the bow of the boat, he in the stern, with Mr. Depew at the oars. He even continued teaching the boys how to swim, by sitting on the edge of a pool and holding out a long pole. He did a good deal of carpentry, and, lying on his back hour after hour, played with his stamps and started a catalogue of all his books. Early in 1923 he began to write a little; he started a History of the United States (the text of which may be found in the second volume of his letters) and his book on John Paul Jones. He refused to be downhearted, and never conceded that he would not be able to walk again.

The legend is that his morale, his spirit, were so good that he was never even irritable. Of course that is not true; he *had* to be fretful on occasion. Once or twice he lost his temper with Anna, whom he loved best; she would weep and, overcome by this frightful tragedy that had assaulted her father, rush wildly from the room. But on the whole he was indefatigably patient, indomitable, and serene. He made his own bed of Procrustes bearable. Above all he was never bored; at the very deepest moments of strain and irritation he could save himself by his own curiosity and technical interest in what was being done for his cure; even when the heavy casts were stretching his legs slowly and painfully into shape he was fascinated by every detail of the treatment. Mr. McGaughey, one of the Hyde Park servants, is willing to swear that he never once saw him angry, plaintive, or seriously discouraged.

A member of the family tells of one series of episodes almost too painful to be borne. FDR got a considerable amount of exercise by crawling. This man over forty who had been one of the most graceful, vital, and handsome youths of his generation spent hour after hour crawling over his library floor like a child. Then he determined to learn how to get upstairs by himself; day after day he would haul his dead weight up the stairs by the power of his hands and arms, step by step, slowly, doggedly; the sweat would pour off his face, and he would tremble with exhaustion. Moreover he insisted on doing this with members of the family or friends watching him, and he would talk all the time as he inched himself up little by little, talk, talk, and make people talk back. It was a kind of enormous spiritual catharsis—as if he had to do it, to prove his independence, and had to have the feat witnessed, to prove that it was nothing.

Much of his energy went in the early days into experiments with such things as a kind of pincers on a stick, to reach for books, and a leaf-picker's device with which he could lift papers off the floor. Sometimes he would carry a book with his teeth. His wheel chairs were usually small, so that they would fit the narrowish corridors both in New York and Hyde Park, cushionless, and armless; underneath the seat was a concealed ash tray on a swivel, so that he would not drop ashes on the floor. Big casters made them easy to steer. He seldom wheeled himself, but when he did he scooted from room to room at a considerable rate of speed.

Roosevelt had after his illness four means of locomotion: (a) he could walk on somebody's arm with the braces and a cane, (b) he could walk with braces and crutches, (c) the wheel chair, (d) he could be carried. He hated to be carried, and Louis Howe laid it down as an iron rule that he must *never* be carried in public. But in private he was carried, like an infant, thousands of times. For instance in later years, at dinner in the White House or elsewhere, he would usually be carried in to his place at the table before the company arrived, as described earlier in this book. Often, however, he used the chair. His servants and helpers acquired a marvelous dexterity in manipulating the change from the wheel chair to another so quickly and unobtrusively that few people ever noticed.

He could get around fairly well by these means after a time, and went daily for a few hours to his office with the Fidelity and Deposit Company. Temporarily he gave up his work at law, however, because his firm was housed in a building with particularly steep steps; to negotiate them twice a day was too exhausting. His confidence was rising; he said he would return to public life as soon as he could throw the crutches away. In the spring of 1923 he took a long cruise in Florida waters on a houseboat, the *Weona II*; this gave him great encouragement. The next winter he took a similar cruise, with Missy LeHand and a group of friends, and he wrote his mother from Miami, "I took the motor boat to an inlet, fished, got out on the sandy beach, picnicked, swam, and lay in the sun for hours. I know it is doing the legs good, and though I have worn braces hardly at all, I get lots of exercise crawling around, and I know the muscles are better than ever before."[3]

One of FDR's secretaries contributes this reminiscence. He was about to sign some checks in his capacity as head of the Woodrow

[3] *Letters*, Vol. II, p. 543.

Wilson Foundation and he said, "Wait a moment. I want to show you something." Then he proceeded to pick up one leg by the trouser crease and crossed it on the other one. "Now what do you think of that!" he exclaimed happily. Later she rode back to 65th Street with him. "He asked me to sit still when the car arrived home. He got out of the car and moved on crutches up the ramp that had been laid down to the front door. Then he gave the crutches to the chauffeur, and, using the railing along the ramp as support, *pulled* himself to the door. It was something he had just mastered."

Roosevelt, with great detachment and objectivity, once wrote a very good account of his own illness. His advice to fellow sufferers from polio was to go in for gentle exercise, skin massage, sun-bathing, and swimming in warm water; and to avoid overexertion, cold, deep massage, and getting fat.

Miracle of Warm Springs

In the autumn of 1924—I am skipping political developments to which we will return soon—began the great adventure of Warm Springs. Here again we confront the extraordinary capriciousness of history; or perhaps it was determined by fate ten thousand years ago that (a) a dilapidated hotel with an adjacent warm pool should exist at Warm Springs, Georgia; (b) Dr. Lovett should have found that swimming in warm water helped some of his patients; (c) Roosevelt became a friend of a New York banker named George Foster Peabody; (d) Peabody bought the Warm Springs resort and leased it to a friend, Tom Loyless, a former editor of the Atlanta *Constitution*; (e) Loyless wrote Peabody that a Southern lad named Louis Joseph had been stricken by infantile paralysis two years before and had benefited greatly by the Warm Springs water. Who was this boy Louis Joseph? What has ever happened to him? Every human life is somehow associated with every other human life. Not one person in twenty million has ever heard of Louis Joseph; yet, by this combinative play and thrust of circumstance, this inextricably conjoined and mysterious chain of events, he became, by the mere fact of his existence, a major factor in the Roosevelt story.

Peabody thought that Roosevelt might be interested in the Joseph case, and passed on what information he had. At first the water did the boy little good; then after a summer he was able to stand up in the pool; then a year later "he could walk on land with the aid of

canes." At once Roosevelt, breaking everything else off, set out for
Warm Springs to see what this miracle might mean.

The Warm Springs pool is fed by a subterranean spring which gives
it a constant temperature of about 88 degrees; the water, full of
mineral salts, is of exceptionally high specific gravity. Its peculiar
property is that patients can stay in it for extended periods, up to
two hours or even longer, without the enervation or fatigue that
usually accompanies bathing in water at this temperature. Immersion
in *any* water will help a paralytic to some extent because water re-
moves the weight of gravity. If, in a polio patient, any musculature
remains at all, or any vestige of the neuromuscular coordinating
mechanism, *some* degree of rehabilitation is possible if the muscles
are exercised in circumstances where the force of gravity does not
operate. But the beneficent effects of the Warm Springs pool seemed
to go far beyond this minimum.

Roosevelt stayed six weeks on his first visit, and made more progress
than in the preceding three long years. "He felt life in his toes for the
first time since August, 1921." Not only did he help himself; he helped
other patients too, by working out a series of underwater exercises.
A good deal of publicity, contrary to his wish, attended his first visit;
when he returned the next spring a dozen crippled persons had arrived
without warning or invitation and were waiting for him. This provoked something of a crisis in the affairs of the local hotel; the healthy
visitors were afraid to mix with the invalids, for fear of "catching"
polio. Roosevelt took this in hand, arranged for the paralysis sufferers (his "gang" as he expressed it) to eat at a separate table, and
even saw to it that a new segregated pool was built. Promptly he
became "Dr." Roosevelt and, in close cooperation with the local physician, took effective charge of the establishment. He has recorded his
struggle teaching two very fat ladies to get their feet down to the
bottom of the pool, for a special exercise he invented. "I would take
one large knee of one of the ladies and I would force this large knee
and leg down. . . . And then I would say, 'Have you got it?' and she
would say, 'Yes,' and I would say, 'Hold it, hold it.' Then I would
reach up and get hold of the other knee very quickly, and start to put
it down and then No. 1 knee would pop up again. . . . But before
I left . . . I could get both those knees down at the same time."[4]

But Warm Springs was not the only therapy FDR tried. Only some-

[4] Rosenman, Vol. III, p. 488.

one in the grip of an intolerable illness can know with what soaring hope, tempered with anguished skepticism, one clasps at every straw. In 1925 he heard of a neurologist named William MacDonald of Marion, Massachusetts, who had devised a "walking board" for polio patients; he spent two summers with Dr. MacDonald, trying to walk round and round on this apparatus. One incident of this period is described by Mrs. Charles H. Hamlin, a close family friend: "One night Franklin and Eleanor came to visit me in Mattapoisett. Two men carried him in to a seat at the dining room table. He told the men not to return until 9:30. When dinner was over, Franklin pushed back his chair and said, 'See me get into the next room.' He got down on the floor and went in on his hands and knees and got up into another chair himself." Dr. MacDonald had taught him how to perform this feat, so that he "would have a feeling of freedom to move, if necessary."[5]

But Warm Springs remained his chief hope. Not only did he return again and again (usually his only companions were Missy LeHand and a valet); he rented a house there, and eventually built one; it is striking that he should have named it the "Little White House," though his mother testifies that this was not because of any future "aspirations." Warm Springs became, in fact, his winter home. More and more he came to love the bland, soothing Georgia sun and the gentle quality of the countryside. Oddly enough Eleanor Roosevelt was somewhat lukewarm about all this. She wrote early in 1926:

. . . My only feeling is that Georgia is somewhat distant. . . . One cannot, it seems to me, have *vital* interests in widely divided places, but that may be because I am old and rather overwhelmed by what there is to do in one place and it wearies me to think of even undertaking to make new ties. Don't be discouraged by me; I have great confidence in your extraordinary interest and enthusiasm. It is just that I couldn't do it. . . .[6]

Roosevelt was utterly convinced by this time (he had twenty-three "patients" at Warm Springs by the spring of 1926) that the curative properties of the resort were all that he had hoped, and he determined to enlarge his activities and regularize them. He felt that an impartial medical board should go into the whole matter; such a board was set up, under the chief of orthopedics of the New York State Board

[5] *Letters*, Vol. II, p. 590.
[6] *Letters*, Vol. II, p. 611.

of Health, and it reported favorably. Thereupon FDR took the decisive step of buying the whole Warm Springs property, hotel, cottages, pools, and all, with 1,200 acres of land, for use as a hydrotherapeutic center; the institution was incorporated as a nonprofit enterprise known as the Georgia Warm Springs Foundation, and it has been functioning ever since. He himself put something like $200,000 into the enterprise, which was a substantial part of his total fortune.

Lifelong Toll and Tribute

It is time now to estimate some of the results of this extraordinary experience to Roosevelt. First, in the realm of the purely physical. Nobody with legs can easily appreciate what it is like to be without them. I do not mean in such obvious realms as that FDR could never take a hike, kick a football, dance, climb a fence, skate, or play with his toes in the sand. So long as he lived, he was never able to climb a stair more than two or three inches high, lean deeply to kiss a child, crouch to catch an object, scuff with his feet, squat on the grass, tap a foot, do a deep bend, or kneel in prayer. Beyond this were countless other deprivations and discomforts. Consider the thousands of times a day a man with normal legs and feet uses them instinctively, without thought: to hold balance in a veering automobile, to give emphasis while speaking, to brace the body in all manner of reflexes. All this—and much else—Roosevelt lost.

I do not even mention such items as that his physical movements were of necessity severely circumscribed; that special ramps and the like had to be set up whenever he traveled; that, by and large, he could not speak in halls where the platform was not easily accessible from street level; that the simple business of getting in and out of an automobile was an almost intolerable strain; that he could not completely dress or undress himself; that he wore a cape instead of an overcoat, and a sweater instead of a bathrobe, because they were easier to get into; that he could never fulfill one tenth or one twentieth of all manner of ideas that came to him. It was a pleasant notion that, when President, he should call on Mr. Justice Holmes. But just how he could be lugged up the narrow stairs in the Holmes dwelling had to be carefully planned out. It was imperative at the Atlantic Charter conference that he should visit Mr. Churchill on the *Prince of Wales*. But *how* to get him up the side of that battleship!

Hundreds of thousands of people saw Roosevelt wave or heard him say a few words from the observation car of his campaign train. The torture caused by these appearances, particularly toward the end, is seldom realized. Before each stop Pa Watson or Sam Rosenman would come into his compartment and say something like, "Mr. President, we'll be in Springfield in about ten minutes." FDR would put down what work he was doing, call for his valet, and his trousers would be taken off (sometimes he did this himself); then the braces were put on, and he locked and tested them; then, this accomplished, he got into his trousers again. During all this he talked incessantly. He would walk to the end of the car when the train eased to a stop, squeezing sideways down the aisle on the arm of a companion; then hold himself erect on the platform, smile, and say his few words or perhaps make a speech of some length; then be slowly turned around by whoever was helping him and return to his compartment where the process was duplicated in reverse (if you were one of those holding him you had to learn to let him down in his seat very carefully); he would whip off his trousers and unlock the braces with the greatest delight; then dress again and go back to work until it was time for the next stop.

Many people have watched him arrive somewhere for a ceremony. First, his legs would project from the automobile; second, he would snap them forward stiffly; third, he would lift himself out on his arms, then lean on whoever was helping him. During this, for a few seconds, his face would be absolutely grim and concentrated; then, becoming aware of the crowd, his features would automatically flash into a public smile.

If he were making a speech in a hall he had to brace himself accurately on the lectern. This was always tested beforehand, to see if it would bear his weight.[7]

He slipped, almost fell, or fell not more than five or six times in more than twenty years, a remarkable record. Once, crawling in his houseboat off Miami, he tore several leg ligaments in a bad fall. During the first presidential campaign, while making a speech in Georgia, he toppled over when the table against which he was leaning slipped. Members of his entourage quickly helped him to his feet; he kept on

---

[7] There were hundreds of unexpected minor problems. For instance at the first inaugural he picked up his silk hat the wrong way so that, if he put it on, it would be backward on his head. He was walking on the arm of his son James, and could not stop, so laboriously, little by little, he worked the brim of the hat around with the fingers of his free hand until it was in the right position.

with his speech at the exact point where it had been broken off, and made no reference to the mishap; the audience cheered wildly. In Philadelphia four years later, a bolt in one of the braces became unlocked just before he was to address the Democratic convention, and he lost balance. The pages of his speech splashed to the floor, but Gus Gennerich, his bodyguard, and Mike Reilly caught him before he actually fell. They reached down and relocked the brace while Jim Farley and his son James closed in around him to keep the mishap from the eyes of the crowd. But there was a good deal of confusion and the President was badly shaken; his words to Reilly were a curt snap, "Clean me up!"

But the worst agony lay in subtler fields. For instance the President could never, except when he slept, be left alone; once he told Ambassador Winant that his utter lack of privacy was the hardest single thing he had to bear. Occasionally, by error, he *was* left alone. Once Frances Perkins was with him in the Oval Room just before he was going to bed; he rang, but unaccountably no one answered; finally he turned to Miss Perkins and said, "Please find Prettyman [the valet]; I am helpless without him." Also it was difficult for him to dismiss a visitor who overstayed his time, since he could not employ such ordinary gestures as rising from the chair or leading the visitor to the door. Again, as I mentioned in a previous chapter, his immobility made it tedious, even arduous, to do routine business in a conference —he could not rise suddenly, move from chair to chair, talk standing, or otherwise do what everybody else does all the time, to relax the mood of a gathering, stiffen an argument, or emphasize a point. Try sitting for four or five hours in serious conversation with an argumentative group without once moving from your chair.

Psychologically one can trace dozens of minor characteristics that developed as a result of the paralysis. He loved gossip so much because he himself could not get around; talk was an outlet for all his suppressed energy. He loved holding the tiller of a boat because this gave him a sense of controlling motion. He had the close consciousness of time, of the passage of time and the intervals in time, so characteristic of people who have had prolonged illnesses; for instance his meals had to be served on the split second. He had a very serious conception (no matter how much he dallied in conversation) of the difference between 7:29 and 7:30.

Another point is that—understandably—he was somewhat timid

of minor illnesses; when he had a cold, he needed to be babied a good deal. He hated to be near sick people, except Howe and Hopkins.

Roosevelt's own attitude to his affliction, as this became cemented into his character during the years, was to disregard it completely so far as externals were concerned. He had the special type of courage of the cripple who will not admit that he is crippled; this was a kind of defense mechanism since, at all costs, he had to protect himself from the invasion of any doubt or underconfidence. Almost never did he refer to his disability; for instance his mother testifies that she never once heard him mention it, incredible as this may seem. The artist Walter Tittle quotes him with an offhand remark, "Oh, yes, I could walk with crutches then," but even such casual references were very rare. He never under any circumstances used the illness as a political weapon. One minor point is that, for years, he would not say the word "golf" aloud, and nobody who knew him well ever talked about golf; it wounded him too deeply to think that he could never play again.[8] He never returned to Campobello, much as he loved it, until 1933, because its associations were too painful. He wanted to discard utterly from his mind anything that had to do with the illness. He tried to seize everything that was normal. Above all he wanted to live like a normal man.

Nor would he permit anybody else to be sorry for him or show pity; nothing irritated him so much as special solicitude from friends or visitors. "No sob stuff!" was his stern warning to reporters who saw him after the attack, and he once told a biographer, "It's ridiculous to tell me that a grown man cannot conquer a child's disease." Above all, he never traded on his affliction, no matter how it might, as Mr. Ickes once put it, be exhausting his emotional reserves. Even healthy presidents ask for sympathy on occasion; Roosevelt never did. His attitude was, "I'm on top, I need your help, let's work together."

FDR himself could ignore his illness; other people couldn't. Members of the family had little, if any, self-consciousness about his disability, if only because he had no self-consciousness himself. But outsiders seeing him and his methods of conveyance for the first time were almost always profoundly shocked; even hard-boiled newspaper men who knew that he could not walk as well as they knew their own names could never quite get over being startled when FDR was sud-

[8] Another detail perhaps relevant is that till the end of his life he hated to throw shoes away, and it is somehow odd that one of his favorite similes was "funny as a crutch." Cf. Tully, *F.D.R., My Boss*, p. 320.

denly brought into a room. The shock was greater when he wheeled himself and, of course, was greatest of all when he was carried; he seemed, for one thing, very small. Beyond this it was impossible not to feel emotion at realizing tangibly that the President of the United States was powerless to move. Yet in a few seconds, so relaxed was Roosevelt himself, the feeling of disconcertment would pass away. One reason why many visitors were so dumfounded was the voluntary conspiracy of silence about his illness that the newspapers maintained for many years. Caricatures never stressed his lameness; photographs were usually taken from the waist up; news stories seldom, if ever, mentioned that he was a cripple; and the fact that he used a wheel chair was never printed at all until the very end. In fact many people never even knew that he was paralyzed. During the 1930's when I lived in Europe I repeatedly met men in important positions of state who had no idea that the President was disabled.

Nobody but the most crassly callow visitors to Roosevelt ever made reference to his handicap. Madame Chiang Kai-shek, however, once committed the *gaffe* of telling the President, when she was about to leave the room, not to bother to get up. He "thanked her for the compliment."[9]

Other Results of the Illness in Varying Fields

1. When he returned to public life he was sometimes forced to unnecessary exertion and he sometimes took unnecessary risks in order to prove that he was perfectly fit physically.

2. Probably the illness had something to do with turning him to the Left politically. A psychiatrist might say that his physical disability was displaced into an absorption with economic disability in others. He learned that there were inferiorities other than those purely physical.

3. An unfriendly critic, pursuing similar hypotheses, has suggested that Roosevelt's conquest of himself, through braces, led him to put braces on the economic life of the entire nation, and that he tolerated the atrophy of American "principles" even as he had to adjust himself to the atrophy of his own legs. The whole country became "paralyzed."

4. Without the slightest medical justification, scurrilous haters of FDR used the illness as the "basis" of a whispering campaign about his health in general. It was even charged on one unutterably weird

[9] *White House Physician,* by Vice-Admiral Ross T. McIntire (New York, G. P. Putnam's Sons, 1946), p. 4.

and silly occasion that what he really had was a disease of the horse, equine encephalomyelitis.

5. Roosevelt's struggle with polio was that of a pioneer, and his intrepid example helped thousands of victims of the disease. Later, during the war, he was an inspiration to paraplegic cases in particular. He seemed to be a living symbol of the conquest of affliction.

6. His own recovery removed all traces of fear from his character, and helped induce his optimism. He learned to concentrate and conserve his energy. Above all the loss of his legs increased vastly his sensitiveness emotionally and intellectually.

7. Finally, he compensated for the fact of being paralyzed by an immense, overwhelming will to power. He, a cripple, would do what no other human being in the world had ever done, be President four times.

Parallels, If Any

The number of important personages in history who have had severe physical disadvantages is, of course, considerable. Most of these, it seems, are artists; it is as if the hair shirt of illness gives boundless stimulus to creative activity. But political figures have had some famous handicaps. Choosing in all fields one need only think of Milton, who was blind, Beethoven, who became deaf, or Lord Nelson, who, mutilated by wounds, had to fight pain all his life. Julius Caesar suffered from epilepsy, Alexander the Great was a drunkard, and Nietzsche died insane. Gibbon had a famous hydrocele, Marat suffered frightfully from a skin disease, and Charles V had gout, arteriosclerosis, and dropsy. Many eminent men had syphilis (Henry VIII, Benvenuto Cellini, Baudelaire), and sufferers from tuberculosis can be listed without end—Voltaire, Kant, Keats, Dostoevsky, Molière, Schiller, Descartes, Cardinal Manning, Spinoza, Cicero, St. Francis. But in the realm of physical deformity names are not so numerous. Several celebrated writers were eunuchs or eunuchoid. Peter Stuyvesant lost a leg and buried it in the West Indies, Toulouse-Lautrec had abnormally short legs, and Talleyrand was lame. Goebbels had a clubfoot, and Kaiser Wilhelm a withered arm. Lord Halifax has a withered hand.[10]

[10] Emil Ludwig mentions some others—medieval German warriors like Götz von Berlichingen (who fought with an iron arm) and Prince Christian of Brunswick. A Greek hero, Alexander Ypsilanti, had only one hand, and James II of England and Philip II of Spain were both lame. One of Gladstone's ministers was blind, and in modern times Philip Snowden was a hunchback.

The closest analogy to Roosevelt in some respects, my friend Jay Allen suggests, is of all people St. Ignatius of Loyola, the founder of the Jesuit order. Loyola was a brilliant and worldly youth, a page at court, an armed warrior in the service of the Duke of Najera, and a lively and successful lady's man. His birth was noble, and he was rich. His early life was one of ease and dissipation. Then in 1521, at the age of thirty, during the siege of Pamplona, a cannon shot smashed both his legs, and he became a cripple for life. During a prolonged and agonizing convalescence, during which he could not walk, he turned to literature and meditation, and gradually took on the characteristics which made him famous. He forswore carnal desires, prayed seven hours a day, scourged himself, and set out on his massive travels, lame. He taught himself Latin, became ordained as a priest in 1537, and promptly got into trouble with the high authorities of the Church for his independence of mind and vigor; then came the formation of the Society of Jesus, under his burning guidance. The analogies to Roosevelt, *mutatis mutandis*, are suggestive throughout the whole life span, since Loyola too was a propagandizer, a popularizer, a political leader, and a spiritual force almost beyond comprehension, whose impact jarred the world for years, and whose work lived after him.

Loyola aside, there are few close parallels. In fact so far as I know FDR is the only man in all history who could not walk who reached a commanding position in world affairs.

The Realm of Compensation

Several consolations and compensations attended Roosevelt's affliction. For instance it is an extraordinary fact that, paradoxical as it may seem, the blight of illness made him robust.

FDR had always been somewhat given to illness and very thin; now all the energy of his body seemed to go into a prodigious development of the torso, neck and arms. His face had been sensitive and narrow, with some marks of weakness; now it broadened out. Almost overnight, the head became Herculean. A minor contrary point is that he lost two inches in height. Jack Dempsey once said that FDR had the most magnificent development of shoulder muscles he had ever seen; on one occasion—and with no power in his legs, remember —he landed a 237-pound shark after a two-hour fight. Ask any fisherman what that means.

There is a curious double paradox here. His illness made him robust, yes, and for many years he was one of the sturdiest and healthiest men alive. Yet something oddly perverse attends a man who, wonderfully healthy, cannot walk.

Other compensations were more orthodox. He always had a good excuse not to do things that might bore him. He dropped out of society altogether and had time to work things out and evaluate; he discovered that what he previously thought was "thinking" had been merely "looking out of the window." He didn't have to exhaust himself on games, celebrations, and interminable public functions and private gatherings. Once he said to an ambassador, "How do you stand all the dinner parties?—I'll bet my stomach is in better shape than yours!" Once he confided to his son James, "The reason I get so much done is that I don't have to waste time with my legs." He said to Bernard M. Baruch once, "I save a lot of energy. What does a fellow need legs for, if we have elevators?"

But the more important transformations occurred in the ripe realm of the spirit. Roosevelt learned what suffering was; he learned compassion. Just as the muscles of his chest acquired a superdevelopment, so did he grow colossally in such attributes as serenity and will. He could not balance on his legs; he did learn to balance with his mind. Maybe he couldn't walk; but his feet were certainly on the ground. He learned the need for courage, and hence could transmit courage to the nation. In some respects it might almost be said that polio was God's greatest gift to him. Through the fires of this ordeal he established a power over his own mind that he had never had before, and this gave him power over the minds of others. The supreme experience of his life was to beat Death off, and then conquer indomitably the wounding traces that Death left.

Before the illness, all his charm and accomplishment notwithstanding, Roosevelt had something of the lightweight in him; even friends like Henry Stimson called him "an untried rather flippant young man." (Of course, later, he was to have another teacher almost as Draconian as illness—the Presidency.) But many people will testify to the fact that until the middle 20's, they liked FDR very much but thought that he was nothing more than an attractive, somewhat spurious, and highly amiable young man—almost a glad-hander, a playboy. He had promise, yes, but no great stature. He had brilliance, yes, but it was superficial. They were stunned, two or three years later, to discover that the ribs underneath this affable exterior had become steel; that the tremendous struggle he survived had etched ineradicable lines of power in every aspect of his character.

One interesting result of all this was superconfidence. Because he had beaten his illness, Roosevelt thought that he could beat anything. "The guy," Harry Hopkins once told Raymond Swing, "*never* knows when he is licked," and Hopkins thought that this was his chief defect.

Illness Did Not Make Him President

Finally, one should reject the notion that it was primarily illness that made Franklin Roosevelt President. Obviously he must have had a good deal of character in the first place, not only to reach the stations in life that he did reach before illness struck him, but to have been able to get through the shattering ordeal of the attack itself. There are, after all, plenty of victims of infantile paralysis who never become great men. Once a friend asked Mrs. Roosevelt if she thought he would have been President if he had not been ill. Her answer was, "He would certainly have been President, but a president of a different kind."

Chapter 14

BACK TO LIFE

The line he must walk is a hair's breadth.

—RALPH WALDO EMERSON

Roosevelt's formal reentry into political life came in 1924, when he nominated Alfred E. Smith as Democratic candidate for President. The next four or five years of his life are inextricably involved with Smith; his relations with that formidable and picturesque character, in all their fluid ups and downs, are the leitmotiv of much of FDR's career until he reached the White House.

Al Smith is largely forgotten these days; a new generation has grown up that scarcely knows his name. It is a pity. Smith was a true original. He was, as Walter Lippmann once pointed out, the first American of "the new immigration" to reach commanding stature in our national politics; Smith was a man of the streets, Irish of the Irish, a Catholic, a wet, a realist to the roots, and for many years a people's man, the "gorgeous knight of the brown derby and the cocked cigar." He served four terms as Governor of New York, and was one of the best governors any American state has ever had. He split the Democratic party not merely because he was a Catholic (the Ku Kluxers said that if he were elected the Pope would sit in the White House) or because he stood vehemently for repeal (nobody of the new generation can possibly realize what a torrential issue Prohibition was), but also because he represented what seemed to be new, dangerous, and unpredictable urban forces never before unleashed upon the nation at large.

Roosevelt and Smith, though they had close political relations for many years, were never intimate. Probably Smith, who had never even been graduated from primary school, liked FDR, the Groton-Harvard product, better than FDR liked him; Al had been fond of him since 1911 or 1912, and always thought that he would "go far." He got his first great political chance when FDR refused to run for Governor in 1918, and he ran instead. Socially, Roosevelt was put off by Smith's Irishness, by his atmosphere of hoodlumism, and by the fact that he was so emotional; the personal friendship was not easy. Also Roosevelt's mother "strongly disapproved" of Smith, and at this time Sara still "wanted to direct FDR's every thought and deed," as Eleanor records. Many of Smith's relatives and friends, on their side, thought that Roosevelt was an "awful stuffed shirt."

To come back to politics was the greatest single decision Roosevelt ever made. This, if any one turning point can be chosen as the most vital of his whole career, was it. Mrs. Roosevelt was, as we know, the most important factor prompting this decision, and to encourage him further she entered politics herself; Louis Howe was a close second. Instead of retiring to Hyde Park as a pleasant despot, a cripple who would be well cared for all his life, as his mother wished, FDR threw himself with full strength into the crossfire of the political arena, his disability ignored. Eleanor contributed to this in more ways than just intellectually. For instance no atmosphere of invalidism was permitted at 65th Street or even at Hyde Park, and there were no nurses or other paraphernalia of illness once he started to get well.

Even before 1924 FDR had been active on the sidelines, though he was little known to the public at large during this period. For instance in 1922 he took a strong stand against national isolation, and he was a major factor that year in persuading Smith, who had given up politics temporarily to go into business, to run for Governor again. William Randolph Hearst wanted the governorship, and FDR thought that Al was the only man who could beat him; Smith heeded this call, smashed the Hearst candidature, and won an impressive victory. In turn, Smith asked Roosevelt to run for Senator. But FDR did not think he was fully enough recovered, and refused. He wanted to conserve every scrap of vitality for the fight against his illness.

In February, 1924, both Franklin and Eleanor called publicly on Smith to run for the Presidency; Al then asked FDR to be his campaign manager, and he accepted. Mrs. Roosevelt seconded the resolution that formally pledged the New York Democratic leadership to Smith, and both Roosevelts worked hard in the campaign. Smith wanted FDR to nominate him at the convention, though it was against precedent for the manager to make the nominating speech, and FDR agreed to do so. One day in June, 1924, Roosevelt's old neighbor, Moses Smith, came across him sitting on a blanket stretched on the side of a road near Hyde Park, a pad of paper in his lap. "What do you think I'm doing?" FDR boomed in greeting. "I'm writing my nominating speech for Al Smith!"

This was the celebrated "Happy Warrior" speech, delivered at Madison Square Garden, New York, on June 26, 1924. It was the only speech of consequence Roosevelt made in the whole seven years of his convalescence, from 1921 to 1928, and it created a sensation.[1] The phrase "Happy Warrior" to describe Smith came from Supreme Court Judge Joseph M. Proskauer. (Of course William Wordsworth had used it before that.) FDR was carried to the platform in a wheel chair, and then took his place near the rostrum on crutches; his son Jimmy, then seventeen, held his arm, while Cordell Hull, the chairman of the Democratic National Committee, stood close by. Roosevelt whispered to Joe Guffey of Pennsylvania, who was seated next to him:

"Go up to the pulpit and shake it, will you?"

"Why?"

"I want to see if it will surely support my weight."

One of the reporters covering this event for the New York *Times* was none other than Elmer Davis. His story describes how a Connecticut tetrarch, now forgotten, announced that his state yielded to the great Empire State of New York. "Citizens of the great Empire State of New York . . . cheered themselves for three minutes while Franklin D. Roosevelt, former Assistant Secretary of the Navy, was assisted to the platform. He has been ill, he had to swing on crutches as he took his place at the speakers' stand, but nothing was the matter with his voice or his enthusiasm." Roosevelt said, "Corruption will be the overshadowing issue of this campaign, and our candidate must be able to stand on that." Davis commented, "This slanting shot at the McAdoo-Doheny connection was meant to excite the delegates but excited only the Tammany clique." Roosevelt said, "He [Al] has a record of law-enforcement; he stands for the whole constitution." Davis commented, "Feeble cheers." When, having talked thirty-four minutes, FDR named his man by calling him "the Happy Warrior of the political battlefield" the lid blew off the Garden and a demonstration took place in "such a din as it had probably never heard before." The band "made four false starts" as Roosevelt tried to finish his oration. The cheering lasted for one hour and thirteen minutes until

[1] In 1926 Roosevelt spoke at the Democratic State Convention when he was again pressed to run for Senator. but this hardly counts as a major speech.

the chairman attempted to call the convention to order. "He was helped by Franklin Roosevelt, who held up his hand and stilled the demonstration almost instantly."

But Smith never got the nomination; he and McAdoo killed each other off after interminable rancid balloting, and John W. Davis was finally accepted.

Roosevelt did not play much of a role in the actual campaign, with his man out. The Republicans nominated Coolidge and Dawes. It appears, interestingly enough, that this was one of the rare times when his political judgment erred; his letters indicate that he thought the result would be so close that the third-party candidature of La Follette might throw the election into the House of Representatives. But, as is firmly written in the history books, Coolidge won by an overwhelming landslide.

FDR got important prestige from the Happy Warrior speech. When the convention wound up its dingy, agitated course the New York *World* wrote that, no matter what happened to Smith, FDR would stand out as the "real hero" of the event. "Adversity has lifted him above the bickering, the religious bigotry, conflicting personal ambitions, and petty sectional prejudices. . . . It has made him the one leader commanding the respect and admiration of delegations from all sections of the land."

Immediately after the convention FDR was invited again to stand for Governor of New York. He declined on the ground that he would not run for public office until he could walk without crutches.

Interlude in Other Fields

Meantime Roosevelt busied himself with other activities in so far as circumstances permitted. Perhaps these activities were halfhearted. His soul was in his legs. But for the record it should be put down that he maintained his interest in the Boy Scouts (he was chairman of the New York organization) and in Harvard (he was the youngest overseer ever elected in the history of the University). Also he worked with the American Legion and the Woodrow Wilson Foundation, was a trustee of Vassar, acted as chairman of the organization to raise funds for the Cathedral of St. John the Divine, and headed the Taconic Park Commission. In January, 1925, he started a new law firm with a man who was to become a lifelong friend, Basil O'Connor; the offices were in the same building that housed his insurance company, so that the physical problem of getting there was not too onerous. His insurance business doubled in these years, which would seem to indicate that he was not too bad a businessman.[2] Contrariwise he took several fliers into other businesses, all of which turned out badly except one. The failures included something called the Consolidated Automatic Merchandising Corporation, a holding company in the field of vending machines, and, of all things, an organization he promoted to fly fast freight between New York and other cities by dirigible. The success—a modest one—was the United European Investors, Ltd., which dealt in German marks. I have heard an unfriendly critic say, with monstrous distortion, "Roosevelt failed in Wall Street seven times. When he became President he closed all the banks in revenge." (Of course he did not "close" the banks; most were closed when he reached office.) FDR certainly did not "fail" seven times. The truth about his brief Wall Street period is simply that he was no great success. He was much more interested in other things than making money. He was an unlucky speculator, and so wisely gave up speculation for the rest of his life. And he learned to dislike heartily two Wall Street phenomena—the monolithic corporations that ate up their competitors, and the gamblers.

Perhaps FDR was hard pressed financially at this time; his illness cost a large sum and he hated to have his mother pay the bills. At any rate he auctioned off some of his naval models and prints early in 1925; the sale was held at the Anderson Galleries, and was duly noted in the New York *Times*; it brought $4,537.

One little-known fact is that FDR wrote a newspaper column during several brief periods. His close friend at Warm Springs, Tom Loyless, was forced to give up writing the column he did for the Macon (Georgia) *Telegraph*, on account of illness; FDR volunteered to step in as a substitute, and wrote gratis a dozen or so articles under the title "Roosevelt Says." They dealt with such themes as taxes, conservation, and the civil service, and are not particularly original or interesting; one is subtitled: "We Lack a Sense of Humor if We Forget That not so Long Ago We Were Immigrants Ourselves." It is an incidental minor point that many years later this same newspaper, the Macon *Telegraph*, was one of those last-ditch, white-supremacy Southern organs that demanded FDR's impeachment as President. Later FDR did a second series of columns, again as a favor to a friend, for the Beacon

---

[2] Yet some people said that he was a mere "front," that his employers were using him only for his name.

(New York) *Standard.* These are better stuff and got considerably more attention; they are full of pith and salt, and papers all over the country asked for permission to reprint them. These interludes as a newspaperman taught FDR one thing, which he was wont to mention gaily: "My experience as a columnist proves that no one can write a column on public affairs once a day, or twice a week!"

During this period 1925-28 Mrs. Roosevelt's influence on FDR continued to be high, and her own political activity expanded fruitfully. Also she continually brought in new people to see him. His golf and old-school-tie companions began to drop out; perhaps they reminded him too poignantly of his affliction or he found out that, when not playing games, most of them were bores; at any rate, largely through Eleanor, he met a whole new world of men and women—teachers, social workers, research students, editors, intellectuals, and plain simple people, not necessarily radical at all, who had ideas. At first FDR appears to have been puzzled by these strange and novel types; he thought that some of them were "pretty wild." Then he grew to discover that they "had" something. Gradually, almost imperceptibly, he developed a new circle of acquaintances and interests, and new sources of information and new objectives began to irrigate his mind.

Never, of course, did he move far from politics. Here Howe continued to be the major mentor. Several of his Warm Springs friends tried to tempt him to run for Governor of Georgia, though as a Northerner he would have faced an unmanageable handicap in such a race. After Smith's defeat he worked hard to unify the riven Democratic party; for instance he wrote not less than a thousand letters to prominent Democrats all over the country, urging harmony, unity, and an aggressive common program to be worked out at a national conference in 1925.

Another point is that, during all the aftermath of his illness, his political friends stuck close. It is easy enough to remain loyal to a leader in his days of promise and expansion; it is not too easy when the leader is smitten, and it is an interesting tribute to FDR that almost everybody who had been in his camp in 1920 was still there in 1928.

Houston, 1928

From 1926 on FDR devoted most of his time and energy to working for the nomination of Al Smith in 1928. He did not handle the pre-convention campaign (by gradual degrees Smith was veering toward more conservative elements in the party) but, as in New York in 1924, he made the nominating speech; this was the third time FDR had put Smith's name before a Democratic convention. The convention met at Houston, and was a mess. Nevertheless Smith did finally win the nomination. Roosevelt's nominating address did not electrify the crowd as did the Happy Warrior speech, but it signalized his full return to political life. His recovery was now so far advanced that he was able to walk on the platform with the aid of canes. Roosevelt gave a note in this speech that was to become famous later; his manner was intimate and civilized, and he became fully aware of the power of his radio voice for the first time. The New York *Times* commented that he spoke "like a gentleman speaking to gentlemen . . ." with nothing "strained, fantastic, or extravagant." And listen to this eyewitness account from Will Durant, who was covering the assembly for the New York *World-Telegram*:

Here on the stage is Franklin Roosevelt, beyond comparison the finest man that has appeared at either convention; beside him the master minds who held the platform at Kansas City were crude bourgeois, porters suddenly made rich.

A figure tall and proud even in suffering; a face of classic profile; pale with years of struggle against paralysis; a frame nervous and yet self-controlled with that tense, taut unity of spirit which lifts the complex soul above those whose calmness is only a stolidity; most obviously a gentleman and a scholar. A man softened and cleansed and illumined with pain. What in the name of Croker and Tweed is he doing here? . . .

Hear the nominating speech; it is not a battery of rockets, bombs and teardrawing gas—it is not shouted, it is quietly read; there is hardly a gesture, hardly a raising of the voice. This is a civilized man; he could look Balfour and Poincaré in the face. For the moment we are lifted up.

After the shouting Roosevelt was offered the national chairmanship of the Democratic party. He declined. But he was by no means finished with the year 1928.

First Run for Governor

He went to Warm Springs in September, intending to stay most of the winter there. The Edsel Fords made a substantial contribution to the Foundation, and the pool had been roofed so that it could be used in cold weather. FDR was continuing to improve, and on one occasion he even walked a few steps unsupported. He felt that if he could devote all his time to Warm Springs he might—dizzy hope!—be able some day to dispense with the braces. This hope was never realized. One reason was that Al Smith talked him into running for Governor. Smith, in a manner of speaking, cost him the further use of his legs. Had he not run at this time his recovery might well have been much more substantial than it ever was. From October, 1928, when he finally and with extreme reluctance entered the gubernatorial race, he never had one minute out of public life until his death.

The background is roughly this. At least three writers on Roosevelt give long accounts of the crucial conversations with Smith that took place. They agree on the essential details, and I will try to blend them together.

Smith was running for President; therefore somebody had to be found to succeed him as Governor of New York. Roosevelt was the obvious candidate, but he refused to run. The New York State convention was about to meet, with no candidate in sight; Herbert H. Lehman consented to run for Lieutenant Governor, but the governorship was wide open. Smith wanted Roosevelt for the most urgent reasons: he himself could not hope to win the Presidency without New York's huge bloc of forty-seven electoral votes, and FDR would help him get them. In fact, without Roosevelt in New York, Smith's campaign was hopeless. FDR not only had a great reputation with the public at large, but substantial roots of power in every Democratic faction; he was a Protestant and thus complemented Smith's Catholicism; he had strong rural connections whereas Smith was a creature of the cities; he had influence with the old Wilsonians, and was not too much committed on the stark issue of Prohibition. From almost every point of view, in fact, Smith or no Smith, he was an ideal choice.

But Roosevelt, with absolute sincerity, did not wish to run. Probably there were three reasons for this: (1) he wanted desperately to finish the treatment at Warm Springs; (2) he thought he might well be defeated; (3) he thought that it was too early for him to make a serious bid for power on the national scene. Louis Howe in particular, whose sagacity he trusted implicitly, urged him to hold off. Howe once told Warren Moscow of the New York *Times* his reasons for hoping that FDR would delay. Herbert Hoover, he felt, would certainly become President in 1928 and probably serve two terms; therefore Roosevelt should not run for Governor until 1932, with the idea that the Presidency itself would finally become ripe for him in 1936. How different

American history would have been if FDR had followed Howe's advice!

Smith, meantime, kept right after FDR. In the midst of his own campaign he telephoned FDR from Milwaukee on September 26 pleading with him "for the last time" to reconsider his decision and run. Roosevelt sent him a long telegram on October 1—the text is available but it is hardly worth repeating in full—flatly declining on the grounds: (a) Smith's record was so good that he would carry New York anyway; (b) he was only forty-six and he owed it to his family to "give the present constant improvement" in his health a chance to continue; (c) he just didn't want to. Still Al did not give up.

Then came two of the most complex, pregnant days in Roosevelt's life. Smith, Mrs. Roosevelt, Lehman, and others assembled at Syracuse where the New York convention was opening. Late in the afternoon of October 2 Al began to try to get FDR on the telephone. The first call came through while Roosevelt was in the Warm Springs pool; he sent a message that he was "out somewhere on a picnic, and would be away all day." That evening he had an engagement to speak for Smith at the nearby town of Manchester. More calls came in, but FDR simply refused to accept them. He got a telegram from his daughter Anna, "Go ahead and take it [the nomination]," and he found time to reply, "You ought to be spanked." But he declined to answer the telephone, no doubt fearing that, voice to voice, he might weaken. Smith, after Lehman and Tom Lynch had failed, finally got Mrs. Roosevelt to try to get through to him, though she insisted that she would not attempt to influence him in any way, and that he must make his own decision. Roosevelt was sitting on the platform in Manchester when a messenger reported that Smith himself was on the wire. The nearest telephone was in a drugstore a block away. Roosevelt refused to budge. Half an hour later the messenger returned with word that Smith was still on the wire, and would not get off till Roosevelt answered. But it was difficult for FDR to get out of the crowded hall, and Smith waited a solid hour. Then laboriously FDR got to the phone—and found Mrs. Roosevelt at the other end. Stories differ as to exactly what went on in the next few minutes. Apparently Lehman promised to assume the major burden of the governorship, and John Raskob, the automobile tycoon who was chairman of the Democratic National Committee, pledged himself to contribute $25,000 to Warm Springs so that Roosevelt need not worry about further financing of the Foundation. The telephone connection in the drugstore broke at this point; it was resumed in Warm Springs after a maddening delay. Roosevelt talked to Mrs. Roosevelt, to Raskob, and finally to Smith once more. He gave a final flat refusal. Then Smith, before he could hang up, shouted the question whether he would actually decline to run *if* nominated. FDR hesitated, and this was all that Al needed. He snapped off the talk. The convention nominated Roosevelt by acclamation the next day, and FDR read in the papers that he was candidate for Governor.

A good many people expressed worry about FDR's health. Smith said to newspaper reporters, "A governor does not have to be an acrobat. We do not elect him for his ability to do a double back flip or a handspring."

One of the happiest months of Roosevelt's whole life followed. Howe was right (even if he had had doubts about this particular campaign): what FDR needed was a sound, exciting dose of politics. He threw himself into running for office with total fervor; he hurled his whole buoyant weight at the New York electorate. His mother recalls that he was so happy to be back in the thick of a fighting campaign, and throve so lustily on the rigors of speechmaking and the like, that he exclaimed exuberantly, "If I could campaign another six months, I could throw away my canes."

This is a sample of his talk late in October. He mentioned first the commiseration of some newspapers about the "unfortunate man who had to be drafted for the governorship." Then:

We started off nearly two weeks ago from the City of New York. . . . We started in in Orange County and we went on through Sullivan, Delaware, Broome, Steuben, and so forth, out through the Southern Tier, all the way to Jamestown. One day we covered 190 miles by automobile and made seven speeches. Then we worked our way up to Buffalo and back to Rochester and Syracuse; because we were getting into our stride, we took a little side trip up to Oswego and Watertown, and then we dropped back to Utica. We got to Herkimer, where we all made speeches; then we expected to come through to Schenectady, but when we got to Fonda, there were forty or fifty automobiles in line blocking the road, and we were literally kidnapped. We were told that up in that neck of the woods, Gloversville, where in the past there had been occasionally two Democrats and sometimes three, that had gone to the polls, there were two thousand people waiting for us on the street, so we changed our plans a little and went up to Gloversville. We got to Amsterdam. We expected to go through Amsterdam just as fast as the traffic cops would let us, but there were sixteen hundred people in the theatre in Amsterdam, waiting. They had been waiting there two hours.

And then, for good measure, we just dropped into Schenectady and spoke there earlier in the evening, and now here we are in Troy. Too bad about this unfortunate sick man, isn't it? . . .

It was during this campaign that Roosevelt first met Judge Rosenman, who was to render him incomparable service for the next seventeen years. FDR asked Maurice Block, his manager, to recruit a campaign helper who was thoroughly erudite on recent developments in New York State politics. Block suggested Rosenman, and so did Mrs. Belle Moskowitz, Al Smith's great friend and political adviser. Rosenman prepared a heavy file of material, and set out to meet FDR at Binghamton. FDR, though very affable, paid no attention whatever either to Rosenman or to the material for about three days. All of his speeches were about Al Smith and the national picture; he scarcely mentioned himself and the struggle in New York. Then, before a speech at Buffalo, Block wired Rosenman to "remind Roosevelt that he is running too." Rosenman at that time thought that FDR was very "courtly," and had "liberal tendencies," but he did not think much else. He showed Block's telegram to FDR, and the candidate replied, "Very well. Suppose we talk about labor. Will you help me?" They hammered out a labor speech together, which was the beginning of their remarkable association. From that day till 1945, FDR scarcely made a speech without Rosenman's sound and judicious help.

Rosenman got a new glimpse of his man's mettle and scrapping quality on election night. As the returns came in it was only too evident that Hoover and the Republicans were giving Smith a decisive beating, both in the nation at large and in New York. The run for the governorship was, however, turning out to be close, although at midnight it seemed certain that Roosevelt had lost by a narrow margin. His opponent, Albert Ottinger, was so far ahead upstate that the morning newspapers went to press saying that he had won. Most of FDR's advisers gave up and went home. But he himself, sitting in campaign headquarters at the Hotel Biltmore and buttressed by the sage advice of Edward J. Flynn, refused to concede defeat. He had the wild thought that some ballot-stuffing might have taken place in remote counties not yet reported, and as a last resort he picked up the telephone and until 6 A.M. put in call after call to every sheriff in the state, demanding the strictest supervision of the returns. If FDR had not done this he might have lost. Both Mrs. Roosevelts, Sara and Eleanor, had gone to bed thinking he was beaten. In the morning they found that, although Smith had lost New York by 103,481 votes, FDR carried it by 25,564. Franklin Delano Roosevelt outran Smith in Al's own native stronghold, and was the Governor.

Thus Roosevelt won this crucial race by 25,000 votes out of more than four million; his whole future career was made possible by less than 1 per cent of the electorate. What would have happened to America in the turbulent 1930's—and later—if this minuscule handful of voters had gone the other way?

Also FDR might not have won had not Ottinger offended some of the local chieftains of his party, which caused a serious Republican split; just enough disaffected Republicans voted for Roosevelt—out of spite at Ottinger—to put him in.[3] Another curious item is that he lost Hyde Park, his own home town, by a narrow margin, some 200 votes.

Roosevelt as Governor: Brief Conspectus

Roosevelt was a good Governor, not a great one; this is the easiest way to sum up his record from 1928 to 1932. The best accounts of the period are in Lindley and Gerald W. Johnson. As the latter says, Smith had been such a vigorously successful Governor, especially in cleaning house and opening the way to sound social reforms, that Roosevelt had little to do administratively except carry on his work; strictly as Governor FDR was, in fact, an anticlimax after Smith. His years in Albany, worthy as they were, gave little indication that as President he would be one of the most tremendous men who ever reached the White House.

The governorship of New York is generally conceded to be the second biggest job in the nation, being outranked only by the Presidency itself. It was certainly the biggest job FDR had ever had. I would like extremely to write an essay some day on the politics of New York State. Suffice it to say now that, classically, the struggle for power in New York is between the upstate legislature, which is usually Republican, and the Democratic forces in New York City; no governor can be effective unless he has anchors in both the countryside and the urban political machines. The chief executive of New York State learns rapidly to be a juggler, if he isn't one already. We can do no more than

[3] Interestingly enough FDR won his first race for State Senator partly as the result of a similar Republican split.

mention in passing some of the seminal facts about New York which must be in every governor's consciousness every minute of the time. Every tenth citizen of the United States is a New Yorker. Every twentieth citizen is an inhabitant of New York City. But even forgetting considerations of mere heft and bulk, New York is unparalleled for the interlocking complexity and vitality of its problems. It contains what is by all odds the greatest city in the world, yet it has more dude ranches than Wyoming, and there are deer passes forty minutes out of Manhattan. It contains what is by all odds the greatest industrial and financial nucleus in the world, but it lives on agriculture. It has the glories of West Point and the degradation of the Bowery; the handsome campus of Cornell and the slums of Troy; the hydroelectric power of Niagara and two of the most powerful labor unions on earth; millionaires by the shovelful and public schools in Buffalo where children come of twenty-six different racial stocks. Interesting terrain for a good inquisitive governor!

Roosevelt's first problem lay in his relations with Al Smith. It became apparent presently that Smith, from his hotel suite in Albany, thought that he, not FDR, was going to run the State; he seemed to think that Roosevelt would be a kind of stopgap or part-time "governor" spending most of the year at Warm Springs. FDR had no such intention, and Al became aggrieved; his attitude was, more or less, "I created you, and now what are you doing to me!" Roosevelt was patient, clever, and extremely firm. The first quarrels came over appointments; Smith expected FDR to keep in office his own chief friends, like the redoubtable Robert Moses and Mrs. Moskowitz. Of course this would have meant that Smith, not FDR, would hold the real power; so Roosevelt insisted on making his own appointments. Perhaps he was ungenerous to Al. But it should be understood that he was under no pledge to be a seat warmer for Smith or to be nice to his official family or kitchen cabinet. He had made no promises. He had outrun Smith vastly (for which the Smithites could not forgive him) and was on his own.

Early in the governorship people who watched him attentively, like Rosenman, discovered that the "courtly" Roosevelt had unsuspected guts. The legislature objected to his first executive budget, on grounds too technical to go into here; what was really at stake was who was going to run the administration. Roosevelt vetoed the budget as revised by the legislature, and the legislature was not strong enough to pass it over his veto; the result was a complete impasse. Finally the deadlock went to the courts, and FDR won, after a vicious, convoluted fight. This may seem a small affair now. But read headlines in the New York papers during February and March, 1929; people in the whole state were agog, and took sides with the utmost violence. Right or wrong, Roosevelt always had this electric capacity to get people excited and aroused by what he did. Listen to the following. It is a foretaste of much to come. The Republicans called him "sinister." They said:

The very foundation of the state is in danger with this message of avarice, usurpation and presumption [by FDR]. . . . The rights of the people must be preserved from the arrogance and presumption of an overzealous executive. . . .[4]

Around Roosevelt now had clustered a good many of those who were to serve him till the end of his life, or theirs. Missy LeHand and Grace Tully were firmly fixed in the official family; so was Rosenman, who became his counsel. He selected Frances Perkins as chairman of the State Department of Labor, and Henry Morgenthau, Jr., became head of the Agricultural Advisory Commission. Jim Farley, who did more to make him President than any single man, came into the picture, and above all Mrs. Roosevelt and others called to his attention one day a young reformer named Harry Hopkins. Soon Hopkins became chairman of the organization FDR set up to deal with emergency relief, a precursor of many subsequent New Deal agencies. Mrs. Roosevelt herself divided her time between Albany and the Todhunter School in New York. Usually she came up to Albany Thursday night, and stayed the week end. Missy LeHand was, in effect, hostess at the Executive Mansion when Eleanor was not there. Then too FDR met a considerable number of able Republicans who were opposing him vigorously at the time but who entered his service later and had great careers, like General "Wild Bill" Donovan, John G. Winant, Henry L. Stimson, and in a different category Fiorello H. LaGuardia.

Came FDR's second run for Governor in 1930. After a good deal of scratching around, the Republicans chose a lawyer named Charles H. Tuttle to oppose him. One signpost to the future was that, in literally hundreds of campaign speeches, FDR never once mentioned Tuttle's name, or gave any other indication of recognizing his existence. Roosevelt won this time by an immense, unbelievable, unprece-

[4] *Franklin D. Roosevelt,* by Ernest K. Lindley, p. 246.

dented majority; instead of carrying the state by 25,000 as in 1928, he
carried it by 725,000. Nothing like this had ever been known in New
York history. He even swept the rock-ribbed Republican territory
upstate, which had never been won by a Democrat before; even if New
York City had gone against him, he would have been elected. What
caused so sensational a victory? First, beyond doubt, the undeniable
power and attractiveness of his personality. This was strictly a *Roosevelt* triumph. The Republicans still held control of the legislature and
many other Republicans won various offices. Second, the hard times
that were eating insidiously into the fabric of the nation. The result
of this election was, of course, to transform FDR overnight into (a) a
nationally celebrated figure; (b) the outstanding Democratic candidate
for the Presidency in 1932.[5]

Much of what FDR did as President was clearly foreshadowed in
the Albany years; in fact the gist of the New Deal was implicit in
several of his gubernatorial decisions. The great Wall Street crash
came in the fall of 1929, and changed the whole focus of his attention
and activity. Depression began to grip the State and country; this was
a real crisis he had to cope with, and he groped for a solution. He
learned fast. The line he developed, under pressure of the mounting
emergency, was quite different from that taken by Mr. Hoover in the
White House; his basic approach, which was to be elaborated in one
of his most famous speeches a little later, was that the state *is* the
people; that if the rank and file of the people, through no essential
fault of their own, are deprived of the opportunity of earning a living,
the state owes them a livelihood not as a matter of charity, but as of
right. This is the way he put it, the actual terminology being partly
Rosenman's:

In broad terms I assert that modern society, acting through its government,
owes the definite obligation to prevent the starvation or the dire want of any
of its fellow men and women who try to maintain themselves but cannot.

While it is true that we have hitherto principally considered those who,
through accident or old age, were permanently incapacitated, the same responsibility of the state undoubtedly applies when widespread economic conditions render large numbers of men and women incapable of supporting either
themselves or their families because of circumstances beyond their control.

[5] Roosevelt knew he would win; but he underestimated by how much. He joined
a pool of newspaper correspondents betting on the election, and guessed his plurality
at 435,000. And this, almost 300,000 short, was by far the highest bet in the pool.
"The Governor," in the *New Yorker*, by Milton MacKaye, August 22, 1931.

This sounded—and was—revolutionary at the time; now it is accepted almost universally. Moreover Roosevelt, with his instinct for concreteness, went beyond words into action; he called a special session of the legislature, and New York was the first state in the union to vote public money for unemployment relief. Pause briefly to consider the implications of this. The whole gravid phenomenon, that of Roosevelt as a man of the Left, had begun to take shape. One speech, entitled bluntly "What Is the State?"—and the die was cast. One brief session of the New York legislature—and the United States started out on a new, uncharted experimental era.

Not everybody liked FDR by any means, and he was accused of being "all things to all men" even as Governor. Some critics dismissed him as a "goo-goo," i.e., a flaccid do-gooder. Here is a typical unfriendly view as written by a newspaperman of the time:

Although advanced as a liberal . . . his liberalism is born of impulse rather than intelligence or conviction. It moves him, except when he can see a definite gain in sight, only slowly and sporadically.

He is indecisive, indiscreet, and impulsive. Ever ready to embrace the newest fad . . . he surrenders himself wholeheartedly to momentary men and issues. . . . He needs balance and ballast. Expediency rules him.

Through some vagary in his nature, he cannot stay put. He is not dependable. Political correspondents at Albany do not trust him, although they like him. . . . He denies and deserts them whenever he deems it necessary.

His heart, more often than not, is in the right place, but he cannot coordinate his head.

Largely FDR's second term was overshadowed by his campaign for the 1932 presidential nomination and the Jimmy Walker affair, which were closely connected because the Walker case was political dynamite. The picturesque James J. Walker was Mayor of New York City; he was a Catholic, a Tammany stalwart, an Al Smith devotee, and a character full of the most fetching idiosyncrasies. Whether or not he himself was corrupt, or simply a gay dog having a wonderful fling, is difficult to determine; but underneath him flourished such corruption as has scarcely been known since the days of Heliogabalus. Scandals burst out into the open, and Roosevelt, as Governor, found himself in a trying predicament; either he had to turn a blind eye to what was being revealed, or throw Walker out. To choose the latter course meant that he would mortally affront Tammany and prejudice his political power in the indispensable key stronghold of Manhattan. There were other

angles. Tammany ran New York City; but Democrats elsewhere in the
nation, particularly the dry South, hated Tammany. So Roosevelt had
to decide, as it has been well put, whether to risk sacrificing his New
York support for the sake of his prestige in the country at large, or
his national prestige for the sake of maintaining control of New York.
Another item was that many conservative Democrats had become
bitterly anti-Roosevelt by this time, and naturally, along with the
Republicans, they sought to smear him with the Walker mud. Roosevelt did not dislike the Mayor personally, and Walker has blamed
himself for his churlish behavior to the Governor. In any case this was
one of the most ticklish tests FDR ever had to face, and he stalled as
long as he could. It took him an unwarranted time to make up his
mind. At last, after the most bizarre and kaleidoscopic developments,
with the newspapers screaming bloody murder and the presidential
campaign getting under way, he formally interrogated Walker in a
series of public hearings, and Walker finally resigned when it was
obvious that FDR would remove him. Thus he performed the complex
miracle of getting rid of Walker and buttressing his position in the
country without losing popular support in New York City, even
though Tammany fought him at the 1932 convention.

Perhaps, to repeat, Roosevelt was no great governor, but the record
of his accomplishment was not negligible. He fought for control of
public utilities, created the State Power Authority, established old-age
pensions, and worked hard for social security, reforestation (over which
he had a serious quarrel with Smith), and the idea that the water power
of the state should belong to all the people. It is revealing to learn
that—only twenty-odd years ago—he and Robert F. Wagner were
called "Communists" for saying that a fifty-four-hour week was too
long! He was not afraid to spend money (another view into the future);
he raised the State income tax 50 per cent, and it was certainly a foretaste of what was to come that when he became Governor the State
had a surplus in the treasury, and a deficit of $100,000,000 when he
left. But, of course, this was because he established the first unemploy-
ment-relief system in the country. When an economic system breaks
down, it costs money to repair it. Albany was, all in all, a fruitful
training ground for Roosevelt. He traveled prodigiously through the
State; no governor ever did so much road work, and he saw all fifty-
seven counties. Then too he evolved most of the working techniques
that were to be so useful to him as President, and the executive routine

of his day became fixed; how he arranged his appointments and so on in the White House exactly duplicated the system he set up in Albany. The later Fireside Chats grew naturally out of his innovation of direct radio talks to the New York electorate. In Albany he customarily held a press conference twice a day; so it was no great burden, in Washington, to do the same thing twice a week. Also he learned something of the incisive role he could play as a teacher, an educator, both to the public at large and to his immediate political associates. Politically, too, he had his first real contacts with labor, and conversely he gained good experience in the art of handling a hostile legislature. Again, his fights with the power lobby gave him a useful background for the great struggle to come over TVA, and his researches into the plight of agriculture led directly to subsequent New Deal legislation in this field. Finally, by incessant explorations among people he became for the first time intimately conscious of the concrete miseries of the underpossessed, and of the cruel realities of unemployment as the depression spread and smothered the productive capacity of the whole nation.

In his last months at Albany, however, Roosevelt had little time for state affairs. The sight of a much brighter, bigger goal transfixed him.

Chapter 15

THE SPRINGBOARD QUIVERS

Private economic power is a public trust.
—FRANKLIN DELANO ROOSEVELT

Roosevelt had probably wanted to be President all his life. One of his fellow law clerks has stated that FDR thought that he had "a real chance" to be President as long ago as 1907. Once he told a representative of the *Times* of London, "For twenty years I had a perfectly natural and laudable ambition to become president, and was obliged to behave like a man who wants to be elected president."

But illness knocked out the hope, and so far as I can gather from close friends he did not resume thinking seriously of the White House until 1928. His son James believes that it was only after the Houston convention that FDR began to consider that, even though crippled, he might have a chance again. On one occasion Roosevelt told one of his old friends, Dr. Adolph Miller of the Federal Reserve Bank, "You know our party is a minority party. Think of Cleveland and Wilson. Only fate gives us a president!" But, according to a well-known anecdote, FDR prophesied to John W. Davis back in 1922 that he, Davis, would be the nominee in 1924; Mr. Davis is supposed to have replied, "You might get it yourself," and FDR answered "No, I won't be ready till 1932." In any case, by 1930 or thereabouts, Roosevelt had become a paramount candidate. Mass meetings in the Bronx and elsewhere hailed him as the "next President" even before the second gubernatorial victory, and immediately after that the boom burst out in full force. The first two important Democrats outside New York to call openly for his nomination were, of all men, Senators Burton K. Wheeler of Montana and David I. Walsh of Massachusetts, both of whom became strong isolationists later and his bitter antagonists. Democratic committeemen from all over the country began to line up, Roosevelt clubs were organized in various states, and party dignitaries like Colonel House and Mr. Hull of Tennessee got on the band wagon.

Ed Flynn recounts that FDR called him to Albany late in November,

1930, for a long talk and said frankly, "Eddie, my reason for asking you to stay overnight is that I believe I can be nominated for the Presidency in 1932."

Flynn, Farley, and Louis Howe formed a kind of triumvirate, though Howe was jealous as an adder of anybody else close to Roosevelt, even Rosenman. Farley did the hard state-to-state travel lining up delegates, and Howe was the indispensable mastermind. An FDR "Pre-Convention Committee" was organized to direct strategy, collect funds, and the like; among its sixteen or seventeen original members were Frank D. Walker (later to become, in a special way, one of the closest of all people to Roosevelt), Laurence A. Steinhardt, Robert W. Bingham, Jesse Straus, James W. Gerard (who, as we know, had beaten FDR in the long forgotten senate race of 1914), Joseph P. Kennedy, the Morgenthaus, William H. Woodin (a converted Republican), Colonel House, and Lehman. Mrs. Sara Roosevelt was a member of the committee, and Eleanor helped staunchly. FDR did a great deal of active work himself. For one thing, systematically and progressively, he kept in touch by letter with every Democrat in the country who could possibly be of use. He made it a definite business to cultivate the best of relations everywhere, and during his second term as Governor he must have written at least five thousand letters to this end.

Later the original group expanded, and its members came to be known as "Roosevelt-Before-Chicago" men, like Homer Cummings, Joseph E. Davies, Breckinridge Long, Dave Hennen Morris, and a good many others who were well known then but are now forgotten. The biggest financial contributors were Woodin, who gave $10,000, and Frank Walker and Henry Morgenthau, Sr., who gave $5000 each. Ed Flynn[1] prints a fascinating list of the rewards the original Roosevelters got. Cummings became Attorney General, Harry M. Durning became Collector of Customs in New York, Robert Gore got the governorship of Puerto Rico, W. A. Julian became Treasurer of the United States, Cordell Hull became Secretary of State, Joe Kennedy served in many posts, and Davies, Long, Bingham, Morris, Steinhardt, and several others became ambassadors. Perhaps this bestowal of jobs for support may seem crude. But it is inescapably part of the American political tradition, and nobody ever claimed that Roosevelt—quite aside from the fact that he thought these were first-rate men—did not play politics to the last fraction of an inch.

[1] *You're the Boss*, pp. 123-24.

But opposing him were some extremely powerful Democratic chief-tains, especially the right-wing conservatives and big-city bosses. They thought that he was not "big enough" to be President, that he did not have enough "capacity for leadership," and above all that he was too liberal. One politician famous in the period gave vent to the considered estimate that "all" Roosevelt had was a good name, a winning smile, and nice diction. Raskob, the chairman of the National Committee, flatly opposed him, as did Frank Hague of New Jersey, the Kelly-Nash machine in Chicago, Pendergast in Kansas City, and all the New York leaders except Flynn. The most important and delicate problem was Al Smith. Smith, as the candidate in 1928, was still titular leader of the party. Roosevelt sent Flynn to sound him out; Smith at this time, according to Flynn's story, insisted that he was not in the running himself, and did not object to Flynn and the others lining up behind FDR. Lehman too went to Smith, and got the same response.

But FDR and Smith themselves did not meet for a long time, and bitter ill-feeling developed; Smith accused Roosevelt of betraying him. Al did become a candidate after all and an aggressive one, and so Roosevelt, on his side, felt that Al had let *him* down. Probably he cleared his conscience vis à vis Smith by a rationalization to the effect that Al could not possibly win if nominated (five states of the dry, Protestant, so-called solid South had deserted the tradition of half a century to vote *against* him in 1928); that he, Roosevelt, could win; and that it was the manifest duty of all good Democrats to get together, pick a sure winner, and elect a President without any chance of a slip. Then too Al steadily came more and more under the influence of Raskob and the du Ponts and was so far to the right by this time that FDR could not possibly go along with him politically.

As the depression continued to grip the country more mercilessly and as the Republican administration steadily lost more and more public confidence a whole covey of Democratic candidates naturally sprang up. Roosevelt was well in the lead, but he had to be careful not to get too far ahead, for fear of being prematurely knocked off. Among men, aside from FDR and Smith, seriously mentioned for the nomination were Ritchie of Maryland, Byrd of Virginia, Barkley of Kentucky, Reed of Kansas, "Alfalfa Bill" Murray of Oklahoma, Joe Robinson of Arkansas, John N. Garner of Texas, Owen D. Young, Newton D. Baker, and literally dozens of others, including no fewer than four hopefuls from the state of Ohio alone.

Roosevelt was a long-minded man. To the end of his life he maintained a zealous loyalty to almost all members of the small original clique of his supporters, and indeed to most others who came out for him before the actual nomination. They remained his trusted friends for years. Conversely, he never forgave some leading Democrats who opposed him, or were lukewarm, before the Chicago convention. It is striking in the extreme that he never gave any really big job to any Democrat, no matter how eminent or potentially useful, who did not think he was fit to be President early in 1932. He maintained friendly relations with men like Baker, Cox, Davis, and Young, but he never took them into his official family. If a man, no matter how deserving otherwise, was on the 1932 blacklist, Roosevelt would not make him a dogcatcher. He never even offered Bernard M. Baruch a truly first-class post. (Baruch is supposed to have said that Roosevelt was a "wishy-washy" Governor and at that time favored Smith or Ritchie for the Presidency.) Of course one reason why FDR slighted so many of the party elders was that they were too conservative; it was not *only* a matter of personal pique. For instance the real reason (years later) for the split with Farley was identical with that over Smith; both became so unsympathetic to what he stood for, and vice versa, in the whole field of social reform and the like, that harmonious relations were impossible.

Roosevelt became an avowed candidate in January, 1932, and proceeded to beat Smith in the New Hampshire primaries and then to clean up in North Dakota against Alfalfa Bill Murray and in Georgia against Jack Garner. But he lost California, Connecticut, and Massachusetts, and very powerful figures like Hearst and McAdoo came out against him. One of his most famous pre-convention talks was the "Forgotten Man" speech; after this, every liberal in the country knew that, if words meant anything, he was their man. But the opposition of the big bosses increased in the same proportion. It was even necessary for FDR to outmaneuver Raskob and the National Committee on such a matter as where the convention was to meet.[2] Nowadays we are apt to assume that Roosevelt became President by a kind of process of inevitability. But when the convention finally met in Chicago in June the fight was by no means won, and a hard, tense struggle still lay ahead.

[2] Raskob wanted Atlantic City, where the proceedings would be dominated by the New York and New Jersey machines.

Matters of Health

During the campaign there was much surreptitious talk that Roosevelt was still a sick man; one rumor, scotched promptly by reputable physicians, was that infantile paralysis attacked the brain in the end, and that FDR was in danger of going crazy.

In actual fact he was in superb health during all of this period; he slept like a baby, and could work hour after hour, day after day, without a stop. He took out $560,000 in life insurance, with the Warm Springs Foundation as beneficiary; twenty-two different companies participated in this insurance, and that he was able to get such a substantial amount after the most rigorous physical examination proved how well he was. Then, during the second term as Governor, he took the unprecedented step of suggesting that a panel of impartial doctors look him over and make a public report. Three eminent physicians did so (Dr. Samuel W. Lambert, a diagnostician, Dr. Russell A. Hibbs, an orthopedist, and Dr. Foster Kennedy, a neurologist) and found him perfectly sound and fit. Part of their report was published as follows:

We have today examined Franklin D. Roosevelt. We find that his organs and functions are sound in all respects. There is no anemia. The chest is exceptionally well developed, and the spinal column is perfectly normal; all of its segments are in alignment, and free from disease. He has neither pain nor ache at any time.

Ten years ago, Governor Roosevelt suffered an attack of acute infantile paralysis, the entire effect of which was expended on the muscles of his lower extremities. There has been progressive recovery of power in the legs since that date; this restoration continues and will continue. . . . We believe that his powers of endurance are such as to allow him to meet all demands of private or public life.

The manner in which FDR behaved during this examination greatly impressed the doctors. He was perfectly cooperative, but otherwise paid no attention to them. The house was full of secretaries, politicians, and reporters; the doctors were several times interrupted as telegrams came or the long-distance telephone rang. Roosevelt did not seem to be in the least interested in his condition, or curious about it; in other words he knew perfectly well that he was in first-class health.

Following is the technical part of the report, which has never been printed before:

Heart: regular; rate, 80; no increased cardiac dullness; no murmurs; aortic dullness is not widened. Blood pressure 140/100.

Pulse: Regular 80—after examination by three physicians rate is 84, returning to 80 after 3 minutes. Electrocardiogram—left preponderance. Inverted T_3. PR and QRS intervals normal.

Lungs: No dullness, no changes in respiratory murmurs, no extraneous sounds or rales; no abnormalities in voice sounds or fremitus. Chest expansion good.

Abdomen: Liver and spleen, not enlarged, no pain, no masses. Abdominal muscles show slight bulging on left. No hernia. Umbilical excursion upward.

No evidence of columnar degeneration of spinal cord. Both optic nerves normal. A false Babinski reflex is present on both sides (old "polio" symptom). Right knee jerk absent. Left shows responses in upper and outer portion of quadriceps extensor.

Some coldness of feet below knees; cocktail makes them right. The lower erector spinae are slightly affected. Gluteus medius partial R. and L.

Wassermann—negative with both alcoholic and cholesterinized antigen.

No symptoms of *impotentia coeundi.*

Anybody who may have doubted FDR's physical fitness had only to observe him campaigning; he could tire out an ox. But do not think that his physical handicap made things easy. The following[3] is from a recent article by his daughter, Anna Roosevelt Boettiger:

During that campaign I learned what terrific physical effort *was* involved for Father. He was to speak at a big rally in a huge hall—in Brooklyn, I think. When we arrived there that evening, it was discovered that there was no ground-floor entrance to the stage and only a broad flight of stone steps leading up to the main entrance of the hall, with no railing to hang on to. Father didn't want to walk slowly up the long center aisle, for fear people might think he was trying to develop sympathy for himself—a sympathy aimed at making people vote for a physically courageous man rather than for one with the political and statesmanlike qualities necessary for the office.

We discovered there was a steep, iron fire-escape stairway, leading up from the ground to the stage, which was raised well up above the floor of the auditorium. In those days Father's steel braces were very heavy. But by using his strong arms and shoulders he could, slowly but surely, swing first one leg and then the other, up one step at a time. It was a tough, slow climb, and

[3] "My Life with F.D.R.," in *The Woman,* August, 1949.

Father paused for breath a couple of times. Each time he made a wisecrack to break the tension for those of us who were watching.

We weren't worried that he might fall. But we knew how he hated to have people watch him doing something that was as much effort as this and that drew attention to his paralysis. When he reached the top, his face was streaming with perspiration, and his white shirt was soaked. He paused just long enough to mop his face and catch his breath. Then he walked out on to the stage and faced the audience with a humorous remark about the fact that it was quite warm in the hall.

Enter the Brain Trust

The father of the Brain Trust was FDR himself; its first recruiting officer was Sam Rosenman; its effective head was Raymond Moley. As the campaign got under way Roosevelt saw that he must have more help. He had to talk about new issues daily, and Rosenman could no longer take the whole brunt of speech writing. Howe and Farley had their hands full (the former always at Roosevelt's elbow, the latter traveling with massive zeal) and besides they were not the type that had become needed. FDR asked Rosenman to bring in some new people, experts on every aspect of the national life, and the worthy judge suggested that, since the fat cats, big businessmen, and professional politicians had either lost their usefulness or were antagonistic, he might turn for a change to the universities. Of course Roosevelt had been in touch with several academic friends right along. One of these was Moley, professor of public law at Columbia, who had served on the State Crime Commission and helped him on several important speeches with great ability. In any event, just before he went to Warm Springs for a brief holiday early in 1932, FDR instructed Rosenman and Moley to assemble a team. The idea was to get a really first-class man in every field the campaign would touch, to dig out material for speeches, submit ideas, and otherwise give succor and advice.

Originally this Brain Trust consisted of Rosenman, Moley, Basil O'Connor, Professor Rexford Tugwell, Professor Adolf A. Berle, Jr., Professor Joseph D. McGoldrick, and Professor Lindsay Rogers. All four professors, as well as Moley, came from Columbia. Later Hugh Johnson, a protégé of Baruch's, became an important member of the group, and McGoldrick and Rogers dropped out. Others were on the fringes, like the late Charles W. Taussig, a Wall Street man with big interests in, of all things, molasses; Donald R. Richberg, the railways expert; and Joseph B. Eastman of the Interstate Commerce Commission. Moley mentions one campaign speech on which no fewer than twenty-five different experts worked. But the core of the organization, from the convention to Roosevelt's inauguration as President, remained Moley-Rosenman-Berle-Tugwell-Johnson.

So two camps grew up around Roosevelt, with the politicians in one and the professors in the other. Relations between them were outwardly amicable, but the first group looked with considerable distaste and apprehension at the influx of professors. By and large the politicians assuaged their uneasiness by deciding that, after all, these "theoreticians" like Tugwell and Berle could not count in the long run and had no relevance except in the innocuous field of speech-making. Later, when Roosevelt took them to Washington and tried to turn them into administrators, resentment grew. Louis Howe in particular held the Brain Trusters in something close to contempt, and one of Moley's jobs was to appease him and keep smooth relations between the rival camps. The phrase "Brain Trust" came originally from Howe; he threw it off in irony, as a term of ridicule. Then it was picked up by James Kieran of the New York *Times*, and instantly caught on throughout the nation. FDR's own name for it—in the early days at least—was the "Privy Council."

Now this development, this deliberate attempt by a presidential candidate to make use of expert brains, had great suggestive importance. Of course all other presidents have used experts; no president could get along without experts of one kind or another. But the way FDR did it struck an original and useful note; here, it seemed, was the application of scientific techniques to the problems of government in a new way, a tapping of the intellectual energy of the nation by scrupulously well-informed men that might bring a healthy irrigation to the whole realm of public thought. Roosevelt, by creating the Brain Trust, started out on his provocative role as elucidator and educator.[4] Also he laid the ground for violent future controversy, because a great many sound Americans thought that the Brain Trusters were dangerously radical.

Chicago, 1932

Climax came in June. Nine candidates were put up in the broiling hot convention hall, and one of the most exciting and confused fights in the history of American politics began; FDR might well have been

[4] One authority even says that nothing like the Brain Trust was known to political science since the reign of a reformist Chinese emperor in 1069.

beaten except for some fancy footwork and the convergence of some extraordinary forces. Tammany fought him to the last ditch, on the not inappropriate ground that he was a "reformer," and at least three other candidates had powerful backing; McAdoo was for Garner, and Hearst, who controlled California and Texas to some extent, held the balance of power for a time.[5] Some Southern delegations began to back away from Roosevelt, and, incredible as it may seem, FDR might have had grave or even mortal losses except for the intervention of Huey Long, who, even more incredibly, was brought to his side by Wheeler of Montana. Also the FDR managers were almost totally inexperienced in the technique of handling such an internecine fracas as a national convention. One looks back now and thinks what a master of strategy Farley was, and with what consummate skill Roosevelt himself always handled affairs of this kind, forgetting that there was a period when they had to learn. Chicago was their baptism.

Smith, the chief opponent, came to Chicago confident that he could stop FDR; his strategy was to try to force a deadlock. Roosevelt, even then, was detested so savagely by several candidates that they would have been perfectly glad to cut their own throats if that would keep *him* from the nomination, after which some compromise candidate like Ritchie or Newton D. Baker could be chosen. Roosevelt himself stayed in Albany, but he decided every major step; he talked for hours on end with Farley, Flynn, and other subchieftains on the telephone. One clever business was to hook up a loudspeaker in Howe's room, connected to Albany by private wire; here visiting delegates from various states would assemble, and cheerfully FDR would boom out a greeting to them. It was excellent politics for him to stay away. It gave him prestige, and anyway he was always a great believer in remote control.

On the first ballot FDR got 666 votes, which was 104 short of the 770 necessary. During a hot, tense night two more ballots were taken, and he edged up to 682. But there was drastic fear that this great lead might be considered as his maximum strength and, if the convention lasted long enough, be eaten away. Roosevelt did not have New York, New Jersey, Massachusetts, or Connecticut, and could not get them.

[5] A wonderful example of self-blindness in even so experienced a politician as Hague of New Jersey was his prophecy that Roosevelt, if nominated, would not carry a single state west of the Mississippi! Farley, p. 14.

His fate, it became clear, depended on California (McAdoo) and Texas (Garner). Farley desperately tried to pull Garner over by talks with Texas satraps like Sam Rayburn, Silliman Evans, and Tom Connolly. Then he telephoned Hearst at his ranch in San Simeon, California, and persuaded him that if he, Hearst, did not put pressure on McAdoo to support Roosevelt, the convention might break to Newton Baker, whom Hearst loathed, or even Smith. Hearst was in a quandary. He didn't like Roosevelt but he hated Smith. Exactly what Hearst said to Farley—and to others who got through to him on the telephone—has never been revealed fully. But his intervention was important. One story is that Hearst himself called Garner and told him that he would have to be satisfied with the Vice-Presidency. If, indeed, Hearst was the decisive factor in throwing the nomination to FDR, one would have to go through all history with a microscope to find a more striking irony.

McAdoo finally gave California to Roosevelt on the fourth ballot, and Garner released the Texas delegation; Roosevelt got 945 votes and won. Smith's vote held at the not inconsiderable figure of 190, and Al's delegates, bitter and disgruntled, refused to make the nomination unanimous or join in the victory parade. Then Garner was nominated for Vice-President. Roosevelt did not care much, at this stage, who got second place. Of course a promise to give Garner the Vice-Presidency must have been part of the Farley-Hearst-McAdoo "deal"; McAdoo was offered a reward too in the shape of a Cabinet post, but he turned it down.

With this episode, the caustic, tragic figure of Al Smith begins to pass out of history. FDR and Al maintained outwardly courteous relations, but Smith never got over his bitterness. It was, however, very important for the party and the ensuing campaign that, on the surface at least, the rift should seem to have been patched up, and at the New York convention, when FDR nominated Lehman as his successor for Governor, he and Smith publicly shook hands. Al's greeting is supposed to have been, "Hello, you old potato!" Roosevelt replied, "Al, I'm glad to see you—and that's from the heart." But they saw little of one another after that, though whenever in later years Smith called at the White House as a matter of courtesy, FDR received him cordially.

While the convention was still in session Roosevelt broke all precedent by flying to Chicago and accepting the nomination in person.

The band played "Happy Days Are Here Again." It was in this speech that he first used the phrase "New Deal."

Campaign and After

Roosevelt's campaign was a masterpiece. Of course the unfortunate Hoover was a dead duck anyway, but it is not quite correct to say, as some writers have said, that all FDR had to do was hold off and let him defeat himself. He was aggressive first, last, and all the time. Very seldom—and this was clever—did FDR attack Republicans as such; he only attacked the party's "leadership." And as a result great numbers of Republicans voted for him. Several of his advisers, including Howe, thought that he should conduct a front-porch campaign; FDR overruled them, and put on an extensive country-wide tour. One motive of this was to show himself to the people, and thus dispel any lingering rumors that he was not physically fit. He traveled 27,000 miles, and visited all but seven of the states.

Though few people knew it, FDR and Hoover had once been quite close friends. In Washington during the First World War, they met regularly as members of an informal dining club; the Hoovers and Roosevelts were both bored by the ritual of Washington society, and set aside Sunday night as an occasion when they might dine and exchange ideas privately. Sometimes they met at the home of the Franklin K. Lanes, sometimes at the Adolph Millers. FDR had high regard for Hoover as an administrator—then—though he was appalled at his lack of social tact. One interesting story is that FDR ardently tried to make Hoover declare himself as a Democrat in the early 1920's because he thought he would be a perfect candidate to succeed Wilson. In fact Roosevelt was astounded when Hoover, after a long period of refusing to take sides, suddenly announced that he was a Republican. Then the two men saw little of one another for many years, and after 1932 any semblance of personal friendship disappeared.

Everybody thinks nowadays of that 1932 campaign as a walkover; yet the Democrats faced several disadvantages. For one thing, as Flynn records, the party was gravely short of funds. (When the battle was over it was found that the Republicans had spent $2,670,000, the Democrats $1,170,000. Politics cost money in the United States.) Roosevelt's own confidence was superb; in fact, several of his speeches had been written and then filed away for use—before the nomination! The Brain Trust did its work so well that much of the material assembled was useful to FDR right into the Presidency and, indeed, up to about 1935.

The Democratic platform, which was brief and explicit, foreshadows the New Deal. It called for a greatly expanded program of public works and unemployment relief, old-age pension laws, increased control of public utilities, reform of the banking structure, repeal of Prohibition, an advanced agricultural aid program through control of crop surpluses, independence for the Philippines (an issue which had given Hoover terrible headaches), and—laughter should not be too immoderate—a 25 per cent cut in government expenses and a balanced budget.

Few people remember it now, but almost the whole of FDR's future politico-economic creed was embodied in a remarkable speech he gave at the Commonwealth Club in San Francisco on September 23, 1932. This, like his address to the New York legislature on the function of the state, should have told any attentive voter what was coming. (And voters by the million liked what was foretold.) The gist of the Commonwealth Club speech, which was written by Berle in part, was a plea for the growth of closer and more workable relations between government and people, for the furtherance of more effective and complete economic democracy, and for the "development of an economic declaration of rights." "Every man has a right to live," Roosevelt said, "and this means that he has also a right to make a comfortable living. He may . . . decline to exercise that right; but it may not be denied him. . . . Our industrial and agricultural mechanism can produce enough and to spare. Our government, formal and informal, political and economic, owes to everyone an avenue to possess himself of a portion of that plenty sufficient for his needs, through his own work." Also: "A glance at the situation today only too clearly indicates that equality of opportunity as we have known it no longer exists." Then, in another address a little later: "I believe that the individual should have full liberty of action to make the most of himself, but I do not believe that in the name of that sacred word, individualism, a few powerful interests should be permitted to make industrial cannon fodder of the lives of half the population of the United States."

Industrial cannon fodder! This was certainly a new note. Those who lived in caves in Central Park took heed; the shivering paupers selling apples took heed; so did the miserable lines of hungry waiting before the soup kitchens. There were, it might be mentioned, no fewer than fourteen *million* unemployed in America by this time; the entire economic machinery of the country seemed to have broken down. So it is not difficult to understand why the great mass of people lifted their hearts to Roosevelt's spirited cry for reform, recovery, and faith. FDR was elected by an overwhelming margin, 22,813,786 votes to 15,759,266 for Hoover, and was the first Democratic President in eighty years to get a clear majority of the popular vote—57 per cent. The extent of the victory was much greater measured in terms of states; FDR got 472 electoral votes to Hoover's 59. He carried, in fact, all states but six; he carried *every* state south and west of Pennsylvania. Seldom in American history had the people spoken with such emphasis. But not one in millions could have dreamed that the man they had just elected would remain in the White House almost thirteen years.

Man of the Left

The 1932 campaign confirmed once for all, if any confirmation was necessary, that FDR was a phenomenon rare in American politics, a man of imposing stature more to the Left than Right. In an era when the geographical frontier was closed, when it was no longer possible for an economic crisis to be solved by a natural movement of the unemployed to the west, and when the whole financial and industrial structure had collapsed in an atmosphere of gloom and panic, Roosevelt proposed to *do* something, first by government-administered relief in the period of emergency, then by a vast structure of ameliorative reform. FDR sought to replace economic anarchy by a society at least partially planned, to set up a system of controls which would forfend further disaster. Of course the nation had had what is now called "statism" before. What are public schools and public roads if not examples of statism? But Roosevelt enormously accelerated the process by which the United States started out on a road that may lead some day to the full welfare state. This is his chief contribution to domestic American affairs, and the one for which he is most vociferously defamed.

The spectacle of a patrician, an aristocrat, becoming a man of the people is rare in history, and hence challenging. The number of genuine aristocrats who became mass leaders and made their leadership effective is small in the extreme. One may call to mind Mirabeau, the Gracchi, Cavour, Pericles, and, above all, Lord Buddha. In contemporary times the closest analogy to Roosevelt is probably Jawa-harlal Nehru, the Indian Prime Minister. Nehru, an aristocrat of impeccable lineage who became a socialist, a man of the masses who at the same time remained the most sophisticated and rational of individualists, has many points of close resemblance to FDR. One parallel is that Nehru spent so many years—fourteen—in jail. The paralysis that constrained Roosevelt, the braces that made him a similar prisoner, had much the same effect on his character that actual prison walls had on the Indian, in producing vision, fortitude, and temperance. And, in a way, the case might be made that just as Nehru brought India to political freedom, so did Roosevelt give America a type of economic freedom it never had before.

In a totally different direction another historical juxtaposition needs further mention, the fact that Adolf Hitler came to power in Germany just five weeks before Roosevelt came to power in the United States. Moreover both men died within a few weeks of one another in the spring of 1945, after more than twelve uninterrupted years in office. Had it not been for Hitler, of course, FDR almost certainly would not have run for the third and fourth terms. And Roosevelt became Hitler's worst enemy, and a principal author of his plangent doom.

How much of Roosevelt's leftness was "sincere"; how much did he adopt a leftist position to gain votes? This sounds like a trick question. In fact it is. Of course Roosevelt was sincere; a test of this is that, once he got the votes, he never let the voters down. Internal belief and external opportunity merged to fit his hand. Also one should point out that FDR's leftist sentiments go far back, long before he was an important politician; he worked for a "Progressive Democratic" party and founded a reformist movement known as "the Empire State Democracy" way back in 1920. Of course he was happy to have the votes people gave him. What politician wouldn't? But the plain fact is that the more he stayed himself, the more votes he got.

In the interregnum between Roosevelt's election and inauguration what remained of the nation's financial order collapsed. Unemployment rose to seventeen millions, agriculture was prostrate, privation became desperate, and people were almost completely gripped by panic and despair. On March 4, 1933, at six minutes after one in the afternoon, with the nation thus smitten by the most unpredictably menacing crisis since the Civil War, Franklin Delano Roosevelt became the thirty-second President of the United States. He was fifty-one years and thirty-three days old.

Chapter 16

PEACE PRESIDENT

*I believe that our industrial and economic system is
made for individual men and women, and not individual
men and women for the benefit of the system. I believe
in the sacredness of private property, which means I do
not believe that it should be subjected to the ruthless
manipulation of professional gamblers and the corpo-
rate system.*

—FRANKLIN DELANO ROOSEVELT

To try to compress the presidential years of Franklin D. Roosevelt into
a chapter or two is like trying to squeeze a football into an inkwell. A
proper study of Roosevelt as President during the colossal epoch 1933-
1945 would, it is only too manifest, take volumes. Anyway this part of
his life is so well known that I do not apologize for skimping it. Let us
confine ourselves to the sparse and minimum essentials.

First, however, no matter how briefly, it may be wise to outline the
main divisions of this titanic period: (1) the banking crisis, resolution
of the emergency, and the "Hundred Days"; (2) the experiments of the
first New Deal; (3) the consolidation of the New Deal into permanent
social legislation; (4) the Supreme Court fight; (5) the growth of preoccupation with foreign affairs; (6) the third term crisis; (7) industrial
mobilization and the transition from peace to war; (8) winning the
war; (9) preparing for the peace.

Expressed in another dimension the presidential years fall into three
fairly well-defined segments, though with considerable overlapping:
(1) the period 1933-39, when technically at least most of the world was
at peace; (2) 1939-41, when Europe fought but America did not; (3)
1941-45, the years of universal war. Then I have heard a shrewd student
of Roosevelt proffer still another classification: (1) the period of orderly
change, which lasted till the late 30's, when FDR ruled by the ordinary
processes of popular and Congressional majority; (2) an ensuing period
of education and persuasion, during which he had to cajole and
manipulate public opinion into following him, despite his majority;

276

(3) the period of rule by what came close to mass consent, after 1941.

Second, we should have at least a word on the presidency in general. The president is commander in chief, he appoints Federal judges and multitudinous other officers, he directs foreign policy, he may veto bills passed by Congress and issue executive orders that have the force of law, and so on ad infinitum as every schoolboy knows. Moreover he is not merely chief of the American nation but also the leader of the majority party, which means that he fulfills a difficult double role in what is anyway by far the most complex job in the world. Administration is not the biggest task of a president; his biggest task is to gain consent on as wide an arc as possible. The basic objectives of a good president should be to find out what the people want, and then get it for them. But, of necessity, the president is not merely the personage on whom all pressures converge; he is a political pressure himself as well. Also, though his powers are majestic and incomparable, he has to know how to make use of them to be effective. A weak president has exactly the same constitutional powers as a strong president. Mr. Truman, in theory, can do everything that his predecessor did. But as we are well aware, few presidents ever exert the command that FDR exerted; one of his prime secrets was the marvelously skillful *use* he made of presidential power.

Third, a word about the White House, which became the Roosevelt home from 1933 to 1945. From the outside it was, and is, a building of surpassing dignity, grace, and calm distinction; inside, it was old-fashioned, seedy, and from the housekeeping point of view almost impossible to maintain. Mrs. Nesbitt, the Roosevelt housekeeper, has described pungently how, when she took over, she was faced with such a problem as squeezing two and a half crates of lemons with an old-fashioned hand squeezer, how she could not work up any enthusiasm for the cockroaches in the antiquated wooden kitchen, and how the public rooms were intolerably difficult to keep clean (the chandeliers in the East Room alone contained 22,000 pieces of glass each). The living quarters were cramped and uncomfortable, and the place was overrun day in and day out by visitors. Until 1891 the White House had only one bathroom; until the regime of Theodore Roosevelt at least, it was full of rats. Mr. Truman discovered, on taking the mansion over, that it was actually unsafe; today the whole structure is being carefully pulled apart and put together again. One striking minor point is that, until FDR, the home of the President of the United States had no library. Belated shame overcame the publishers and booksellers of the country in the 1930's, and they contributed enough books to start one; most of these are still housed in temporary cases along the halls. Another point is the friendly ease and informality that have always marked the atmosphere of the first home of the nation. For instance the front doorman for many years doubled as the President's barber, and how often the sheets should be changed and what the cook should do with leftovers were just as acute problems as in any well-run house in Chillicothe, Ohio, or Burlington, Vermont.

The Hundred Days

The keynote of the Hundred Days was Roosevelt's phrase, "The only thing we have to fear is fear itself." The first duty of the new President was, obviously, to restore confidence to the stricken nation, lift it to its feet. FDR had to be soothing, hortatory, calm, decisive, and strenuously practical all at once. He blew hope into the deflated body of the country like a boy blowing up a balloon. The people listened to the inaugural address and then to the first Fireside Chat a few days later, and felt that the man in the White House was their friend, as well as leader, who would save them from further catastrophe no matter what. Almost audibly, a sigh of relief went up through the entire land.

FDR summoned Congress for a special session on March 9, 1933, and this remained sitting until June 16—hence the locution "Hundred Days." Seldom in any parliamentary history has so much been done so quickly.

It is interesting to recall that Roosevelt's first emergency powers, which were of unprecedented range, were based on an obscure item of financial war legislation in 1917; FDR was, in a sense, a war President from his first day in office. It is interesting, too, that the Banking Act, the first of all the multitudinous bills that he signed in thirteen years, and which among much else gave him control of all transactions in foreign exchange and the right to sequester all the gold in the country, as well as to keep any bank closed for any period he directed, was not only passed by Congress in a single day's session, but was passed without any debate or even a roll call in the House, without any committee consideration at all, and with only the briefest treatment in the Senate.

Roosevelt, it might be mentioned parenthetically, always strove to work *with* Congress; this is a point often forgotten these days, but it was vital. No president ever approached the prerogatives of the legislative body with more scrupulously delicate attention. But the pressure of the emergency was so electrically intense and the power of Mr. Roosevelt's voice so universally persuasive that Congress did anything—or almost anything—he wished. In fact, if FDR had not taken the lead in vigorous emergency legislation, Congress itself would have seized the initiative and done the job, well or badly. The country, as never before, was in a mood for action. And action was what it got.

Immediately the Banking Act was signed Roosevelt sent his Economy Bill to Congress; it cut Government salaries 15 per cent, drastically reduced pensions to war veterans, imposed excess profit and dividend taxes, and promised a budget reduction of 25 per cent. Then things came thick and fast. The banks began to reopen. On March 13, Roosevelt asked for repeal of Prohibition. On March 15, the Stock Exchange reopened. A day later the framework for the first of the great New Deal agencies, the Agricultural Adjustment Administration (A.A.A.), went before Congress. This only two weeks after the inauguration! On March 21 FDR asked for the creation of the Civilian Conservation Corps, to provide work for youthful unemployed, and a few days later came the Securities Act which paved the way for the Securities and Exchange Commission (S.E.C.) and sounded the death of the old Wall Street forever. On April 3 the President laid the Farm Relief Act before Congress, and a week later the bill to create the Tennessee Valley Authority (T.V.A.), the most enduring of all New Deal agencies, was formulated. On April 13 came the act creating the Home Owners Loan Corporation (H.O.L.C.), to finance small mortgages. On April 20 the country went off the gold standard; people gasped as if the end of the world had come.[1] Early in May FDR proceeded with the first Federal Relief Act and the Railway Reorganization Act, and then came an appropriation of $3,300,000,000 for relief through public works—an utterly unprecedented sum—and, above all, the National Industrial Recovery Act, which produced the stupendous experiment of N.R.A. Finally, on the last day of this extraordinary session, came the Glass-Steagall Act which created the Federal Deposit Insurance Fund and guaranteed bank deposits.

Lytton Strachey wrote once that all great men of action have to be empiricists; certainly Roosevelt was. What he wanted was something that would *work;* he didn't care how; he moved by intuition and cared

[1] Lewis Douglas actually said, "This means the end of western civilization." Mr. Douglas is at present Ambassador to the Court of St. James's.

for little but results. He was perfectly capable of advocating the policy of the Good Neighbor with one hand at one moment, and scuttling the London Economic Conference with the other at the next; of proposing inflationary legislation on one day, and deflationary legislation the day after. All that really counted in his mind was pulling the country out of the grimy abyss into which it had fallen—and quickly. In any case, for good or ill, he did more to alter the basic structure of the nation's economic life in one hundred days than anybody else had done in one hundred years. And through the whole prodigious upheaval he remained debonair, unalterably sure of himself, level-tempered, and relaxed.

Lord Bryce wrote in *The American Commonwealth*: "The federal executive has no influence on legislation, and even in foreign policy and in the making of appointments it requires the consent of the senate. That any man should acquire so great a hold on the country as to secure the election of two houses of Congress subservient to his will, while at the same time securing the Presidency . . . for himself, is an event too improbable to enter into calculation." That, written in 1893, made strange reading in 1933, as it makes strange reading now. One well-known Washington correspondent wrote an article after FDR had been in office a few months outlining "the living facts of the new dictatorship," and listing seventy-seven specific grants of power given him which no president had ever had before.

Nevertheless the Hundred Days were a honeymoon, and like all honeymoons it came to an end. Before the year was out Roosevelt was having trouble aplenty, and a hard burning core of hatred for all he stood for became immovably fixed in the minds of many, though millions continued to adore him.

New Deal: Atmospherics

All this happened only fifteen years or so ago; time softens the sharp contours of yesterday; much that was sensational then is generally taken for granted now. Even the comparatively innocuous proposal to remove hungry, loitering boys off the streets and put them to useful work in the C.C.C. camps was considered outrageous, if not actually revolutionary, by most conservatives in 1933. (Some conservatives still think it was outrageous and revolutionary.) It is difficult to recapture fully the exalted excitements, frustrations, and confusions of Washington in 1933 and 1934. The city simmered and boiled.

Also it became what it had never really been before, the capital of the United States.

I remember arriving one evening and registering at a good, sound, conservative hotel and telephoning a New Deal friend; he asked me where I was staying and when I told him he replied in a shocked voice, "But that's the haunt of our enemies!" I remember an irreverent newspaperman saying that what the forlorn Republicans were awaiting was the "second coming of Capital"; I remember another friend furiously calling a millionaire an "anarchist" because he lined up with the NRA; I remember the idealistic fanaticism with which an intimate of the White House told me, "What we have here is an alliance of King and Commons against the Lords!"

Dorothy Thompson, in the early days of NRA, wrote a famous and brilliant article proving that the New Deal was Fascist. The late Frank H. Simonds wrote a famous and brilliant article proving that it was Communist. John Maynard Keynes wrote a famous and brilliant article proving that it was neither.

What could the opposition do? When the Republicans made jokes about "From New Deal to New Dole" it did not win them the votes of the hungry; when they said that fifteen or more million unemployed could be absorbed "naturally" everybody knew that this was blind nonsense; they could not sabotage the New Deal by making a panic because this would irretrievably complete the destruction of what Roosevelt hadn't got around to "destroying" yet, and after all they were capitalists even before they were Republicans; they faced a world in which the depression, so it seemed, had made practically everybody a Democrat, and "Hunger" was a bad slogan as against "Relief."

I met one shrewd conservative in 1934 who said, "FDR is simply trying to patch up the works, like Mussolini. He will pull the nationalist card essential to Fascism out of the top drawer some day and then we will have war with Japan."

I met one shrewd liberal who said, "The New Deal is simply the effort of a lot of half-baked Socialists to save capitalism for the dumb capitalists." (This, be it noted, was before the neat locutions "free enterprise" and "management" had replaced "capitalism" and "capital" in the conversation of polite society.)

Fermentation and experiment, wild hope after wild despair, conspiratorial glee and conspiratorial hatred, jealous suspense and volatility—these were keynotes. "Don't you know what FDR is doing?"

I heard a distinguished judge exclaim passionately in 1934. "Playing tiddlywinks with the entire universe!"

New Deal: Personalities

Roosevelt had his Cabinet picked before the inauguration; the two men he chose first, and whom he never had any doubt about, were Farley for Postmaster General, and George H. Dern of Utah, whom he had met and liked at various governors' conferences, for Secretary of War. State went to Hull, the Treasury to Will Woodin, Agriculture to Wallace, Labor to Perkins, Commerce to Daniel C. Roper of South Carolina (a gesture of appeasement to McAdoo), Navy to Swanson of Virginia, and Interior to Ickes. Homer Cummings of Connecticut became Attorney General, when Walsh of Montana died two days before he was to be sworn in. Of these no fewer than three—Wallace, Woodin, and Ickes—were, or had been, Republicans. Two were senators; FDR had a close eye for Congress. Of the whole group only two, by conventional definition, could be called true New Dealers, Ickes and Frances Perkins.[2]

The leading New Dealers came out of the Brain Trust, though this ceased meeting as a regular body after the inauguration. Moley became Assistant Secretary of State, Tugwell Assistant Secretary of Agriculture, and Johnson head of the NRA. Others conspicuous were Jerome Frank, Donald Richberg, Mordecai Ezekiel, Hopkins of course, and two lively and attractive young lawyers, Thomas G. Corcoran and Benjamin V. Cohen. Later came Leon Henderson, Thurman Arnold, William O. Douglas, and a host of others. Senator Wagner of New York was always a close influence. At the beginning FDR kept good relations with several advisers much more orthodox and conservative, like Lewis Douglas who was the first Director of the Budget, and Dean Acheson whose abrupt departure from the Treasury we have already recorded. Sumner Welles and William Phillips were pillars of the State Department. The New Dealers were, in fact, an actual minority in the official family. Men who could not be called

---

[2] It may be useful, even if it means jumping ahead of our story, to list all Roosevelt's Cabinet members. In his total Presidency he had two Secretaries of State (Hull, Stettinius), two Secretaries of the Treasury (Woodin, Morgenthau), and four Attorneys General (Cummings, Murphy, Jackson, Biddle). War had three men (Dern, Woodring, Stimson), Navy three (Swanson, Edison, Knox), Commerce four (Roper, Hopkins, Jones, Wallace), and Agriculture two (Wallace, Wickard). Frank Walker replaced Farley as Postmaster General in 1940. Only two, Miss Perkins and Harold Ickes, stayed the whole route in their original jobs.

New Dealish by any stretch of the imagination—Jesse Jones, Leo Crow-ley, Joe Robinson, Hull, Garner, Farley, and a dozen more—often overshadowed them.

Of those men who had heretofore influenced Roosevelt and whom we have mentioned in the course of this book, several began to drop out. Howe became ill, had to keep to his bed, and lost much of his usefulness. But he died happy; he had made a President. FDR's two other secretaries, Early and McIntyre, rose correspondingly in im-portance, though neither was ever much of a New Dealer, and Missy LeHand's influence grew. One powerful sustained force was Felix Frankfurter, who served as a kind of recruiting officer for the whole Administration, particularly in finding young lawyers for the mush-rooming net of new Government agencies. Among Frankfurter "men," at this time and later, were Stimson, Acheson, Biddle, MacLeish, Jerome Frank, Ben Cohen, Lloyd Garrison, who became head of the National Labor Relations Board, and James M. Landis, who filled usefully a variety of important posts.

Of all the early New Dealers the most pungent and useful was probably Tom Corcoran. For a few years after 1934, in fact, the New Deal could scarcely have continued to exist without him; he "operated on a shoestring" and often pretended to have more White House authority than he really had, but he got things done. His vivacity was an almost universal stimulus. His star began to fall, how-ever, as that of Harry Hopkins rose. The last big job he and Cohen did for FDR was organization of the Temporary National Economic Com-mittee (T.N.E.C.) in 1938. But by that period the New Deal was on its last legs, because the war was coming, and during the war itself Cor-coran played no substantial role.

It is highly suggestive and interesting to note that many New Dealers who were denounced by the conservative community as howl-ing radicals and "purveyors of revolution" in the 1930's have become pillars of contemporary respectability. Corcoran and Arnold are prosperous corporation lawyers, MacLeish holds one of the most venerable and respected of chairs at Harvard, and Frankfurter him-self has become one of the most conservative justices the Supreme Court has ever had.

New Deal: What It Was

The first great pivotal structures were, as already pointed out, the AAA and NRA. The former was designed to promote agricultural recovery and reform, the latter industrial recovery and reform. The gist of the AAA, a complicated measure improvised far too hastily and ambitiously, was its effort to raise agricultural prices and bring a tolerable livelihood back to the farmer by (1) curtailing production and (2) subsidizing certain crops. No Roosevelt measure in the domestic sphere ever caused more bitter criticism, in part because millions of young hogs were slaughtered to keep production of pork down. In fact the AAA was vulnerable on several scores, and FDR was probably delighted when the Supreme Court declared it unconstitutional in 1936. Then, in 1938, came a second and much more workable AAA, the content of which is still fundamental to our agricultural policy; for instance American farmers still get tremendous subsidies without which many of them could not survive, and the Government still controls and supports farm prices. Roosevelt's AAA set in motion forces which, in other words, are only now coming into full play.

The NRA was designed to stimulate industrial recovery by a whole set of new processes, some of them half-baked in the extreme, and some dangerous in that they encouraged price-fixing and monopoly. Industry was to be "codified" under the Blue Eagle, almost in the pattern of the corporative state. But also NRA contained provisions for eliminating unfair competition, raising wages, improving working conditions generally, and in effect abolishing child labor. What is more, its famous clause 7(a) provided for collective bargaining, which meant that labor was legally assured the right "to bargain with employers through representatives of their own choosing," i.e., their unions. This was a historic landmark. For out of it came the whole contemporary development of the American labor movement, from the birth of the CIO to the proliferating economic—and political—power now held by the major unions. The NRA, like the AAA, was declared unconstitutional by the Supreme Court, and died presently; but, again as in the case of agriculture, it laid seeds which still sprout headily today. The Wagner Act followed it in 1935.

Something that did survive intact from the earliest days of the New Deal was what, in final estimate, may prove to be its most permanent monument, the Tennessee Valley Authority. Defined in the simplest way TVA was a project for harnessing a hitherto savage and obstreperous river in seven states and developing its valley for the service of the people as a whole. TVA was mercilessly attacked. It represented the concept of decentralized government planning on an extremely ambitious scale, and touched everything in its watershed from reforestation and reclamation to cheap electric power, from flood control and rural education to the most advanced techniques in agriculture. Its real essence, which FDR seized at once, was its attempt to get man and nature working together to restore life to the land. TVA has, so far, saved some three million acres from destruction by soil erosion; it has raised the average income in the valley by not less than 495 per cent in fifteen years. The project was, in part, the brain child of Senator George Norris of Nebraska, Roosevelt became an enthusiastic foster parent, and its chairman for many years was David E. Lilienthal, who later became head of the Atomic Energy Commission. (Incidentally, the atomic bomb could never have been produced when it was except by virtue of the enormous supplies of electricity made available by TVA.)

After the Hundred Days came a bewildering succession of other measures. The Federal Emergency Relief Administration (F.E.R.A.), under Harry Hopkins, got under way with a $500,000,000 appropriation for direct relief. This was followed by the short-lived Civil Works Administration (C.W.A.), also run by Hopkins, which gave four million men temporary work and which cost roughly a billion dollars—such figures may seem small now, but they were considered monstrous then. The period of acute emergency had passed; what Roosevelt was trying to do was "prime the pump," i.e., increase the purchasing power of the consumer to the point where "it would percolate upward and start the factory wheels again." The Public Works Administration (P.W.A.) was set up under Ickes, by authority of a clause in the NRA act; this took a million men off the relief rolls by early 1934, as a public building program started slowly. Finally in this field came the creation of the Works Progress Administration (W.P.A.), in 1935, with Hopkins as administrator. Within a few months some 3,000,000 men and women had WPA jobs—everybody will remember stories about the leafpickers and ditchdiggers—and the largest public works program ever attempted by any government was inaugurated. We are tempted to neglect these days some concrete accomplishments. These projects cost a colossal amount of money; of course there were scandals and abuses; yet PWA and WPA between them did a great deal to improve the physical plant of the United States. Think not merely of Bonneville Dam and the Triborough Bridge in New York but of ten thousand schoolhouses, ewers, culverts, athletic fields, post offices, airports, and swimming pools in towns and villages all the way from Maine to California.

Nor is this all. In various fields came at one time or another the Fair Labor Standards Act, the Pure Food and Drug Act (which was savagely attacked by those whose feathers were being clipped), the Commodity Credit Corporation, the Export-Import Bank, and the Public Utility Act. One seminal development was establishment of the Rural Electrification Administration, to assist electrification of the countryside; another was the setting up of the Farm Security Administration. Then there were multitudinous acts and regulations having to do with everything from soil conservation to civil aeronautics, from the merchant marine to railway pensions, from soft-coal mining to crop insurance. Many of these measures in the field of socio-economic amelioration were bitterly fought at the time; almost all are now so deeply embedded into the fabric of American life that no one even thinks of them. Above all there came the great Social Security Act of 1935, which FDR called the "supreme achievement" by his Administration. It is indeed odd to think back fifteen years and reflect that, until Roosevelt, old-age and unemployment insurance did not even exist in the United States.

New Deal: Opposition

The New Deal alienated a large segment of the business community of the country, most of the propertied class, roughly 80 per cent of the newspapers, and most of the rich, the archaic, and the privileged. Two main reasons account for this. First, fear that Roosevelt's "deficit spending" would result in a permanently unbalanced budget and wreck the finances of the country. Second, indignation at soaring taxes. "Tax the wealth" was, quite frankly, FDR's keynote. Then too many citizens perfectly honest, decent, and patriotic felt acute worry that the New Deal, if its implications were fully pursued, would produce new, frightening, and revolutionary changes in the very bedrock of American society. "Let us make America over," said the New Dealers, "let us establish a system of production for use, not profit." But this, said the anti-New Dealers, would eventually mean regimentation, socialism, the collapse of free enterprise, and an end to the American dream of rewards based on individualism and competition.

Almost all Americans believe in the free enterprise system—

when it is working. What made suspicion and fear of Roosevelt so rancorous was the fear that he would kill the spirit of the country so thoroughly that free enterprise would never get a chance to work effectively again.

Roosevelt's spending in the New Deal seems, however, puny in the perspective of today. Even Hoover left a deficit of some four billion dollars. FDR, it is true, spent enormously more than any president in history, but by far the greater part of the debt his administrations piled up came unavoidably as a result of the war. In 1940 the public debt of the nation was 42 billion dollars; in 1946 it was 270 billions. Even in the later days of the New Deal the naval expansion program cost as much as relief and public works together. Today the budget for defense alone (roughly 13.3 billions in 1950) is more than twice the *total* Roosevelt budget of 1934. The foreign aid program alone from 1945 to date has cost $24,000,000,000, which is more than three times the *total* Roosevelt expenditures of 1938. Today's budget of some 42 billions compares to New Deal budgets of 6 to 7 billions. And servicing of the public debt, huge as this is and granting that it should be pruned, only takes a comparatively small percentage of the national revenue today.

Did Roosevelt's spending wreck the country? In 1949 the national income reached 220 billion dollars, which is twice what it was in any prewar year. Some 60,000,000 persons were employed, and revenue from taxes alone was almost as great as the *total* national income during the depression. "We live under conditions of prosperity that a decade ago would have appeared impossible to achieve. . . . The country has come through a time of spending by whose standards President Roosevelt's New Deal profligacy was Lilliputian."[3] Wreck the country, indeed!

Business, particularly big business, hated Roosevelt with ferocity; but it has much to thank him for. He did, at least, help to resuscitate the nation out of collapse. His role was that of a receiver in bankruptcy. Controls of some new sort were as inevitable—and necessary— as traffic lights.

It is easy to understand why Roosevelt was detested so tenaciously (except by enough Americans to elect him President with large majorities four times); plenty of people today hate him dead even more than they ever hated him alive. Dislike of FDR produced some marvelous wishful thinking. As distinguished a political commentator as Mark

[3] Raymond Swing in the *Atlantic Monthly*.

Sullivan predicted in 1935 that he would be a "one-term president"; a historian formerly so well respected as Charles A. Beard wrote in the same year that "Roosevelt's spell of leadership has been definitely broken."

One item often neglected in retrospect is that Roosevelt faced opposition not merely from the Right but from the crackpot Left. Huey Long, Father Coughlin, Gerald L. K. Smith, and all the demagogues of that moldy variety were at the peak of their influence in the 30's; if they had combined and organized to capture the vote of the discontented the danger to FDR could have been formidable. Nevertheless he would have no dealings with them (except for some brief political contact with Long) and he despised and condemned almost all that they stood for. Some of his own advisers wanted him to support the Townsend Plan for old-age pensions; it might have brought him millions of new votes. He would have none of it, and worked out instead the more moderate, sensible, and humane social security statute that is in force today.

New Deal: Roosevelt's Own View

What did FDR himself think of these sweeping and irreversible developments? One thing to say is that he did not seek to impose a new system on the nation to demonstrate a theory. Quite the contrary. Events produced his policy; policy did not produce the events. Roosevelt was no revolutionist, if you mean by revolutionist someone who forcibly seizes power and by peremptory methods alters the form and structure of a regime. He was a Dutch burgher at heart, and his fundamental motive was not to smash the existing order, but to save it. But if by "revolution" one means a permanent, if gradual, shift in the basis of economic power in a community, the progressive transfer of wealth from rich to poor, then certainly Roosevelt made one. Only a man of the Left *could* have saved capitalism, because what capitalism needed was reform. FDR fought off socialism, so to speak, by reforming capitalism—but in the process he let a lot of socialism in.

Roosevelt knew that reform and defense of the nation against future economic catastrophe would cost money, but in the beginning at least he always thought in terms of a balanced budget. Many of his early critics, far from accusing him of extravagance, thought that he did not spend enough.

FDR was always pragmatic, and, as we know, a compromiser. This was no fanatic preaching authoritarian doctrine; he was a man of reason gripped by fierce crisis who looked for practical ways out. "Mr. Roosevelt," wrote John Maynard Keynes, "has made himself the trustee for those in every country who seek to mend the evils of our condition by reasoned experiment within the framework of the existing system. If he fails, rational change will be gravely prejudiced throughout the world, leaving orthodoxy and revolution to fight it out. But if he succeeds new and bolder methods will be tried everywhere."[4]

Indeed, as time went on, FDR saw that the crash of 1929 was not merely a catastrophe but "the end of an era," and that "recovery was not enough." He became spokesman for the doctrine, altogether new to American history, that the Government had the duty and obligation to *provide* jobs for its citizens in distress. He said forthrightly that a government "that cannot take care of its old, that cannot provide work for the strong and willing, that lets the black shadow of insecurity rest on every home, is not a government that can or should endure," and that "a new and fairer order" must be established on "a wider distribution of wealth and property."

The New Deal (1) installed the beginnings of a system of planned economy without ever resorting to police power or terror; (2) it achieved in a few years, during a great depression, and without any violation whatsoever of civil liberties, by popular mandate of the people, what it had taken Great Britain (as an example) several generations to achieve; (3) it was one of the few successful gradualist revolutions in history; (4) it had profound emotional results in lifting up the mental climate of most of the nation, stirring citizens to new hope and faith, and in particular giving courage and reinforcement to the younger generation; (5) it is the essential precursor of the basic struggle in American politics today between Mr. Truman's "Fair Deal" and his opponents who cry out against "statism" and the welfare state.

Consider what has happened in twenty years elsewhere in the world. In the United States the free enterprise system, though restricted and modified, still survives and works, and it is working terrifically well. We have virtually full employment, and national income is at an all-time high. But Hitler wrecked Germany, Mussolini wrecked Italy, the war lords wrecked Japan; China has disintegrated into chaos and gone Communist, and Great Britain has had five years of a Labor gov-

[4] The *Times*, London, January 2, 1934.

ernment; Italy is shaky, and in France the Communists are the largest single party.

Nobody should think that the hundreds and thousands of honest men and women who opposed the New Deal were villains or criminals; the opposition contained millions of good Americans of the utmost decency. They disliked the spasmodic and chaotic quality of much of Roosevelt's policy; they were suspicious of his "opportunism" and his tendency to fly off half-cocked; they hated his seeming recklessness with both principles and dollars. Much Roosevelt legislation was indefensible from the point of view of consistency, and the New Deal certainly did not solve the problem of unemployment; there were still 9,300,000 unemployed in 1940. What solved unemployment was defense and the rearmament program.[5]

But to return to FDR's own words. I know no better, simpler expression of his general point of view than the following, which was an extemporaneous statement thrown off at a press conference in 1935:

The social objective, I should say, remains just what it was, which is to do what any honest government of any country would do: to try to increase the security and the happiness of a larger number of people in all occupations of life and in all parts of the country; to give them more of the good things of life, to give them a greater distribution not only of wealth in the narrow terms, but of wealth in the wider terms; to give them places to go in the summer-time—recreation; to give them assurance that they are not going to starve in their old age; to give honest business a chance to go ahead and make a reasonable profit, and to give everyone a chance to earn a living.[6]

Years later, in 1943, at another press conference, when "Dr. New Deal" had given way to "Dr. Win the War," FDR reminisced briefly about the torrential early days and ad-libbed a list of major New Deal accomplishments:

Old Dr. New Deal saved the banks of the United States and set up a sound banking system. We don't need to change the law now, although obviously there are some people who don't like saving the banks . . . so that banks would have the great privilege under American freedom of going "bust" any time they wanted to again.

[5] On the other hand the amount of recovery FDR *did* produce should not be minimized. The national income went up from 46 billions to 68 billions between 1932 and 1936, gross farm income from 4½ to 8½ billions, and wages and salaries from 31 to 42 billions. "Even net profits of corporations went up from 4 billion in the red to 6½ billion in the black." Alan Barth, "F.D.R. as a Politician," *Harper's Magazine*, February, 1945.

[6] Rosenman, Vol. IV, pp. 236-37.

In those days, another remedy was saving homes from foreclosure, through the HOLC; saving farms from foreclosure by the Farm Credit Administration. I suppose some people today would like to repeal all that and go back to the conditions of 1932, when the people out West mobbed a Federal Judge because he was trying to carry out the existing law of the land in foreclosing a farm; rescuing agriculture from disaster—which it was pretty close to—by the Triple A and Soil Conservation; establishing truth in the sale of securities and protecting stock investors through the SEC. And yet I happen to know that there is an undercover drive going on in this country today to repeal the SEC, and "let's sell blue-sky securities to the widows and orphans and everybody else in this country." A lot of people would like to do that, take off all the rules and let old Mr. Skin skin the public again.

Well, we have got slum clearance—decent housing; and there hasn't been enough done on slum clearance. I don't think that people who go into slums in this country would advocate stopping that, or curtailing the program, although of course a small percentage of real-estate men would like to have slums back again, because they pay money.[7]

Then he proceeded to make a long list of other reformist legislation—old-age insurance, unemployment insurance, the principle of a minimum wage and maximum hours, reduction of farm tenancy, abolition of child labor, the reciprocal trade agreements, stimulation of private home building, the breaking up of the utility monopolies, the resettlement of farmers from marginal lands, flood control, drought control, water conservation, assistance to farm cooperatives, and the ever-normal granary.

Finally, FDR was convinced that by having saved the system of private profit and free enterprise "after it had been dragged to the brink of ruin," he also saved democracy itself, by giving it a proper chance to work. He thought of himself, in fact, as the savior of capitalism and democracy both. "The President's highest hope," an intimately informed interviewer wrote in 1937, "is to leave democracy stronger than he found it and set an insurmountable barrier against the encroachments of other systems. In the long view of history he wants this to be his political epitaph."[8]

The Kerensky Analogy

Several writers on Roosevelt have suggested a contrary view, namely that his role in history may have been that of Alexander Kerensky, that far from being remembered as the savior of democracy he may

[7] Rosenman, Vol. XII, pp. 571-72.
[8] Arthur Krock in the New York *Times*, February 28, 1937.

turn out to have opened the path to its destruction. Of course this analogy does not hold water. Kerensky was a failure and was succeeded by the Communists largely because during his period in office he did *not* achieve substantial reform, which—above all—was what Roosevelt did.

It amused FDR to be compared to Kerensky, and he enjoyed learning that he was actually called "Kerensky" in the secret code of one foreign power before the war. One day he had a talk with the ambassador of this power, and casually handed him a memorandum which he signed with a flourish, "A. Kerensky Roosevelt."

Personal Interlude

Roosevelt went at the job of the Presidency as if he had been Chief Executive all his life; he loved the job and throve on it. He was the first president in more than eighty years to be at home in the White House when he got there, and he became more at home day by day. The country might be sick, the times might be out of joint, but his optimistic hopes and sanguine temperament were not affected. He took up burdens of responsibility such as no president had had to face since Lincoln, and flourished on them as if he were having the best time of his life.

Dr. Foster Kennedy, one of the physicians who had looked him over in 1931, dropped in at the White House late in 1935 and found him in better shape than he had been three years before. Kennedy laughed and said, "Nothing seems able to kill you; we will have to take you out in the yard and shoot you like an old horse."

Roosevelt smiled, "Oh, no, you can't do that! Too many of those fellows out there watching!" He pointed to the guards. Then he grew serious and turned to Kennedy, "Really, Doctor, do you think this carcass of mine will stand the racket a while longer?"

Kennedy replied: "Yes, it will—but I have a lot of high-flown Wall Street friends who are quite sure that the country cannot." FDR tossed his head back and laughed heartily.

A year or two later Dr. Kennedy saw him again, and once more found him to be in first-class spirits and condition. Roosevelt said on this occasion, "You know, Doctor, I could never have done it all except for the help of my dear wife."

Second Term and After

Mr. Roosevelt was nominated by acclamation for a second term, even though powerful conservatives of his own party fought him fiercely, like Raskob, Al Smith, and some of the Liberty Leaguers. He was put in nomination, as in 1932, by his old friend and Poughkeepsie neighbor, Judge John E. Mack. In his acceptance speech FDR animatedly attacked the "economic royalists," and told his listeners that they had "a rendezvous with destiny." Of course every American president starts running for his second term early in his first, and FDR had carefully nurtured his political support from the beginning. The Republicans nominated Landon and Knox, and the only interesting thing about the election as we look back to it today is that anybody thought there could have been any other outcome. Roosevelt was re-elected by the most stunning vote in American presidential history. He lost only two states, Maine and Vermont, and won by the totally unprecedented total of 523 electoral votes to 8. The landslide was so enormous that the new Senate had 75 Democrats as against only 21 Republicans; the house was Democratic 334 to 89.[9] In the words of a British observer, Roosevelt had become anthropomorphic, a virtual god.

He announced, "I should like to have it said of my first administration that in it the forces of selfishness and lust for power met their match. I should like to have it said of my second administration that these forces have met their master."

FDR's second inaugural, delivered on January 20, 1937, radiated confidence, challenge, and reformist zeal. This was the speech in which he said:

I see millions of families trying to live on incomes so meager that the pall of family disaster hangs over them day by day.

I see millions whose daily lives in city and on farm continue under conditions labeled indecent by a so-called polite society half a century ago.

I see millions denied education, recreation, and the opportunity to better their lot and the lot of their children.

I see millions lacking the means to buy the products of farm and factory and by their poverty denying work and productiveness to many other millions.

I see one-third of a nation ill-housed, ill-clad, ill-nourished.

[9] The Republicans spent about $9,000,000 on this election, the Democrats $5,194,741. Organized labor contributed $770,218 to the Roosevelt campaign fund. Harvey Wish, *Contemporary America* (New York, Harper & Brothers, 1945), p. 471.

But though his electoral majority was so immense FDR met more opposition in the early years of the second term than at any other period, and suffered his only damaging defeats. 1937 and 1938 were the two least successful years he ever had. Perhaps this was an inevitable reaction from the extravagant successes of the early years, or perhaps overconfidence prompted him to go too far. The pendulum of American public opinion can travel a wide arc swiftly. Also, as a British observer pointed out, the mere fact that a considerable recovery *had* taken place opened the door to criticism. "The patient, being convalescent, no longer needed to turn a look of dumb devotion upon the doctor"; the very fact that he no longer was "the full and unquestioned arbiter" of the previous term proved, in a curious way, how substantial his accomplishment had been. In any event Roosevelt lost the great Supreme Court fight, lost the "battle of the purge," and in the 1938 midterm elections the Republicans won eighty-one seats in the House and eight senatorships. Also FDR had his first serious tussles with labor in the period of the momentous sit-down strikes and quarreled mortally with John L. Lewis. Congress, which had been so docile, became turbulent and even mutinous. Finally, midway through the term, there came a sharp, severe business "recession."

The Nine Old Men

The Supreme Court fight was a struggle for power, no more, no less. The issue was who should make the laws, or, to be more precise, whether or not the Court, which had not been elected to anything by anybody, and all members of which had reached their lofty station before Roosevelt became President, could justifiably continue to obstruct and in fact nullify the will of the nation as expressed by the Chief Executive and Congress. Was it proper, in other words, that nine men should withhold from the great mass of the American people legislation which the American people clearly wanted? Was this democracy? Could nine men be permitted to continue thwarting the New Deal indefinitely? Up to January, 1937, the Supreme Court had invalidated nine out of eleven major Administration measures; the only ones to survive were the TVA and the devaluation of gold, and this latter had only scraped through on a 5-4 decision.

The age of several leading justices exacerbated the dispute. Brandeis was at that time eighty, Van Devanter seventy-seven, McReynolds seventy-five, Sutherland seventy-four, Hughes seventy-four, Butler seventy, Cardozo sixty-six, Stone sixty-five, and Roberts sixty-one. The last-ditch "horse-and-buggy" obstructionists were Van Devanter, McReynolds, Sutherland, and Butler; Roosevelt had to get around them somehow, or get rid of them. But how? He contrived a stratagem. On February 5, only a few weeks after the inauguration, he proposed a bill whereby he would have the right to appoint one new justice (up to a total of fifteen) for each member of the Court who refused to retire at full pay within six months of reaching the age of seventy. Such legislation, if passed, would eventually give him a comfortable majority on the Court, whether the obstructionists took the hint and retired or not. Judges already over seventy who retired would be replaced in the normal manner, without any increase in the size of the Court. We may grant that the desperate nature of the legislative deadlock made some action by the President necessary, but his manner of presenting the bill showed, it seemed, his worst qualities. It looked devious to most people; it looked half-baked; it looked dishonest. American public opinion is apt to be very sharp about something about to be slipped over on the country. Moreover the proposal was bitterly unfair to Brandeis and Cardozo, who—even if old men—took the New Deal side on most judgments. FDR and Homer Cummings, his Attorney General, wrote the bill in utter secrecy; nobody in Congress was informed till almost the last moment. Tom Corcoran (despite much talk to the contrary) never even heard of the bill until the day before it was to go to the Hill; horrified, he rushed to Missy LeHand and tried to stop it, partly on the ground that Brandeis and Cardozo would be bitterly affronted. But it was too late, the bill reached the legislature, and a tornado of vehement opposition swept the country.

Now the root of this matter goes back as far as American history goes back. As a writer put it in the *Times* of London, "a no-man's land of sovereign power" exists in the United States between president, congress, and the judiciary. Roosevelt was accused by his enemies of steady encroachment into this no man's land, and packing the Court was the last straw. Of course there had been quarrels between president and Court since Van Buren. President Grant added two members to the Court. And all strong presidents have initiated legislation of doubtful constitutionality; Lord Bryce, in fact, once wrote that two of the greatest achievements of American presidents, Jackson's Louisiana Purchase and Lincoln's Emancipation Proclamation, were probably unconstitutional.

The acuteness of the fundamental dilemma was once presented by the opposition of the two following syllogisms:

First Premise: The people have made the Constitution, established the departments of government, and assigned powers to each of them, and this Constitution is declared to be the supreme law of the land.
Second Premise: The Supreme Court has taken an oath to uphold the Constitution.
Conclusion: When an act of Congress (admittedly inferior law) conflicts with the superior law, the Supreme Court cannot enforce it, but must declare it null and void.

In rebuttal:

First Premise: The people have made the Constitution, established the departments, and assigned powers to each of them, and this Constitution is declared to be the supreme law of the land.
Second Premise: The President has taken an oath to uphold the Constitution.
Conclusion: When a decision of the Supreme Court (admittedly inferior to the Constitution itself) conflicts with the superior law, the President cannot enforce it but must declare it null and void.[10]

If Roosevelt had been more candid, if he had explored opinion more subtly and taken Congress into his confidence, the result might have been different. But people could not get over the feeling that the proposal had been cooked up in an underhanded way. If he had said without equivocation, "It has become necessary to pack the Court, and I am going to pack it," he might have won. Many men of good will agreed that something had to be done to stop usurpation by the courts of the legislative function; but they could not stomach the way Roosevelt did it. The struggle went on for 168 violent days. Eventually, despite tremendous pressure from the President, the bill was rejected by the Judiciary Committee of the Senate by a vote of 10 to 8, and it had to be dropped. The fight all but tore the Democratic party asunder, and the whole issue is still furiously alive to many people. A celebrated American general told me in 1949, "My blood still boils when I think of that court-packing scheme!"

Strangely enough Roosevelt won his objective, even though the bill was cast out. He lost the battle, but won the war. The Court itself must

[10] "The New Deal on Trial," London *Times*, July 10, 1935, paraphrased from Charles A. Beard.

have felt something of the inexorable pressures that led FDR to propose
the bill, because actually while the struggle was going on it approved
the constitutionality of two supremely important measures, the Wagner
Act and Social Security, although by 5 to 4 decisions. Then Van
Devanter retired, and Roosevelt got his first chance to appoint a new
justice. He chose Hugo Black. By 1940 the Court was FDR's. Brandeis
and Cardozo were gone; so were Sutherland, Butler, and McReynolds,
to give way to Reed, Frankfurter, Douglas, Jackson, Murphy. In 1941
Roosevelt elevated Harlan Stone to Chief Justice, who had been one of
his teachers at Columbia. Today it is almost unthinkable that the
Court, no matter how constituted, could refuse to march in spirit with
the times or deliberately frustrate the clearly expressed will of the
people. But the struggle cost FDR a good deal. I have heard the episode
described as "the bravest" thing he ever did, but he lost face and magic
by it. Never again, on the domestic scene at least, did he have quite the
inordinate prestige, the halo undimmed by any defeat or setback that
he had had before.

Blunder of the Purge

Congress remained restive throughout 1937 and 1938, and on several
measures—including one to reorganize the Federal machinery in the
interests of economy—FDR was actually beaten, despite his unprecedented majority. He set out to punish the conservative Democrats who
obstructed him and took the stump himself to urge the defeat in the
approaching elections of senators like George (Georgia) and Tydings
(Maryland), and congressmen like John J. O'Connor of New York, who
he decided must be got rid of even though he was his law partner's
brother. FDR's sanctimoniousness during this episode was considerable.
At the very moment that he invited the electorate to dismiss Walter
George he said to the intended victim, who was sitting on the platform
with him, "God bless you, Walter." The chief influence behind the
purge was probably Corcoran. The party regulars, like Farley, viewed
it with vigorous distaste for the obvious reason that it ruined unity,
patronage, and discipline.

The purge was a failure. O'Connor was beaten, but the others on
the FDR blacklist came in handsomely, and some of the best New
Dealers in the country, like Maury Maverick of Texas, were casualties
because people resented so much the way that the President seemed to
be interfering in strictly local politics.

In all this we see an issue that survives angrily today. The Democratic party, under Roosevelt, grew so large and amorphous, its frontiers became so fluid and ill-defined, that no one—except FDR himself—could possibly hold it together. It was bound to split, or at least spread in the seams. Northern labor and Southern reactionaries simply would not lie down together, unless Mr. Roosevelt tucked them in. Ask Mr. Truman about the Dixiecrats.

*

But by this time domestic affairs were taking second place in the imagination of Mr. Roosevelt and the world. The ugly breath of war blew from across the seas.

Chapter 17

INTO WAR

One doesn't put a time limit on things any more. That's the last century.

—FRANKLIN DELANO ROOSEVELT

To serve the public faithfully and at the same time please it entirely is impossible.

—BENJAMIN FRANKLIN

During the first term FDR paid comparatively little attention to foreign affairs; during his second they devoured him. Until 1936 or 1937 he scarcely gave the rest of the world a thought, except to pat Sumner Welles on the back for the Good Neighbor policy. He had, of course, received visits early in his Presidency from various prime ministers like MacDonald and Herriot; he maintained a close sentimental interest in China, pushed for independence of the Philippines, and recognized the government of the Soviet Union; but, this aside, the world beyond American shores did not concern him much. The totality of his activity was concentrated on the New Deal in the United States, and so far as possible he left everything else to the State Department.

In 1933 Eleanor Roosevelt asked Anne O'Hare McCormick of the New York *Times* to dinner at the White House. "I wonder if you would try to get the President more interested in foreign affairs," Mrs. Roosevelt suggested. Certainly the Roosevelts could not have chosen a better-informed or more perspicacious guide.

In 1940 a friend asked Robert H. Jackson, then the Attorney General, whose province might be assumed to be far away from foreign affairs, if the President ever talked to him on foreign policy. Jackson replied drily, "He never talks about anything else."

Such was the gamut that history forced FDR to travel. Even before World War II he had become the acknowledged leader not merely of American democracy but of that of the entire world.

Isolation, Hitler, and the Crisis

Roosevelt knew perfectly well that the intellectual climate of the United States was overwhelmingly isolationist; many reasons accounted for this, some quite legitimate—dislike of embroilment in European affairs, disillusion at the results of World War I, and above all distaste for the evil of war itself. Isolationism is, always has been, and always will be a perfectly authentic expression of one phase of the American national spirit. Not only was the leadership of the Republican party almost solidly isolationist in the 1930's; many prominent New Dealers, like Hugh Johnson, Jerome Frank, and even Harry Hopkins, were isolationists. Important businessmen and industrialists had ties to Germany; many conservatives had surreptitious (if not open) sympathy for Fascism; Mussolini was a hero to millions of respectable but thoroughly misguided Americans. Congress passed a series of so-called neutrality acts designed to keep the United States out of war at almost any cost, and it seemed, in the words of an epigram of the day, that the foreign policy of the United States was to have no foreign policy. Confusion, greed, cowardice, inertia, paralyzed the drifting public mind.

Meantime the dictators were on the march. The slippery Japanese proceeded with their undeclared conquest of the giant body of China, Italy attacked Ethiopia, and civil war savagely broke out in Spain when a military junta overthrew the legally constituted democratic government. Here Hitler and Mussolini conducted their crude, villainous rehearsal for World War II; Stalin also played a role in Spain, but only later and with much less weight. Hitler took over the Rhineland in 1936, shook the pillars of Europe with threat and braggadocio in 1937, absorbed Austria in 1938, and got ready for the Czechoslovak coup later that year. Spain went down the drain (this was the worst failure in the whole record of Roosevelt's foreign policy), and the Japanese got bolder. Even a blind man must have known that war was coming, and that it would be impossible in the long run for America to keep out of it. The blind were, however, blind.

Roosevelt's first consequential attempt to define these catastrophic issues was the Quarantine speech delivered in October, 1937.[1] With foresight and precision he outlined the point at stake—"whether our

---

[1] The term "quarantine" was suggested by Harold Ickes. (*Saturday Evening Post*, July 17, 1948.) FDR was disappointed because the public at large did not respond to the speech as strongly as he had hoped.

civilization is to be dragged into the tragic vortex of unending militarism punctuated by periodic wars, or whether we shall be able to maintain the ideal of peace, individuality, and civilization as the fabric of our lives"—and called for the "quarantining" of aggressors.

Next FDR pursued a both-sides-of-the-coin policy; intermittently he appealed to the dictators to modify the course of their aggression (for instance in his various appeals for peace during the Munich crisis, and in his later somewhat naïve messages to Hitler and Mussolini) while at the same time he bent every effort to reveal to the American people the reality of the acute danger they faced, exhort them to the cause of democracy, and give them something of his own stamina and confidence.

FDR understood Hitler, and this was a highly important contribution; he managed to communicate to the United States how dangerous and menacing he really was. Plenty of people knew that Hitler was a nuisance; plenty thought that he was disgusting; few, even in the late 30's, realized that he was capable of incinerating the whole world. The isolationists, whose vehemence rose steadily, accused Roosevelt of "exaggerating" the danger of war; nowadays it is only too painfully obvious that they were those who exaggerated wildly. It was they, not Roosevelt, who did not have "imagination" enough; it was they who were "unrealistic"—the term is mild—and not the President.

What is more Roosevelt understood the philosophy behind Hitler, the state of mind that produced this ugly genius and monster. He appreciated—more by instinct than by reason perhaps—that Hitler combined in one movement two of the most powerful conceptions that can attract the minds of men, nationalism and socialism; he knew that the rock-bottom basis of Hitler's support was agonized dissatisfaction by the rank and file of people at the circumstances under which they lived; he knew that the failure of laissez-faire economy and the consequent collapse of nineteenth-century ideals of freedom and justice were the twin fuels on which he waxed hot; he knew that Hitler's real "secret weapon" was the ineptness, the complacency, and the selfishness of the democracies. Finally FDR sensed how vulnerable Hitler really was, despite his triumphs; he knew, in Jan Masaryk's phrase, that dictators always look good—until the last ten minutes.

Hitler never fooled Roosevelt; nor did he ever frighten him. Think by contrast of how Hitler both fooled and frightened Neville Chamberlain, the British Prime Minister of the period.

Japan was, however, during most of this tumultuous interval a more intimate and awkward embarrassment to Washington than Germany. Hitler blustered and took territory by poaching; the Japanese were actually fighting in the field. The predicament for Roosevelt was intricate and dangerous. If he followed one great wing of American opinion and cut off all shipments of oil and scrap iron to Japan, he might well provoke Japan to war. (Which, in effect, was what finally happened.) If he did nothing to check Japanese aggression, the Japanese would conquer Asia. Tokyo took full advantage of this dilemma. For one thing Japan signed the Tripartite Pact; thus the three Fascist powers became full allies. Roosevelt temporized a good deal as regards the Japanese, but during most of this period he was in an extremely isolated position. Russia played its own colossally double-handed and secretive game; France joined Britain in the Munich appeasement; Britain, to conciliate Japan, took measures like closing the Burma Road, which had become the only effective route for aid to stricken China. We do not sufficiently appreciate today how Roosevelt had to act almost *single-handed*, as the putative defender of world democracy, such as it was, in this global struggle between tyranny and freedom.

The President's correct appreciation of the malign forces then at work is the more remarkable in that he was so inadequately—even evilly—served by some of his own ambassadors. Several notable emissaries were as isolationist as senators like Nye and Wheeler. Then too FDR had to wage a running battle with venomous "minor league Metternichs" in his own State Department, some of whom came close to sabotaging their own chief.

Roosevelt, let it be understood beyond doubt, did not at this point want a war. No sane or decent American wanted war. But he was certain that war was coming, that America was bound to be drawn into it no matter what people wanted, and that we had better get ready before it came. He set himself with every weapon of persuasion to teach the country that a continued policy of isolation was *not* of itself capable of producing security. The mood of the country became almost schizoid. "We know we *will* have to fight, but won't," summed up the prevailing attitude, and people gave way to the narcotic thought, "We can beat the Axis without fighting." Apparently FDR himself became convinced finally that war was unavoidable after the German *Anschluss* with Austria. For instance he told Admiral

Leahy, in the most casual sort of way, "Bill, there is going to be a war, and I am going to need you." Henry Stimson, adjudicating the whole issue with all his great elevation of judgment, gives the verdict that FDR did his best for the cause of peace, but that events were too strong for him, and even states that if he is to be blamed for anything, it is that he moved too slowly toward war, not too fast. Indeed, as the record shows, Roosevelt—far from being a firebrand—still continued to falter and vacillate a good deal. Many Americans today consider soberly that he might have, and should have, taken a much stronger line against the Axis than he did, in 1939, that he was not "worried enough"[2] about the imminence of war, and that his hesitations gave stimulus to the enemy, who may have been deluded into the notion that we would not fight no matter what. FDR, it seemed, forever tiptoed to the edge of a decision, then seesawed away. His "lack of leadership," a member of Mr. Truman's present Cabinet once told me, "seemed almost criminal." The reason was of course that he had to continue to make every possible effort for peace in order to placate antiwar and isolationist sentiment, and his hold on Congress was getting shaky.

Germany invaded Poland and the most tragic catastrophe ever to smite mankind came on September 1, 1939, which, by odd coincidence, was the very day on which George Marshall was sworn in as Chief of Staff.

Ambassador William C. Bullitt got through to the President from Paris at 2:50 A.M. that morning, Washington time. "I've just talked to Tony Biddle in Poland. The German army has started marching," Bullitt said. Mr. Roosevelt's answer was calm: "Then it's happened!"

The Bomb

As early as October, 1939, though it was unknown at the time, FDR gave a potent demonstration of his vision, courage, and accessibility to new ideas. On the eleventh of that month a distinguished New York economist and amateur of scientific affairs, Alexander Sachs, called on him to report on recent developments in the field of nuclear fission. Roosevelt had as much knowledge of the possibility of splitting the uranium atom to produce a chain reaction as the corner cop. But he promptly seized on the suggestion. He was not only receptive; he ordered action. Here, incontestably, he demonstrated one of his

[2] This became FDR's own view later. See Rosenman, Vol. X, p. 61.

peculiar qualities of greatness—the capacity to see mysteriously forward, to grasp at unpredictable unknowns.

Dr. Sachs went to see Roosevelt on his own responsibility and his own initiative. This picturesque figure, and indeed Dr. Sachs is picturesque, deserves well of the republic. He was prompted to his visit by knowledge of what progress the Germans had recently made in nuclear physics, and he was armed both by a letter from Dr. Albert Einstein and a memorandum by Dr. Leo Szilard, who had recently completed successful experiments in the same arcane and pregnant field. It is interesting that both Szilard and one of his close associates, Dr. Enrico Fermi, were refugees from Fascism. Also Dr. Sachs carried a scientific paper by Szilard that had appeared in April in the *Physical Review*, entitled "Instantaneous Emission of Fast Neutrons in the Interaction of Slow Neutrons with Uranium." Sachs and Roosevelt began to talk. The President was preoccupied and inattentive. Sachs interrupted gently to the effect that he was paying for the trip to Washington himself and couldn't deduct it from his income tax and would FDR please pay attention. Then, because he feared that the President might drop the scientific memoranda into his tray without studying them carefully, the estimable Sachs insisted on reading them to the President *aloud*, word by word. FDR listened. Then Sachs told him more about what German physicists were doing.

Roosevelt: "Alex, what you are after is to see that the Nazis don't blow us up." (In other words his first thought was defensive, and it is interesting to speculate whether he would ever have used the bomb on Japan as it was used.)

Sachs: "Precisely."

Roosevelt: "This requires action."

The President called Pa Watson in, gave him relevant instructions, and then ordered, "Don't let Alex go without seeing me again." That same night Sachs returned to the White House, and Roosevelt put him in touch with Dr. Lyman J. Briggs, director of the Bureau of Standards.

Some of the military were not impressed; officers would say, "Well, this thing is so remote; what is this thing?—let's wait and see." But Watson would reply firmly, "The Boss wants it, boys. Get to work."

FDR set up an "Advisory Committee on Uranium," with army, navy, and scientific members. Within six months the groundwork for the future Manhattan Project had been laid; on June 15, 1940, the very day after the fall of Paris when "it seemed that Christian civilization was coming to an end,"[3] FDR ordered Dr. Vannevar Bush, chairman of the newly constituted National Defense Research Council, to take charge. Practically before anybody could blink a vast organization had been set up, the best military, engineering, and scientific brains in the country applied themselves to a problem without parallel in magnitude and complexity, the whole world of technology was turned upside down, and the President found himself committed to the expenditure of two billion dollars—for what might have turned out to be nothing more than a grandiose mirage. But we know now that it was no mirage.

Third Term

Youngsters growing up today may not remember the storm and crisis caused by the third term controversy only ten short years ago. I talked to a group of students recently; they appeared to be puzzled that there had even been a crisis. "What was it about?" they asked. Which goes to indicate that once a tradition is broken, no matter how deeply rooted, the new generation is apt to forget that it ever existed. This was exactly the point of many who opposed the third term so intransigently; they felt and feared that if Roosevelt ran again, the cherished principle that a president should not serve more than eight years might indeed be forgotten, and that the path would be opened to permanent acquisition of power by anybody ambitious or aggressive enough to attempt to seize it.

The third term grew out of two things, the New Deal and the relentless crisis over war. Probably Roosevelt would not have run for a third term if war had not been imminent. Not only did war— or the threat of war—make the third term inevitable; the possibility that he might have to run for a third term strongly influenced FDR's conduct of affairs in regard to war. He had to have public opinion with him.

On constitutional grounds opponents of the third term had little leg to stand on; there is no legal inhibition to a president seeking as many terms as he wants. In fact two presidents, Grant and Theodore Roosevelt, had sought third terms, though Grant only made his third try after another term had intervened (he failed by a narrow margin to get the nomination); and TR, running in 1912 against Wilson

[3] Sherwood, p. 154.

and Taft, could state that he was not seeking a third "elective" term since his first had followed the assassination of McKinley. On the other hand a deeply fixed and important tradition held against a third term—especially a third consecutive elective term. Washington quit office after eight years (true, he was ill and he once wrote Lafayette that, in an emergency, there was no reason why a man should not serve longer) and Jefferson transformed this precedent into firm practice. Twice Congress passed resolutions against any third term, once in 1875, once in 1928. But these did not have the force of law.

Those opposing the third term did so for reasons that seemed to them scandalously obvious. They cried "Caesarism"; they talked about the *Führer Prinzip*; they said that democratic principles were being destroyed. "The tradition against the perpetuation in office of the Chief Executive is as sacred as anything the American boy learns at his mother's knee," wailed Alf Landon,[4] "the third term is fatal to the future of the republic . . . odious . . . and not American." Debate raged with utmost truculence. Adherents of the President, like Harold Ickes, pointed out that (a) no matter how long a man stayed in the White House he remained subject to the checks and controls of Congress, a free press, public opinion, and the electorate; (b) the founding fathers themselves, after prolonged debate, had refused to put any limits on presidential tenure in the constitution; (c) nobody objected to life terms for judges, or to the fact that many senators and congressmen were re-elected time after time; (d) the will of the people is the highest law in a democracy, and, as Ickes put it, "if the people want President Roosevelt for another four years, they are well within their rights in taking him."

The main element in this controversy was intense personal feeling about Roosevelt, pro and con. Many of those who opposed him would not have objected so strenuously if, let us say, it had been Mr. Hoover, or even Mr. Garner, who was running for a third term; conversely, what united people in the Roosevelt camp was passionate love for FDR; his person outrode any constitutional issue. Nevertheless we should not minimize other factors involved. Many good citizens came to support Roosevelt in the end, but only after the most soul-searching agony and reluctance. It seemed to them that only the imminent possibility of war and *force majeure* could justify so grave a breach with

4 New York *Post*, July 13, 1940. The quotation from Ickes below is from the same.

a fine tradition, and even so that it was almost shameful that a tradition so valuable had to go. Some liberals deeply pro-Roosevelt were almost as horrified as the strait-laced conservatives. For instance a writer in the *New Republic* said in 1939 that if FDR ran again the shock would be as great as if Mahatma Gandhi should turn to beer and sausage.

Third term talk began, not during the entrance-to-war period, but considerably earlier. People asked, "Will the President run again?" from about 1937 on; it seemed fairly obvious even then that, to consolidate the New Deal into permanent legislation, FDR might need time in the White House beyond 1940. What added to the excitement as time went on was complete uncertainty about the President's own intentions. People split for and against; FDR himself said not a word. The country exploded in curiosity and agitation; he stayed mum.

Roosevelt's coquetry in fact, all but drove the nation frantic during this period. There were several reasons for his silence: (1) If he declared he was not a candidate, he would substantially lose power to conduct policy. (2) If he admitted that he was a candidate, his prestige as President would suffer. (3) He didn't make up his own mind until the very end.

Other Democratic candidates for the Presidency were, as was inevitable, killed off by this, since they could make no headway until it was known what FDR himself was going to do. Perhaps this was one reason why he waited. In January, 1939, he announced that he could not support for the Presidency any Democrat not a New Dealer; the country, he said, "would be in a sad state if it had to choose in 1940 between a Democratic Tweedledee and a Republican Tweedledum." Since most leading Democratic aspirants were lukewarm, if not cool, to the New Deal, he must have felt that he had a legitimate reason for frustrating them by not declaring his own plans. Farley and Garner were gelatinously interlocked in a camarilla to get the nomination for one of themselves, and FDR simply did not think that either was fit to be president.[5]

Roosevelt appears for a time to have thought of grooming Hopkins as his successor, but Hopkins' health failed. Mr. Ickes once told me that every member of the Cabinet except himself and Miss Perkins

[5] Garner said on one occasion to Farley, "Jim, the two of us can pull together to stop Roosevelt." Farley, p. 172.

was, at this time, "running" to succeed their chief. A minor wisecrack credited to the President shows how harassed he had become. Somebody asked him if he wanted a third term and he replied, "I don't know, but I'd like a second one."

Before 1939 I do not think FDR ever dreamed of running in 1940, though indication exists, as is pointed out in Sherwood, that he flirted with the idea that he might run again in 1944, if the country wanted him, after an intervening term. Many factors contributed to his disinclination. For one thing Mrs. Roosevelt, who was still a strong influence, did not want him to run. He was getting tired, and the Washington climate gave him sinus. After eight tremendous presidential years he needed a change of tempo. What he wanted was to loaf in Hyde Park, fish in Florida, build a house, and write. At any rate, though no announcement was made one way or other to the country at large, he told a good many people in private that he would *not* run —Farley, Hull, Miss Perkins, and Dan Tobin of the Teamsters Union, among others. John G. Winant said to him on one occasion that he "must offer himself to the electorate again"; he rebuffed Winant with "cold anger." From all this derive the "duplicity" charges of Farley and his group. They took him at his word (though they must have been fully aware that circumstances might force him to change his mind) and Farley broke away—probably he would have broken away anyhow—to build up his own candidature.

One conclusive piece of evidence that FDR had firmly determined to quit the White House has never been published before, so far as I know. Thomas H. Beck asked him to become a contributing editor of *Collier's* when he left the Presidency in January, 1941, at a salary of $75,000 per year, and Roosevelt accepted with alacrity. A contract was drawn up, dated January 27, 1940; a photostat of it may be seen today, signed by FDR, Beck, and William L. Chenery of *Collier's*. A few days later, the President introduced Chenery around the White House as "my future boss." The contract ran for three years (as drawn, it was for two, but Roosevelt scratched out the "two" and wrote in "three" instead); FDR was to have several editorial assistants, and would write twenty-six articles a year "subject to editorial control." *Collier's* offered him more than $75,000, but Roosevelt thought it would not be proper to get as an editor more than he had received as President of the United States.

After the contract was signed Mr. Beck said to FDR, "Since you're not going to be a candidate for a third term, who will it be?"

Roosevelt: "Whom would you suggest?"

Beck: "I suppose it will have to be Henry Wallace."

Roosevelt: "No, he cannot make up his mind on anything."

The forces that made FDR change his mind may be recapitulated: (a) War was obviously coming closer. (b) Refusal to run would have played straight into the hands of the Japanese and Hitler. (c) He could not afford to disrupt the American defense program then getting under way. (d) No other strong candidate who would protect the New Deal was available with a ghost of a chance to win.

Probably Roosevelt did not make his final decision until May, 1940, while France was being overrun. He had the tempered courage to decide to run again at the very moment when the Blitzkrieg was at its most efficient and savage peak and when many people thought that Hitler had already won the war.

Convention, Willkie, and the Campaign

However worthy were FDR's motives his methods were somewhat slippery. On July 17, when the convention opened, Senator Barkley, who was permanent chairman, read a message which can scarcely be said to have conveyed the whole or literal truth:

Close friends of the President's have long known that he has no wish to be a candidate again. We know too that in no way whatsoever has he exerted any influence in selection of delegates or upon opinions of delegates.

Tonight at the specific request and authorization of the President, I am making this simple fact clear to this convention.

The President has never had and has not today, any desire or purpose to continue in the office of President, to be a candidate for that office or to be nominated by the convention for that office. He wishes in all earnestness and sincerity to make it clear to all that this convention is free to vote for any candidate.

That is the message I bear to you from the President of the United States.

The story of this convention has been told too often to need recountal here. Roosevelt sent Hopkins out to superintend operations, because he distrusted most of the professionals, though Hopkins had never even been to a convention before. Farley and Garner were open candidates, and Paul McNutt, if he had made a fight, could have made trouble. Of course FDR won hands down, though not by acclamation;

the paraphernalia of loudspeakers and the like rigged up by the Chicago bosses were not necessary. He could no more have been stopped than Niagara could be stopped.

Roosevelt insisted that Wallace, for all his cloudiness and Hamletism, be nominated for Vice-President, thus displacing Garner; here the struggle was more vivid, and had it not been for effective intervention by Mrs. Roosevelt, Wallace might not have got the nomination. An odd point is that young Elliott Roosevelt opposed his father by plugging for Jesse Jones for Vice-President, and had to be held off by Eleanor. There were seventeen Vice-Presidential candidates in all. FDR's own first choice for this post had been Hull; virtually he had gone on his knees to Hull—and Mrs. Hull—asking the Secretary of State to accept, but he refused.[6]

About Wallace, Roosevelt always had an ambivalent attitude. FDR blew hot on him, and then cold. First he did not want Wallace as Vice-President. Next he changed his mind so emphatically that he wrote a note in longhand, ready for transmittal if necessary, stating that he himself would not run if the convention refused to accept Wallace as his running mate. Then during the campaign Wallace brutally embarrassed him. Letters became available which apparently proved that Wallace had the closest and silliest associations with a variety of crackpot folk; the Republican high command got possession of these letters, and if they had been published the effect could have been damaging. As it happened the letters (which may possibly have been forgeries) were not published. Anyway Roosevelt was angry; he even demanded that Wallace withdraw from the race. But legal experts found out that, even if Wallace had agreed to withdraw, this was not constitutionally possible, since there was no legal provision whereby a vice-presidential candidate could be replaced. Then, *after* the election, FDR softened; he and Wallace resumed a period of close association, and Wallace was put in charge of tasks far beyond his normal province as Vice-President.

Meantime the Republicans nominated Wendell L. Willkie. This fabulous Hoosier stole the nomination from the party leaders like an unruly child getting away with a pot of jam. He was one of the most lovable, most gallant, most zealous, and most forward-looking Amer-

---

[6] Fascinating details may be found in Hull's memoirs as to the above. For instance FDR once said to Hull, after hours of pleading and urging, "If you don't take it, I'll have to get Henry Wallace to run." Hull continued to refuse, replying, "That's all right with me." Cf. Hull, Vol. I, p. 861.

icans of this—or any—time. One thing peculiar was that he had been a registered Democrat until a few years before; he had even been a delegate to the 1924 convention at which FDR made the keynote speech! FDR liked him extremely. He once told his son James to tease the party regulars by saying that, come the next election, he and Willkie would run together, and even that he would make Willkie Secretary of State. But also he had a healthy respect for his powers as an opponent, if only because Willkie shared in great degree some of his own most marked qualities. Also FDR thought that Willkie might well win if Great Britain should suffer the fate of France, because his own policy of aid to Britain would be discredited. If the Nazis had won the war that summer, they might have beaten Roosevelt too.

Willkie was far too confident—at the beginning; when he went out to Colorado after the nomination, he even thought that he could win "without a campaign."[7] He based this hope on the wild miscalculation that he could break up the Democratic party; he spent weeks telephoning leading Democrats all over the country, some 300 in all; but not one budged. Some disgruntled Democrats did desert FDR, mostly because of the third term issue; Al Smith, Moley, and Hugh Johnson were among them. Also John L. Lewis came out for Willkie. It was a reckless, violent campaign. The shadow of war hung over it. There was much nastiness. The desperate Republicans even advertised in the *Daily Worker*, because at this time the Communists opposed the "imperialist war." Willkie was gravely handicapped both because he was honest and liberal enough to accept some New Deal reforms and because he agreed patriotically with much in Roosevelt's foreign policy, as was handsomely proved by his subsequent trips to England and around the word, and his testimony on the Lend-Lease bill. FDR demonstrated once more in this 1940 run what a sublimely masterful campaigner he was. I hope that some young student at Hyde Park will write some day a really comprehensive and minutely detailed account of Roosevelt's techniques as a vote getter. The record deserves close attention. FDR won by a popular vote of 27,751,597 to 22,304,755 and an electoral vote of 449 to 82. But Willkie carried ten states, which was equivalent to a man staying ten rounds with Joe Louis, and his popular vote was higher by some 300,000 than that of any other Republican who ever ran for president.

[7] But one contemporary joke, attributed to Bob Hope, said, "Willkie has his eye on the presidential chair, but look what Roosevelt has on it."

In his third inaugural Mr. Roosevelt made a strange slip of the tongue. He said that if the nation did not recall what its place in history was, it would "risk the real peril of isolation." The text read, not "isolation," but "inaction." Dr. Freud would have been amused.

"Again and Again and Again"

The "smear Roosevelt" experts have paid more attention to this phrase than any other of the period. FDR spoke in Boston on October 30, 1940, toward the climax of the campaign; it was a slashing, aggressive speech mostly attacking the Republican record on preparedness. Roosevelt was under insistent pressure from the orthodox politicians to give a new reassurance to the nation that American boys would not have to fight overseas. Somewhat reluctantly, because it had all been said many times before, he consented to include in his speech the passage, "And while I am talking to you mothers and fathers, I give you one more assurance. I have said this before, but I shall say it again and again and again, your boys are not going to be sent into any *foreign* wars" (italics mine).

Sam Rosenman, as the story is authoritatively told in Sherwood,[8] suggested that the President add the words that had followed this identical phrase in the Democratic platform—"except in case of attack." FDR scoffed at the proposal; his feeling was that "except in case of attack" was too obvious to need stating. He turned to Rosenman and Sherwood, "Of course we'll fight if we're attacked. If somebody attacks us, then it isn't a foreign war, is it? Or do they want me to guarantee that our troops will be sent into battle only in the event of another Civil War?"

Disingenuous? Perhaps. It was obvious that we would have to fight if we were attacked and that in such an event American troops would have to go overseas.

End of the New Deal

Of course the New Deal helped considerably to make the American war effort possible. The miracles of production the factories of the United States performed with only a minimum of labor trouble would not have been so easily achieved except for the groundwork FDR laid in the years of peace. Emotionally too the people had been prepared for

[8] *Roosevelt and Hopkins,* p. 191.

this stupendous crisis by the positiveness, the educational impact, and the reformist energy of the New Deal.

Some good New Dealers, however, viewed the onset of war with anguish, on the ground, first, that full mobilization would cost so much that social reform would have to be sacrificed; second, that entrance into war might gravely imperil American democracy itself. What was the good of a war, fought ostensibly in the name of "freedom," if its net result might be to produce totalitarianism? Were we, in the United States, subjecting our own democracy to greater risk by fighting or by staying out? If we fought Fascism, might we not become Fascist ourselves? So spoke many on the New Deal side.

As war came closer FDR had to let more things go in the domestic sphere, and the New Deal inevitably dwindled off. If the United States was going to fight a war (this was the argument of Felix Frankfurter among others), every ounce of the nation's productive effort must be mobilized. To get production going in a really big way FDR had to conciliate big businessmen, industrial leaders, and the Detroit and Pennsylvania tycoons; the New Dealers correspondingly lost prestige and influence. He *had* to have industry, and he had to assure it a handsome profit. The way Roosevelt made it known—later—that he wanted to drop the New Deal slogan has interest; as always, he liked the casual and oblique approach. A columnist for a Scripps-Howard newspaper in Cleveland was a guest at a White House press conference, and was introduced to the President as somebody friendly to the New Deal; they had never met before. Roosevelt began chatting and said that he wished newspapermen would quit talking about the New Deal as such. The columnist thought this over for a day or two and then wrote a guarded and entirely legitimate story, not quoting the President but giving the substance of his views. It made a national sensation. This was the trial balloon FDR wanted. So at another press conference the next week he let his full opinion become known. It was that "Dr. New Deal," the good old family physician and internist, had had to call in his partner and consultant, an orthopedic surgeon named "Dr. Win the War."

The Energizing Glow

Roosevelt, now almost sixty, began to have spells of being tired—no wonder!—and sinus and minor throat infections bothered him. He had too many colds, and one prolonged bout of stomach trouble.

Nevertheless his basic health remained excellent throughout this period. He boomed to one visitor, "I can take anything these days!" Even when a particularly hard spell of work wore him down temporarily, he gave the impression of indestructible elasticity and power. "Come on in!" he would say to a guest, with the familiar sweeping gesture famous to millions—the commanding head arched back, the right arm stretched up and out. Energy is contagious, and Roosevelt's own glow of energy was energizing. He made almost everybody close to him feel bigger, heartier, more vigorous, by reason of his own luminous expansiveness.

Two things grew in him at about this time. First, his ego and the feeling that he was indispensable. Second, the physical beauty of his face, which had become mellowed and tempered by the immensity of the burdens he shouldered, and made stronger and more rugged too. It is suggestive to trace the change in Roosevelt's photographs from, say, 1932 to 1940. He became mature.

Last Steps on the Road to War

During this entire time—even before the President's nomination, well before his election—convulsive developments continued to take place. The onrush of war in Europe and Asia—the Japanese were penetrating into Indo-China and Siam—intensified the demand of a large body of American opinion that, at all costs, the United States must stay out. The third term campaign did not eliminate the Vallandighams and isolationists. Quite the contrary. The America First Committee was organized in October, 1940, the German-American Bund flourished, native Fascist and Nazi groups expanded, such senators as Borah and Johnson and representatives like Hamilton Fish moaned and raged, isolationist newspapers like the Chicago *Tribune* spat venom, and above all Colonel Lindbergh preached a steady doctrine of defeatism, passivity, and appeasement. Lindbergh said early in 1941, *after* the Battle of Britain, "This war is lost. It is not within our power today to win the war for England, even though we throw the entire resources of our nation into the conflict"; he said later that only "the British, the Jews, and the Roosevelt administration" wanted war.

Against this trend FDR worked incessantly; he refused utterly to kowtow to the defeatism that was preached on almost every side. The Hitler flail demolished country after country; indeed he seemed irresistible. But the President never budged or faltered in his conviction that Hitler could and would be beaten, no matter what people said of his "invincibility" and the "inevitability" of Nazi triumph. At the very moment when he took the supreme decision to arm Britain after Dunkirk his closest advisers said that the British had only one chance in three of pulling through. FDR simply wouldn't believe it. Men of such stature as Mr. Hoover said, "Does any sane person believe that by military means we can defeat two-thirds of the military power of the whole world in even years and years?" Roosevelt paid no attention. He was not an easy man to scare.

Dr. Luther Gulick, the well-known publicist and administrator, called on the President to discuss problems in social welfare. FDR kept straying off the subject (he hated the word "welfare") and would talk about nothing except industrial matters in Great Britain and Germany. He slid open a desk drawer and pulled out a tabulation, partly in pencil, partly typed, showing what aircraft production was in each country month by month. Roosevelt's own estimates of German capacity were greater than the British estimates, and Gulick said that the figures from London ought to be trusted. FDR scolded him, "No, no, the British don't understand mass production!"

Interestingly enough it was not his English blood or any sentimental feeling about the British that prompted FDR to his general stand. Actually, in most matters, he was not pro-British in the emotional sense at all; in fact he rather disliked the British in some ways. What interested him was the safety of *America.*

Something to startle the soberest historian today is the effort by several Republican leaders to build up a case that Roosevelt erred by not preparing for war promptly or efficiently enough. (Dewey did this, too, in the 1944 campaign.) Senator Brewster of Maine stated with a straight face recently that FDR was responsible for the loss of "thousands of lives and millions of dollars because he *delayed* [italics mine!] putting into effect the industrial mobilization plans . . . drafted prior to the outbreak of war." The hate-Roosevelt philosophy, particularly after his death, approaches at times the frontier of lunacy. That isolationist senators can charge nowadays that *they* worked for preparedness and that Roosevelt obstructed it is double talk so monstrous that it can only be explained on the grounds of actual intellectual deformity, as well as the rankest prejudice.

Go back and summarize the whole record briefly. Immediately after the outbreak of war in September, 1939, in a Fireside Chat, FDR gave prompt warning to the Axis, saying that America could not be expected to be neutral in thought. He declared a limited national emergency, and a few weeks later called Congress into special session to amend the Neutrality Act. The embargo was dropped, and the cash-and-carry principle extended so that Britain and France could buy munitions in America. When the Blitzkrieg in the west ended the Phony War FDR set on foot all sorts of defensive measures. He renovated the War and Navy departments and put Republicans (Stimson and Knox) in charge. His correspondence with Churchill became closer and more intimate. On the very day that Hitler invaded the Netherlands he stunned the country by demanding the production of 50,000 airplanes a year.[9] The foundation of the complex structure that eventually became the War Production Board was laid, and OPA and multitudinous other agencies associated with defense were set up. Immediately after the fall of France FDR started sending munitions to Great Britain, and that summer, during the election campaign, he worked out the "destroyer deal"—his own special "baby"—whereby the British got fifty overage destroyers in return for naval bases turned over to our use in the western Atlantic; this was announced to a startled Congress on September 3. Leadership? There is no other word for it. Roosevelt thought that this destroyer trade was "the most important thing that has come for American defense since the Louisiana Purchase." He sent American officers and technicians to Great Britain in great number; British aviators were trained in the United States and British warships secretly repaired here. In September came the first peacetime conscription (Selective Service) act in American history,[10] and day by day the Navy was put in better order. The year closed with preparations for the Lend-Lease bill, and on December 29 came the great Fireside Chat on the need for the United States to become the "arsenal of democracy."

The record of 1941 is, of course, even more closely packed; its keynote was the Four Freedoms speech on January 6. The Lend-Lease bill was introduced on January 10, and passed on March 11. It was presented by its adherents as a bill that would keep the United States out of war; its effect was to change American foreign policy more than anything since George Washington. (FDR's first name for it was the

[9] It was Mr. Hull who suggested the figure 50,000. Roosevelt was at first "speechless" at the idea. Hull, Vol. I, p. 767.

[10] A year later extension of this act passed the House by exactly one vote. Even at such a moment of extreme peril to the nation the isolationists were within an ace of being strong enough to wreck the whole Selective Service System.

"Lend-Spend" bill.) In April Roosevelt got from Denmark permission to set up naval and military establishments in Greenland, and the occupation of Iceland followed. On May 5 he gave orders for the construction of a strategic-bomber fleet, and on May 20 established the Office of Civilian Defense; a week later came the speech announcing an unlimited national emergency. All Axis ships in American ports were seized, the twenty-four German consulates in the country were closed, Axis credits in American banks were frozen, and the embargo on Japan was tightened. Lend-Lease aid was extended to the Soviet Union after Germany attacked that country, and to China.[11] Meantime the entire face of the country was transformed by war production; the nation's factories buzzed and hummed on a 24-hour-day basis. On August 12 came the Atlantic Charter meeting with Churchill, and on September 11 FDR delivered another major Fireside Chat, warning the Germans that if their submarines continued to attack American ships they did so at their own peril. By October a convoy system was in operation, and on November 7 the Neutrality Act was modified again to permit among other things the arming of American merchantmen. At this time the Tojo government took power in Japan, and it seemed certain that the Japanese would presently attack Malaya, the Dutch East Indies, and the Philippines. The Nomura-Kurusu negotiations began in Washington, and on December 6 FDR made a final appeal for settlement to Emperor Hirohito. As to December 7 we all know what happened, and Hitler and Mussolini declared war on the United States three days later.

Was Roosevelt "Neutral"?

Of course not. Until 1939 the course he pursued was cautious and correct enough—perhaps too cautious; I have said that he did not want war, and that is correct; but once war broke out, and particularly after its full force struck Britain and France, the situation sharply changed. If there was ever any doubt about this one has only to read carefully Mr. Churchill's latest memoirs. For instance when Hopkins first visited London early in 1941 he told the Prime Minister frankly, "The President is determined that we shall win the war

---

[11] At a press conference after Lend Lease was approved a reporter asked if there would be aid to China; FDR's reply was, "Oh, I guess so." It all seemed very casual. Rosenman, Vol. X, p. 50.

together. Make no mistake about it. He sent me here to tell you that at all costs and by all means he will carry you through."[12]

Does this mean that Roosevelt was a warmonger, and should have been impeached for violating the letter of his oath? Equally—of course not. He can be accused of lack of candor, though almost every domestic circumstance forced him to adopt a circuitous course in order to get anything achieved at all. But he cannot be accused of lack of patriotism or of failure to prepare conscientiously for the country's defense. If he had *not* been as aware as he was of the realities of the stern dangers confronting the United States he would be much more open to criticism than he is now. What would be the verdict of history if Roosevelt had done nothing whatever to help the British, or delayed until it was too late, with the result that the Axis won the war?

Did Roosevelt dupe the public? Only a citizen blind, deaf, and dumb could have failed to catch on to what was happening, and the opposition certainly had full opportunity to express itself. Moreover, by 1941 a substantial majority of the country had come around to supporting the President's own views, largely as a result of his leadership. For instance a Gallup poll in April shows that roughly three quarters of the people favored going to war if it were certain that there was no other way to defeat Germany, and four fifths thought that entry by the United States was inevitable, though they did not want to go in at once.[13]

Did Roosevelt break promises? As Professor Samuel Eliot Morison has pointed out, the presidential oath of office to preserve, protect, and defend the United States overrides any political platform or campaign promise.

Nowadays we know a great deal more than FDR did about the detailed aims and designs of the Axis powers, in consequence of revelations at the Nuremberg trials and at the trial of Tojo in Japan. The Luftwaffe called for planes able to bomb New York as early as in 1938, and Hitler and the Japanese foreign minister Matsuoka worked out joint plans for attacking the United States on both oceans early in 1941. If Roosevelt had *not* taken measures to stave off assault he should have been impeached.

The dictators ran wild for year after year before FDR acted at all. In fact the case might be put that, after Pearl Harbor, we were forced

[12] New York *Times*, January 26, 1950.
[13] Stimson, p. 374.

to fight to get back much that we had already thrown away. China was gone; Spain was gone; France was gone. Things that the Administration did in the 30's tore the hearts out of good democrats all over the world. FDR refused to apply the Neutrality Act to warfare in the Far East and for years the Japanese war effort was made possible only by *American* shipments of oil and scrap. He did nothing to check Italy in Ethiopia, snubbed the League, threw cold water on plans for collective security, and encouraged the appeasement of Hitler and Mussolini at Munich, though things had gone so far by then that he had little choice.

As to Japan the United States was obliged in the end by every moral, strategic, and political consideration to freeze Japanese credits and embargo war materials, but once we did so, war was bound to come. Rather than retrench at home or give up China, Japan would strike—and everybody knew it—though nobody knew exactly when or where. But this does not mean that Roosevelt was a warmonger.

At 1:47 P.M. on Sunday, December 7, the President, wearing an old sweater belonging to one of his sons, sat at his desk chatting amiably with Harry Hopkins. They had just finished a light lunch. FDR had set aside this as a lazy day and planned to deal with arrears in his stamp collection. The telephone rang, and the operator said apologetically that Frank Knox, Secretary of the Navy, insisted imperatively on being put through. FDR said, "Put him on" and then, "Hello, Frank." Knox said, "Mr. President, it looks as if the Japanese have attacked Pearl Harbor!"

FDR's answer was *"No!"*

He spent eighteen minutes, so far as we know, doing nothing whatever. At 2:05 P.M. he put in a call for Mr. Hull at the State Department, and the war was on.

Chapter 18

WAR PRESIDENT

He serves me most who serves his country best.

—ILIAD, X, *l.* 201

That nefarious villain Abraham Lincoln assassinated a worthy citizen named John Wilkes Booth, and the electric light invented Edison. The Belgian armies invaded peaceful little Germany in 1914, the liner *Titanic* sank an onrushing iceberg, and Hitler appeased Chamberlain at Munich. Reversals of fact like these may seem humorous, if not monstrous; they are no more monstrous than the legend assiduously propagated by an outer fringe of "smear-Roosevelt" addicts that FDR, not the Japanese, sank the American fleet at Pearl Harbor.

The argument, if one may dignify it by any term so sober, goes like this. Roosevelt, out of ambition to perpetuate himself in power and because he personally wanted war, had long plotted to drag the United States into hostilities and so, when other stratagems failed, he set up major units of our Asiatic fleet like sitting ducks in Hawaii and contrived that the Japanese should attack them. There is, of course, no serious evidence whatsoever to support this contention. The Japanese warlords themselves must have been somewhat staggered to hear of it. It is noteworthy that those stubborn Roosevelt haters who support the "plot" thesis were also those who viewed with perfect equanimity the spectacle of Germany and Japan advancing together to conquer all Europe and Asia, regardless of the vital interests of the United States. They preferred to see almost the entire world go under rather than lift a finger; seemingly it did not occur to them that the United States could not have survived long in peace if the Axis won the war. Hence, in their last-ditch blindness, they were not only enemies of FDR, they were outright enemies of America itself. Parenthetically it is interesting that the most ferocious isolationists vis-à-vis Germany and Japan in 1940 and 1941 are, by and large, the most ferocious interventionists today, begging the United States to attack the Soviet Union. The resultant implication is hard to resist that they were Fascist sympathizers then, and something close to Fascists now.

To return to Pearl Harbor let us repeat frankly that the attack did indeed come because American policy—even though it was a defensive policy—had made the Japanese desperate. The case may be further made that FDR, as Sherwood points out, was "rescued" by Tokyo from an impossible dilemma. But this is far from saying that the President "plotted" war or that he himself "provoked" the Japanese assault. In the last negotiations it was the Japanese, not the Americans, who presented the ultimatum that made an outbreak certain. The United States wanted a settlement, and offered terms; the Japanese did not want a settlement, and therefore fought. What we were playing for was time. FDR had told Churchill that he thought he could "baby the Japanese" along for another few months. It was very much to the American interest strictly from the technical point of view of defense that war should not come until 1942.

Roosevelt was, indeed, so cautious about committing this country to armed action that he said at a White House luncheon, as quoted in one of the Pearl Harbor investigations, that he doubted if the United States would become a belligerent *even if the Japanese attacked the Philippines.* But events were too strong for him. Mr. Stimson has revealed that on November 7, 1941, a month before the attack, FDR polled the full Cabinet to ask whether we should fight if the Japanese committed aggression against British or Dutch possessions in the Pacific; the unanimous answer was Yes, and that the country would support such a move. On November 28 the Cabinet definitely agreed to fight if Japan invaded Malaya. But first Roosevelt insisted on pushing negotiations further and appealing personally to Emperor Hirohito.

When, at last, the period of agonizing, insupportable suspense was terminated by the Japanese, who, we know now, had been itching to fight all along, and whose conduct had for years made war inevitable, the atmosphere was clarified as if by a burst of lightning, the country precipitated itself together under Roosevelt's leadership, the long and debilitating period of equivocation was brutally ended, and all dubieties were wiped away. Only such a fiercely overt act as Pearl Harbor *could* have plunged the United States into actual war. I have heard inflamed interventionists say that we should, in fact, erect some kind of monument of gratitude like the Statue of Liberty to the

Japanese for getting us into the war finally and thus making global victory certain. Once the United States was in, Hitler was irrevocably doomed. The Japanese assault on the bland beaches of Oahu made Germany's eventual defeat and collapse inevitable. And Germany was by far the more serious enemy.

Proceeding to the actual events of Pearl Harbor day we should point out that, all the above being true, it is also true that nobody expected the attack to come on Hawaii of all places, that the defenses of the Islands were wretchedly botched and that the United States Army and Navy were caught in a gross state of unpreparedness. Millions upon millions of words have been written pro and con on the responsibility for this shocking state of affairs. The defeat was the most formidable in American history. The seed of the Mukden incident, the mother of all incidents, bore bitter fruit at last. Very broadly, two points may be fairly made. (1) Even though negotiations with the Japanese were reaching a climax in December, the focus of high American interest was so much on the Atlantic that the Pacific was neglected. This is not an excuse, of course. But the national eye was too adhesively fixed on Europe to have sharp vision elsewhere. (2) Almost universally the Japanese were underestimated, and it was anticipated that if they did strike they would attack Malaya or the Dutch East Indies, not commit suicide (for this was the eventual result) at Pearl Harbor by making full American participation in the war inevitable.

There have been three major investigations of the Pearl Harbor disaster so far: that headed by Mr. Justice Roberts immediately after the event (the Roberts report became public on January 25, 1942), the double inquiry instituted by the Pearl Harbor Army Board and the Naval Board of Inquiry (August 29, 1945), and the joint Congressional investigation which followed and made its report in July, 1946. All boiled down roughly to the same conclusions: (a) the administration did its best to avert war with Japan, and the Japanese were of course responsible for the attack; (b) the local commanders in Hawaii failed to make adequate preparation despite a number of warnings of a general nature from Washington; (c) faulty liaison, slackness, and bad management existed on the spot; (d) the supreme chieftains in Washington should have made their orders more explicit and seen that they were more efficiently carried out.[1]

---

[1] The Congressional Committee's minority report, which Mr. Stimson for instance calls "twisted and malicious" (though Stimson does not by any means exonerate himself or the War Department), went much further in blaming Washington.

What began as a Congressional "investigation" became, before long, a noisy "trial" of the dead Roosevelt himself. The President was malignantly defamed, but the proceedings as a whole did little, if any, damage to his reputation.

Interestingly enough the Roosevelt haters who have been most avid to accuse FDR of responsibility for Pearl Harbor seldom mention that General MacArthur in the Philippines was caught in exactly as awkward and exposed a state of armed nakedness as the commanders in Hawaii. MacArthur's planes at Clark Field were destroyed on the ground exactly as were the planes in Oahu, some hours *later,* but MacArthur is a hero to most of those who malign Roosevelt, and so is never blamed by them. MacArthur himself appears to have thought even more definitely than the War Department that a Japanese attack was unlikely at the moment; according to General Wainwright, he did not anticipate any armed action at all until April, 1942.

Pearl Harbor: Aftermath

Already we have mentioned Roosevelt's steadiness on Pearl Harbor day, the elasticity with which he met this shock, and above all his courage. That the crisis was at last resolved must have been a relief. "He demonstrated the ultimate capacity to dominate and control a supreme emergency, which is the rarest and most valuable characteristic of any statesman," is the testimony of Sumner Welles.[2] Mr. Welles has told me that, shortly after the news was received, he seemed "tense, but not drawn," and that he showed "confidence and mastery" in every gesture, though at that moment it was thought that Japanese troops were actually landing in Hawaii. Also FDR was seriously concerned over the safety of the Panama Canal. As the day wore on the strain naturally increased; by evening, when FDR met the leaders of Congress, he was somewhat jumpy. Bits of the stenographic report of that conference show how excited everybody was. Hopkins wanted FDR to make a long and emotional declaration of war. Roosevelt turned to Welles because he knew Welles' advice would be "cold and precise," and this was the mood adopted. The speech delivered the next day, with its celebrated phrase, "a day that will live in infamy," was drawn up partly by Welles, and it was Welles who urged FDR to make it to Congress in person.

The last person to see Roosevelt that night was Edward R. Murrow

[2] *The Time for Decision* (New York, Harper & Brothers, 1944), p. 296.

of the Columbia Broadcasting System, who had just returned from London. Mrs. Roosevelt had asked him to supper at the White House; when Murrow heard the Pearl Harbor news, he assumed that the function would be called off, but he was told to come anyway. The President did not appear at dinner. But he sent a message to wait, and Murrow sat in the hall outside the Oval Room for an hour or two, while Cabinet ministers and Congressional leaders erupted in and out. One distinguished senator yelled at an equally distinguished admiral, "You're not fit to command a rowboat!" Hopkins saw Murrow and asked him quietly what he was doing there and he replied, "I don't know. Should I wait?" Hopkins said, "If the boss said to wait, wait." Finally Roosevelt received Murrow toward midnight. He did not seem nervous at all, and his talk was poised and quick. A bell rang, and General Donovan entered. The President boomed out a greeting that Murrow thought was choice: "What do you know, Bill?" Donovan didn't, of course, know anything; promptly the President told him all. Donovan suggested a scheme for emergency defense of the Philippine beaches. Murrow's memory is that the President's last remark was an outraged, indignant, "To think that all our planes were *caught on the ground!*"

If anybody ever doubted that Roosevelt was a good bluffer, events after Pearl Harbor should put the record straight. For almost a year the United States had no fleet worthy of the name in the Pacific, but no one, least of all the Japanese, ever caught on to how miserably defenseless we really were.

The few days after Pearl Harbor provide the only known interval when FDR was not loquacious to visitors. He was businesslike and even curt to everybody; appointments were brief, the clock had no mercy, and the President kept time with time.

FDR—Some Major Contributions to the War

First, he picked a first-class military team, and never interfered with it. Leahy, Marshall, King, Arnold, made a quadrumvirate that lasted straight through the war.[3] When one thinks by comparison of the innumerable shifts and tergiversations in high command that have occurred in almost all other countries during a great war (e.g., Great Britain in World War I, Germany in World War II) this record is

---

[3] Leahy became Chief of Staff to the President as Commander in Chief in July, 1942, largely on Stimson's recommendation.

the more notable. Moreover there were remarkably few difficulties with commanders in the field. Relations were harmonious from first to last with men—among countless others—as spirited as Eisenhower, Nimitz, Spaatz.

Did Roosevelt ever directly overrule a major strategic decision by the Joint or Combined Chiefs? "Never," Admiral Leahy once told me. On the other hand two offensives in the Asia theater were abruptly countermanded at the Cairo Conference of 1943, largely by the President's decision.

On the tactical level FDR seldom gave actual orders at all; he paid little attention to what was going on in local actions provided the grand objective was being fulfilled, though he was always intimately informed. Occasionally, however, he did make decisions of the most specific kind on comparatively minor enterprises, if they had a strategic aim; for instance General Arnold reproduces one of his written memoranda suggesting, as a result of a talk with T. V. Soong, the bombing of the Shanghai electric-light plant from bases in India. His function as a layman was not, as he said himself to a conference of newspaper editors one day, to stick pins in generals; but whenever it was necessary that a general be stuck, the pin was ready. Only once during the entire war did he even so much as have a talk with a general so eminent as Omar Bradley. On that occasion (before the invasion of Italy) he took Bradley aside to warn him secretly about developments in atomic energy and that the Germans might spring a surprise by the use of new weapons.

Roosevelt's proper caution in these matters may have arisen from an experience in World War I, when he visited Marshal Foch on the Western Front. He marveled at the simple efficiency of Foch's headquarters, and the French generalissimo replied:

> If I concerned myself with details, I could not win the war. I can consider only major advances or major retirements. The knowledge of movements of two or three kilometers here or there would confuse me by diverting my attention from the great objective. Only major results and major strategy concern the . . . commander-in-chief.[4]

After the fall of Tobruk in June, 1942, with all the disaster this seemed to foretell, FDR said to an acquaintance that this catastrophe

[4] Rosenman, Vol. IV, p. 251.

taught him one thing above all—never to interfere in purely military decisions.

Second, though FDR by and large gave full leeway to the military, prodding them the while, he never remotely became their dupe or creature. He was the boss—Commander in Chief in much more than mere name. He enjoyed with the ardor and curiosity of a small boy the secret paraphernalia of the White House Map Room, but he never, as I heard it put, "became a sucker for military mystery." The generals never dazzled him. He remained a civilian first and last, and yet retained smooth and steady control of the most complex series of military operations ever known to history.

Moreover FDR played a substantial role as moderator and conciliator vis-à-vis other forces than our own. A coalition war is the most difficult of all types of war to fight, for the obvious reason that unity of effort and aim must be welded out of so many diverse and often conflicting points of view. Roosevelt had American as well as foreign public opinion to think about too, since the United States is notoriously "noncoalition-minded." We had the money, the munitions, and the machines. In Washington early in 1942 I remember asking a high authority just how the Combined Chiefs of Staff acted. This body, the supreme directing organ for the whole allied military effort, had just begun to function. Answer: "In essence the Combined Chiefs are the White House."

Third, Roosevelt's strategy was sound. It was he (in conjunction with Churchill of course) who took the decision within a few weeks of Pearl Harbor that Germany, not Japan, must be beaten first;[5] it was he who pressed for TORCH, the invasion of North Africa, as a preliminary to the assault on Europe, against the opposition of some of his own best advisers, like Stimson and Marshall; it was he who insisted that American ground troops must be put into combat against German ground troops as soon as possible; above all it was he who

[5] The reason for this was mainly that Germany was the more serious enemy. Hitler could destroy the whole world; Hirohito couldn't. Also if Germany was beaten, the fall of Japan would follow inevitably, whereas the obverse of this was not true. Again, Germany was the only enemy state which could be attacked by all the chief allied powers. Eisenhower testifies in *Crusade in Europe* (New York, Doubleday & Company, 1948) that "no real student of strategy" has ever questioned this decision, though it was often attacked by armchair strategists who thought that Japan should be polished off first, largely for political reasons and because Japan was weaker.

maintained persistent pressure on Churchill for the launching of OVERLORD, the second front in France. (This is not to minimize Churchill's own profound, brilliant, and far-seeing contributions to allied strategy.)

Problems of the most infinite variety and comprehensiveness afflicted FDR without end. He was manager of the entire apparatus of government, and at the same time had to run the war. The sense of balanced values, to say nothing of merciless responsibility and capacity to see the whole picture the whole time, that his task demanded for year after year is almost beyond comprehension. Not only did he, and he alone, have to decide whether Marshall or Eisenhower should command OVERLORD; he himself had to decide whether or not to call off the Army-Navy football game![6] In an incredibly interlaced complexity of fields and enterprises, the final decision was the President's. It was he who had to stiffen MacArthur in the immediate post-Pearl Harbor period, when Filipino morale was bad; it was he who had to decide later to order MacArthur out of Bataan. It was he who determined just how large the Army should be (because he saw clearly that *too* big a military establishment would be tantamount to isolation; i.e., the United States would not be able to continue large shipments of supplies to our allies) and it was he—to choose one example on the domestic front out of literally thousands available—who had to decide whether the War Department or the War Manpower Commission should have charge of the mobilization of civilian labor. And always politics!— senators to cajole, tycoons to encourage, local bosses to coax, administrators to propitiate, rival authorities to juggle, and windspouts to calm down.

Fourth, Roosevelt knew that, in the long run, the outcome of the war would be decided by the power of American industrial production. We do not need to trace the tedious and at times sinuous evolution whereby the National Defense Advisory Commission became the Office of Production Management, which became the Supply, Priorities and Allocations Board, which finally became the War Production Board. But we may note that, early in 1942, FDR had the courage— and foresight—to establish a building program for 60,000 planes that year, 45,000 tanks, 20,000 antiaircraft guns, and 8,000,000 tons of shipping, along with much else, and to raise these stupendous figures to

[6] This was in the era, be it remembered, when the Navy refused even to share the Pentagon Building which the Army had built.

100,000 planes, 75,000 tanks, 35,000 antiaircraft guns, and 10,000,000 tons of shipping in 1943. By the end of the war all known records for production anywhere in the world had been surpassed. And the cost! Early in 1943 Roosevelt asked for war appropriations totaling one hundred *billion* dollars; by the end of that year total expenditures on the war reached $225,000,000,000 which "was more than the whole cost of our government since the inauguration of George Washington."

Fifth, Roosevelt's bouncing energy and highly keyed optimism contributed much to national morale. Nowadays, perhaps, people take it too much for granted that we were bound to win. But particularly in 1942 the military situation was black indeed. The Germans were bearing down on the Nile; the Japanese, having occupied Burma, were at the gates of India. It did not seem that the Soviet Union could hold out much longer, and the life of Britain was being gutted by the U-boats. If the British had given way, if Moscow and Stalingrad had not held, if the Nazis and Japanese had ever been able to make a junction in Asia, the war would probably still be going on. The President had acute awareness of these dangers. They did not daunt him.

When Mr. Willkie undertook his trip around the world FDR told him that "probably" Cairo would have fallen by the time he got there. American production was enormous and unprecedented, yes, but it took a long time for it to gather momentum. Willow Run, for instance, had not produced a single airplane by October, 1942.

Sixth, FDR did everything possible while warfare was still going on to assure American participation in the coming peace. Today the United Nations is pretty much of an old shoe, whether or not we like it, and that the United States is a member is no matter for excitement. But think back to 1919, to 1940, or even 1943! Roosevelt considered, in fact, that the stiffest fight of his entire career would be to get the Senate to ratify American participation in the new world organization. The heirs of the old gang that had killed the League were still powerful isolationists. He was wrong; there was very little fight. But a principal reason for this was the work he did while the war was still being fought; if he had waited it might have been a different story. San Francisco, he told one interviewer, was to be the crowning act of his whole life; full, forceful, and constructive American adhesion to the new peace structure was his dearest wish. Moreover he did not think of "peace" in theoretical or abstract terms; his ideas were concrete and positive; what he hoped for was "the end of the system of unilateral action and exclusive alliances . . . and other expedients that have always failed."

From mid-1944 on FDR paid, in blunt truth, comparatively little attention to military matters; Eisenhower and other witnesses testify that the Commander in Chief was much more interested in postwar problems than the war itself. Yalta, and to a lesser extent Teheran, were peace as well as war conferences, and Roosevelt was actually a postwar President, even though he died before the war was over. He was asked what the United States would do if Russia or any other great power repudiated its United Nations pledges; his answer was, "I do not think that will happen, but if it does, we must go ahead anyway—alone, if need be."[7]

Finally consider the demerit side. For one thing the President, whose best quality was never administration, often refused to delegate authority accurately or define spheres of influence precisely. This was a familiar failing. Everything had to come to *him*. Even Mr. Stimson records how, late in the war, in order to cut through the existing confusions, he had to adopt the extreme technique of getting "his camel's head McCloy[8] into the President's tent of personal government." The President, as is notorious, often gave men contradictory instructions, sent out irresponsible emissaries without consulting the regularly constituted authorities, and played favorites. He had too great confidence in his own durability and charm, he worked far too hard, and non-essentials took a fantastic amount of his time. "One man simply could not do it all," as Stimson says, "and Franklin Roosevelt killed himself trying."

From TORCH to Teheran

Bare chronology need not detain us long. But it may stimulate the jaded memory and put us more in tune with Roosevelt's overwhelming responsibilities, and those of others, to recollect such a miscellany of events packed close together early in the war as the fall of Singapore on February 15, 1942, the Battle of the Coral Sea on May 4, the Japanese landing in the Aleutians on June 12, the Battle of Midway in June, the American assault on Guadalcanal on August 7, the be-

---

[7] Anne O'Hare McCormick in the New York *Times*, April 30, 1945.

[8] John J. McCloy, Assistant Secretary of War and later American High Commissioner in Germany.

ginning of the battle for Stalingrad in September, and the splendid British victory at El Alamein a month later.

Immediately after Pearl Harbor Mr. Churchill arrived at the White House for the first of the great war conferences. We know from his latest memoirs what magnificent sageness he brought to Roosevelt, on everything from the setting up of the Combined Chiefs to the plans for TORCH. Manifestly the primary preoccupation was to keep from being beaten. But strategic plans were so competently grounded, industrial production progressed with such promise, an army was trained with so much dispatch, and the general diplomacy of coalition warfare so acutely negotiated that, by November, 1942, American troops in great number had landed in North Africa in an operation which was unprecedentedly risky but which from a military point of view went forward almost without hitch, and which prepared the way for the ejection of the Axis forces from Africa by the spring of 1943. So the route was laid bare for the subsequent Anglo-American invasions of Sicily and Italy.

During this evolution one considerable embarrassment to the President was the Darlan affair, and one considerable steppingstone was the announcement of the unconditional surrender formula at Casablanca.

Admiral Darlan—to summarize the story in the briefest possible space—had been a Vichy stalwart, and therefore from any reasonable point of view our enemy. But, it appeared during the African landings, he was the only Frenchman who could call off continued fighting by the French. Eisenhower therefore employed him to this end, and Darlan became our man until he was assassinated shortly thereafter. No political murder in history, it may be safely said, ever brought greater relief to practically everybody concerned. One should note further that we were forced into the position of having to utilize Darlan by serious miscalculations as to the quality of other French talent available, like General Giraud, and by utter confusion as to the potentialities of General de Gaulle. The State Department's Vichy policy still handicapped decent or fair judgment on the "so-called" Free French. A biting storm of criticism about Darlan burst out in America and England. Until this time it had been generally conceded that the allies were fighting a "clean" war. But now it seemed that we did not hesitate to make deals with Fascists if this suited military expediency, and to work amicably with quislings if this happened to be convenient. Purists all over the world, who had assumed that we were fighting in the name of freedom, were mortally shocked. Not only purists. Almost everybody was shocked. Harry Hopkins once told me, "No matter what victories he wins, Ike [Eisenhower] will never live that one down." This is unfair to Eisenhower. He was completely unskilled in political affairs and his only motive was to drive ahead quickly and save American lives. But for weeks thereafter he had little time or energy for military business, so harassed was he by protests about Darlan from Washington and elsewhere and appeals to straighten the matter out. Roosevelt himself had no direct role in the Darlan fracas. But the responsibility was ultimately his, and it worried him. He didn't want "his" war to go sour politically; he did not like to think that his generals were doing business with a notorious collaborator of Hitler. Even Churchill called the French admiral "dirty Darlan." Yet FDR had to concede that from any sound military point of view the Americans in the field had no choice but to do what they did. Hence he supported Eisenhower vigorously on the understanding that Darlan was not to be "trusted" and that all arrangements must be "temporary." Discussing the whole episode later he summarized his point of view by quoting a Balkan proverb, that you can let the devil himself help you over a bridge if you drop him on the other side. It is not a particularly ennobling proverb.

In January, 1943, immediately after TORCH, the President journeyed to Casablanca. This, except for the Atlantic Charter meeting, was the first of the presidential war conferences held off American soil, it broke all manner of precedents, and it gave Roosevelt a spirited, glamorous experience he enjoyed to the utmost. Casablanca had pivotal importance for several reasons, mostly strategic and psychological. It cemented the close friendship now linking Roosevelt and Mr. Churchill; it attempted to loosen the exasperating deadlock in French political affairs; it proved that the Allies, not the Axis, had at last firmly attained the military initiative; and it laid concrete plans for the great offensives to take place later in the war.

Also it produced the unconditional surrender formula, the tale behind which is tangled in the extreme. The version commonly accepted is that FDR, without consultation with Churchill, tossed off this major strategic tenet, on which the whole course of the war and the peace to come might rest, extemporaneously at a press conference following a nerve-racking interview with Giraud and de Gaulle.

Roosevelt himself gave this story wide currency; he even said that he thought up the formula on the spur of the moment out of his memory of Grant and the Civil War. Certainly the State Department, which ought to have been informed, knew nothing of it. Mr. Hull was dumfounded. And Mr. Churchill is on record as having stated that "the first time I heard that phrase used it was from the lips of President Roosevelt." But the Roosevelt version of the spontaneous origin of the phrase cannot be wholly true. For, discussing the matter in the House of Commons years later, Churchill conceded that he and FDR had talked it over informally "at meal times," and we know now, in fact, not only that there had been some sort of consultation but that the actual proposal for unconditional surrender had been communicated to the British War Cabinet, with a proviso by Churchill that Italy be excluded. But the mystery grows. Mr. Bevin, who was a member of the War Cabinet, has angrily stated in the Commons that the Cabinet never had a chance to say a word on the issue, and that he "would never have agreed to such a thing." Yet against this is Churchill's subsequent statement declaring frankly that he had informed the War Cabinet that "he and Roosevelt intended to issue an unconditional surrender demand but to exclude Italy," and quoting a reply from Attlee and Eden to the effect that the "British Cabinet unanimously believed that Italy should be included," i.e., should get the same treatment as Germany and Japan. Obviously this proves that Roosevelt's declaration was not spur of the moment or haphazard. But why did he pretend that it was? Why did he cook up such a story? Was this carelessness, distrust of his own advisers, or sheer bravado? Did FDR want to protect Churchill, who might have been embarrassed by joint responsibility for the statement at that time? Or was Churchill protecting Roosevelt?

Whatever the eventual solution to this mystery, the President had several motives in making the initial declaration. (1) To encourage Russia. At that time the Anglo-American high command had serious fears, not merely of Russian collapse, but of a negotiated peace between the Soviet Union and Germany. A vital paragraph in the Casablanca communique stated that "the President and Prime Minister realized up to the full the enormous weight of the war which Russia is successfully bearing along her whole land front, and their *prime object* [italics mine] has been to draw as much weight as possible off the Russian armies." To cap this the unconditional surrender statement was designed to tell Stalin that we too, beyond any doubt at all, were going to fight through to a real finish. (2) Some silly people had been whispering about negotiations between the western allies and Hitler, and Roosevelt wanted to shut them up. (3) FDR hoped that the statement would tighten things up on the home front, and tell anybody still lukewarm about the war that it was going to last a long, long time. (4) For the sake of future peace, he felt that it was necessary for Germany to be beaten actually *in the field*, so that the German people would never again be able to say, as they had said after World War I, that their armies had not been legitimately defeated. (5) He wanted to encourage the submerged peoples in France, the Balkans, and elsewhere, who had suffered most from Hitler, by telling them that they would be avenged.

Probably, too, unconditional surrender was meant to be an answer to the Darlan scandal. It would, it was hoped, serve notice that even if we had dealt with a quisling like Darlan, we would not repeat the mistake in Germany and Japan.

In any case the formula did little if any harm. It had small effect on the major course of events. Mr. Bevin has said that its consequence was to leave the Reich without a government and that as a result Germany could not be grappled with after the war, but this would have happened anyway. Unconditional surrender did not prolong the war; Hitler, we know now, would have fought to the last gasp anyway, and so did the Japanese.

Militarily FDR had to keep his eye on much during the rest of 1943. The problem above all problems was that of the Second Front, which Stalin and the Russians pressed for sternly. Decision to make a beachhead in Normandy and invade German-held France had been reached in April, 1942, but its execution was repeatedly delayed, first because of the inordinate difficulties of amassing sufficient forces in Great Britain for the assault, secondly because the British, with plenty of justification, thought it might be too dangerous if premature. As FDR himself said at a press conference late in 1942, "You can't walk down the street and buy a second front in the department store." Stalin pressed Roosevelt to advance. Churchill pressed him to be prudent. This was the background of the historic conference that gathered at Teheran in November, 1943, when Roosevelt, Churchill, and Stalin met together for the first time.

FDR Versus Stalin—First Round

Once, a good many years ago, I wrote that Stalin was the most powerful single human being in the world. He still is. Among sources of his power, I mentioned, were qualities like perseverance, tenacity, and concentration. "Stalin," I said, "is about as emotional as a slab of basalt. If he has nerves, they are veins in rock."

For years Roosevelt had wanted to meet Stalin, and transform his Herculean duets with Churchill into three-power talks. Over a prolonged interval Stalin had delayed the climax of a meeting for several reasons, among them his own suspiciousness and basic hostility to the West and also the fact that he was the active military leader of the Russian forces and could not spare time out of Moscow during a period of supreme crisis. The route to Teheran was prepared by several other conferences, like Molotov's visit to Washington and Hull's to Moscow; also FDR and the Russian dictator secretly exchanged longhand letters.[9] For a time it appears that Stalin suggested Fairbanks, Alaska, as the meeting place. When, finally, the three leaders did meet at Teheran, the world carefully paid heed. It has been well said that this conference in Persia, bringing together for the first time the effective spokesmen of the United States, the Soviet Union, and the British Empire, represented a concentration of physical power and political authority unique in the whole history of mankind.

FDR's Russian policy had, from its inception, been on the basis of calculated risk. He was torn between twin fears (a) that Russia might be beaten; (b) that Russia might win too much and conquer Europe. "In all our dealings with Stalin," he once told the former Polish Prime Minister Stanislaw Mikolajczyk, "we must keep our fingers crossed."

Never before had a President of the United States traveled so far while in office; never before had a President resided, so to speak, on foreign soil, because he slept at the Russian Embassy, not our own. (Facilities for protection were better within the Russian compound, and to be Stalin's guest saved him fatiguing travel within the city.) Not for thirty years or more had Stalin, on his side, ever set foot out

[9] See Forrest Davis, "What Really Happened at Teheran," *Saturday Evening Post,* May 13 and 20, 1944. These articles are packed with material of the utmost value on FDR's foreign policy and Teheran.

of Russia, and one contemporary account states that he had never flown before.

There were all manner of festivities. Churchill presented Stalin with a handsome sword, the gift of the King of England, as a memorial to Russian heroism at Stalingrad; Stalin toasted Roosevelt, saying that without American supplies and munitions the Russians could not have won their victories. Churchill insisted on being host at one dinner because he was the eldest of the three, because his name came first alphabetically, and because it happened to be his birthday. A great concourse of Brobdingnagian underlings met and merged— Hopkins, Marshall, Voroshilov, Eden, Leahy, Clark Kerr, Molotov, Harriman, Elliott Roosevelt, Sarah Oliver (Churchill's daughter), and enough brass to equip a brace of battleships. The Teheranese knew nothing at all of this, except by peeking at a distance. Even the young Shah of Iran had no role except as onlooker, though theoretically he should have been the host.

Roosevelt was, of course, meeting Stalin for the first time, whereas Churchill had encountered him before. The President made all-out efforts to win the Soviet dictator's esteem; it pleased him that he and Stalin got along personally better than Churchill and Stalin did. But I have heard from several participants at the conference that Stalin was seemingly perplexed by Roosevelt, though he treated him with great deference. Churchill he could grapple with. Stalin gave the impression that he understood Churchill perfectly, and that there was even a community between them, as between lusty fellow rogues. But FDR was much more difficult, a new type of phenomenon puzzling to the glacierlike Russian's mind, nervously elusive, too optimistic, strangely discursive, and perhaps naïve.

This celebrated Teheran Conference about which so much nonsense has been written had the simplest kind of overriding aim—to consolidate the military effort of the three powers, establish incontrovertibly the fact that the western allies would invade France the next year and thus inaugurate the Second Front, and make derivative preparation for the peace by settling, if possible, the German problem.

Much that happened in the dingy Persian capital was in the realm of the curious, and some is in the lonely domain of the forgotten. For instance Roosevelt shocked Churchill on one occasion (and pleased Stalin) by suggesting that the area around the Kiel Canal should be permanently internationalized, i.e., de-Germanized into a "free state."

And—contrary to most belief—it was at Teheran, not Yalta, that Stalin promised to enter the war against Japan as soon as the German war was over. It requires the most careful reading of various authorities—like Sherwood, Deane, Byrnes, Forrest Davis, and others—to resurrect the political and spiritual atmosphere, not to mention the chronology, of what went on in such a Neolithic period as six or seven years ago. For instance great numbers of Americans think that Stalin pushed Roosevelt around very roughly and crudely and got exactly what he wanted on this business of when he should enter into the Japanese war. Actually our chief worry at this time—the fact may seem incredible but survey of the relevant records will prove it—was that the Russians might become a belligerent against Japan *too soon*. Reason: Germany was by no means beaten at this time, neither was Japan, and if Russia was suddenly forced to fight on another front, the Germans might have recouped their Russian losses and together with Japan knocked the Soviet Union out of the war.

But the chief issue at Teheran, which still sings around the very word "Teheran," and its chief result, was OVERLORD, the invasion of western Europe by Great Britain and America, the killers' thrust against Germany straight through France.

FDR's motive for pushing OVERLORD was double: (1) He accepted the unanimous advice of his principal military advisers that this was incomparably the best of all possible ways to smash Germany once for all, win the European war, and to save countless thousands of American lives; (2) he wanted to work just as closely and amicably as possible with the Soviet Union in order to bring it wholeheartedly into the new international organization and a decent, lasting peace.

Churchill's point of view was much more subtle and complex. Instead of a single giant lunge across western Europe, he also favored attack on Germany through the "soft underbelly"—Italy, southeastern Europe, and the Balkans. Of course he wanted to win the war quickly too, but also he was thinking in long-range terms of what would be the balance of power in those regions after the war. In part, at least, he stubbornly urged the underbelly campaign for political reasons. He wanted to keep Russia out of eastern Europe, or at least to check her influence there, and thus preserve the Continent from further infection by the Red Army and/or Communism.

Stalin naturally wanted the overwhelming emphasis to be on Normandy, and he too had obvious political reasons. Churchill wanted Normandy plus the Mediterranean. FDR (though he was not averse to subordinate action in the south) cast the deciding vote, and took Stalin's side. Of course, it was all but impossible for Churchill to overrule FDR; he always had to keep in mind the preponderance of American manpower and industrial potential. "Roosevelt," General Deane has said, "was thinking of winning the war; the others were thinking of their relative positions when the war was won."[10]

Historians will argue about the rights and wrongs of this for decades to come, or until an atomic bomb destroys us all. The case may well be made that Roosevelt was 100 per cent right, even from the point of view of the immediately contemporary European situation. Because if the chief weight of the allied armies had struck at Germany from the south instead of the west, there might have been nothing in the west itself to stop the Russians when they really started moving, and the Red Army might—conceivably—be in Paris and Milan today, as well as Berlin and Budapest.

But Roosevelt was certainly wrong, or shall we say overoptimistic, in some of his political estimates. That the Russians let him down badly is undeniable, and we shall see presently what happened at the next conference at Yalta.

The Same Old Roosevelt

Joseph Eastman, the railroad administrator, asked him to resolve a bitter dispute on the price of steel rails. The railroads wanted to pay $36 per ton, whereas the steel men held out for $40. FDR picked up a pad and scrawled:

$$\begin{array}{r} 40 \\ 36 \\ \hline 2\overline{)76} = 38 \end{array}$$

Then he told Eastman, delighted, "The price will be $38."

George Backer, the publicist, was a guest at a Hyde Park picnic. Cars were unloading along the road, and the President noted Backer's chauffeur hovering respectfully on the outer edges of the group. "Sit down here!" FDR commanded; the chauffeur dutifully took his place to eat on the grass a few feet from the President.

Walter Nash, the Deputy Prime Minister of New Zealand, suggested

[10] *The Strange Alliance,* by John R. Deane (New York, The Viking Press, 1947), p. 43.

at an important conference that American forces occupy a small island in the Pacific area that New Zealand was interested in. Roosevelt said, "No, not that island; an island nearby called Mangareva would be better." Nash had never heard of Mangareva, and confessed his embarrassment. "Oh, it's in the Tuamotu Archipelago, in the postal administration of Tahiti," the President smiled cheerfully. "I know the place because I'm a stamp collector."[11]

Dr. Foster Kennedy, the neurologist, brought his ten-year-old daughter Isabel-Ann to call on FDR. The President showed her the knick-knacks on his desk and the mantelpiece nearby, where scores of figures of donkeys were on display. Isabel-Ann professed that she too liked to collect toy animals, but that she had all kinds, not just donkeys. "Oh," the President smiled, "I'm just like your father—I have to be a specialist."

Once Frances Perkins heard him answer a question put to him by a young man about his philosophy. He responded, "I am a Christian and a Democrat—that's all!"

Professor Charles E. Merriam dropped in on FDR one day, and found him slouched forward on his desk, head in hands. FDR said, "Professor, did you notice who just left the office?" Merriam said he had seen Ickes in the anteroom. FDR proceeded, "Did you see the other fellow who was in here?" Merriam shook his head.

"Wallace. He and Ickes were in here for an hour arguing as to who should have a couple of sticks of timber along the Cumberland River. And do you know—neither of them controls a single vote!"

The strain of war made little difference to the fundamentals of Roosevelt's character. He was still as friendly, irreverent, wily, agile, full of dash, and devoted to the art of politics as he had been ten years before when he reached the Presidency. But there was a difference. Ten years in the White House take a toll. Roosevelt was getting old.

The War: Affairs Domestic

During this whole period FDR faced home-front problems of bewildering variety. People grumbled at rationing of foodstuffs and gasoline; the cost of living skyrocketed; Congress ruthlessly cut various appropriations; savage political feuds broke out in the Administration;[12]

---

[11] The *New Yorker*, March 30, 1946.

[12] At one point FDR had to issue a formal order instructing "every government department and agency" to stop bickering and airing confusions and disagreements in public.

railways were overloaded, inflation threatened, stoppages occurred, shortages became acute; and almost everything important enough to be a problem at all could, it seemed, only reach settlement by being dumped in the President's own tired lap.

The White House circle needed new blood. FDR's chief lieutenants were shuffled from job to job and overworked to prostration. "The President either appoints four men to do one job, or one man to do four," it was said. Some old faces remained; some new faces appeared. Fred M. Vinson, who succeeded Byrnes at the Office of Economic Stabilization; Harold D. Smith, who rendered incalculable and incomparable service as Director of the Budget; Chester Bowles, who took over OPA;[13] Robert P. Patterson in the War Department and James Forrestal in the Navy; Admiral Land (shipping) and Donald Nelson (WPB); Byron Price (censorship), Milo Perkins (BEW), and White House intimates like Wayne Coy, Isador Lubin, Lauchlin Currie—the list is endless. But the most spectacularly rising star was that of James F. Byrnes. Roosevelt made him Director of the Office of War Mobilization in May, 1943; he became "assistant President" in charge of the domestic front. Some conception of the unparalleled magnitude of his job—and Roosevelt's—may be gathered from the fact that, before the war was over, no fewer than 156 different main war agencies existed in the executive branch of the government *alone*. To list them all takes fourteen pages in a book published by the Bureau of the Budget. Does anybody remember today the Advisory Board of Just Compensation of the War Shipping Administration? Or the Alaska War Council? Or the British-American Joint Patent Interchange Committee? Or the Committee for Congested Production Areas? Or the Interdepartmental Committee for the Voluntary Payroll Savings Plan for the Purchase of War Bonds? Or the President's Soviet Protocol Committee? Or the Office of Fishery Control?

One vexatious, envenomed feud was that over the Board of Economic Warfare, which brought into conflict gladiators like Henry Wallace and Jesse Jones, to say nothing of the State Department and a round dozen other embittered agencies. To settle this FDR had to oust both Wallace and Jones from their respective jobs in this province and set up a new organization, the Office of Economic Warfare (OEW),

---

[13] An index of Roosevelt's political troubles is that it took Congress six months to set up OPA.

which presently gave way to still another, the Foreign Economic Administration (FEA).

Another remarkable example of tangle, botch, and fractiousness came with the development of information services. One agency was the Office of Facts and Figures (OFF) which was organized and run by Archibald MacLeish, then the Librarian of Congress, but the scope and resources of which were severely limited. Others were the Office of Government Reports (OGR), under Lowell Mellett; the Division of Information of the Office of Emergency Management; and the Office of Civilian Defense, run for a brief time by Mayor La Guardia of New York. Also General Donovan had the most important role of all as Coordinator of Information. His organization operated independently of OFF, but it shared certain functions with OCD. If the reader thinks this is difficult there is much more confusion to follow. After stormy troubles the Donovan establishment (COI) split like a writhing amoeba and two new agencies emerged, the Office of War Information, under the admirably efficient leadership of Elmer Davis, and the Office of Strategic Services, again with Donovan as head, but now under the jurisdiction of the Army. The trembling frontier between OWI and OSS was by no means clearly marked; some men in COI elected to go with OWI (like Sherwood, who became director of its all-important Overseas Branch); some stayed with Donovan. Then all manner of internecine feuds began. Davis and Sherwood had a long-drawn-out fight; it went all the way up to FDR himself. To keep publicity down, both men came into the White House secretly one day, through the tunnel from the treasury; FDR quite properly said that a disagreement on this level was not his business, and that the two contestants should straighten it out themselves. As to the OSS it was, of course, primarily a military agency, but it got into several long disputes. For one thing it needed Latin America badly as part of its sphere of activity, but this whole continent belonged to Nelson Rockefeller, who was Coordinator of Inter-American Affairs. The FBI (under the Department of Justice) had highly important business in Latin America too, with the result that Donovan and J. Edgar Hoover became allies, more or less, against Rockefeller's CIAA. Meantime the Joint Chiefs held supreme authority at one end of the field, and the State Department fought tenaciously for its privileges at the other. Then heated jealousies developed between OSS and OWI, and OWI itself had a savage crisis when three valuable members of the New York staff,[14] who had been directing short-wave

[14] Joseph Barnes, Edd Johnson, and James P. Warburg.

propaganda, were forced to resign because of broadcasts attacking Badoglio and the "moronic little" King of Italy; it had suddenly become Roosevelt's policy to play with these gentry (though nobody knew this clearly) and the innocents at home had to be ruthlessly sacrificed. Also a prolonged, bitter struggle took place over control of something that became a cross between the Holy Grail and the Golden Fleece—PWB, the Psychological Warfare Branch of the Army. One group (led by Sherwood) thought that our propaganda and psychological warfare should be "white," i.e., should so far as possible tell nothing but the truth. The military favored "black," which made no bones about being deceptive whenever necessary. "Black" won.

A book might be written about what I have just attempted to sketch in a paragraph. I go into the matter at all only because it is a convenient example of the type of jurisdictional complexity Roosevelt had to handle. An executive order was, in those days, a kind of hunting license. You got your precious order; you hoped it was a "good" order, because many were contradictory; then you rushed full speed to Harold Smith at the Budget to implement it. Administration became a mad, pell-mell race. Victory went to the fastest or the cleverest. Why did FDR permit such extravagantly inefficient performances? Probably there were four reasons: (1) This is the way democratic government often, alas, has to work. (2) There was great lack of good men, and even the best of men have frailties. (3) By seeing what fledgling administrator got to the Treasury or the Senate Appropriations Committee first with the best results, FDR learned which of his assistants were the most nimble and would survive best in future crises. (4) To an extent he actively *liked* the stress, the competition, and even the confusion.

No single hour was without a task or duty. FDR exchanged greetings with President Vargas of Brazil in January, 1943, and on February 1 submitted to Congress a treaty relinquishing American extraterritorial rights in China. A few days later he proposed to limit all salaries in the country to $25,000 a year, and on February 9 by executive order set the minimum work week at forty-eight hours. He vetoed a bill on agricultural parity early in April (because its tendency was inflationary), and then issued the famous "hold the line" order on prices and wages. He visited Mexico later that month, and on May 2 seized the coal mines. A new committee on Fair Employment Practice was established by executive order on May 27 and on June 25 he vetoed the Smith-Connally (War Labor Disputes) bill. He had to untangle a snarl in the Food Administration a little later, and transfer what was left of the PWA to the Federal Works Agency. He vetoed a bill that would have crippled the Commodity Credit Corporation, and on July 28 (after the invasion of Sicily) came a notable Fireside Chat. In August he pledged himself to independence for the Philippines when they were liberated from Japan, launched the Third War Loan, and protested spiritedly to Congress over a rider on an appropriations bill that involved personal injustice to Professor Robert Morss Lovett and two other individuals. In September he sent Congress a long message on the progress of the war, and recommended self-government for Puerto Rico. In November he established UNRRA, and in December (while he was at Teheran) vetoed a bill to make December 7 a national holiday.

1943 became 1944, and the tempo quickened; every event was hydra-headed; pressure, scope, and velocity all increased. Always FDR exhorted his subordinates to get things moving, to get things done. The chief occurrence of 1944 was, of course, the D-Day of all D-Days, June 6, when American and British forces at last crossed the Channel to open the second front in France. Steady advances by MacArthur and the Navy meantime took place in the Pacific. But also the President had to occupy himself with such matters as the short-lived resignation of Senator Barkley as majority leader, the seizure of Montgomery Ward in Chicago, legislation for a projected authority like the TVA for the Missouri, Federal aid to education, worry over the possibility that Mr. Stimson might resign, veto of a bill about the Jackson Hole monument in Wyoming, the biggest budget of any nation in the history of the world, a moratorium for insurance companies, a program for postwar scientific research, secret negotiations with both labor and management over Oak Ridge where the first atomic plant was being built, a mayoralty election in New York City, the GI Bill of Rights, and the staying of a court-martial sentence inflicted on a young marine for shooting a wounded calf.

Chapter 19

FOURTH TERM AND YALTA

The historian is a prophet looking backwards.
—SCHLEGEL

Time and change; change and time; remorselessly these imponderables bit into Roosevelt. He was older now, thinner, gaunt, grayer, more wont to be abstracted and even peevish. He was older now—past sixty —and lonelier. It was inconceivable that the years would not take their toll, and they took it at a leap. Age clamped down on him. If one looks at photographs taken month by month it seems that he became white-haired almost overnight. But in some respects nobody could accuse him of losing grip; in fact as he grew older he held the reins of power even more tightly, as if to compensate for fatigue and growing weakness. Nothing was going to budge him from the driver's seat except death. Soon, death did.

Toward the Last Phase: Fourth Term

The United States of America is, as is well known, a country gripped immutably by the calendar; punctually every four years the electorate goes to the polls to choose a new president no matter how inconvenient the date may be. No other important nation has this system. Come death, hell, or high water, the election with its attendant turmoil must occur on the dot; these colossal leap-year cataclysms are ordained like the movement of the tides. It is a good thing too. But only once before in American history—in 1864—had this circumstance produced an election in the midst of a tremendous war, and it is a striking tribute to the health of American democracy that an utterly free national poll, with no holds barred, did duly register its untrammeled verdict with little cost to the war effort during the culmination of the greatest struggle ever to engage the nation. A lot of energy spouted off into partisan electioneering, and people who should not have been interrupted in their war duties were forced to waste appalling amounts of time. This does not affect the basic beneficent fact that the American people were offered full opportunity to switch teams and appoint a new commander in chief if they so willed, during the very climax of the war.

FDR did not want to run in 1944, but he had to. Four years before, he might well not have offered himself to the electorate; this time he had little choice. I have just looked through an elephantine mass of old newspaper clippings; the fourth term (except in the Hearst press, the New York *Daily News,* and so on) was never an issue of itself to the degree that the third term was. Roosevelt was not criticized so much for the bare fact of running. At least this disproved the specious charge that he was a "dictator." Also if he were truly indispensable as war leader, there was no point to objecting on theoretical grounds to the fact that he was running again. The fourth term was the inevitable consequence—penalty, one might almost say—of the third. The former Vice-President, Mr. Garner, gave it as his conviction at the time that FDR would keep on running as long as he lived, and even Josephus Daniels stated after his death that he might well have been a fifth-term candidate if he had survived the fourth. This is pure conjecture. White House correspondents who seldom left his side are convinced that FDR did not "want" to run in 1944, if only because his health was failing. One may discount Roosevelt's own statement that all he wanted was to retire but not the evidence of so many of his close collaborators. Why, then, did he run? Ego and the conviction that he was indispensable had something to do with it. But also he truly conceived it as his minimum duty to see the war through. He could not possibly quit the job. Whether or not the state of his health should have kept him from running is another question. Perhaps he should have been prevented from exerting himself with this last effort. But by whom?

The commander-in-chief issue was fiercely argued, particularly after the nomination in June when FDR and his entourage took a trip across the country and then journeyed to Hawaii. Thousands of people saw him and heard him speak, though no report of the trip appeared in the newspapers till it was over. He had announced that he would not run "in the usual partisan, political sense," but developments made this seem disingenuous. Obviously the fact that he was showing himself to large crowds of war workers and to GI's at our military installations and elsewhere was not exactly an electoral disadvantage, particularly in view of the soldier vote. Mr. Dewey, his opponent, had no such opportunity to address troops. The fact was that the President had become a divided personality; he was Commander in Chief in one role, and presidential aspirant in another.[1] That both roles should be held by one man infuriated the opposition; he was accused of "gross impropriety," "bad sportsmanship," and the like. He was even accused of setting the date of D-Day to jibe with political developments (the accusation is just plain silly), and to have worked out details in Pacific strategy to favor his campaign. Admiral Leahy among others has denied this authoritatively. Roosevelt's reputation for cleverness was so blinding that people always looked for sinister motives in the most innocent circumstances. One Republican maneuver was an attempt to raise a constitutional issue; it was asserted that FDR was "Commander in Chief" of Army and Navy, yes, but not of the civilian population. Dewey himself was in a quandary because, as Governor of New York and a patriotic citizen, he had called for "unswerving loyalty" to the Commander in Chief when war broke out. But now the Commander in Chief was his hated rival in a hot political race.

Some conservative Democrats fought FDR in 1944 as in 1940, but with less effect. The Democratic party had become, in effect, Mr. Roosevelt. It was the person of the President, little more or less. Before the convention a movement came to nominate General Marshall, but quite properly this good soldier would have none of it. Groups like the so-called Texas "Regulars" were inflamed antagonists to FDR, but their opposition did not amount to much. At the convention itself Senator Byrd of Virginia got 89 votes and Jim Farley exactly one. Roosevelt got 1,066.

What really interested the convention was the Vice-Presidency. This is an involved and not very edifying story. In 1940, even though he was in excellent health, FDR had enough realization of the mortality of man to take acute interest in the choice of his running mate. That was one reason why, in the end, he insisted on Henry Wallace, whom he considered to be the ablest liberal candidate available, especially on foreign policy. But in 1944, when FDR was four years older after withstanding the merciless pressure of the Presidency for twelve solid years, and at a time when his own physical condition had sharply deteriorated, he seemed to take no decisive interest at all in the person of whoever might have to succeed him. Certainly this is strange.

We face once more the puzzling subject of FDR's relationship to

[1] One joke was that the President's political tactics were so aggressive that he should be called "commando in chief."

Wallace. That he dropped Wallace in 1944[2] was a blessing to the country, as subsequent events manifestly proved, but more remarkable than the dropping itself was the brutal, circuitous manner in which it was performed. The ostensible reason was that the big-city politicians and organization chieftains said that Wallace would no longer go down with the country and would be a serious handicap to the ticket. Perhaps FDR had premonitions as to Wallace's future as a fellow traveler. But this is doubtful, because on July 14 he wrote the chairman of the convention that although he did not want to dictate to the assembly he, personally, if a delegate, would vote for Wallace. A few days later he saw Wallace off to Chicago and whispered to him, according to Wallace's own story, "Henry, I hope it's the same old ticket." Then on July 19 Roosevelt came out for two other people!—without letting Wallace know. His hand may have been forced by dramatic exigencies within his own party, but even so (and conceding fully that Wallace would have been a disaster as President) this can hardly be considered other than as the worst double-cross in Roosevelt's history.

One reason why FDR cooled to Wallace was that, during the four years he had been Vice-President, Wallace had made little effort to get along with the politicians, even the senators over whom he presided every day. Roosevelt simply couldn't understand this. He thought: (a) it was Wallace's duty to have played politics; (b) it should have been fun.

If one can solve the riddle of this performance over Wallace at the convention, one can solve the riddle of Roosevelt as a whole. It is not enough to say merely that the President equivocated, played two ends, and gave conflicting promises. Probably the true explanation, as indicated above, is that FDR did not care much *who* was Vice-President. He was beyond all that. He was not deliberately devious or opportunistic; he was bored. Nothing whatever interested him but winning the war and peace, with himself in the saddle as a creature of circumstance. He was no longer capable even of caring much for his own life, let alone for what might happen after. He did not compete against destiny; he was willing to let fate play the cards as it willed, without regard to his own survival or what came later. Was this irresponsible? Or Olympian?

There were at least a dozen active candidates for the Vice-Presidency,

[2] As Vice-President. Roosevelt rewarded him later by making him Secretary of Commerce.

and Roosevelt encouraged more than one. He even pulled old Mr. Hull out of the bag once more and told him he could have the position for the asking. Jimmy Byrnes certainly thought that *he* was bound to be the candidate, if only because he expected to be rewarded for having stepped down from the Supreme Court to become economic mobilizer. But Byrnes was too conservative and he had other disadvantages; labor opposed him hotly. Busy with the war and as always hating to be disagreeable, FDR could never quite steel himself to telling Byrnes that he was unacceptable, and Leo Crowley was given the job of breaking the lamentable news. When he did so Byrnes, angry and disappointed, telephoned FDR direct demanding to know if it were true that he was out. The President, uncomfortable, dodged the question. Then someone else was assigned the duty of "taking care of Jimmy" to keep him quiet.

Meantime the convention met. It was run, not by Hopkins this time, but by the old-line professionals, Ed Flynn, Frank Walker, sundry urban bosses, and the new chairman of the Democratic National Committee, Robert E. Hannegan, with labor as a strong and growing influence. Particularly Sidney Hillman, head of the Political Action Committee of the CIO (which was to play a vital role in the campaign), held a commanding position. Ed Kelly of Chicago, Hannegan, and Walker all thought firmly that Byrnes should be chosen. They sent a message to this effect to FDR, who apparently accepted their decision but at the same time washed his hands of the whole matter by saying, "What you fellows decide will be all right, but clear it with the labor men," i.e., Sidney Hillman. Then Hillman refused to approve Byrnes. This meant that the whole field was open again, and Wallace gained a rapid lead. Then on July 19 the President wrote Hannegan that he would be glad to run with "either Harry Truman or Bill Douglas." The bosses refused absolutely to accept Wallace, and both Truman and Douglas were acceptable to Hillman. One person who played a considerable role in this singular development was Anna Boettiger. As originally drafted the phrase in Roosevelt's letter was "Bill Douglas or Harry Truman." Hannegan persuaded Roosevelt to change this wording at the last moment so that Truman's name would precede Douglas's, on the grounds that Truman was the stronger candidate and that the convention would go for whomever the President named first. Of such magical power was Roosevelt's most casual word! And out of such fantastic procedures in the practice of American democracy did Mr. Truman eventually become President of the United States!

Notable is the irony that Mr. Truman himself intended to nominate Byrnes. In fact—the circumstances are all but incredible—Truman actually had the text of a nominating speech for Byrnes in his pocket when he was told that he, not Byrnes, was to be the candidate.

The phrase "clear it with Sidney" haunted FDR during the campaign, but it did not hurt him much even though it was compared to a famous alleged indiscretion by Hopkins years before, "We will tax and tax, spend and spend, and elect and elect." There was nothing improper in FDR's remark. Any president is, in fact, duty bound to see that a leading vice-presidential candidate should be acceptable to a powerful wing of his own support.

Roosevelt and Truman never became close, although the President admired greatly his record as senator and particularly the good job he did as chairman of the committee keeping tab on the national defense program. Even so, FDR met him only once in the entire time between the convention and inauguration. In all manner of ways the President had shunted himself into aloofness.

We need say little about the campaign itself, which was poisonously bitter. One minor point I remember is that many voters who were employed in banks, big corporations, and the like were afraid to wear Roosevelt buttons while at work; coming down the elevators and going out in the streets at five P.M., they would take their Dewey buttons off and put on instead FDR buttons they had concealed behind their lapels.

Mr. Dewey was at a grave disadvantage on at least three counts. In the first place he was running against Roosevelt as war president. Second, he was forced before November, in order to make any kind of headway at all on domestic issues, to endorse much New Deal legislation, and hence opened himself to the charge of "Me-tooism." Third, the Republican record was excessively vulnerable on foreign policy. For instance Republican congressmen had voted against repeal of the Arms Embargo by 129 to 5; against extension of Selective Service on the eve of war, 135 to 24; against arming merchant ships, 137 to 22; against Lend Lease, 135 to 24. Mr. Dewey himself had said something preposterous about Lend Lease, that it "would bring an end to free government in the United States and would abolish the Congress for all practical purposes." Moreover Roosevelt gained great effect by pointing out that if Dewey were elected, chairmanships of several important Congressional committees would go to the most rabid isolationists, like Johnson and Fish. Dewey was, in effect, in a cleft stick during the whole campaign. He could not possibly take a defeatist line, which would have been suicide; yet he had to attack the way the war was being conducted—and it was being conducted very well indeed.

Most people thought the result would be close. Dr. Gallup's poll had Dewey in the lead almost until the last minute, and a magazine like *Time* even predicted that it might be weeks before the winner could be announced, on account of the soldiers' vote. FDR himself forecast that he would get 335 electoral votes to Dewey's 196; actually he got 432 and Dewey 99. Roosevelt carried 36 states, and his strength was so strategically placed that he would have won even if he had lost the entire solid South. The President's popular vote was, however, considerably cut down; his majority was only 3,000,000, the smallest in any presidential election since 1916. The Dewey experts calculated that a shift of some 300,000 votes in a few key states would have given the Republicans an electoral majority. But it is also true that a switch of only 282,000 in the states Dewey won would have given Roosevelt a clean sweep of all 48.

Why did Roosevelt win? The simplest explanation is that you don't change pitchers in the last inning with overwhelming victory in sight. But this does not tell the whole story because, even with the country at war, domestic considerations played a substantial role. It is significant that Democrats all down the line won their biggest Congressional victory since 1932, and that immediately after the election FDR told a press conference that his domestic policy was still "a little left of center."

But what exactly was the center to be left of? What did these terms mean in a country where the national income had multiplied enormously overnight? Center, as was aptly said, had moved right.

Toward the Last Phase: Personal

One of Roosevelt's ambassadors saw the President during the conference with Chiang Kai-shek at Cairo, after Teheran in late 1943. He had not met him since Pearl Harbor and was dumfounded at the way he had aged. He asked him to autograph a portrait; FDR's hands shook so that he could hardly write, and he looked up wryly, grinning, with the comment, "Not so steady as they used to be!" Yet during the conversation that followed, the ambassador, who had known him well for many years, thought that he was as acute, adroit, and intellectually energetic as at any time they had ever met. This paradox became standard throughout 1944. In some respects Mr. Roosevelt seemed very well; in others not. Some days his vitality seemed superb, and on others low.

During the campaign sinister whispers climbed up about the President's health, although few people could have shown more durability while it was going on. It was no sick man who delivered the great Teamsters Union speech, or the one in New York to the Foreign Policy Association, before which he drove for 56 miles in an open car in freezing rain. Many witnesses among people who saw him daily will testify as to his vim and spirit. He always loved campaigning, and he actually gained weight during the tour. But we know now that he had been forced to cut down on work considerably, and needed far more rest than he was able to get. Everybody around the President tried to make him "take it easy," but this was a difficult thing for him to do.

Many devoted Roosevelt followers heard rumors that he was far from well during the campaign and, even if they believed them, voted for him anyway. Sick or well, they were glad to have him. They counted on his superb resilience, as did he. I heard one citizen say something that crystallized a general attitude, "I would vote for him even if I knew he was going to die tomorrow. I hope he will stay President as long as he lives." Other people, who knew his lustrous voice so well, became frightened when they thought it sounded weak or fuzzy. Contrariwise still others thought that he should not have been permitted by his doctors to run, if only because they loved him and felt that it was inhuman to subject him to this further, final strain.

One factor was that he was somewhat lonely. But the President, even in his failing days, had such hearty spark and intense pleasure in people that it was difficult to appreciate this. Anna Boettiger moved into the White House (and accompanied him to Yalta); this was a delight. Hopkins was still close, but frightfully debilitated by illness; Rosenman, Early, Miss Tully, and a few others whose service dated back twenty years were still close, Pa Watson was a pillar of strength, and Sherwood had become a real friend. But the atmosphere was changed, particularly after Hopkins left the White House. Mrs. Roosevelt was away a good deal of the time; the sons were overseas fighting; James had been very ill. Missy LeHand was dead, Marvin McIntyre was dead, and Watson was soon to die. FDR seldom had time to see Morgenthau or Frankfurter these days, Sumner Welles was out, Byrnes was cool, and only two members of his first Cabinet remained. Luckily George Marshall was still at hand. FDR once explained that he had given Eisenhower, not Marshall, command of OVERLORD because he did not think he could sleep at night with Marshall out of the country. But Marshall was not an intimate friend, a crony.

A British dignitary saw Roosevelt at Teheran in 1943 and then at Yalta a little over a year later. He was shocked beyond belief at the way the President had "deteriorated," as he put it to me, in fourteen months; he who had been a picture of exuberance had become "a broken shell." An American plenipotentiary saw how stunned the Englishman was, and took him aside to whisper, "Don't tell anybody back home how ill the President is. It's temporary. He always bounces back." The Englishman said, "It is a tribute to how he has toiled."

Indeed Roosevelt was a sick man at Yalta, though not so sick as his enemies have subsequently alleged. There was no "sellout" at Yalta because of ill-health on the part of the President. He was far from being perfectly well, and he was mortally tired, but there is no faintest evidence of intellectual breakup, advanced senility, or sudden mental decay as the detractors charge. The story of Yalta is far more complex than that. FDR knew exactly what he was doing, and his behavior stemmed from perfectly rational and precise motives and aspirations. Let us explore.

Mystery and Climax at Yalta

Of all controversies over FDR that involving Yalta is the most exacerbated. For some time Roosevelt had been preparing for another meeting of the leaders of the Grand Alliance (though he could not admit this openly for security reasons), and after prolonged consultations Yalta, in the Crimea, was chosen as the site, and appropriately enough ARGONAUT became the code name. Churchill disliked Yalta as a meeting place because of its inaccessibility and other disadvantages; Roosevelt agreed to it largely on the urging of Harry Hopkins, since Stalin, as usual, refused to leave Russian soil. As a matter of fact it was Hopkins who suggested the Crimea in the first place. FDR sailed on the cruiser *Quincy* on January 22, 1945, met Mr. Churchill and picked up some of his own advisers at Malta in the Mediterranean ten days later, and flew the 1,400 miles further to Yalta on February 3. The conference lasted until February 11, and was by all odds the most formidable gathering of leaders the war had yet known, outranking even Teheran; this was the first meeting at which the three heads of government met accompanied by their ranking chiefs in foreign affairs—Stettinius, Eden, Molotov. In Roosevelt's entourage besides Stettinius were such dignitaries as Leahy, Hopkins, Byrnes, Ed Flynn, Marshall, King, Land, Harriman, Somervell, Deane, Early, Bohlen—and Alger Hiss.

Question over Hiss may be disposed of briefly. Mr. Hiss was at that time deputy director of the Office of Special Political Affairs in the Department of State. The Roosevelt haters had a gorgeous holiday when, five years later in 1950, he was found guilty of perjury by a Federal court in New York; they used the Hiss trial as they had attempted to use the Pearl Harbor investigations as a "smear-Roosevelt" springboard. For instance in the report of the verdict in one Hearst paper FDR was conspicuously mentioned twice in the first two paragraphs; commonly Hiss was called his close friend, "confidant," and the like. It is perfectly true that Mr. Hiss was a member of the Yalta delegation. But it is not true that he had power or influence to move the President in any way. Roosevelt had no contacts of any importance with technical advisers like Hiss; he did not move personally on that level at all. It was hard enough even for men like Byrnes or the highest generals to get to Roosevelt at Yalta. The President did not write any policy out of Hiss's mouth. Hiss had no function at all in that exalted realm, and it is probably doubtful that FDR was aware of his existence even when they were in the same room.

Charges that Roosevelt himself was a secret "Communist" or fellow traveler, or that he deliberately fostered the development of communism in the United States, are of course so fantastically absurd that they do not need the dignity even of a cursory denial.

That whole-souled and sagacious anti-Communist, Mr. Churchill, we sometimes forget, was a cosignatory with Mr. Roosevelt on every decision reached at Yalta, even though he may have argued strenuously against several before they were signed. The British Prime Minister and the President worked out every written and verbal detail together in close collaboration, they agreed fully on the Yalta terms, and they have joint responsibility. But nobody in his right mind in London ever dreams of calling Churchill a "Communist," or of charging that what *he* did at Yalta, which was exactly what Roosevelt did, constituted a "betrayal," a "sellout," or anything remotely of the kind. If Roosevelt lost the peace at Yalta, so did Churchill, though the Prime Minister *had* to follow him in most matters. If FDR was guilty of sacrificing any substantial interest, Churchill was guilty too. But American defamers of Roosevelt never mention this, because most of them have got themselves into the position of being fervently pro-Churchill while still hating FDR.

In fact Churchill was much more deeply involved in deals with Stalin than FDR ever was. For instance Stettinius reveals that the British Prime Minister and the Russian dictator reached an arrangement in Moscow in October, 1944, which reduced to actual percentages "the degree of influence each would have in the Balkans." The Soviet Union was to get a 75–25 or 80–20 predominance in Bulgaria, Hungary, and Rumania; Yugoslavia was to be divided between them 50–50; Britain was to have 100 per cent responsibility in Greece.[3]

Primarily Yalta was a military conference, held while stiff fighting still went on both in Europe and the Far East. The agenda was triple: (1) to consolidate final plans for beating Germany; (2) to arrange terms for Russian entrance into the war against Japan; (3) to prepare policy on all manner of matters having to do with the peace, from the organization of the United Nations conference at San Francisco to settlement of the Polish frontiers.[4]

What Roosevelt wanted above all was to bring Soviet Russia firmly into a lasting peace. He thought that good relations *were* attainable; he wanted to make a peace that would really stick. His ambition was too great, perhaps; yet to be the architect of the first truly effective multinational peace structure in the history of the world was a respectable enough ambition. The secret of Yalta is simple; to achieve this ambition, he gave too much away. "He broke my trader's heart," one of his advisers said frankly later. In addition FDR was moved by considerations of chivalry and gentlemanliness. Russian bad manners and aggressiveness make us forget nowadays the Soviet contribution to the war. Roosevelt thought that a generous reward to Stalin would be meet and fitting. Besides there were sound

[3] *Roosevelt and the Russians,* by Edward R. Stettinius, Jr. (New York, Doubleday & Company, 1949) pp. 12–13.

[4] But even at a conference like this FDR had to keep his eye on domestic affairs. For instance on February 8 he took time out to write an executive order about taking over a factory in Detroit.

military reasons for being nice to Russia. General Marshall has calculated that had it not been for the Soviet resistance on the eastern
front, the United States would have had to put in France twice the
force we did put there. This would have meant another sixty American
divisions overseas, or well over a million combat troops. The Nazis had
just made their last terrific counterattack in the Ardennes, and nobody
knew what other strokes they might deliver.

Roosevelt was guilty of bad judgment; so was the judgment of a
lot of people bad. He was both overconfident and underconfident in
a peculiar way. When close friends commiserated with him just before
he left Washington about how "tough" Stalin was going to be, he
replied acerbly that it was Uncle Joe who should be commiserated,
because *he*, Roosevelt, was just as tough. "Everybody expresses sympathy with me for having to do business with Churchill and Stalin,"
he protested with a pained look, "I wish somebody once in a while
would extend their sympathy to Churchill and Stalin too." Preparing for the conference he had moments of superficiality, frivolity, and
even cynicism. "Stalin?—I can handle that old buzzard!" he told one
intimate. But also he erred grievously in underestimating several
factors. For instance he was convinced that the United States could not
be counted on to keep an army of occupation in Germany for more
than two years after the peace; hence he wanted a hard and fast
agreement on international control of the Reich at almost any price.
He still brooded over the possibility that the Senate might not ratify
the peace; therefore it was more than ever essential to make haste
and get the structure of the new world organization approved before
opinion cooled off. FDR was in a hurry; perhaps he had premonitions
of his own death. And to be in a hurry is always prejudicial to a
negotiator. Moreover Stalin knew Roosevelt's weakness in this respect;
that FDR was not absolutely sure of his own backing at home
strengthened the Russian's hand. Stalin had no such problem. Finally,
the President was certainly naïve in accepting some of the Russian
postures at face value. The Declaration on Liberated Europe guaran-
teed "free elections" in eastern Europe, but nobody, even at that time,
should have been deceived by this. Later we shall make brief mention
at least of Roosevelt's subsequent disillusion.

Roosevelt (and Churchill) talked of what "grand allies" the Russians were, but they were not duped or unwarrantably pro-Russian.
FDR began to see how the Russians were playing their own deep game

and were grabbing for every illicit advantage immediately after Teheran, when Soviet officials double-crossed him on the time of release of an important document. Perhaps, all in all, the best summary is to say that FDR was gambling at Yalta. His eyes were open, and he knew perfectly well the risks he was taking. What he was gambling for was permanent peace on a moral, idealistic, one-world basis. Unfortunately he lost. But if he had lived to see the peace through it might have been a sharply different story and the whole world might be in a far happier state than it is, because after his death no single person was able to provide the leadership he gave.

Stalin was profoundly shocked by the President's pallor and gaunt appearance; he told FDR at their first meeting that had he known how fatigued he was, he would have gladly waived his refusal to leave Russian territory and would have met him at some point more convenient to him. No doubt Stalin was worried over his health not merely out of personal solicitude but because of what it might cost future Russian policy. But, even though sick, FDR was well enough to run the conference. He and Stalin got on very well, better than at Teheran. Roosevelt told him that he saw no inherent reason why the USA and the USSR should not similarly get along in the evolution of the years, as both countries changed gradually. During one conversation he asked Stalin, as if idly, "What will happen when we two are gone?" The Russian replied that in the case of the Soviet Union he could state categorically that the decision had already been made and that the succession to himself was fixed; Roosevelt neglected, however, to ask who the successor was. Even today, it would be interesting to know! Stalin gave FDR a signed portrait; the inscription runs to about one hundred words of small, tightly written Cyrillic script. I saw this portrait in an inconspicuous corner of the White House on one occasion, but, unable to read Russian and not being in a position to summon a translator, I never found out what Stalin's message was. Probably it was no more than a conventional salutation.

The main burden of accusation about Yalta is that the United States (and Great Britain) made grossly disproportionate concessions, and indeed the case is strong that FDR and Churchill did give too much away. But the Soviet Union, on its side, made several concessions too; Yalta was by no means an unqualified "Anglo-American defeat." For one thing the Russians wanted final settlement of German reparations on an astronomical level; they did not get it. They wanted the firm exclusion of France from participation in the control of postwar Germany; they did not get it. They wanted more leeway for their political maneuvering in the liberated areas than they got, though in the long run the result was the same. Also they accepted the American suggestion about Polish boundaries, the American formula for the Security Council, and most American proposals in regard to San Francisco. It should never be forgotten that, so far as eastern Europe was concerned, the Anglo-American negotiators were at a crippling disadvantage in that the Red Army was already there. It was difficult, to say the least, to talk about the future of Poland with Russian forces already occupying Poland. What the Soviet Union "got" at Yalta, its armies already had. And nobody could possibly push them out.

One specific charge against Roosevelt (and inferentially Churchill) is that, had not the Yalta deliberations held the generals in the field back, Bradley and Patton could have taken Berlin and Prague and there would have been no such nonsense as later developed over the military control of Germany and Czechoslovakia. This charge hardly holds water, though Patton could easily have taken Prague.[5] There was never any political agreement that the Russians should take Berlin first. The division of Germany into zones of occupation was decided upon long before Yalta, and the line at which our troops stopped was determined largely by the generals themselves. Actually the American high command seriously underestimated our own military prowess, and we were delighted to accept the Elbe as part of our line of demarcation, because the supposition was that when Germany gave in the Russians would in general be *west* of the Elbe, not that we would be in a position to strike east of it. To get this agreement would, it was thought, give us a gain at Russian *expense*; in a word, the United States outsmarted itself. Nobody dreamed that our own armies would unleash such immense force with such devastating speed or that Germany itself was so near collapse.

Another sore point was the business whereby Russia got two extra seats in the United Nations, one for the Ukraine, one for Byelorussia. (The Russians started with a request for sixteen seats in all, one for each constituent "republic"; FDR scotched that quickly enough by stating that he would be delighted to agree provided that the United

[5] Harry Butcher says that Eisenhower saw "no military sense" in taking Berlin. *My Three Years with Eisenhower* (New York, Simon & Schuster, 1946), p. 804.

States got forty-eight.) But he could not easily refuse to grant Russia two more seats, inasmuch as the British Empire had more than two. What was infuriating is that, for some mysterious reason known only to himself, he kept this agreement secret.[6] It leaked out in March, two months later, and the fact that it *had* been secret naturally made people assume that something ominous or dishonest must be involved. Probably FDR felt that, in this instance, the Russians had got away with a bit of chiseling, and it annoyed him to have this known; also he feared that, if announced prematurely, the arrangement would play into the hands of American isolationists and Russia-haters who might still make trouble in the Senate.

Much more important was the accord by which the Soviet Union agreed to enter the war with Japan within "two or three" months after Germany's surrender. This accord (signed by Roosevelt, Churchill, and Stalin) was not made public until a year later, on February 12, 1946; it was so secret that even Byrnes never heard of it till months afterward. That Russia *would* enter the Asia war was decided upon at Teheran; what Yalta did was fix the date and terms. The price paid was, among much else, returning the southern half of Sakhalin Island to Russia and giving the Kurile Islands to the Soviet Union outright, as well as opening North China to Russian penetration. A bad bargain? Perhaps it may seem so now. But as of that time, early in 1945, it seemed very good. Both Roosevelt and Churchill, it is vital to recall, thought that the Japanese war would last *till 1947*; we did not know how tremendously punishing had been the incendiary raids on Tokyo and the atomic bomb had not yet been successfully tested; we were not sure that Japan could be defeated at all without Russian aid; our military plans called for an invasion of the main islands of Japan that, by our most cautious predictions, would cost *one million* American casualties alone. Of course the point may be argued that, once the struggle with Germany was over, the Soviet Union would have been bound to enter the Asia war anyway. Be that as it may the Yalta accord was based on what were then assumed to be the soundest possible military estimates, with the British concurring. FDR was a prisoner of his own military on this issue, and if anybody is to blame it is the military intelligence of our own high command.

[6] Hopkins wired Byrnes, who had flown home while FDR was en route by ship, "The President is extremely anxious that no aspect of this question be discussed even privately." *Speaking Frankly,* p. 41.

Roosevelt has been severely criticized for not informing the Chinese leaders of the secret agreement concerning Japan. But it was impossible to let them know, if only for the reason that the Chungking government was so notorious for leaks and betrayals of information.

Yalta itself, to sum up, was no treasonable "sellout" or "betrayal," even though FDR and Churchill gave Russia more than they need have given. The tragedies that followed did not derive so much from the conference itself as from the brusque alteration in Soviet policy later and direct, callous Russian violation of what had been agreed upon. But this should have been foreseen.

The conference wound up, the great men of state scattered, and FDR flew back to Egypt to pick up the *Quincy*. Then after a few days began the long journey home. Roosevelt and his advisers, military as well as diplomatic, were bright with jubilance; the mood was even one of "exultation," because it seemed to these sober and conscientious men of high rank not merely that the final stages of the war had been charted ahead to certain victory, but that a fair and lasting peace had been assured. The irony is grim.

Reaction from his efforts struck Roosevelt cruelly on the voyage back to the United States. His fatigue was crushing, and he had intermittent periods of being virtually comatose. In fact his exhaustion was so complete that, on occasion, he could not answer simple questions and talked what was close to nonsense.

Chapter 20

DEATH THE END

The world goes on by peaks and valleys, but on the whole the curve is upward. . . . Let us move forward with strong and active faith.

—FRANKLIN DELANO ROOSEVELT

It happened that I was a guest in the White House twice in the last days of March, 1945. I was doing research for my *Inside U. S. A.*; Mrs. Roosevelt asked me to tea, and I had a long talk with her and Anna Boettiger. The Earl of Athlone, the Governor General of Canada, and his wife, Princess Alice, were present. I mention this only because one of the scurrilous "medical" stories about FDR alleges that he had a serious "stroke" on exactly this occasion; almost the only point that can be pinned down is that the "stroke" was supposed to have occurred during the Athlone visit. Mr. Roosevelt died three weeks later, but he certainly had no stroke on or about March 25. Mrs. Roosevelt is a woman of many great qualities, but that of being a supreme actress is not among them. She talked about the President with the utmost candor, detachment, and discernment for an hour. If he had just had a stroke she is Garbo, Duse, and Sarah Bernhardt rolled into one.[1]

Mrs. Roosevelt asked me if I would like to have a look at the President's private study on the second floor of the White House. I spent an hour there on March 27, prodding around. The room was spacious, friendly, filled with a great amount of miscellaneous material, and faintly shabby. A large portrait of the President's mother hung on one wall, and one of his wife faced it; dozens of naval prints took every inch of space not occupied by bookcases. Behind FDR's desk was a sheaf of roll maps, set into the wall so that they could be pulled

[1] On another occasion when the President was supposed to have had a "stroke" he had just caught a ten-foot sailfish which is preserved in the Hyde Park library. Another stroke story may have originated from the minor fact that, back in 1938, he fainted once at Hyde Park. But he was well enough to go in to dinner fifteen minutes later. Tully, p. 273.

out like window shades, and a contraption like a pouched blanket, full of pockets holding other smaller maps.

These were some of the things on the desk, aside from the usual gadgets and knicknacks:

A book, *Palestine, Land of Promise,* opened at page 40.

Scribbled memoranda—"228 from Stockholm," "Marshall," "2627 File & Copy"—in FDR's hand.

A wooden statue of Winston Churchill smoking a large cigar, and a paper-weight marked "Penalty for removal, $250, F.D.R."

A letter from Jonathan Daniels.

A carefully folded copy of the Washington *Post.*

Notes for a speech the President was writing—"Voting Procedure," "Proposal Slight Justification," and "Such a Charter . . ."

Across the room were a nest of card tables; stamp albums; a radio; a table with a T-square, oil paper, drawing paraphernalia; and some books. These were titles I noted down:

Guide to the U.S. Army
How to Win at Stud Poker (in a brilliant orange jacket)
Lanterns on the Levee, by W. A. Percy
A Dictionary of International Slurs
The Good Neighbor Murder, by Eleanor Pierson

In the cozy twilight I began to reflect on the character I would have assigned to the man whose sanctum sanctorum this was, if I had never heard of him. Obviously an extrovert; a man with sharp and eager curiosities; a restless man who liked ships, travel, his family, games, and hobbies; a man with a strong sense of both past and future; a practical man who liked to do things with his hands and who loved life. Then I began to notice clusters of other objects; the room had an almost disorderly appearance. On one group of three unmatched chairs was a pile of loosely tied bundles, and on the floor were spreading heaps of books, files, papers. I saw old Government reports and copies of obscure technical magazines I had never heard of. Then more maps, strung together, and old-style letter files, wrapped in yellow paper and tied with cheap string. Finally, a small tower of phonograph records, sitting on the floor. Among them were the *Oklahoma* album, something called "Presidents of the United States," and the hymn "Lead Kindly Light."

Leaving the room I reflected again. It seemed to be the room of a man who was packing up, who knew that he was about to go away.

Summary to Begin

Unless I have been grossly deceived it can be stated categorically on the highest medical authority that:

1. Roosevelt never had a stroke until the one that carried him off.
2. He never had any malignancy.
3. The manner of his death was not anticipated by anybody. The family and his physicians were taken completely by surprise.
4. He died of a massive cerebral hemorrhage.
5. He might have lived years longer if he had been able to get more rest.
6. For some time he had been suffering from a heart complaint, but this ailment was responding well to treatment, and was under control so long as he took good care of himself.
7. His old poliomyelitis had nothing to do with the fatal stroke.

1945

On January 3 President Roosevelt sent to Congress the annual budget message (estimating expenditures at 83 billion dollars) and a few days later came a speech on the state of the union. These were hard chores. But in a Fireside Chat on January 6 he seemed to be in excellent form. The fourth inaugural followed, and then the trip to Yalta. On February 12 FDR sent Congress a long and complex message about the new International Bank, and on February 28 issued his invitations to San Francisco. Then on March 1 he addressed Congress in person on the results of Yalta. This speech was the first indication to many that something might be gravely wrong with the President. He spoke sitting down, and almost for the first time in twenty years made public reference to his disability.

"I hope that you will pardon me for this unusual posture of sitting down," FDR began, "but I know that you will realize that it makes it a lot easier for me not to have to carry about ten pounds of steel around on the bottom of my legs."

The President seemed to have considerable labial difficulty during this speech. His voice was weak and hurried, and the incomparable old resonance of delivery was obviously impaired. But this may be partially explained by the fact that, sitting down informally with members of his audience only a hand's breadth away, he ad-libbed a great deal. In fact never in his whole career had he ad-libbed so much in an important speech; he departed from his prepared text no fewer than forty-nine times. This phenomenon too was disconcerting to those who were worried about his condition.

Yet, as had happened before, many people close to him did not think he was in bad shape at all. Experienced newspapermen listened to his speech and wrote that "he looked tanned, refreshed, and in the best of health." Admiral Leahy says that he was not conscious of "any marked deterioration" in the President on the trip to Yalta, and that he did not appear "very ill."[2] Bob Sherwood has testified that at this time he seemed to be "on top of the wave," and Sumner Welles has said that he had never known his mind to be sharper. Roosevelt himself chuckled at one gathering, "Old age hasn't crept up on me yet," and at his next-to-the-last press conference, on March 13, he was gay, provocative, and full of pepper and badinage on subjects ranging from relations between Churchill and Stalin to affairs on the St. Lawrence River and night baseball. Eleanor Roosevelt wrote Franklin, Jr., who was in the Pacific, that the President had gained weight, looked better, and was feeling fine. This letter was written just a week before FDR died, and young Franklin did not receive it until a few days after his death.

On the other hand there is much contrary testimony. On the day of the inauguration the President's hands shook so violently that James Roosevelt, standing next to him, was afraid that he would not be able to hold the pages of his brief speech, much less read it. (But, although it was a bitterly cold morning, FDR refused to let James slip a cloak or cape over his shoulders.) Miss Perkins was among those profoundly shocked by his haggard appearance on this occasion. Several people thought that they noticed a slight droop or lag in the corner of the lip, and Miss Tully records that the President dozed occasionally while reading his mail. He spoke off the record at a dinner of the White House Correspondents' Association; veteran newsmen were perturbed by what seemed to be a slight impediment in his speech. Once or twice, in talk with friends, he "drew a blank," and could not remember the thread of his discourse; once he introduced Bob Jackson to a visiting dignitary as the "Attorney General," though Jackson had long since given up this post. At one small White House gathering he told guests that they were going to see a movie about Yalta; his daughter Anna whispered to him, "No, Father, not Yalta, but Casablanca." People meeting him for the first time, like General Clay, were dumfounded by

[2] "I Was There," by Fleet Admiral William D. Leahy, *Saturday Evening Post*, February 25, 1950.

his shakiness. Jimmy Byrnes was deeply worried. When his military entourage called on his ship at Malta, en route to the Crimea, Admiral King and others were troubled by something that seemed to them totally new and disconcerting—the President listened, but did not talk. They saw that he wanted to get rid of them as soon as possible, and they left quietly and in a hurry. Anna Rosenberg saw him just before he went to Yalta, and again on the day he returned; she was horrified at the way he had deteriorated precipitously, and he complained to her—again something new—that he couldn't sleep. He was bothered by a penicillin rash. Anna Boettiger became seriously alarmed on the journey home from Yalta, and intervened with the medical authorities to insist that he get more rest. Mrs. Roosevelt's own solicitude was marked; she said to several friends in the middle of difficult negotiations, "Please do not push the President too hard."

How is one to explain these discrepancies and varying views? For one thing FDR's condition varied sharply from day to day; he always picked up and bounced back quickly. For another his inner vitality, even though weakened, was so radiant that, after a few moments' talk, he could make almost any visitor completely forget that he seemed ill. For still another many people who knew him well, including those who tried to build a kind of protective screen around him, had come to think in a peculiar way that he was indestructible. Life was inconceivable without Roosevelt as President; FDR was immortal and eternal; it was just not possible that he could be sick enough to die.

One anguishing shock to Roosevelt was the sudden death of Pa Watson on the *Quincy* en route home from Yalta. Not only did he profoundly love Watson; he relied physically on Watson's exuberant and robust strength. It was Watson who almost always held his arm and helped him walk and stand. Watson had apparently been in perfect health, and the suddenness of his death added to FDR's consternation, grief, and sense of loss.

Meantime everybody agreed that this was going to be "the toughest term." There was still a lot of war being fought. Congress was, as usual, troublesome, and FDR had to wrestle with two standard headaches, debt and taxes. The war was costing more than $300,000,000 per day and yet he had to fend off inflation; there were 60,000,000 promised jobs to find when reconversion got under way; he had important appointments to make in a dozen posts; he wanted to expand social security, health insurance, river development, and housing; he had to keep both labor and industry in harness. A sample day in March, 1945, went like this. He saw the Canadian Prime Minister, and then the Chinese ambassador. He spent a quarter of an hour on a problem having to do with the recreation of troops, and then forty-five hard minutes with Harold Smith, Director of the Budget. He talked with an emissary from Brazil, had lunch with Stettinius, and conferred lengthily with General Marshall and Admiral King on major strategy. Then came a home-front talk with Jimmy Byrnes. During all this there were perhaps twenty important phone calls, each requiring some sort of decision, incoming reports to handle, mail to read, and documents to sign. He dined with Anna Boettiger, and then put in two hours on paper work. How could a sick man possibly do it all?

Mainly what bothered FDR was Russia, because the reaction following Yalta had set in. Gone were the days when Roosevelt had said that he and Stalin, once the ice had cracked, got on so "beautifully." The Russians were making trouble over the United Nations, and had patently begun to violate the agreements on eastern Europe. Mr. Vishinsky had set up a puppet government in Rumania and the promise of "free" elections in Poland had vanished into empty air. Roosevelt was angry. He cabled Churchill on March 27 over his "anxiety and concern" at the way the Soviet attitude had changed since Yalta, and on April 1 sent an almost peremptory message to Stalin expressing his disappointment at "the lack of progress made in carrying out . . . the political decisions which we reached at Yalta, particularly those relating to the Polish question." Also Stalin exasperated the President by charging that the United States and Britain were secretly contriving to arrange for the surrender of the German Army in Italy behind Russia's back; Roosevelt called this a "vile misrepresentation." FDR has been so viciously attacked about Yalta that it is important to set the record straight in these last particulars. He had by no means given up hope of coming to a satisfactory agreement with Russia eventually; he told one distinguished interviewer that he worked all the time to keep "the doors open"; but this, he said, took time and patience, and he was "only one of three." Roosevelt, to the end of his days, never conceded that there was *anybody* he couldn't win over and work with, if he really tried. Certainly if he had lived there would have been another meeting with Stalin. He would have gone to Moscow himself if necessary.

But let us repeat the immediate point; the President was disappointed and angry at the way the Russians had let him down. For a time he did not believe that what he was getting from Moscow could be from Stalin himself. Then incontrovertible evidence received from Ambassador Harriman proved the contrary. FDR's mood was to fight back. He exclaimed to one close acquaintance, "All this proves one of two things. Either Stalin has been deceiving me all along, or he has not got the power I thought he had."

Incidentally Stalin told General Bedell Smith, when Mr. Truman subsequently invited the Russian dictator to visit the United States, something that has interest: "I would like very much to visit the United States, but age has taken its toll. My doctors tell me that I must not travel long distances, and I am kept on a strict diet. I will write to the President and tell him why I cannot now accept his invitation. A man must conserve his strength. President Roosevelt had a great sense of duty, but he did not save his strength. If he had, he would probably be alive today."[3]

The Last Day

Roosevelt left for what was his last visit to Hyde Park on March 24, spent a day in Washington, and then traveled to Warm Springs on the 29th. That nothing untoward was anticipated is proved incontestably by the fact that Admiral McIntire, his chief physician and the most faithful and assiduous of watchdogs, was not there, and that Mrs. Roosevelt did not come down. If anybody had thought he was on the point of death, they would certainly have been present, and Anna Boettiger too. Mrs. Boettiger's young son happened to be very ill; several members of the family were more worried about him than about FDR. In the President's party were two of his beloved cousins, Laura Delano and Margaret Suckley, who often accompanied him on holidays, and Mrs. Winthrop Rutherfurd, one of his oldest friends. The entourage included Mike Reilly, the chief of the Secret Service detail; William D. Hassett, one of FDR's secretaries; Grace Tully and Dorothy Brady, her assistant; Louise Hackmeister, his chief telephone operator; Commander George Fox, who had been his physical therapist for many years; and Dr. Howard G. Bruenn, a heart specialist who was a commander in the Navy, and who the year before had been assigned by

[3] New York *Times*, November 6, 1949.

McIntire and others to keep close to the President. Roosevelt was somewhat tired, but relaxed and happy; he motored through the quiet Georgia valleys and loafed in the placid sun. Also he spent some time working on the agenda for the San Francisco Conference, which he intended to open on April 25, and wrote a speech which he was to give at the annual Jefferson Day dinner the next week; its final sentence was, "Let us move forward with strong and active faith." The President inserted this phrase in the dictated script with his own hand. He got a cable from Churchill asking advice on what he should say about Poland in the House of Commons, and replied, "I would minimize the general Soviet problem as much as possible because these problems, in one form or other, seem to arise every day and most of them straighten out. . . . We must be firm, however, and our course thus far has been correct."

Henry Morgenthau dropped in for dinner on the evening of April 11; most of the talk was about "the good old days," and Roosevelt kept referring to Pa Watson and how sadly he missed him. Another guest was Madame Elizabeth Shoumatoff, a well-known artist who had painted him once before, and was now doing his portrait again. The party was quiet, and broke up early. FDR was feeling fine—Warm Springs always picked him up—and went to bed for a good night's sleep. Plans were made for a barbecue the following evening, with hillbilly music, and friends bought two small hogs, a lamb, and a side of beef.

The next morning he complained of a slight headache, but nobody thought that this was of any moment. Dr. Bruenn saw him at 9:30 A.M. and put in a call to McIntire in Washington; it was routine procedure for him to report to the Admiral every day. Nothing was thought to be amiss. Roosevelt worked on his mail—he called it "the wash"—and signed a good many documents, including some postmastership appointments. According to custom the President's signature is never blotted, but must be allowed to dry, and Hassett spread the papers over the room. Then FDR signed a bill extending one of the old New Deal agencies; he joked with Hassett, "Here's where I make a law."

Next he turned to his stamps, picked up the telephone, and called Frank Walker in Washington asking him to be sure to get him the first issues of stamps commemorating the forthcoming United Nations conference. This was about half an hour before the fatal seizure. FDR filled an envelope with duplicate stamps, which he marked "To give away," and then inspected some issues put out by the Japanese during their occupation of the Philippines. (Manila had been liberated by MacArthur on February 3.) Then he tossed in a basket some other stamps and also—a strange and striking point—his draft card, which he must have taken out of his wallet as if thinking he didn't need it any more. But his spirits were good. He summoned Madame Shoumatoff, and asked her to get to work. He wore a Harvard-red tie, because she wanted a touch of color in the portrait. Lunch was about to be served, and the President said, "Now we've got just about fifteen minutes more to work." While she painted he was reading some reports with what she has described as "intense" attention.

This was the last thing the artist heard him say. Just as lunch was ready the President groaned, put his left hand to his head, and pressed his temple hard. He kept circling his hand over his forehead as if he were in acute pain and then, without other warning, fainted backward in his chair. Madame Shoumatoff screamed and rushed out of the room to call for help; Joe Espencilla, the Filipino house boy, and Arthur Prettyman, FDR's valet, leaped to his side. The President was heard to mutter feebly, "I have a terrific headache." Madame Shoumatoff herself did not hear this remark because she and Laura Delano had darted out to find the nearest Secret Service man, who was stationed at the door. The two servants carried FDR to the bedroom adjoining the dining room. He was unconscious. The Secret Service man got word to Dr. Bruenn, who was swimming at the pool two miles away, and who instantly sped to the Little White House in a Secret Service car. Care was taken not to alarm anybody; even Mike Reilly, at the pool, did not know for the moment whether it was the President who had suddenly been taken ill, or someone else. When he got to the Little White House, a few minutes later, Bruenn was working over the President, who had been undressed and was lying unconscious in his pajamas.

Reilly had no thought that the President was going to die, but the day before he had been worried because he seemed "heavy." Only once before in all their years together, on a fishing cruise to the Tortugas in 1937, when Roosevelt was ill of a dental infection, had Reilly felt that FDR was dead weight when carrying him.[4]

Bruenn did what he could. While FDR was being undressed his heart stopped, and then started again. Obviously he had had a cerebral

[4] See *Reilly of the White House*, pp. 229 *et seq.*

seizure; a vessel had burst in the brain, or a thrombus or clot had formed. Bruenn managed, while starting artificial respiration, to have a call put in to McIntire in Washington; he told McIntire that the President was "pale, sweating profusely, and totally unconscious."

At almost that instant, by striking coincidence, McIntire had rung off from a talk with Dr. James Paullin of Atlanta, one of the President's doctors who had been in consultation before; McIntire planned to go to Warm Springs that week end, and take Paullin with him. Urgently McIntire put in another call to Paullin, told him what had happened, and ordered him to get to Warm Springs as soon as possible.

Dr. Bruenn then called again, to say that, although the President seemed to have had a cerebral hemorrhage, there might still be hope, since his heart was holding up and his breathing was good. But everybody in the hushed room knew how close Death might be. Bruenn continued to give artificial respiration and other emergency measures. Then Paullin arrived; he had made the eighty miles to Warm Springs from Atlanta in ninety minutes. Bruenn called McIntire again, now to report that in spite of everything FDR was sinking fast; while he was on the telephone McIntire heard him "utter a startled exclamation," and he knew that the President must be dead.

This is Dr. Paullin's report, as quoted in McIntire's book:

The President was *in extremis* when I reached him. He was in a cold sweat, ashy gray, and breathing with difficulty. Numerous rhonchi in his chest. He was propped up in bed. His pupils were dilated, and his hands slightly cyanosed. Commander Bruenn had started artificial respiration. On examination his pulse was barely perceptible. His heart sounds could be heard, but about three and a half minutes after my arrival, they disappeared completely. I gave him an intracardiac dose of adrenalin in the hope that we might stimulate his heart to action. However, his lungs were full of rales, both fine, medium and coarse, and his blood pressure was not obtainable. There were no effects from the adrenalin except perhaps for two or three beats of the heart, which did not continue. Within five minutes after my entrance into the room, all evidence of life had passed away. The time was 3:35 o'clock.

Miss Tully gives a profoundly moving account of these events. With Miss Brady and Miss Hackmeister she had gone to the pool before lunch. They had a swim, and then Miss Hackmeister thought she might check with her switchboard. At that precise moment a call came through from Miss Delano and Miss Suckley asking for

Dr. Bruenn. Miss Hackmeister asked innocently if the President wanted him for lunch. There was a moment of confused silence and then Daisy, the Negro cook at the Little White House, got on the phone and called out, "No, he's sick. The President is sick." The race to the bedside started. Miss Tully proceeds, "By the time I reached the house, both Bruenn and Fox were with the President in his bedroom. Miss Suckley was in the living room, Miss Delano entered from the bedroom as I walked in. There were sounds of tortured breathing and the low voice of the two men attending him. Miss Delano and Miss Suckley looked shocked and frightened."

After the death Hassett, Miss Tully, and the others, waiting in the next room distraught, tried to restrain their grief and incredulity. Merriman Smith of the United Press and the two other correspondents covering the President entered. Miss Tully and Miss Brady were on the couch "crying softly and literally wiping their eyes on each other's shoulder." Hassett announced that the President was dead in a strained voice, and there came a hot scramble for the telephone. Then Miss Tully, without saying a word, "walked into the bedroom, leaned over, and kissed the President lightly on the forehead." Bruenn, according to Smith's account, mopped his face with a handkerchief and said, "It was just like a bolt of lightning or getting hit by a train."

Fala had been sitting in the room all along. Suddenly the dog leaped from his corner, shook himself, crashed through a screen door, and ran outside barking frantically till he reached the top of a nearby hill. There he stood vigil.

So died Franklin Delano Roosevelt, in the 63rd year of life and the 169th of the republic he strove so undeviatingly to serve. His face was composed and peaceful, without any indication of struggle; there was no swelling or discoloration, and no trace of unhappiness or pain.[5]

Post Mortem

No autopsy was held, and the body did not lie exposed in state. The cause of the death was obvious, and the family saw no reason why, in wartime, the funeral ceremonies should be sumptuous or prolonged. As a result stupid rumors began to circulate, some of which are still

[5] In case it is of any interest I happened that afternoon to be talking to old Josephus Daniels in Raleigh, North Carolina. At almost the exact moment of Roosevelt's death Daniels started talking about him and about how the three greatest things of life—birth, love, and death—were mysteries beyond control.

heard today—that FDR had shot himself, that he had been shot, that he had fallen off a cliff, and even that he didn't die, but had been packed off to a sanitarium as a mental cripple. To deny stories as childish as these is hardly necessary.

Mainly the attempt to make a mystery out of Roosevelt's death is of political derivation. Critics strive to prove (a) that he was much sicker than he ever was; (b) that he should not have been allowed to run for the fourth term, considering his condition; (c) that members of a White House camarilla concealed the true facts from the public, and foisted a dying Roosevelt on the country out of their own ambition and greed for power.

Among the ailments the President was variously supposed to have been suffering from were "coronary thrombosis, a brain hemorrhage, a nervous breakdown, an aneurism of the aorta, and a cancerous prostate."[6] Also "reports" were repeatedly heard that he had been spirited off to the Mayo Clinic for an operation for a malignant tumor of the liver or rectum. Of course no such operation ever occurred.

Admiral McIntire, who had been Roosevelt's doctor for many years, vigorously refutes these charges. The President, he insists, was in good enough health for the proper discharge of all his duties until the end. McIntire takes full note of the frequent sinus attacks, the debilitating bout of bronchitis and intestinal influenza in early 1944, and the pallor, fatigue, and loss of weight, but he denies strenuously that any of this had any critical importance. A wen was surgically removed from the back of FDR's head in 1944, but he had had this wen for twenty years or more; the operation was minor, and it had no significance.

Question about the President's health became so widespread, particularly during the fourth-term campaign, that McIntire issued several statements denying rumors and attesting to his good health. On October 12, 1944, for instance, he stated flatly, "The President's health is perfectly OK. There are absolutely no organic difficulties at all." McIntire admitted that he was "eight or nine pounds under his best weight," but said that this was a good thing, and that FDR was delighted that he had lost his slight paunch and was justifiably proud of his new "flat—repeat, f-l-a-t tummy."

Naturally, as the responsible doctor in charge, McIntire wants to

[6] This list of alleged ailments is from an article by George Creel in *Collier's*, March 3, 1945, which is a staunch defense of Dr. McIntire.

explain the course he took. In his book he stresses that no medical man can predict with accuracy when a given patient may, or may not, have a cerebral hemorrhage. Such a hemorrhage, known commonly as a "stroke" or apoplexy, can descend like a bolt of lightning on a perfectly healthy man without warning, though this is unusual; as a rule there is a previous history of arteriosclerosis or high blood pressure. But McIntire denies that FDR's blood pressure was "alarming at any time," or that his arteriosclerosis was more than what was "moderate" for a man of his age.

Here there would appear to be mysteries. It was widely known that *some* type of heart ailment might be afflicting FDR if only because he was forbidden to fly at high altitudes, and because Dr. Bruenn saw him every day. Indeed McIntire says frankly that it was quite natural to worry about his heart. "Here was a man of 63, under terrific strain for years, who had been coughing heavily for more than two months in the spring of 1944. Time proved that our fears were groundless, for that stout heart of his never failed." But also he writes, "The problem now was to protect the President's reserve strength, with constant watch on the heart, and this became the particular business of Commander Bruenn." McIntire reproduces in his book two reports of physical examinations given the President, each signed by five doctors. In the first (May 10, 1944), the blood pressure reading is, oddly enough, omitted. The second, covering the period from September 20 to November 1, 1944, says of the heart, "No cardiac symptoms at any time; electrocardiogram shows no changes from that of May examination." The blood pressure is normal. "Patient more relaxed and at ease; it is noted that only small annoyances cause any rise in systolic pressure." Also: "Cardiovascular system shows moderate arteriosclerosis."[7] But if this was only moderate, if the blood pressure was normal, and if there were no cardiac symptoms at any time, why were such elaborate precautions taken to watch the heart?

The actual course of events appears to be more or less as follows. Several members of the family, particularly Anna Boettiger, became concerned about the President's health early in 1944—so was Miss Tully—and they asked McIntire to call other doctors into consultation. There was no lack of confidence in McIntire. FDR himself adored him. McIntire, originally a nose and throat man, was particularly gentle

[7] All quotations in this paragraph are from *White House Physician* (New York, G. P. Putnam's Sons, 1946).

and adept in treating his sinus passages, and FDR loved to have his sinuses drained by a careful hand. But Roosevelt needed someone who could lay down the law to him, with no holds barred; he needed to be kept in check, not babied and encouraged. Besides it was thought that if new physicians were summoned they might give a fresher, more objective view. So on March 26, 1944, the President went to the naval hospital at Bethesda for an exhaustive checkup from top to toe.

Here a group of Navy doctors most distinctly did not like what they saw. One, in fact, thought the President should have been taken in firm hand and obliged categorically to rest at least a year before; another thought that his weakened condition (he had a racking cough) was "a bombshell." Two distinguished physicians were then brought in from outside: Paullin of Atlanta, whose specialty was the heart, and Dr. Paul Dickens, clinical professor of medicine at George Washington University. "Some changes in the cardiograph tracing" were found. The result was that the President was told in the sternest terms that he must rest, rest, rest. McIntire worked out a schedule which cut his working day by about half; he was forbidden to have business guests at luncheon, and ordered to take it completely easy for a full hour between two and three in the afternoon and again for an hour before dinner. Night work was excluded, and ten hours of sleep prescribed. The President then set off for a month's recuperation at the Baruch plantation in South Carolina, and he began to feel a great deal better almost at once.

What had McIntire and the other doctors found? One guess is that the President had a familiar form of heart disease known as chronic myocarditis, which sometimes produces cardiac decompensation, or what is known colloquially as heart "failure." Myocarditis is an inflammation of the muscular part of the heart wall. The medical history before this would indicate some such condition, because obviously his heart was tired and strained. Also his occasional moments of "drawing a blank" (temporary cerebral aphasia) and labial difficulties might have arisen indirectly out of such a heart condition. Moreover, the fact that all the doctors agreed that *rest* was the prime therapeutic necessity would seem to point to chronic myocarditis as the ailment.

McIntire reported after ten days in South Carolina, "Blood pressure dropping down; very interesting fact that the readings are lower in the evening than in the morning; moreover, posture seems to have a great deal to do with fluctuations in the systolic pressure." When the President returned to Washington he was even more strikingly improved. Dr. Paullin came up to see him again, and Dr. Frank Lahey, a surgeon and head of the well-known Lahey Clinic in Boston, was called in. Paullin was surprised and delighted at the degree of recovery made. But, again, what the President needed and imperatively had to have was rest, rest, rest. Paullin laid down the law like a Dutch uncle. He told him that he *must* slow down, and not continue "burning up the road." The President thereupon promised to behave.

Then what happened was, of course, that FDR did not behave. He could not. He had too much to do. It was his duty to do it all. He would obey orders for a few days, then disregard them. It was extremely difficult for the doctors, or even members of the family, to give orders to the President of the United States. They worked in a vacuum. Mr. Roosevelt, it was once said, had "a whim of iron." When he disobeyed a doctor it was not easy to rebuke him or force him to mend his ways. What Navy doctor could have dared tell the Commander in Chief, at the supreme climax of the war, that he had to quit? Doctors are human beings; it would have been unnatural not to have trembled before the throne. Moreover almost all the medical decisions were compromises among several doctors. It is easy to see how a physician could say to himself, "Have *I* the right to alarm the President further—is it *my* duty to make him stop work?" Millions of men were risking their lives in combat; Roosevelt had to take risks too. It is a fair guess nowadays that FDR never knew how near the danger line he was, and it is doubtful if the implications and significance of the medical findings were known fully to the family. Few doctors tell the *whole* truth to anybody. Roosevelt knew that he needed rest, but he did not know how badly he needed it. To most warnings he paid scant attention. To the very end, he always thought that a few days in Warm Springs would fix him up.

Several doctors are convinced today that Roosevelt could have been saved if he had taken a period of stringent rest *much* earlier, and kept in bed for a period of at least three solid months. But it was utterly impossible, at that time, to order the President to stay in bed for three solid months.

He was a good patient, friendly to the doctors and cooperative; but he simply refused to take enough rest steadily. He seldom asked questions about treatment, and was almost never inquisitive on medical matters. As we know, he hated illness. He gave the impression of thinking that he was in the hands of fate, destiny, and that it was not

his province or that of anybody to interfere. Once, however, he astonished one physician by saying (though not on grounds of ill health)
that he might resign the Presidency after San Francisco. The doctor
protested, "But, Mr. President, you can't do that!" FDR replied, "I do
a lot of things I can't do."

Certainly he had no idea in Warm Springs that he was going to die,
though it is a macabre detail that the detective story on his bedside
table the last night was titled *Six Feet of Earth*. He had decided to
visit England after the UN conference, and then possibly China. He
was full of ideas for a cooling-off period after the peace, during which
small neutral nations might act as trustees for occupied countries; he
talked incessantly of operations like the TVA in the Danube valley,
Africa, and the Middle East; he wanted to work out an elaborate
regime for colonial peoples whereby they would advance more quickly
toward self-government; what he hoped for was independence, security,
social decency, for all mankind.

Funeral and Aftermath

The events that immediately followed FDR's death—the cloudburst
of grief that descended on the country and the world—are fresh in the
minds of almost everybody. Citizens saw the headlines and burst into
tears on the street.

Mrs. Roosevelt that afternoon was a guest for tea at the Sulgrave
Club in Washington. Previously she had been in touch with Warm
Springs and had been told that the President had had a hearty breakfast and was looking forward to the barbecue that evening in fine spirits.
Then Laura Delano called her to say that he had fainted while sitting for his portrait, but, as Mrs. Roosevelt herself puts it, "Dr. Mc-
Intire was not alarmed."[8] Next came an urgent call from Steve Early
summoning her back to the White House where he broke the news to
her. Early, McIntire, Jonathan Daniels, and Anna Rosenberg happened to be together when the news came. McIntire was staggered.
Mrs. Roosevelt's first words were, after the initial shock, "I am more
sorry for the people of the country and the world than I am for us."
Then, after Mr. Truman was sworn in as President, she flew down to
Warm Springs, arriving late that night. Reports have been heard that
the FBI and Secret Service had cleared all the guests out of the Little
White House by "spiriting them away." Actually most of the guests left

8 *This I Remember*, p. 343.

voluntarily and at once, not wanting to be in the way at such a moment. The next morning the funeral train started back to Washington, traveling slowly for twenty-three hours across the route the President had taken so many times, and knew so well. Before enormous throngs, the coffin on a black caisson moved through the densely packed, almost totally quiet streets of the capital until it came to temporary rest in the East Room of the White House.

Here, on the fourteenth, a simple and brief funeral service was held according to his own instructions given years before. It lasted only twenty-three minutes. Two hymns were sung, and an Episcopal bishop repeated the words of the President's first inaugural, "The only thing we have to fear is fear itself." Mr. Truman, Mrs. Roosevelt, and those of her family who could gather in time stood solemnly by the flag-draped coffin. The grandchildren were not asked to attend because several were so young. Harry Hopkins, near to the point of death himself, managed to leave the Mayo Clinic to be present. Jimmy Roosevelt flew back all the way from Manila, but was too late; Elliott was the only one of the sons who arrived in time. The next day, as the mourning of the nation rose, the body was taken to Hyde Park for burial. Some of Roosevelt's fiercest political antagonists fought to cadge rides on the funeral train. The President's body was committed to the earth in the place he had chosen for it long before, a few yards from where he was born, while a quick spring breeze swept off the Hudson, and the great men of the nation watched with bowed heads and hearts. Some throughout the land yelped in glee that FDR was dead; his friends and neighbors, meaning most of the world, mourned with mute intensity.

In Warm Springs, Daisy Bonner, the President's cook, hung up a sign over her stove: "Daisy Bonner cook the first meal and the last one in this cottage for the President Roosevelt."

Tributes, it is needless to add, poured in from every quarter. It was as if he had been President of the World. He was gone, and it seemed impossible to believe it. FDR's belief in the basic goodness of man, his work to better the lot of humble people everywhere, his idealism and resourcefulness, his faith in human decency, his unrivaled capacity to stir great masses and bring out the best in them—to realize that all this was now a matter of memory was hard to absorb. Above all the grief of those who grieved was intimate and personal. One great newspaper, which had often opposed him, wrote, "Men will thank God on their knees, a hundred years from now, for Roosevelt's leadership." One close friend, who had often argued with him heatedly, said sadly, "Now we are on our own."

And so to End

This whole book is in the nature of a summary; therefore we need add little further summary now. Roosevelt was a man of his times, and what times they were!—chaotic, catastrophic, revolutionary, epochal— he was President during the greatest emergency in the history of mankind, and he never let history—or mankind—down. His very defects reflected the unprecedented strains and stresses of the decades he lived in. But he took history in his stride; he had vision and gallantry enough, oomph and zip and debonair benevolence enough, to foresee the supreme crises of our era, overcome them, and lead the nation out of the worst dangers it has ever faced.

Roosevelt was the greatest political campaigner and the greatest vote getter in American history. Thirty-one out of forty-eight states voted for him each of the four times he ran. His influence, far from having diminished since his death, has probably increased. When Mr. Truman won his surprising victory in 1948, which was made possible in part by the political influence left behind by FDR, it was altogether fitting that a London newspaper should head its story, "Roosevelt's Fifth Term."

Roosevelt believed in social justice—and fought for it—he gave hope and faith to the masses, and knew that the masses are the foundation of American democracy. He turned the cornucopia of American resource upside down and made it serve almost everybody. Mrs. Roosevelt has said that in the whole course of his career there was never any deviation from his original objective—"to make life better for the average man, woman, and child." I have heard men of the utmost sober conservatism say that they think FDR saved the country from overt revolution in 1932. He created the pattern of the modern democratic state, and made it function. To be a reformer alone is not enough. A reformer must make reform effective. This certainly Roosevelt did. Yet, as we have pointed out, he was a conservative as well as a liberal; he believed in free enterprise and the profit system. It is not beyond the bounds of possibility that thirty or forty years from now the country will have swung so much further left that what FDR stood for will be thought of as almost reactionary.

Also Roosevelt's career nicely disproves an essential constituent of Marxism, namely the principle of class war. His entire life refutes the Marxist thesis. He was a rich man and an aristocrat; but he did more for the underpossessed than any American who ever lived. Moreover, as we know, FDR always operated within the framework of full democracy and civil liberties. He believed devoutly in the American political tradition. Much of the world outside the United States during his prodigious administrations had political liberty without economic security; some had security but no liberty. He gave both.

Mr. Roosevelt was the greatest war president in American history; it was he, almost singlehanded, who created the climate of the nation whereby we were able to fight at all. Beyond this he brought the United States to full citizenship in the world as a partner in the peace. He set up the frame in which a durable peace might have been written and a new world order established; if he had lived to fill in the picture contemporary history might be very different.

Above all FDR was an educator. He expanded and enlarged the role of the Presidency as no president before him ever did. "The first duty of a statesman is to educate," he said in his Commonwealth Club speech back in 1932. He established what amounted to a new relationship between president and people; he turned the White House into a teacher's desk, a pulpit; he taught the people of the United States how the operations of government might be applied to their own good; he made government a much abler process, on the whole, than it has ever been before; he gave citizens intimate acquaintanceship with the realities of political power, and made politics the close inalienable possession of the man in every street.

One result of all this is that the President, though dead, is still alive. Millions of Americans will continue to vote for Roosevelt as long as *they* live.

BIBLIOGRAPHY AND ACKNOWLEDGMENTS

ADAMIC, LOUIS. *Dinner at the White House.* New York: Harper & Brothers, 1946.

ALLEN, FREDERICK LEWIS. *Since Yesterday.* New York: Harper & Brothers, 1940.

AMERICAN GUIDE SERIES. *New York.* New York: Oxford University Press, 1940.

ANONYMOUS. *The Mirrors of 1932.* New York: Brewer, Warren, and Putnam, 1931.

ARNOLD, GEN. H. H. *Global Mission.* New York: Harper & Brothers, 1949.

ASHBURN, FRANK D. *Peabody of Groton.* New York: Coward-McCann, 1944.

BARCK, OSCAR THEODORE, JR., and BLAKE, NELSON MANFRED. *Since 1900.* New York: The Macmillan Company, 1947.

BARGERON, CARLISLE. *Confusion on the Potomac.* New York: Wilfred Funk, 1941.

BEARD, CHARLES A. *President Roosevelt and the Coming of the War 1941.* New Haven: Yale University Press, 1948.

BINKLEY, WILFRED E. *President and Congress.* New York: Alfred A. Knopf, 1947.

BOOTH, EDWARD TOWNSEND. *Country Life in America as Lived by Ten Presidents.* New York: Alfred A. Knopf, 1947.

BRANDEIS, ERICH. *Franklin D. Roosevelt, the Man.* New York: American Offset Corporation, 1936.

BRYCE, JAMES. *The American Commonwealth.* New York: The Macmillan Company, 1901.

BULLITT, WILLIAM C. *The Great Globe Itself.* New York: Charles Scribner's Sons, 1946.

BUREAU OF THE BUDGET. *The United States at War.* Washington: Government Printing Office, 1946.

BUSCH, NOEL F. *What Manner of Man.* New York: Harper & Brothers, 1944.

BUTCHER, CAPT. HARRY C. *My Three Years with Eisenhower.* New York: Simon & Schuster, 1946.

BYRNES, JAMES F. *Speaking Frankly.* New York: Harper & Brothers, 1947.

CARMICHAEL, DONALD SCOTT, ed. *F.D.R., Columnist.* New York: Pellegrini & Cudahy, 1947.

CHASE, STUART. *A New Deal.* New York: The Macmillan Company, 1932.

CHURCHILL, WINSTON S. *The Gathering Storm.* Boston: Houghton Mifflin Company, 1948.

———. *Their Finest Hour.* Boston: Houghton Mifflin Company, 1949.

CLAPPER, OLIVE EWING. *Washington Tapestry.* New York: Whittlesey House, 1946.

COX, JAMES M. *Journey Through My Years*. New York: Simon & Schuster, 1946.

CRANE, MILTON, ed. *The Roosevelt Era*. New York: Boni & Gaer, 1947.

DANIELS, JONATHAN. *Frontier on the Potomac*. New York: The Macmillan Company, 1946.

DANIELS, JOSEPHUS. *The Wilson Era*. Chapel Hill: University of North Carolina Press, 1944.

DAVIS, FORREST, and LINDLEY, ERNEST K. *How War Came*. New York: Simon & Schuster, 1942.

DEANE, JOHN R. *The Strange Alliance*. New York: The Viking Press, 1947.

DELANO, DANIEL W., JR. *Franklin Roosevelt and the Delano Influence*. Pittsburgh: James S. Nudi Publications, 1946.

DE ROUSSY DE SALES, RAOUL. *The Making of Yesterday*. New York: Reynal & Hitchcock, 1947.

DILLING, ELIZABETH. *The Roosevelt Red Record and Its Background*. Chicago: 1936.

DOWS, OLIN. *Franklin Roosevelt at Hyde Park*. New York: American Artists Group, 1949.

EISENHOWER, GEN. DWIGHT D. *Crusade in Europe*. New York: Doubleday & Company, 1948.

ERNST, MORRIS L. *So Far So Good*. New York: Harper & Brothers, 1948.

FARLEY, JAMES A. *Jim Farley's Story*. New York: Whittlesey House, 1948.

FAULKNER, HAROLD UNDERWOOD, and KEPNER, TYLER. *America, Its History and People*. New York: Harper & Brothers, 1942.

FLYNN, EDWARD J. *You're the Boss*. New York: The Viking Press, 1947.

FLYNN, JOHN T. *Country Squire in the White House*. New York: Doubleday, Doran & Company, 1940.

———. *The Roosevelt Myth*. New York: Devin-Adair Company, 1948.

FOTITCH, CONSTANTIN. *The War We Lost*. New York: The Viking Press, 1948.

FOWLER, GENE. *Beau James*. New York: The Viking Press, 1949.

GEDDES, DONALD PORTER, ed. *Franklin Delano Roosevelt, A Memorial*. New York: Dial Press, 1945.

GOODMAN, JACK, ed. *While You Were Gone*. New York: Simon & Schuster, 1946.

HALLGREN, MAURITZ A. *The Gay Reformer*. New York: Alfred A. Knopf, 1935.

HATCH, ALDEN. *Franklin D. Roosevelt*. New York: Henry Holt & Company, 1947.

HOOVER, IRWIN HOOD (IKE). *Forty-two Years in the White House*. Boston: Houghton Mifflin Company, 1934.

HUGH-JONES, E. M. *Woodrow Wilson and American Liberalism*. New York: The Macmillan Company, 1948.

HULL, CORDELL. *Memoirs*. 2 Vols. New York: The Macmillan Company, 1948.

ICKES, HAROLD L. *The Autobiography of a Curmudgeon*. New York: Reynal & Hitchcock, 1948.

JOHNSON, GERALD W. *Roosevelt: Dictator or Democrat*. New York: Harper & Brothers, 1941.

JOSEPHSON, EMANUEL M. *The Strange Death of Franklin D. Roosevelt*. New York: Chedney Press, 1948.

KENNEDY, JOSEPH P. *I'm For Roosevelt.* New York: Reynal & Hitchcock, 1936.

KINGDON, FRANK. *"That Man" in the White House.* New York: Arco Publishing Company, 1944.

KINNAIRD, CLARK, ed. *The Real F.D.R.* New York: Citadel Press, 1945.

KIPLINGER, W. M. *Washington Is Like That.* New York: Harper & Brothers, 1942.

LASKI, HAROLD J. *The American Presidency, An Interpretation.* New York: Harper & Brothers, 1940.

LEECH, HARPER. *The Surprise President.* Chicago: New Trend Library, 1933.

LEIGHTON, ISABEL, ed. *The Aspirin Age.* New York: Simon & Schuster, 1949.

LINDLEY, ERNEST K. *The Roosevelt Revolution.* London: Victor Gollancz, 1933.

———. *Franklin D. Roosevelt.* New York: Blue Ribbon Books, 1934.

LIPPMANN, WALTER. *Men of Destiny.* New York: The Macmillan Company, 1927.

LONG, HUEY PIERCE. *My First Days in the White House.* Harrisburg: Telegraph Press, 1935.

LONGWORTH, ALICE ROOSEVELT. *Crowded Hours.* New York: Charles Scribner's Sons, 1933.

LUDWIG, EMIL. *Roosevelt: A Study in Fortune and Power.* New York: The Viking Press, 1938.

LYDGATE, WILLIAM A. *What America Thinks.* New York: Thomas Y. Crowell Company, 1944.

MACDONALD, DWIGHT. *Henry Wallace, The Man and The Myth.* New York: Vanguard Press, 1947.

McINTIRE, VICE-ADM. ROSS T. *White House Physician.* New York: G. P. Putnam's Sons, 1946.

MACKENZIE, COMPTON. *Mr. Roosevelt.* New York: E. P. Dutton & Company, 1944.

MACLAURIN, CHARLES. *Post Mortem.* London: Jonathan Cape, Ltd., 1923.

MARSHALL, GEN. GEORGE C. *The Winning of the War in Europe and the Pacific,* Biennial Report 1943-1945. New York: Simon & Schuster, 1945.

MARSHALL, KATHERINE TUPPER. *Together.* Atlanta: Tupper & Love, 1946.

MICHELSON, CHARLES. *The Ghost Talks.* New York: G. P. Putnam's Sons, 1944.

MIKOLAJCZYK, STANISLAW. *The Rape of Poland.* New York: Whittlesey House, 1948.

MILLIS, WALTER. *This Is Pearl.* New York: William Morrow & Company, 1947.

MILTON, GEORGE FORT. *The Use of Presidential Power 1789-1943.* Boston: Little, Brown & Company, 1944.

MOLEY, RAYMOND. *After Seven Years.* New York: Harper & Brothers, 1939.

MOORE, RUSSELL. *Roosevelt Riddles.* New York: Doubleday, Doran & Company, 1936.

MOORMAN, LEWIS J., M.D. *Tuberculosis and Genius.* Chicago: University of Chicago Press, 1940.

MORGENSTERN, GEORGE. *Pearl Harbor.* New York: Devin-Adair Company, 1947.

MOSCOW, WARREN. *Politics in the Empire State.* New York: Alfred A. Knopf, 1948.

MOWRER, EDGAR ANSEL. *The Nightmare of American Foreign Policy.* New York: Alfred A. Knopf, 1948.

MUZZEY, DAVID SAVILLE. *A History of Our Country.* Boston: Ginn & Company, 1948.

NESBITT, HENRIETTA. *White House Diary.* New York: Doubleday & Company, 1948.

PARKES, HENRY BAMFORD. *Recent America.* New York: Thomas Y. Crowell Company, 1941.

PERKINS, FRANCES. *The Roosevelt I Knew.* New York: The Viking Press, 1946.

PRINGLE, HENRY F. *Theodore Roosevelt.* New York: Harcourt, Brace & Company, 1931.

RAUSCH, BASIL. *The History of the New Deal, 1933-1938.* New York: Creative Age Press, 1944.

REILLY, MICHAEL F., and SLOCUM, WILLIAM J. *Reilly of the White House.* New York: Simon & Schuster, 1947.

ROOSEVELT, ELEANOR. *It's Up to the Women.* New York: Frederick A. Stokes Company, 1933.

———. *This Is My Story.* New York: Harper & Brothers, 1937.

———. *If You Ask Me.* New York: D. Appleton-Century Company, 1946.

———. *This I Remember.* New York: Harper & Brothers, 1949.

ROOSEVELT, ELLIOTT. *As He Saw It.* New York: Duell, Sloan & Pearce, 1946.

———, ed. *F.D.R. His Personal Letters.* Early Years. New York: Duell, Sloan & Pearce, 1947.

———, ed. *F.D.R. His Personal Letters.* Vol. II, 1905-1928. New York: Duell, Sloan & Pearce, 1948.

ROOSEVELT, FRANKLIN D. *Looking Forward.* New York: John Day Company, 1933.

———. *On Our Way.* New York: John Day Company, 1934.

ROOSEVELT, MRS JAMES, as told to Isabel Leighton and Gabrielle Forbush. *My Boy Franklin.* New York: Crown Publishers, 1933.

ROSENMAN, SAMUEL I., ed. *The Public Papers and Addresses of Franklin D. Roosevelt.* 13 Vols. New York: Random House, 1938 (vols. for 1928-1936); The Macmillan Company, 1941 (vols. for 1937-40); Harper & Brothers, 1950 (vols. for 1941-1945).

SCHRIFTGIESSER, KARL. *The Amazing Roosevelt Family 1613-1942.* New York: Wilfred Funk, 1942.

SHERWOOD, ROBERT E. *Roosevelt and Hopkins.* New York: Harper & Brothers, 1948.

SMITH, ALFRED E. *Up to Now.* New York: The Viking Press, 1929.

SMITH, GERALD L. K. *The Roosevelt Death.* Detroit, 1947.

SMITH, MERRIMAN. *Thank You, Mr. President.* New York: Harper & Brothers, 1946.

SMITH, WALTER BEDELL. *My Three Years in Moscow.* Philadelphia: J. B. Lippincott Company, 1950.

SMYTH, HENRY DEWOLF. *Atomic Energy for Military Purposes.* Princeton: Princeton University Press, 1945.

STARLING, COL. EDMUND W. *Starling of the White House.* New York: Simon & Schuster, 1946.

STETTINIUS, EDWARD R., JR. *Roosevelt and the Russians.* New York: Doubleday & Company, 1949.

STILWELL, GEN. JOSEPH W. *The Stilwell Papers,* as compiled by Theodore H. White. New York: William Sloane Associates, 1948.

STIMSON, HENRY L., and BUNDY, MCGEORGE. *On Active Service in Peace and War.* New York: Harper & Brothers, 1948.

STOLBERG, BENJAMIN, and VINTON, WARREN JAY. *The Economic Consequences of the New Deal.* New York: Harcourt, Brace & Company, 1935.

SUMMERSBY, KAY. *Eisenhower Was My Boss.* New York: Prentice-Hall, 1948.

TITTLE, WALTER. *Roosevelt As an Artist Saw Him.* New York: Robert M. McBride & Company, 1948.

TUGWELL, REXFORD GUY. *The Stricken Land.* New York: Doubleday & Company, 1947.

TULLY, GRACE. *F.D.R. My Boss.* New York: Charles Scribner's Sons, 1949.

WECTER, DIXON. *The Age of the Great Depression.* New York: The Macmillan Company, 1948.

WELLES, SUMNER. *The Time for Decision.* New York: Harper & Brothers, 1944.

WHARTON, DON, ed. *The Roosevelt Omnibus.* New York: Alfred A. Knopf, 1934.

WINANT, JOHN GILBERT. *Letter from Grosvenor Square.* Boston: Houghton Mifflin Company, 1947.

WISH, HARVEY. *Contemporary America.* New York: Harper & Brothers, 1945.

In addition I tried to read every magazine article of substance published in the United States about Mr. Roosevelt in the past twenty years, and I scoured newspaper files with care. Finally I had access to a considerable amount of privately prepared and unpublished memoranda.

Without making the rule too hard and fast I have attempted to give footnote references in the text to all quotations or citations of any length. Following are additional sources which I did not identify by footnote because the procedure seemed too laborious and pedantic. Mostly these refer to periodical literature. I do, however, also include a good many references to books, even though the books themselves are already listed in the bibliography, as a token of my deep appreciation. The books I used most were Sherwood, Rosenman, both autobiographical volumes by Mrs. Roosevelt, and both volumes of letters, all of which—it is only too obvious—are indispensable to any Roosevelt student. Also of great value in their respective fields are Stimson, Perkins, Tully, Dows, Lindley, Johnson, and Edward J. Flynn.

Chapter 1

By one reckoning Mr. Roosevelt is the thirty-first president, not the thirty-second. It depends on whether or not Cleveland is to be considered as "two" presidents. Hamilton Basso in a brilliant brief article, "That Man in the White House," *New Republic*, July 22, 1940, poses interesting questions about Roosevelt's greatness, liberalism, etc. See also Anne O'Hare McCormick in the New York *Times*, April 14, 1945, and April 13, 1946. See the *Roosevelt Omnibus* for the five members of the Roosevelt family who were assistant secretaries of the Navy. TR's "Square Deal" is mentioned in Milton, p. 259, and the item about TR needing only six hours' sleep is from a portrait interview by S. J. Woolf in the New York *Times*, January 24, 1943. The quotation about sticking to the name of Roosevelt is from Ludwig, p. 44, but Ludwig is an unreliable source. An admirable paragraph comparing Wilson and FDR is in "Mr. Roosevelt and the Future" by Stanley High, *Harpers' Magazine*, September, 1937. The source of Wilson's not keeping score at golf is Ike Hoover, p. 61. Wilson's remark on reactionaries is from Rosenman, Vol. VII, p. 571. His definition of statesmanship is in Milton, p. 199, and his remarks on bureaucracy are from Josephus Daniels, p. 422. That FDR thought in terms of a third term for Wilson is mentioned by Mauritz A. Hallgren in the *Nation*, June 1, 1932. Hugh-Jones, p. 200, is source for the remark that World War I took Wilson by surprise, and that it was caused by "nothing in particular." Wilson's domestic reforms are discussed in Rauch, p. 5, and the phrase "ethical climate" is from Perkins, p. 18. For Wilson as a brake on Roosevelt see Sherwood, pp. 360, 697, 855, and 876. The best discussion of Churchill and Roosevelt I have ever read is "Mr. Churchill" by Isaiah Berlin, *Atlantic Monthly*, September, 1949. The main point that Mr. Berlin makes is that Churchill is a man of the past, Roosevelt a man of the future. The quotation from Stimson is on p. 526. For the Roosevelt-Churchill genealogy see the New York *Times*, June 24, 1942. That Churchill "was struck by FDR's magnificent presence" is from *The Gathering Storm*, p. 440. For details of the first meeting between Churchill and FDR see Sherwood, pp. 350-351 and 945, and *Letters*, Vol. II, p. 354. FDR's statement about the Atlantic Charter is from Rosenman, Vol. XIII, p. 438. Eisenhower in his book gives a slightly different version of Roosevelt's remarks to him about Churchill. The quotation about Churchill as mid-Victorian is in Rosenman, Vol. XIII, p. 563. The quarrel over Newfoundland is mentioned in Forrest Davis's articles about Teheran in the *Saturday Evening Post*, May 13 and 20, 1944, and the Map Room story is from Reilly, p. 68. That "Churchill looked as if he was going to be hit" is in "Roosevelt—Man and Statesman," by Jonathan Daniels, *Liberty*, September 8, 1945. Roosevelt's memorandum to Stettinius is reproduced in Stettinius, p. 184. The Morgenthau quotations are from the New York *Post*, November, 1947, and Churchill's remarks about Roosevelt's health are from the New York *Times*, April 18, 1945. For Roosevelt's powers from Congress see "Long Live the King" by J. F. Essary, *American Mercury*, September, 1933.

Chapter 3

The text of Roosevelt's statement after the Cermak shooting is reproduced in *Omnibus*, pp. 160-163. FDR's fear of fire is discussed in Reilly, p. 15. Byrnes, p. 9, is source for the promotion of Eisenhower over 366 senior officers. For FDR's nightmares see Eleanor Roosevelt's *This Is My Story*, p. 135; for his sleepwalking, *Letters*, Vol. II, p. 98. His freedom from worry is discussed in *This I Remember*, by Eleanor Roosevelt, p. 68. See the Woolf article in the New York *Times* already cited for his temper. FDR mentions the postman at Warm Springs in one of his own speeches. "I like my opponent, the legislature" is from Ludwig, p. 328. FDR's reference to human values during the depression is in his *On Our Way*, p. 62. McIntire, pp. 88-89, mentions how various items of Roosevelt legislation arose from his personal experience. One version of the Eugene Grace story is in Lindley, *The Roosevelt Revolution*, p. 212. For Ickes on Roosevelt as a gentleman see "My Twelve Years with FDR" by Harold L. Ickes, eight provocative articles in the *Saturday Evening Post*, published in 1948. The Rayburn letter is from the New York *Times*, July 7, 1942, and the anecdote about Rayburn is from *PM*, January 24, 1943. FDR's "natural sensitiveness" is mentioned in Mackenzie, p. 179, and for his considerateness to Ickes and Hopkins consult the Ickes articles and Sherwood. The Earle letter is from the New York *Times*, December 9, 1947. Busch, p. 84, describes how FDR was "a leader of the underdog party but always in a very upperdog way." See George W. Martin, "Preface to the President's Autobiography," *Harper's Magazine*, February, 1944, one of the best short articles about FDR ever written, for mention of the quality of his enemies. Roosevelt's remark, "Wouldn't anybody like to be president?" is from Marquis W. Childs, "Mr. Roosevelt," *Survey Graphic*, May, 1940.

Chapter 4

For an example of the President's deviousness about statistics see Arthur Krock, New York *Times*, September 26, 1944. The reference to FDR listening in on Sumner Welles is from Hull, Vol. II, p. 1148. The Hugh Johnson material is from his column in the New York *World-Telegram*, July 22, 1940, and an article called "Third Term ? ? ?" in the *Saturday Evening Post*, December 17, 1938. I am indebted to my friend Jay Allen for the quotation from Karl Marx. The phrase "intellectual and moral precision" comes from an old article by Rebecca West in *Time and Tide*. Roosevelt's disquisition on Byrd is from a private memorandum. Mrs. Roosevelt's remarks about his patience are from an article in the *Saturday Review*. How "he had to take it for everybody" is from an appreciation of the President by Lyndon Johnson, quoted in *Life*, April 23, 1945. The phrase about Garbo is from "Roosevelt, A First Appraisal by Those Who Knew Him," a valuable special supplement to the *New Republic*, April 15, 1946; the article is "Number One Movie Fan" by Melvyn Douglas. The quotation from Anne O'Hare McCormick is from the New York *Times*, November 25, 1934, and that from Dorothy Thompson is from "The President and His Minute Men," New York *Herald Tribune*, October 7, 1936. The anecdote about Steinhardt and Hull is from the New York *Times*, February 10, 1948. For Roosevelt's memory of President Cleveland see Dows, p. 128; other details on his memory are in Eisenhower, p. 138, and Tittle. Also see Anna Rosenberg in the *New Republic* supplement just cited, "He Shared Our Lives." The submerged rock story is in *Time*, June 10, 1940, and a variant of the story about American counties is in Busch, p. 152. The anecdote about the three Spanish names of islands comes from Thomas H. Beck, chairman of the board of *Collier's*, and that about the book in Casablanca is in Elliott Roosevelt, p. 116.

Chapter 5

For Roosevelt's mannerisms while watching a movie see "The President," by Henry F. Pringle, the *New Yorker*, June 16, 1934, and "Roosevelt," an article by Geoffrey T. Hellman in *Life*, January 20, 1941. The quotation concerning lovely ladies is from *This Is My Story*, p. 319. That he never took women on cruises is in Tully, p. 3. Missy LeHand's role in the appointment of Homer Cummings is mentioned in Edward J. Flynn, p. 126. See *This I Remember*, p. 49, and *My Boy Franklin*, p. 22, for details on Roosevelt's attitude toward money. The quotation about the six-dollar pair of trousers is from *Letters*, Vol. I, p. 303. That Roosevelt received a $100,000 bequest from his half brother is from *Omnibus*, p. 145, and also the estimate of his average earnings. For various financial details and tabulations see *Letters*, Vol. II, pp. 350, 511, 567, 603, and 632. The story about Anna Boettiger and the account book is from *This Is My Story*, p. 141, and for items on White House finance see Nesbitt, pp. 79-80, and Jonathan Daniels, "That Poor Man in the White House," *Collier's*, December 1, 1945. Details of servants, automobiles, etc. in Washington are from *This Is My Story*. An Associated Press dispatch from Warm Springs after the President's death is authority for the statement that FDR's cottage had no mechanical refrigerator. That he spent hours tracing a missing nickel is from "Stories and Anecdotes About FDR," by Grace Tully, *Ladies' Home Journal*, July, 1949. Details about the Roosevelt estate are from the New York *Herald Tribune*, September 27, 1946, and the New York *World-Telegram*, September 28, 1946. Some religious details are in *Time*, April 23, 1945, and the joke about "formerly God's" is in Dows, p. 66. Perkins, p. 142, describes Pa Watson's deathbed conversion. The story of the expletive in the voting booth is from the Boston *Post*, November 21, 1944. Anne O'Hare McCormick, New York *Times*, January 25, 1942, describes FDR's pride in never having used troops to quell civil disturbances. Frances Perkins, p. 202, is source for the anecdote about keeping Hugh Johnson "sweet." The quotation from

Prettyman is from "Hyde Park: Moment in History," by Ralph G. Martin, *New Republic*, April 29, 1946. Much else about Howe is in *This I Remember*. The Hopkins munitions story is from Thomas H. Beck. Reilly, p. 65, mentions FDR's interest in birds, and also see the article by Jonathan Daniels in *Liberty* already mentioned. In addition to the Kinkaid story cited in the text, the *New Yorker*, February 2, 1946, has an article about the collection of envelopes called "Brickbats and Bouquets," and several of these are reproduced in *Life*, February 18, 1946. Geoffrey T. Hellman in the *Life* article cited above describes how stamps were "occupational therapy." "The Roosevelt Legend" by Hamilton Basso, *Life*, November 3, 1947, has much additional material in this field. Roosevelt's first sailboat is described in *Omnibus*, p. 114, and for his trip to Maine see a highly informative profile in the *New Yorker*, "The Governor," by Milton MacKaye, August 15 and 22, 1931. The *Half Moon II* is described in *Letters*, Vol. I, p. 396, and the navigation of the *George Washington* by Hugh-Jones, p. 247. See Johnson's *Roosevelt: Dictator or Democrat*, p. 59, for Roosevelt's love of the sea in connection with his political career. That FDR loved to store poker chips in various pockets is from the Ickes articles in the *Saturday Evening Post*, and for his poker playing in general see James Kieran in *Look*, August 19, 1947. An article about Fala by John H. Crider appeared in the New York *Times*, October 15, 1944. That FDR had a digestion like ten oxen is from *Letters*, Vol. I, p. 235, and that he was proud of his early prowess as a cook is in *This Is My Story*, p. 143. Mrs. Roosevelt's list of foods that the President should have is printed in full in Nesbitt, p. 68, and Mrs. Nesbitt describes how he liked "duck just chased under the flame." His instruction about sweetbreads is from *White House Diary*, p. 279. Roosevelt's drinking habits are mentioned in the Hellman article in *Life*, and that he liked fish baked in mud is in Rosenman, Vol. VIII, p. 402. For Roosevelt's luck see Tully, Reilly, and the New York *Sun*, April 13, 1945.

Chapter 6

The Roosevelt house and library are well described in pamphlets issued by the Park Service and the National Archives; see also *Life*, April 15, 1945. I am uncertain of the source of the story about Sara Roosevelt and the Oyster Bay family. Tittle and Dows are interesting sources for some of the background in this chapter. That FDR was a member of the Dutchess County Historical Society for many years is in "The Way He Wanted It," by Daniel Lang, *New Yorker*, April 12, 1947. The poem by Archibald MacLeish, "The Grave at Hyde Park," appeared in the *Atlantic Monthly*. Dows reproduces FDR's design for Top Cottage, p. 170. For collections of Rooseveltiana see the New York *Herald Tribune*, January 31, 1949, and *Look*, August 16, 1949.

Chapter 7

See "Was There Really a Man Named Roosevelt?" by William Harlan Hale, *New Republic*, January 3, 1949, for FDR and the price of gold. His methods with big figures are described in Sherwood, pp. 473-474, and elsewhere. The quotation on compromise is from "How the President Works" by Drew Pearson and Robert S. Allen, *Harper's Magazine,* June, 1936, and for the way FDR "wove" pieces of legislation together see Moley pp. 49 and 177. Edward J. Flynn, p. 212, and Moley, p. 11, have passages on the way FDR passed on other people's opinions as his own, and that he seldom took advice "undiluted" is mentioned in Michelson, p. 11. Sherwood, p. 708, is authority for the item about "Free Ports of information." The Tugwell anecdote is in Lindley, *The Roosevelt Revolution,* p. 31. See Stettinius, p. 180, for FDR's ideas about Iran, and Rosenman, Vol. X, p. 557, for his memorandum to a President of the United States in 1956. Perkins and Elliott Roosevelt both describe Roosevelt's interest in TVA's for Europe and Africa. See "The Man We Remember" by Henry Wallace in the *New Republic,* April 14, 1947, for the shelter belt and the "dimo." The Hannegan anecdote is from the *Washington Merry Go Round,* April 25, 1945. That Roosevelt liked to be called a progressive rather than a liberal is in Lindley, *Franklin D. Roosevelt,* p. 320, and that he all but memorized Mahan is from *My Boy Franklin,* p. 15. The naval bookplate and the family china designed by FDR are reproduced in Dows. His idea for a square coin is mentioned in Kinnaird, p. 12, and the tie pins he designed (which were based on the family crest) are mentioned in *This Is My Story,* p. 124. See McIntire, pp. 52 and 110, for Roosevelt's contributions to battleship design, and Reilly, p. 38, for his design of the vault in the White House bomb shelter. For FDR's own comments on how he couldn't keep a diary see Rosenman, Vol. VII, p. 635. One of FDR's "poems" is in Merriman Smith, p. 71. Grace Tully mentions the movie he wanted to write on the theme of *Old Ironsides.* For the origin of the phrase "New Deal" see Moley, p. 23, and Wecter, p. 53. Rosenman, Vol. IX, pp. 284-285, describes the origin of the phrase "Four Freedoms"; originally the President planned to add a fifth. Tully describes how Roosevelt ad-libbed the "stab-in-the-back" line. The phrase "release, climax, and coherence" is from an article by Diana Trilling in the *Nation,* May 26, 1945.

Chapter 8

Perkins describes, (pp. 161-162) how Roosevelt liked to have ideas presented in brief outline. The quotation from Harold Laski is from the Manchester *Guardian,* April 7, 1934. See the valuable article by Stanley High already cited for FDR's working methods; High also notes how the Treasury Department was closest to his heart. Kiplinger, p. 24, mentions his telephone habits; also see Perkins, p. 131, and an article by Charles Hurd, "As His Third and Hardest Term Begins," New York *Times,* January 19, 1941. Miss Tully describes graphically how the President handled mail; see also "An Old River Friend," by Mrs. Charles Hamlin, a particularly revealing article in the *New Republic* supplement, and the Pringle profile in the *New Yorker.* For FDR's staff see "The President's Job—Biggest in the World" by Richard Wilson and William Mylander, *Look,* July 25, 1944. Binkley, p. 243, describes how FDR kept tab on Congress. See Rosenman, Vol. X, p. 345, for a slightly different version of FDR's visit to the State Department. For the President as administrator see Eliot Janeway, "Roosevelt: The Master of Politics," *Life,* April 30, 1945, and "FDR As a Politician" by Alan Barth, *Harper's Magazine,* February, 1945. The quotation from Beard is from Binkley, p. 274; that from Samuel Grafton is from the New York *Post,* April 12, 1946. That Hull's father killed a man in a blood feud is in Hull, Vol. I, p. 4, and the Secretary of State's reference to FDR as "that fellow" is in Farley, p. 330. FDR's fear of leaks by Garner is mentioned in the first installment of the Ickes memoirs. For Morgenthau on Hull see his reminiscences as they appeared serially in the New York *Post.* Ickes mentions Morgenthau's "divine right" to have lunch with the President alone every Monday. Good background on FDR's relations with the press is in Walter Davenport, "The President and the Press," *Collier's,* January 27 and February 3, 1945. Roosevelt's ideas for editing a tabloid are in *F.D.R. Columnist,* p. 153. Rosenman, Vol. XIII, p. 564, describes FDR's annoyance at Arthur Krock. The item about Boettiger and Hearst is from Rosenman, Vol. VII, pp. 293-294, and the anecdote about Mrs. Craig is from the New York *Times,* December 23, 1944. That reporters were not allowed in the White House until Theodore Roosevelt is in Rosenman, Vol. II, p. 42. The remark "No cross examination, please!" is from Pringle in the *New Yorker.* Details about Colonel Otis Bryan are from the New York *Times,* April 18, 1945. Reilly, p. 105, is authority for the fact that two people "died" in a melee at one of Roosevelt's speeches. For general details of precautions taken in guarding FDR see Reilly, Nesbitt, McIntire, and Tully. The dummy story is from *This I Remember,* p. 226. That FDR's own phone was once tapped is from the New York *Journal American,* December 14, 1948. Sherwood, p. 768, and Arnold, p. 455, give slightly different versions of the torpedo episode.

Chapter 9

Schriftgiesser and Dows are invaluable sources for Hyde Park and family background. For the architecture of Springwood consult the New York volume in the WPA Guide Series, and see *Omnibus,* p. 139, for the original price paid for the Hyde Park property. The item about members of the Roosevelt family in the Netherlands today is from the New York *Herald Tribune,* October 23, 1949. For FDR's relationship to other presidents see *Look,* August, 1937. The calculation that Roosevelt had only 3 per cent Dutch blood is in the Basso article in *Life* cited above, and the quotations about FDR's father are from Schriftgiesser. That "Isaac could not bear the sight of human suffering" is from the Alsop article in *Life* mentioned in the text. The way Roosevelt was named and the detail from his father's will are from Delano, pp. 13 and 174. His father as a "museum piece" is in Alsop. The footnote on butlers is from *Letters,* Vol. I, p. 398, and mention of Hyde Park as a paying proposition is in *Letters,* Vol. II, p. 149. The source of the battleship story is Reilly, p. 84. Tully prints the Huey Long anecdote in slightly different form, p. 324. Also see Ed Flynn, p. 215, for two of the other anecdotes about the elder Mrs. Roosevelt. Sara's remark, "Why, they look like a lot of gangsters," is from Reilly, p. 82. That Sara sat at the head of the table is from Dows, and her remark that she had always planned that Roosevelt should be President is from Busch, p. 49. Her remark that Roosevelt was "grown up and is the governor" is from Perkins, p. 64, and Tittle, p. 59, mentions that her jaw was just like his.

Chapter 10

For early pictures of Roosevelt see Stephen Lorant in *Life*, "The Early Life of Franklin D. Roosevelt," and *Pageant*, October, 1949, "The FDR You Never Knew." The anecdote from Sara on giving orders is from *My Boy Franklin*, p. 26, as are several other items. The examination from Mademoiselle Sandoz is from "A Dutchess County Boy," by Michael Straight, in the *New Republic* supplement already several times cited. For FDR's arrests in Germany see Mackenzie, p. 29, and Hatch, p. 20. The background of Groton is well rendered in the explanatory notes in *Letters*, Vol. I, p. 31; also see this volume for details of FDR's report card and the debate on Hawaii. Mention of the trotter and light runabout is in Hatch, p. 33, and the item about Negro students is from the article by Michael Straight just mentioned. For FDR's letters from Europe when he was still at Harvard see *Letters*, Vol. I, pp. 489-502.

Chapter 11

The quotations about the Roosevelt wedding are from *My Boy Franklin*, p. 64. For Farley on Hall Roosevelt see Farley, p. 60. FDR's remarks about asking Eleanor Roosevelt to a house party are in Dows, p. 63; the meeting of FDR and Eleanor on the train is described in *This Is My Story*, as is the anecdote about Rivington. The Choate detail is from Hatch, p. 42. Quotations about seasickness and others following are from *This Is My Story*, and the honeymoon letters are in *Letters*, Vol. II. The long list of Mrs. Roosevelt's early activities is an addendum to an article by Helena Huntington Smith in the *New Yorker*, April 5, 1930, later reprinted in *Omnibus*, pp. 125-135. Mrs. Roosevelt's remarks about Farley and Trohan are from the *Ladies' Home Journal*, September, 1947. The quotation about Mrs. Roosevelt's sense of duty is from *This Is My Story*, p. 110. See also a profile of Mrs. Roosevelt in the *New Yorker* by E. J. Kahn, Jr., and the Hellman article in *Life*. Mrs. Roosevelt's remarks on the President's attitude toward divorce are in *This I Remember*, pp. 164-165, and James Roosevelt's letter about money is in *Letters*, Vol. II, pp. 615-616.

Chapter 12

Basic sources for this period are Lindley and the second volume of *Letters*. For the fact that he could not break with his mother see *This I Remember*,

p. 18. Consult Lindley, *Franklin D. Roosevelt*, p. 72, for Roosevelt's first encounter with the Poughkeepsie politicians and Busch, p. 75, for his membership in the Hyde Park fire department. Mrs. Roosevelt's testimony that he was more interested in the science of government than the philosophy is in *This Is My Story*, p. 173. The phrase "second coming of Roosevelt to the legislature" is in *Omnibus*, p. 22, and that he voted against appropriations for his own district is mentioned in *Time*, November 29, 1943. The Warn article is reproduced in *Omnibus*, pp. 20-30, as are the first Roosevelt cartoons. H. L. Mencken in "Why Not an American Monarchy?", *Vanity Fair*, November, 1934, mentions that it flattered Wilson to have a Roosevelt working for him. The Daniels colloquies are from *The Wilson Era*, p. 126 ff. For Roosevelt's collection of books on the Navy see "F. D. Roosevelt, Assistant Secretary of the Navy," New York *Times*, March 17, 1940. The letters exchanged between FDR and Sara are from *Letters*, Vol. II. That Daniels never believed what any admiral ever told him and how FDR watched his own admirals are from Lindley, *op. cit.*, pp. 117 and 123. Fuller elucidation of the relations between Roosevelt and Daniels is in *Letters*, Vol. II., pp. 244-45. The excerpts from the war letters to Eleanor are in *Letters*, Vol. II, pp. 246 and 267, and the quote from Sara Roosevelt is from *My Boy Franklin*, pp. 92-93. Rosenman, Vol. I, p. 60, has the text of Roosevelt's talk about labor relations at the Brooklyn Navy Yard. For his prescience about air power see Arnold, p. 97, and for his breaking regulations consult Lindley, *op. cit.*, p. 140. A first-class discussion about Roosevelt and the law on naval matters is in Johnson, p. 106 ff. The quotations from FDR about Daniels are in *Letters*, Vol. II, pp. 233 and 243. That his eyes were not precisely the same size is in Tittle, p. 78. The Wilson quote about FDR is in Josephus Daniels, p. 130. For the background of the San Francisco convention see Johnson, p. 110; that he was not among the 39 candidates mentioned for vice-president is in *Omnibus*. For Cox's meeting with Wilson see *Letters*, Vol. II, p. 496, and Cox, pp. 242-243; and that FDR wanted to sit in on Cabinet meetings is in Cox, p. 258. The Mac-Kaye profile in the *New Yorker* mentions that he made 800 speeches in the 1920 campaign.

Chapter 13

The item about vaulting over chairs is from Perkins p. 27, and that Roosevelt played golf within two strokes of a course record is from *Letters*, Vol. I, p. 345. For Elliott's leg braces see *This Is My Story*, p. 213. Authority for Roosevelt's having fallen overboard is Ludwig, p. 87, and the quotation from Dr. Keen is in *Letters*, Vol. II, p. 524. Roosevelt's own account of his illness is reproduced in *Time*, March 4, 1946, together with his advice to fellow sufferers. For Mrs. Roosevelt's "breakdown" see *This Is My Story*, p. 339. I have drawn on this and *This I Remember* steadily on these matters. That he hated and mistrusted braces is in Reilly, p. 120. Quotations about Roosevelt's first days of recovery are taken from recordings in Hyde Park. Also see Dows, pp. 88 and 95. Louis Howe's instruction that he must never be carried in public is in Hatch, p. 139, and for the early days at Warm Springs see Lindley and *Letters*, Vol. II, pp. 568 and 578. Miss Tully, p. 65, talks about the visit to Mr. Justice Holmes, and Roosevelt himself mentions the difficulty of getting aboard the *Prince of Wales*, Rosenman, Vol. X, p. 321. The anecdote about the hat comes from Thomas H. Beck. For the fall in Georgia see *Omnibus*, p. 7; for that in Philadelphia see McIntire, p. 74, and Reilly, p. 99. For his lack of self-pity see McIntire, and the remark, "No sob stuff," is from Lindley. The quotation about the grown man with a child's disease is in Ludwig, p. 96. Ickes mentions how he drew on his emotional reserves in the *Saturday Evening Post*, July 24, 1948. For unnecessary risks FDR had to take see Lester Markel in *While You Were Gone*, p. 359, and for descriptions of other celebrated victims of disease consult *Post Mortem* and *Tuberculosis and Genius*. The fishing episode is described in "Mr. Roosevelt," by Marquis Childs, *Survey Graphic*, May, 1940. For FDR's definition of "thinking" see Edmund Wilson in the *New Republic*, April 5, 1933.

Chapter 14

Lindley is an indispensable source for this chapter. For Al Smith see Lippmann's *Men of Destiny* and the *Mirrors of 1932*. Smith's early opinion of FDR is given in *Beau James*, p. 262. The quotation from Mrs. Roosevelt about Sara's disapproval of Smith is from *This I Remember*, p. 16. For Hearst in 1922, Eleanor's role in the Smith campaign, and Smith's request to FDR to run for senator see Lindley, *Franklin D. Roosevelt*. The quotations from Elmer Davis are from the New York *Times*, June 27, 1924. Roosevelt's prediction on La Follette is from *Letters*, Vol. II, pp. 566-567. For FDR's various jobs while convalescing, see *Letters*, Vol. II, and Mackenzie, p. 141. An article in *Fortune*, October, 1932, mentions that his insurance business doubled. Details of the 1925 auction are in *F.D.R. Columnist*, p. 164, and that the Macon *Telegraph* urged his impeachment is from Clapper, p. 133. General sources for the telephone talks between Smith and Roosevelt before FDR's run for Governor are Mackenzie, Perkins, and *Letters*, pp. 645-647. Howe's remarks about future plans are in Moscow, p. 15, and the quotation about canes is from Sara Roosevelt, p. 110. Johnson is an admirable source for Smith's jealousy and why. That Roosevelt didn't recognize Tittle's existence is in Lindley, and for Walker's attitude toward FDR see Fowler, pp. 261-263. The quotation about Roosevelt as Governor is from *The Mirrors of 1932*, pp. 78-80.

Chapter 15

For FDR's early ambition to be President see the New York *Herald Tribune*, April 30, 1945, and the London *Times*, March 5, 1934. See Lindley, *op. cit.*, p. 230, for the John W. Davis anecdote and much subsequent material on the campaign. The Ed Flynn anecdote is from Flynn, p. 82. Original members of the committee to help FDR and their contributions are listed in Flynn,

Farley, and Lindley. That Roosevelt called the Brain Trust the "Privy Council" is from an article by Raymond Moley in *Omnibus,* p. 149. For the 1932 convention my main source is Ed Flynn, and the dialogue between Smith and FDR is from Farley, p. 30. The MacKaye profile in the *New Yorker* is authority for the statement that FDR sought to make Hoover come out as a Democrat. For the cost of the 1932 campaign see Wish, p. 437. Moley, p. 63, describes how Brain Trust material was used up to 1935 and (p. 58) how Berle helped to ghost the Commonwealth Club speech. Details on the extent of FDR's electoral victory are in Faulkner, p. 720, and Rauch, p. 46.

Chapter 16

General White House background is in Nesbitt and Ike Hoover. My chronology of legislation during the Hundred Days closely follows Johnson, pp. 223-224. The article about FDR's powers was by J. Frederick Essary in the *American Mercury. Fortune,* March, 1945 quotes Lewis W. Douglas's remark on "the end of Western civilization." The quotation from Bryce is from Volume I, p. 578. Lindley, *The Roosevelt Revolution,* p. 92, discusses how the CCC shocked people, and the quotation about collective bargaining is from Muzzey, p. 836. For the cost of the naval program see "The New Deal in Review," a special supplement in the *New Republic,* May 20, 1940. The quotations from Mark Sullivan and Beard are from Binkley, pp. 253 and 256. For Keynes's view of the New Deal see the London *Times,* January 2, 1934. Binkley, p. 237, mentions that FDR was the first president since Buchanan to be at home in the White House. See George Creel, "Roosevelt's Plans and Purposes," *Collier's,* December 26, 1936, for aims in the second term, and for Government and the right to work see Lippmann, New York *Herald Tribune,* January 18, 1935, a superbly discerning article. Farley, p. 64, mentions that Roosevelt saved the private-property system after it had been dragged "to the brink of ruin"; also see Anne O'Hare McCormick in the New York *Times,* October 16, 1938. For the background of the Court fight see Milton. Both Farley and Flynn tell the story about Walter George, as does Alan Barth.

Chapter 17

Stimson mentions that the foreign policy of the United States was "to have no foreign policy." For reactions to the Quarantine Speech see Byrnes, p. 6, and Rosenman, Vol. VI, p. 423. The conversation between Roosevelt and Ambassador Bullitt is from Hatch. For the atom bomb see Sherwood, Smyth, and an article in the *New Yorker,* December 1, 1945, "The Contemporaneous Memoranda of Dr. Sachs," by Geoffrey T. Hellman, as well as Dr. Sachs' own testimony to the Senate, November 27, 1945. A slightly different version of the bomb story is in Rosenman, Vol. X, p. 245. For the historical background to the third-term issue see Muzzey, p. 870; some interesting contemporary journalism on the subject is an article by R. E. Turpin in the New York

Times Magazine, October 30, 1938; a discussion of Theodore Roosevelt's third-term hopes by W. R. Warn, New York *Times*, June 16, 1940; Lippmann, "The Third Consecutive Term," New York *Herald Tribune*, October 29, 1938; and Donald Richberg, "Why No Third Term," *Forum*, August, 1939. Moley and Tugwell debated the issue before the New York Herald Tribune Forum as early as 1938. The item about Gandhi is from the *New Republic*, June 21, 1939. Sherwood, p. 137, has a fine analysis on the third-term dilemma as seen by FDR himself. The reference to "tweedledum and tweedledee" is from Muzzey, p. 871, and the anecdote about Roosevelt wanting a "second" term is from the *New Republic*, January 11, 1939. For Roosevelt's plans after 1940 see his remarks to Dan Tobin quoted in Perkins, p. 126, and for the 1940 convention and campaign in general see Farley, Michelson, Flynn, and Hull. Cox, p. 328, is authority for the statement that Willkie was a delegate to the 1924 Democratic convention. The Bop Hope wisecrack is from Lydgate, p. 98. That the Republicans advertised in the *Daily Worker* is in Sherwood. Roosevelt's verbal slip about isolation in the third inaugural address is in Rosenman, Vol. X, p. 3. Sherwood, Jonathan Daniels, and *This I Remember* all have cogent remarks on the relationship between the New Deal and preparations for war. The quotation from Senator Brewster is from the New York *Post*, October 24, 1947. That Roosevelt thought that the destroyer deal was more important than anything since the Louisiana Purchase is in Rosenman, Vol. IX, p. 376. The columnist to whom Roosevelt suggested that the term "New Deal" be dropped was Dr. Dillworth Lupton of the Cleveland *Press*; see also John Crider in the New York *Times*, December 24, 1943. A neat rebuttal of Roosevelt's war "guilt" is in an editorial in the New York *Times*, December 12, 1945. The quotation from Professor Morison is from his article "History Through a Beard," *Atlantic Monthly*.

Chapter 18

Roosevelt's remarks about the Philippines are in the New York *Times*, November 20, 1945. For his relation to Pearl Harbor in general see "A Challenge to Historic Truth," by Allan Nevins in the New York *Times*, December 16, 1945, and an admirable review by Walter Millis of George Morgenstern's *Pearl Harbor*, New York *Herald Tribune*, February 9, 1947. The relationship between FDR and his Chiefs of Staff is mentioned in Sherwood, pp. 446, 800, and 948. Arnold, pp. 332-333, is source for the item about bombing of the power plant in Shanghai. For sticking pins in generals see Rosenman, Vol. XII, p. 82. For the decision to beat Germany first see Sherwood, p. 445, and Eisenhower, p. 27. Basic background for all of this chapter is Stimson. For war-production figures see Muzzey, p. 883, and Sherwood, p. 474; the quotation is from Muzzey. The interviewer to whom Roosevelt said that San Francisco would be the crown of his career was Anne O'Hare McCormick in the New York *Times*, April 22, 1945. For FDR as a "post" war President see Rosenman, New York *Times*, April 7, 1946. FDR himself said at a press conference after Yalta, "The first few months were devoted to seeing that we did not get licked," Rosenman, Vol. XIII, p. 556. For the results of Casablanca presciently described see Lippmann, New York *Herald Tribune*, January 28, 1943. The quotations from Mr. Churchill about unconditional surrender are from the New York *Times*, July 22 and November 18, 1949. A penetrating account of this episode is in Sherwood, pp. 695-696, although the full story was not available when he wrote it. If this is a blot on Mr. Sherwood's book, it is as if one flower were mildewed in a garden of 10,000 roses. FDR's remark about "buying a second front in a department store" is in Rosenman, Vol. XI, pp. 462-463. For several details about Teheran see a first-class eyewitness account by Edward Angly in *PM*, December 7, 1943. Hull, Vol. II, p. 1294, is authority for the statement that Stalin wanted to meet in Fairbanks, Alaska. The quotations from Mikolajczyk are from the *Rape of Poland*, pp. 59 and 60, and for other background on Teheran see the Forrest Davis articles in the *Saturday Evening Post* already cited. The anecdote about FDR as a Christian and a Democrat is from Perkins, p. 330. That Roosevelt appointed "one man to do the work of four," etc., is from Arthur Krock in the New York *Times*, December 17, 1942. Good articles on the home front are in *Life*, October 26, 1942, and July 12, 1943. My list of executive war agencies is taken from the Bureau of the Budget's *The United States at War*, and the chronology of Roosevelt's activities closely follows Rosenman, Vols. XII and XIII. "He Shared Our Lives," by Anna Rosenberg, *New Republic*, April 15, 1946, and Jonathan Daniels, p. 2, discuss labor and management problems connected with the atomic bomb.

Chapter 19

For the American system of quadrennial elections see Lippmann in the New York *Herald Tribune*, October 28, 1944, and Herbert Agar in the *Reader's Digest*, October, 1944. Josephus Daniels' remark about FDR and a fifth term is from the New York *Herald Tribune*, December 19, 1947. The phrase "commando in chief" is from Bert Andrews in the New York *Herald Tribune*, July 29, 1944. David Lawrence discusses FDR's "impropriety, bad sportsmanship," etc., in the New York *Sun*, August 11, 1944. Constitutional aspects of the commander-in-chief issue are discussed in the New York *Times*, July 19, 1944. The anecdote about Henry Wallace and the "same old ticket" is from *Time*, January 20, 1947. Tully, p. 276, describes how the names of Truman and Douglas were switched. See Helen Gahagan Douglas, New York *Herald Tribune*, October 19, 1944, for the Republican voting record on foreign policy. Electoral figures are from *Time*, November 20, 1944. For "left of center" see *Fortune*, March, 1945. Reilly, p. 244, mentions the Yalta executive order about Detroit, and Stettinius, p. 127, tells of FDR's fear that the United States would not keep an army of occupation in Germany for more than two years. One of my sources on Yalta is a private memorandum prepared by one of the negotiators. For Yalta in general see McGeorge Bundy, "The Test of Yalta," *Foreign Affairs*, July, 1949; a review by Walter Millis of the Stettinius book in the New York *Herald Tribune*, November 6,

1949; and a masterful article by Raymond Swing, "What Really Happened at Yalta," New York *Times*, February 20, 1949. That Roosevelt thought the Japanese war would last until 1947 is in Stettinius, p. 72, and Eleanor Roosevelt discusses FDR's conception of relations with Stalin after the war in *This I Remember*, pp. 253-254.

Chapter 20

For Roosevelt's alleged strokes see an article in *Look*, February 15, 1949, "The Truth About FDR's Health." It was answered by Elliott Roosevelt in *Liberty*, May, 1949, "They're Lying About FDR's Health." That Roosevelt departed from the prepared text of his Yalta speech 49 times is in Bert Andrews, New York *Herald Tribune*, March 3, 1945. Byrnes, p. 48, describes colorfully how General Clay was shocked at the President's appearance. See Rosenman, Vol. XIII, pp. 233, 546, and 547 for FDR's changing attitude toward Stalin. That he was working to keep the doors open and that he was "only one of three" is in Anne O'Hare McCormick, New York *Times*, April 14, 1945. The routine of a sample working day is in Drew Pearson, March 18, 1945. Roosevelt's last talk with Frank Walker about stamps is in McIntire, p. 78, and other details of happenings just before his death are from a UP dispatch from Warm Springs, April 13, 1945, and an interview with Madame Shoumatoff in the New York *Times*, April 15, 1945; the detail about the draft card is from "The Great Philatelist" by Eugene Kinkaid in the *New Yorker*, March 30, 1946. The quotations from Smith are from his *Thank You, Mr. President*, pp. 182-183, and the details about Fala are from Reilly. The item about the detective story is from Tully, p. 365. McIntire's statement about the President's health is from the New York *Times*, October 13, 1944, and for FDR's plans just before his death see Tully, Marquis Childs in the New York *Post*, April 15, 1945, and Charles Van Devander, New York *Post*, May 18, 1945. For details of the funeral see stories in the New York *Times*, by Frank L. Kluckhohn. Among thousands of obituaries written all over the world two particularly noteworthy are "Twelve Years of Roosevelt" by Henry Steele Commager, *American Mercury*, August, 1945, and "The Happiest Warrior" by Milton Mayer, *Common Sense*, June, 1945. See Rosenman, Vol. XIII, p. 376, for FDR's belief in private enterprise and the profit system, and Stimson for the remark that he was "our greatest war president" and the greatest campaigner in American political history. James Reston in the New York *Times*, November 4, 1948, points out cogently Roosevelt's influences on the 1948 elections.

Finally, as I said in the foreword to this book so many pages past, I owe an immense debt to a great many people who helped me by word of mouth, and I want to thank them for their copious assistance so generously bestowed. For a time I flirted with the idea of printing all their names, as I did with a similar list in *Inside U.S.A.*, but I have given this up because it seems pretentious. But I cannot refrain from thanking particularly a few out of several hundred benevolent friends or acquaintances for their encouragement, assistance, and advice—Frederick Lewis Allen, editor of *Harper's Magazine*, who made available to me the correspondence between Dr. Lovett and Dr. Draper; Sidney Hyman of Washington, D.C., to whom my debt is literally immeasurable; Mrs. Eleanor Roosevelt; Cass Canfield and John Fischer of Harper & Brothers, my publishers, who as in the case of previous books have been miracles of stout and discerning counsel; Gardner Cowles and Daniel D. Mich of *Look* Magazine, who gave hospitality to parts of the manuscript in serial form; Robert E. Sherwood; Morris L. Ernst and Alexander Lindey, attorneys at law; the staff of the library and home at Hyde Park; Jay Allen; Karl Schriftgiesser, author of *The Amazing Roosevelt Family*, who read and checked the entire manuscript; Dr. C. H. Traeger, who was my indispensable guide on medical matters; Miss Nancy Barnett, who typed one draft of the manuscript; and Mrs. Susan Walthew Elliott who typed another and helped prepare the bibliography and source lists.

Finally I want to thank my wife, Jane Perry Gunther, who has been an indispensable co-worker on this book since its beginning, and without whose discerning help and warm cooperation in every detail and throughout every phase of the work it could not possibly have been written.

INDEX